HOUSER

H. Peter Oberlander and Eva Newbrun

HOUSER

The Life and Work of
Catherine Bauer

With a Foreword by Martin Meyerson

UBC PRESS / VANCOUVER

Printed in Canada on acid-free paper

ISBN 0-7748-0720-2

Canadian Cataloguing in Publication Data

Oberlander, H. Peter, 1922-
  Houser

  Includes bibliographical references and index.
  ISBN 0-7748-0720-2

  1. Bauer, Catherine, 1905-1964. 2. Public housing – United States. 3. Social Scientists – United States – Biography. I. Newbrun, Eva. II. Title.

H59.B38023   1999   363.5'85'092   C99-910503-5

UBC Press gratefully acknowledges the ongoing support to its publishing program from the Canada Council for the Arts and the British Columbia Arts Council. We also wish to acknowledge the financial support of the Government of Canada through the Book Publishing Industry Development Program (BPIDP) for our publishing activities.

Canadä

UBC Press
University of British Columbia
6344 Memorial Road
Vancouver, BC V6T 1Z2
(604) 822-5959
Fax: 1-800-668-0821
E-mail: info@ubcpress.ubc.ca
www.ubcpress.ubc.ca

*To Annie Neubrunn and Margaret Oberlander (in memoriam),
our mothers, Catherine's contemporaries,
for their wisdom and compassion*

I see one-third of a nation ill-housed…

PRESIDENT FRANKLIN DELANO ROOSEVELT
SECOND INAUGURAL ADDRESS
20 JANUARY 1937

CONTENTS

ILLUSTRATIONS

FOREWORD

Catherine Bauer was a national treasure. She was the "houser" that
H. Peter Oberlander and Eva Newbrun identify as her calling. She
will always be identified with that set of contributions. But her life
cannot be captured by a single rubric; it was one of contrasts. Even in
housing, although an avid advocate of the public sector, she increasingly
recognized the significance of the private sector. Enthusiastically devoted
to thought and to action, she could change her mind-set – and did so on
many subjects – as circumstances allowed. She heeded details, including
intellectual ones, and at the same time possessed and shared vision. A
committed Democrat, she had her Republican admirers, and there were
those whom she admired. She bloomed in the company of men, but she
was also a feminist and a supportive friend to many women. Part of the
flapper generation, she became a most devoted wife. Thus, she was a
many-faceted gem rather than a single-focused gleam of light.

But national treasures in our complex world tend to be forgotten as
another generation comes to the fore. Oberlander and Newbrun not only
reinforce the memories of those who were enriched by knowing Catherine
as mentor, colleague, student, and friend but also provide an illuminating
portrait of her ideas, actions, and character for those who were never
blessed by having actually met her. There is much information here about
Catherine that even her good friends did not know, and this is a tribute to
the fullness of her life. She was candor personified. Indeed, she was such
a profound critic that those who were the beneficiaries of her sharp eye
and deep but amused voice were more often than not gratified instead of
defensive.

I knew Bill Wurster before I knew Catherine. Bill was twice my age, but
he and I were the two original students in Harvard's newly shaped
Department of City Planning. Then Catherine and I were colleagues in
many settings and policy sessions, including some in Europe and Japan.
Little did I think that one day I would leave Harvard and the MIT-Harvard

Joint Center, succeed Bill as dean of the College of Environmental Design at the University of California, Berkeley, and persuade Catherine to be my deputy dean there. Although I was never her student in a formal sense (Margy, my wife, was), I always believed that Catherine and I were fellow students of policy and action, not only in America but also in the urban world.

Peter Oberlander, who had come from Europe and had been a devoted student of Catherine's, himself became a dominant figure in Canada's housing and city planning. Catherine took great pleasure in his accomplishments, as she did in those of many students.

This book is a tribute not only to Catherine Bauer but also to her generation of doers and thinkers, who helped to shape the physical and social environment of the century. All of us are grateful to the authors of this enchanting book.

MARTIN MEYERSON
EMERITUS PRESIDENT AND UNIVERSITY PROFESSOR
UNIVERSITY OF PENNSYLVANIA
APRIL 1999

PREFACE

Historically in rural societies and agrarian economies, families would build houses for their own use. This required a combination of financial resources and human skills. Nineteenth-century industrialization radically changed the relationship between building, working, and living. Shelters were constructed at market prices for those who could afford them – and poor people lived in hand-me-downs and slums.

The historical trinity of human needs – shelter, clothing, and food – was severely challenged by the Great Depression of the 1930s. Of the three, shelter was the slowest to engage the public policy debate. Catherine Bauer's genius and passion would convert an idea into a legislated national program, when Roosevelt's New Deal embraced public responsibility for shelter. She demonstrated that one person can make a difference.

With a degree in neither architecture nor city planning, Catherine Bauer became the most prominent housing expert of her generation in North America. Her 1934 work, *Modern Housing,* applied what she had observed in Europe to the American crisis. The book became a classic. She searched passionately for social justice and devoted her life to improving housing and planning policies through political action. She co-authored the United States Housing Act of 1937 and advised five presidents, the Ford Foundation, and the United Nations on urban strategies.

I met Catherine Bauer in 1946 when I enrolled in her housing seminar in the Department of City and Regional Planning at Harvard's Graduate School of Design. I had noticed her in the halls, and not just because she was the only woman. She was tall and blonde, with hair piled high and a lock falling over her left eye. She wore swishing skirts and flat-heeled shoes, and she walked with an enormous stride – you had to run to keep up with her – and always smoked. Catherine had a charismatic personality that filled any room as soon as she appeared. I thought of her as "the smiling lady," and what she taught me that spring changed my thinking forever.

Catherine talked about housing not only in terms of architectural or urban planning, but as social responsibility. As a "houser," she saw housing as a *bridge* between architecture and planning. The politics of planning consumed her, and the fire of her personal involvement sparked my own. Following her model, I devoted myself to figuring out how to change the world, not how to accept it. She was largely self-taught and worked outside the system. A person who never followed the conventional path, Catherine was an extraordinarily effective person who taught me to learn by doing.

Today we are facing another crisis in housing. A whole generation of young people is growing up with no memory of a time when homeless folk did not crowd the streets. I cannot help but wonder what Catherine Bauer would have to say about our plight today. I do not believe we would have reached this pass if our nations had followed her thinking. It is with the hope of illuminating her particular vision that Eva Newbrun and I embarked upon this study of her life.

Each human life is a mystery, and only when it is over can its trajectories be mapped. To study a single life is to view a cross-section of history. May this portrait of Catherine Bauer help show how we got to where we are today – and provide a basis to go forward.

H. Peter Oberlander

HOUSER (hau'zr) [Com. Teut.: OE hus] someone committed to raising the quality of urban life through improving availability of and access to shelter for low-income families.

I

Early Years (1905-26)

Home

They're so proud of this clover-leaf right in the middle of town, that I find it hurts their feelings to say that my father did the first ones in America.

Catherine Bauer to her father

Modern-day Elizabeth, New Jersey, lies within New York City's conurbation, located across Newark Bay just a few miles northwest of Staten Island. Elizabeth was the capital of the New Jersey Colony before the American Revolution; Alexander Hamilton and Aaron Burr attended school here. It was also the geographic centre of a large settlement of German farmers who had migrated during the early nineteenth century. By the turn of the twentieth century, Elizabeth was a tidy town with wide, tree-lined streets and rows of large clapboard houses like those depicted in Charles Addams's *New Yorker* cartoons in the mid-twentieth century.

Elizabeth is the birthplace of Catherine Krouse Bauer, born to an affluent family on May 11, 1905. Her father, Jacob Bauer, descended from a farming family that migrated from Bavaria in 1834, settling in Linden, south of Elizabeth. Jacob qualified as an engineer after two years' study at Rutgers University and went on to serve several apprenticeships in highway engineering. At the time the automobile was rapidly replacing the horse-drawn carriage, and road conditions were beginning to receive serious consideration.

Shortly after opening a private practice in 1898, Jacob was appointed Union County Engineer, a post he held for thirty years during which he distinguished himself as one of the pioneers of American highway construction. He was the first engineer in North America to use reinforced concrete in pavement, and he spearheaded the use of macadam impregnated with oil instead of water for road surfaces. During his tenure Union

JACOB BAUER, IN HIS SIXTIES

Jacob Bauer, descended from a farming
family that migrated from Bavaria in
1834, settled in Linden, south of
Elizabeth ... Shortly after opening a
private practice in 1898, Jacob was
appointed Union County Engineer.

County roads grew into an integrated system of highways. Road construction codes were developed and then adopted as a model for the 1927 New Jersey Highway Act, which Jacob helped draft. In 1929 he went on to serve for four years as New Jersey's Chief State Highway Engineer and was responsible for the development of a network of highways that would become the Pulaski Skyway connecting New Jersey with New York, and the elevated approaches to the George Washington Bridge.

Jacob is credited with the first practical application of the cloverleaf interchange (designed by his predecessor, Colonel Sloane) in a major American highway system. Indeed, in 1936 his daughter, Catherine Bauer, mailed a postcard to her father from Stockholm featuring Sweden's first traffic cloverleaf: "They're so proud of this clover-leaf right in the middle of town, that I find it hurts their feelings to say that my father did the first ones in America." The success of Jacob's programs attracted interested engineers to Elizabeth from many parts of the United States and Europe. Germans came to study his methods as they embarked upon plans for the *Autobahn*. Catherine would later travel to Germany to bring back ideas to the United States. She grew up knowing that one person's ideas can change the life of a nation.

He was a handsome, well-groomed man with penetrating blue eyes. In April 1904, at the age of thirty-six, Jacob married twenty-three-year-old Alberta (Bertie) Louise Krouse of Roselle, New Jersey. Like her husband, Bertie was descended from German migrants. An exceptionally bright student, she attended a one-room schoolhouse for twelve years and learned everything her teacher knew. Upon graduation she begged her father to send her to college, but Henry Krouse thought it frivolous for Bertie to pursue post-secondary studies unless she became a school teacher, a vocation that held no interest for her.

So Bertie continued her studies informally. She read everything the library had to offer in her preferred subject areas, including biology and botany. Later she would often guide her children through the woods explaining natural phenomena. It was thanks to their mother that Catherine and her younger siblings, Betty and Louis, developed a love of nature. Although all three were sent to the best schools and colleges, they understood from their mother's example that one need not have a degree to

ALBERTA BAUER, IN HER FIFTIES

In April 1904, at the age of thirty-six, Jacob married twenty-three-year-old Alberta (Bertie) Louise Krouse of Roselle, New Jersey. Like her husband, Bertie was descended from German migrants.

become an expert. From their father they learned to embrace new ideas – and to support them with hard data.

Photographs of Bertie as a young mother show a trim, attractive woman of medium height, with short permanent-waved hair. A prominent nose supported a pair of wire-framed glasses that Bertie never took off except to swim and sleep. She was strong-willed and self-reliant. She headed women's groups, church groups, and the Octagon Literary Society, and made her mark as a bridge master and women's golf champion. Bertie was also the first woman in Union County to obtain a driver's licence, and she drove fearlessly all around the county on her husband's roads.

Jacob too was active in the community. He was a director of the Chamber of Commerce and several professional organizations, and a

BETTY, LOUIS, ALBERTA, AND CATHERINE, C. 1919

It was thanks to their mother that Catherine and her younger siblings, Betty and Louis, developed a love of nature. Although all three were sent to the best schools and colleges, they understood from their mother's example that one need not have a degree to become an expert.

member of the Freemasons and Rotary Club. He and Bertie were congregants of the Second Presbyterian Church, and when their children were young they made church attendance a family tradition, followed by Sunday dinner at home. If the children ever complained of being bored with this routine, Jacob would recount the dark winter mornings of his youth, when he and his seven older siblings were subjected to their father's daily readings from a German Bible followed by a quiz and lengthy prayers.

CATHERINE, TWO YEARS OLD

When their children were young they made church attendance a family tradition, followed by Sunday dinner at home.

Jacob had left the German Lutheran Church when he married Bertie, whose family was Presbyterian.

Both parents were intimately involved in their children's intellectual development, though Bertie took special interest and pride in her daughters. Betty would spend a year as a student of architecture, apprenticing with Frank Lloyd Wright at Taliesin, Wisconsin, in the 1930s. She was curator of architecture at New York City's Museum of Modern Art from 1943 to 1946, and later earned acclaim as a researcher and lecturer in architectural history and as the author of several books on modern design. Jacob devoted himself to mentoring Louis from an early age, often inviting the youngster to help out in his office. He was delighted when his son entered engineering college.

ELIZABETH (BETTY), ALBERTA, AND CATHERINE, C. 1911

Both parents were intimately involved in their children's intellectual development, though Bertie took special interest and pride in her daughters.

The Bauer house at 160 Westfield Avenue was large and comfortable. It was three stories high, with a front porch, pitched roof, and two dormer windows. Typical of countless other upper-middle-class residences in countless other small towns in the United States at the time, it was architecturally very simple and unpretentious, yet warm and spacious. On Sundays after dinner Catherine would find a cozy, private nook – often a window seat – where she would curl up and read. She could pause in her reading, look out the window and down the broad leafy street, and allow her gaze to travel out into the wide world.

Catherine excelled in high school but was only an average student in college. A somewhat unsociable child who preferred just a few close friends, she grew into a young woman remembered for her classroom

BAUER FAMILY HOME, C. 1919

The Bauer house was large and comfortable.

clowning in college. She could always make people laugh, and her own laughter was legendary for its resonance. Like her mother, Catherine was athletic, and from her mother she learned to play golf and swim. Many summers were spent at camp, first as a camper and later as a swimming instructor in charge of lakefront activities. She also excelled at tennis and basketball, and loved taking long bicycle trips in the country, alone or with friends. It was said that she took to sports like a boy and apparently played as hard as one, earning the nickname "Casey" after the mythical baseball slugger. Being captain of the team did not protect her from being sent to the sidelines for aggressive behaviour during high-school basketball games, and Catherine often spent more time on the bench than in play. Her fighting spirit earned her the admiration of friends and siblings and the embarrassment of her mother, who nevertheless attended all of her games.

The Bauer and Krouse families shared a long legacy of family loyalty and stability. After marriage children typically moved only a stone's throw from their parents' homes. Widowed grandmothers moved in with their children. Girls married early, often to older men who had to demonstrate their ability to support a family before asking the father's permission. All this, and much more, would change for Catherine and her generation.

VASSAR/CORNELL

From the time I first came to know your mind, early in your freshman year, I recognized it as predominantly of the masculine type: the sweep, the range, the grasp, the steadiness, and happily (and rather rarely) in combination, the sensitiveness.

MARGARET POLLARD SMITH TO CATHERINE BAUER

Alberta Bauer sent away for an application to Vassar, one of America's most prestigious girls' colleges, when Catherine was still in her freshman year at Vail-Deane High School in Elizabeth. Bertie was ambitious for her daughter and did not want to leave anything to chance. She needn't have worried; Catherine graduated at the top of her class and was welcomed to Vassar's class of 1926. In September 1922 she set out for Poughkeepsie aboard a Hudson River Day Line Steamer with two school chums also bound for Vassar. From them she learned that a $450 deposit had been required to secure a room on campus; her mother had neglected to attend to this detail. So began Catherine's long career of convincing people to bend the rules: upon arrival her first task was to persuade the college administration to provide a room for her on credit. They did, and she was assigned a room in a suite.

"I remember being impressed by the lean, blonde, and blue-eyed, kind of rascally looking girl, who was tall and strong, and moved fast and well," recalls Elizabeth Melone Winston. At Vassar, Elizabeth Melone was known as Lib, and she was one of two suite-mates who became Catherine's

CATHERINE (BOTTOM CENTRE) WITH TEAM MATES AT VAIL-DEANE HIGH SCHOOL

It was said that she took to sports like a boy and apparently played as hard as one, earning the nickname "Casey" after the mythical baseball slugger.

CATHERINE, SEVENTEEN YEARS OLD

Catherine graduated at the top of her class [at Vail-Deane High School] and was welcomed to Vassar's class of 1926.

lifelong friends. The other was Eleanor (Ellie) Kingman, who would later accompany Catherine on her European travels.

Catherine wrote excited letters home from college about bicycle trips into the countryside, hikes in torrential rain, shopping escapades, and bridge parties with her new friends. She was thrilled with the social life at Vassar, with its close community of students and faculty. About her academic experiences, however, she could hardly scare up a positive word. And no wonder. After enjoying top honours at Vail-Deane, Catherine was stunned by mediocre grades at Vassar.

"The queerest thing, tho!" she wrote a few months after school began, "is to have to work so hard just to get a passing mark when at V.D. I felt extremely dumb if I didn't get 90!" Her only A's were in mathematics – a sore point for an English major with aspirations to a career in writing. What she couldn't have known is how valuable those English courses would be regardless of her grade, particularly the speech and voice-technique classes that would serve her well in public life. Nor could she have chosen a better mentor than the English professor, Mrs. Margaret Pollard Smith.

Margaret Smith was a widow with four small children. She sat on civic and university committees, played chamber music on the piano, frequently entertained family and friends from afar, and still managed to maintain a close personal interest in her special students. One rainy afternoon Catherine and Lib Melone ran into Mrs. Smith in downtown Poughkeepsie; their teacher invited them back to her house for tea. Thereafter Catherine became a frequent visitor and often baby-sat the children. The Smiths lived on the south side of town in a rambling, colonial-style clapboard house surrounded by a large and lovely garden. It was Mrs. Smith who triggered Catherine's interest in architecture.

In her sophomore year Catherine got a new roommate, an adventurous girl from Minneapolis named Frances Goetzmann, nicknamed Fritz. With the help of their mothers, the girls created a comfortable nest into which they invited friends for tea and card parties. But this style of life was not entirely satisfying to Catherine. She felt driven, though she didn't know exactly by what. Questions about her future began to haunt her, and she wondered where her studies were leading.

She enrolled in a drawing course just for fun, not for credit, because she drew and painted quite well. This led to her first thoughts of drawing in connection with buildings, and in turn to the possibility of architecture as a vocation. Margaret Smith encouraged this line of thinking and approved when Catherine decided to apply to Cornell University's five-year Bachelor of Architecture program.

"The idea of leaving here simply floors me, because of course it wouldn't be half as much fun at Cornell, but I'm really not working very hard and I feel as if I *could* if only I got awfully interested in something," Catherine wrote to her family. "Mrs. Smith thinks that if one is going to learn anything technical and really accomplish anything, one should begin early."

Mrs. Smith also thought the unworldly nineteen-year-old would do well to spend a year abroad before commencing studies at Cornell, but Catherine chose to ignore this piece of advice. Likewise, her parents' doubts about the wisdom of such a hasty leap into professional school failed to deter her. On September 5, 1924, she was admitted to the Cornell University College of Architecture.

Again, Catherine's first letter home noted her family's lack of attention to detail. "As usual, we overlooked something quite important," she wrote. "When one registers at the treasurer's office one is supposed to bring one's tuition along too." This time she was unable to bend the rules, for which she paid a small price: waiting for a gym locker until her tuition was paid.

Catherine found the Cornell girls to be elegantly dressed, which she attributed to the presence of men on campus. It was the first time she had attended a co-educational school. In letters home, she described the young women's attire in great detail and with the derision she would later use to describe ornate building façades. They wore fur pieces, silk stockings, and impractical high heels, she noted, in contrast to Vassar girls, who wore sweaters, socks, and saddle shoes.

Her staid wardrobe, however, created no social stigma. She was rushed by the sororities, receiving nine bids for various dinners and teas, of which she accepted five then narrowed her choice to two because "they seem to be the only houses where all the girls are natural, unaffected and lady-like.

I certainly do hate this 'rushing' business." She took up basketball again, playing for the junior squad and later for the Alpha Phi Sorority, which she joined that first winter. She also played tournament tennis and took minor parts in theatre productions.

"As for the work, which is really the important thing, I *am* doing it," she informed her parents. "If anyone at Vassar could see my schedule, they'd turn over in their graves!" Her first design assignment was a small museum. "Just imagine yourself never having drawn a building or even a dog kennel before, sitting down and drawing a handsome 'small museum.' Fortunately, everyone else in the class is just as dumb as I am – which is a great comfort."

To Mrs. Smith back in Poughkeepsie, Catherine wrote of her surprise to discover that she was just as smart as her male classmates. Margaret Smith responded that she was not surprised at all: "From the time I first came to know your mind, early in your freshman year, I recognized it as predominantly of the masculine type: the sweep, the range, the grasp, the steadiness, and happily (and rather rarely) in combination, the sensitiveness."

Catherine's design class was so demanding that for days on end she worked from 8:00 a.m. to 11:00 p.m. In addition to the small museum, designs for a national bank and an art gallery were assigned. She would spend hours on details, such as friezes of figures in low relief, ornate bronze doors, egg-and-dart mouldings, and dentils. Although she was having fun, she discovered that such fine, concentrated work required a lot of energy. Indeed, her health was compromised from sheer exhaustion, and several letters were written from the infirmary as she lay recovering from ear infections, conjunctivitis, or tonsillitis.

At the desk next to hers in the design class sat the Emmons boy, who was also from Elizabeth, New Jersey. About twenty years later, this boy's younger brother, Donn, would become the youngest partner in the San Francisco architectural firm of Wurster, Bernardi, and Emmons, founded by the man whom Catherine would marry: William Wurster. But in the spring of that year, Catherine was in love with Douglas King Condie, an architecture student one year ahead of her. He was tall, charming, handsome, and deaf.

Toward the end of her first year at Cornell, Catherine wrote to Mrs. Smith of her infatuation with Doug Condie. The young man's zest for adventure appealed to her, she said, confessing that even his deafness was an exotic attraction. Verbal communication was not a problem because Doug was a fluent lip reader and his speech was well modulated.

Her former English teacher urged caution. "It seemed strange to me that you had not known men at home," Margaret Smith replied, suggesting in no uncertain terms that Catherine spend time getting to know men better on the whole before making a serious commitment to any one. In her own college days, Mrs. Smith recalled, she had "cavorted with the stronger sex" while remaining strictly friends until she had obtained a degree and some professional credentials. At the age of twenty-eight, she engaged and shortly afterward married the man who would be the father of her children. "I never regretted those years by myself, and that much study. So, when life brought me something seemingly unbearable, four years ago, I had a definite profession. Without that – I do not like to think of the difficulties that would have beset me, in getting back to a feeling of security."

These words, from the woman Catherine admired most in the world, would return to haunt her over the next decade. But at the moment she was deeply in love, and by the end of the spring semester Catherine and Doug made a decision to marry. Their informal engagement was greeted with dismay by Catherine's family and with good cheer by her friends. "I salute you," offered her former Vassar roommate, Fritz Goetzmann. "You who have now probed the mysteries of life are in love. If you're in love – for Lord's sake, make the most of it. Stay in love and get engaged and marry him even if it *is* a compromise, in the sense that you'd give up your work."

But Catherine was not prepared for so hasty a compromise and may have had more mixed feelings toward her fiancé than she allowed to her friends. By June she had devised an entirely new plan for herself: to return to Vassar and complete a college degree – not necessarily in architecture – before getting married. Whether this was her way of bowing to Mrs. Smith's advice, or of putting some distance between herself and Doug, or both, was never articulated. But she did discuss the graduation dilemma with her closest friends: If they got married, she would have to leave Cornell at the end of her fourth year because Doug was a year ahead of her and had plans to return to his home near St. Louis, Missouri, following graduation. She would, of course, have to follow, sans degree. Convinced that a general arts degree from Vassar was preferable to no degree at all, she resolved to apply for readmission to Vassar's class of '26. To save face, she would later revise history by attributing her departure from Cornell to intellectual-aesthetic reasons, namely disaffection with its outmoded Beaux Arts curriculum.

Having only a year earlier informed the authorities at Vassar that she was leaving because she really wanted to be an architect, Catherine now faced a challenge winning their approval for readmission – especially since she expected them to transfer credits from Cornell for the year she had missed at Vassar. The admissions board greeted the request coolly. They would determine the merits of her application, they replied, at the final admissions meeting in July, but were quite certain she would not have sufficient credit for graduation with the class of '26. Letters flew back and forth that summer between Cornell University, Vassar College, and Forest Vale Camp, where Catherine served as head waterfront counsellor. The red tape seemed insurmountable, and might have been were it not for the fact that she had two allies on the admissions committee: Mrs. Smith, who spoke for Catherine, and Miss Ogden, who spoke for the value of Cornell credits.

The table turned in mid-July. "How long I am withholding good news!" Mrs. Smith wrote to her protégé. "Your two firm allies were able to turn the rather inflexible Miss Thompson and Miss Sandison from their much-biased attitude." Miss Sandison had been opposed to Catherine's reentry because she smelled romance behind her wish to return to Vassar. The two opponents finally relented, but put so many obstacles in her path to a June graduation that they hoped she would be deterred from returning. Now Catherine was more determined than ever to document her credits and graduate the following June. Under Mrs. Smith's guidance, which included taking a special English examination, she reentered Vassar's class of '26 in good standing.

Ironically, Doug failed so many courses in the 1924-25 college year that he would have had insufficient credits to graduate in '26. He decided to spend the summer of '25 in Europe, an idea Catherine endorsed, though she thought a full year abroad would be even better for him. This suggestion was the first sign that she wanted him far away. He stood by his original plan.

Over the summer Doug visited England, France, and Italy, his letters to Catherine c/o Forest Vale Camp bursting with vivid descriptions of the landscapes, cityscapes, cathedrals, museums, and people he encountered. Clearly, Catherine was in his thoughts at all times: his letters carried quotes from imaginary dialogues he was having with her, and some were signed "your husband." No doubt inspired by Doug's descriptions, Catherine promised herself that next summer she would tour Europe with one of her classmates.

Catherine's letters to her parents during her senior year at Vassar contained more references to classes and marks than ever before, perhaps to reassure them about her decision to return to the women's college. In October 1925 she took up the thread of earlier conversations about a trip to Europe. Fritz's parents had invited her to join them on their summer tour abroad, but Ellie Kingman's plan to join an architect's tour held more appeal. "Mother, couldn't you possibly go for at least part of the trip?" she begged, wishing to emulate her wealthy midwestern friends whose parents guided their first major voyages. Bertie was the more adventuresome of the Bauer parents, but she reluctantly informed her daughter that with two children still at home, such a tour was not possible.

Doug met the Bauer parents early in autumn, shortly after his return from Europe. Although disinclined to welcome a deaf son-in-law into the family, their hearts were quickly won by the young man's genuine warmth and charm. Catherine's little brother Louis was won over to his sister's suitor by his gift of an elaborate construction toy and willingness to spend hours playing with him. Betty was swept up by the romance, too, and her parents were sufficiently impressed to invite Doug to spend Thanksgiving in Elizabeth with them. This would allow Catherine's grandmother and all her aunts and uncles to meet the man she continued to describe as her "unofficial" fiancé.

Thanksgiving plans fell through when Doug's father suffered a business setback, forcing him to return for a time to St. Louis. To compensate, the Condies invited Catherine to spend Christmas with them. Bertie and Jacob Bauer approved of the invitation and showered their daughter with spending money and gifts of clothing and accessories for the trip. Catherine was overwhelmed with gratitude. "I *do appreciate it,* honestly, Mother, (tho I know I don't ever seem to show it)," she wrote. In the past her appeals for money had been met hesitantly at best. The Bauers were more than pleased at the prospect of a wedding in the family.

Catherine was charmed by the elegant Condie house in Ferguson, near St. Louis. It was comfortable and filled with handsome old furniture, "but not in the least ostentatious. They keep a chauffeur and three maids – and three cars but entirely for convenience and comfort and not for show." Doug welcomed her with the gift of a jewelled fraternity pin, which drained his purse over many installments. Mrs. Condie was "*lovely* – you would like her *ever* so much. Just the sort of woman you would have wished," she wrote to her parents. Mrs. Condie and her two daughters were deaf, but read lips and modulated their voices so effectively that their handicap was hardly noticeable. Catherine was also taken with Doug's two younger brothers, especially Churchill, who had just turned sixteen and was wearing his first pair of long trousers. "He is *darling,*" Catherine wrote, and Mr. Condie was "darling" too.

Their fun-filled week was spent in the manner of the *haute bourgeois* of the mid-1920s: small dinners, tea parties, drives to the country, horseback riding, and bridge parties. It culminated in a splendid Christmas dinner for the extended family: fourteen Condies plus Catherine, who was made to feel entirely at home. "You certainly need not worry about my happiness with Doug," she wrote. "He is the finest, keenest, sweetest man I've ever seen – and he really is rather in love with me … I find that being engaged is very good for one's egotism." Catherine was very much in love with the security of being loved by a man and with the fanfare caused by her engagement.

From St. Louis she went on to Minneapolis, the farthest she had ever been from home, to spend New Year's holidays with her Vassar friends, Lib Melone and Fritz Goetzmann. She was still basking in the glow of romance. "I am so much in love with Doug that I can't think of anything else," she wrote, "and he is even more in love with me – so everything is splendid and all we have to do is wait until he gets through and starts to work."

It was as though the honeymoon came – and went – before the wedding date was even set. By the spring of 1926, Catherine's attention was focused entirely on the approaching commencement ceremonies. Her correspondence reflected a preoccupation with the minutiae of travel and accommodation arrangements for her commencement guests. Oddly, Doug was not among them. While the Bauers and Condies awaited word of their children's formal engagement, Catherine's letters home contained barely a mention of the man.

Then, shortly before graduation, an acquaintance of Catherine's from Cornell turned up at Vassar. While he was strolling around campus, Julian recognized Catherine and struck up a conversation. Both were thrilled by the chance meeting, and they spent the next two days wandering about the countryside and dining together in town.

A few days later Catherine was in the infirmary, suffering from severe tonsillitis and an ear infection. She recovered in time to attend graduation, but shortly after her return home was admitted to hospital to have her tonsils removed. A glib letter from Julian arrived while she was convalescing. "How are the old tonsils getting along without you or vice versa?" he wrote. "I just read a story about a 'damsel' who ate breakfast with a guy and was horribly compromised thereby. We must do that again sometime when you find a good excuse for staying in town." In his letter, Julian admitted that a fraternity brother of his accused him of trying to cut Doug out. "Why must people make those prep-schoolish cracks? I told him yes or something." Turning serious, he urged, "Do get well soon and come over. I can almost live on your visits or rather ours. You make me feel so damn splendid that you really must come over."

Doug was working in an architectural firm in Austria that summer. Catherine had no idea how long he would be there, nor did she care – though she admitted to feeling some guilt and even regret about this. Perhaps she could learn to love him more, she thought, wishing she could return his passion. Her classmate and confidante, Lib Melone, sensed the relationship was in serious trouble and said so: you will not be ready for marriage until you both encounter more of life, Lib counselled. This resonated with Catherine, and in August she broke off her informal engagement to Doug.

Her family was stunned. Betty, writing from camp, said, "What a *dam fool* you are to break your engagement. You sap, if you're an old maid it's your own fault." Catherine forwarded this letter to her friend, Fritz, in Minneapolis. "I enjoyed Betty's [letter]. What else, pray, would she think?" Fritz, thinking it was for the best, added:

You're not in love with him. I'm sure of it. You can't help but feel awful now because even fondness and the degree of physical and mental dependence involved in necking and writing continually can leave an awful gap when it disappears. And another thing which I've never said before: Doug isn't particularly right for you – that is, as I consider him. He's ahead of both you and me in personal charm and sensitiveness to beauty, and in his talent, but mentally, he's not up to you on account of his deafness. Thinking and speaking are so fundamentally related that there's no separation between the two. And where you can talk forever about something you've read, or thought, Doug can't. You should marry someone equal or better, my dear girl. Don't let that craving for attention lead you from Kingman's virgin side, in Europe.

And so Catherine finalized plans to join her friend, Ellie Kingman, on a journey to Europe that fall.

She had been able to save some money by living at home and working in her father's engineering firm that summer, an enlightening experience in itself. The firm's main business in those days was laying out residential developments, always rectilinear, with sewers, water, and gas running below the centres of the streets. Outlets from the main lines led to houses lined up like tin soldiers on both sides of straight streets. While this was

CATHERINE'S PASSPORT PHOTO, 1926

Catherine finalized plans to join her friend, Ellie Kingman, on a journey to Europe that fall.

the cheapest way to build and provided the highest profit for developers, Catherine found the checkerboard regularity of the designs dull. In her first critique of planning practices, she suggested that her father's layouts incorporate cul-de-sacs, and Jacob Bauer listened. He assigned her to draft a cul-de-sac plan and to estimate the cost of its utilities versus the costs of the usual grid pattern. Her young brother helped determine specifications that supported Catherine's viewpoint. Jacob was so proud of his two children that he took them on a tour to see new model subdivisions in New Jersey.

On August 21, 1926, a letter came from Ellie outlining their departure plans. "Your passage is engaged and you can't back out. Price: $150. Anytime that you feel like sending a check make it out to Joseph R. Kingman." Ellie's father had booked a cabin for the young women aboard a Cunard liner scheduled to depart on September 25 for Plymouth, where Ellie suggested they disembark so they might see some of the country on their way to London. Knowing her friend's laxness for detail, Ellie reminded Catherine to get her passport, warning "don't put it off too late!"

Three weeks later another letter came from Ellie, this time gently reprimanding Catherine. "Of course I really don't care if you don't go to Europe with me," she wrote, "but it would be easier for me if I knew it now so I could get someone else to go with me." She reminded Catherine to send $150 to her father and to get British and French visa stamps on her passport. Ellie also sent luggage tags and instructions about the disposition of trunks during the voyage. The girl from Minneapolis took care of all the travel arrangements for herself and for her friend who lived only a stone's throw from the harbour from which they would sail.

Catherine and Ellie departed from the United States right in the middle of the Roaring Twenties, leaving behind a lively world of jazz and flapper fashions and a culture obsessed with pleasure. If there was poverty in America, these two had not noticed. Their peers hung out in speakeasies or at Carnegie Hall. The rich clad themselves and their homes gaily, while those less fortunate aspired to do the same. The period following the end of the Great War had produced great private wealth, and optimism was rampant. While Europe worked to pull itself out of the ruins of the war, America's moneyed class multiplied. The Republican administration in Washington offered political stability as major American cities began their outward push into substantial suburbs, and the motor car became the vehicle of choice.

Suburban neighbourhoods, consisting of freestanding, single-family houses designed to look like Mediterranean villas, Swiss chalets, or Grecian palaces, characterized the ideal American way of life. For those who could afford them, or who merited credit from the few financial institutions willing to advance housing loans, life was very good. These included Catherine's circle of friends and family. For the majority of Americans, home ownership meant a crippling down payment that depleted family savings, and/or help from relatives.

It was assumed that a free-market economy would thrive forever on lavish private spending, speculative investment, and minimal government interference or regulation. Taxation for public expenditures was kept to a minimum. A social security net, such as the one evolving in Europe, was deemed unnecessary and even un-American. The most highly regarded social attributes were self-reliance, individualism, and unbridled competition. The least government was the best government: "May the best man win" was the spirit of the day.

Learning Years (1926-30)

Britain

I may be awfully fussy but I do insist that there be a bathtub somewhere in the house.

Catherine Bauer

A few short foghorn blasts signalled the departure of the R.M.S. *Lancastria* on Saturday morning, September 25, 1926. On deck stood Catherine Bauer, a handsome, slim woman dressed in the popular flapper fashion. Her shoes were sensible; twenty-one-year-old Catherine purchased clothes with an eye to durability first, fashion next. These clothes would serve her well for the six months that she planned to stay abroad, she assured her mother, who frowned on modern fashions.

There had been much fanfare at the dock that morning, with the entire Bauer family accompanying Catherine and lingering for a tour aboard the well-appointed ship. Her younger siblings, fifteen-year-old Betty and twelve-year-old Louis, thought it was swell to see their sister off. Her father, an engineer, made a mental note of the ship's fittings. Satisfied that his oldest daughter would be safe and comfortable on her ten-day journey to England, and not given to great shows of affection, he gave her a peck on the cheek followed by a quick hug after the first deafening blast of the foghorn. Urging her to write often, including to her grandmother, Nana, Jacob took his leave and trotted briskly down the gangplank. Given to seasickness, he was happy to be on *terra firma.*

Alberta Bauer was wistful that morning, she later told Catherine, and a little in awe of her daughter's sophistication and courage to take on the world. Bertie longed for this kind of adventure, but domestic duties dictated otherwise. She asked Catherine to write long, descriptive letters as often as possible. Like her husband, she did not enjoy drawn-out farewells, and she quickly descended the gangplank to secure a place behind the barrier that separated visitors from the ship. Bertie wanted an unobstructed view of the liner being pulled out of its berth into the Hudson River, toward the New York City Harbor.

Catherine, a heavy smoker, lit up a cigarette as she shared the thrill of passing the Statue of Liberty with her friend and now cabin mate, Ellie Kingman. Relatives and friends from Vassar College had showered the girls with flowers, candy, fruit, and nuts. Fortunately both were able to enjoy their bounty in spite of stormy seas.

Of the ninety passengers in Cabin Class, seventy were English. Catherine was enchanted by the sophisticated and amusing Englishmen who, she predicted, would spoil her for American boys. In the dining room, the girls were assigned to a table with two young gentlemen: a very funny Englishman and a dull but attractive American architect who had a fellowship to study abroad.

The girls quickly befriended several male passengers, including two British army captains on leave from India, a doctor from Oxford, a businessman from Shanghai, the next heir to the title of Earl of Effingwell, and a delightful "Scotty from Edinbra." All were graduates of Cambridge or Oxford; all were intelligent, attractive, and, as Catherine wrote, "pleasantly able to talk about nothing at all without nervous spaces in between." She raved about their clothes: "How *can* American men have so little imagination? Such blazers, such neckties, such handkerchiefs sticking out of breast pockets. Such 'spohting cuts,' double-breasted effects & baggy trousers! And every one with a mustache." In spite of all that, she found that they did not dance well, did not read much, and gambled prodigiously.

One of the officers, Captain Dutton, offered her his heart and his hand, convinced that she would be a success in Indian army circles. He was an Oxford graduate, thirty years old, and had been living in India for the past eight years. Although she regarded him as the most entertaining man on board, she could not possibly fall in love with him. Still, she was amused at the prospect of a weekend party at his family's home in Exeter, to be held shortly after their arrival. "His mother and sisters will be present ... It *would* be fun – there might be shooting. Jolly decent, daont you know, re-a-ally quite topping," wrote Catherine, mimicking her new friend.

Two lighthearted young women arrived in Plymouth and were helped through customs by their English friends, who directed them to a pleasant and cheap lodging house. In an attempt to impress her parents with her frugality, Catherine translated pounds sterling into dollars. Bed and breakfast cost only $1.75 per person at Hacker's Hotel, where the twosome plunged headlong into Victorian England. The landlady, warning that her gentlemen guests were due to arrive soon for their drinks, and wishing to spare the women the discomfort of dining in a public room, invited

Catherine and Ellie into her private salon. This chamber astonished the girls, even though they grew up in homes that displayed knick-knacks and contained overstuffed furniture. It was a smallish room embraced by thirteen corners and two bulbous bay windows. On top of a pink and green carpet, carefully fitted into all the corners, lay a small rectangular red carpet – and on top of that sat three fur rugs.

The windows, which were nailed shut, were covered by three sets of curtains, one of which was an extravagant lace that draped over the window seats and spread far out on the floor. Three vitrines displayed a jumble of nameless objects made of porcelain, glass, metal, or leather. The small room contained three tables, nine chairs, three clocks that were not running, eleven empty vases, cork and wood carvings, wax flowers, antimacassars, lace tidies, and potted palms sitting beside plush covered chairs. The tables displayed pearl-handled pens, pen wipers, glass inkwells that were dry, and porcelain figurines.

To Catherine, the salon felt more like a backstage storage room, housing props, than a place to entertain guests. That day she found the room exotic, though in the future she would build her career as a critic of design by disparaging such poor taste.

With its old stone houses, narrow alleys, and walled gardens, Plymouth was a typically English town. The morning after their arrival, the girls bought second-hand bicycles for £2 each and set out for Dartmoor, leaving most of their luggage at Hacker's. That week Catherine sent home six picture postcards depicting the landscapes through which she journeyed. Sometimes she drew herself into scenes, other times she circled a house where she ate or slept to supplement her vivid descriptions scrawled on the other side. The first of several packets of cards that she would send home that year extolled the beauty of the moors. "Great long winding hills with nothing on them but heather, gorgeous yellow furze (or gorse), a few jagged rocks, and sheep and wild ponies," she wrote. "Marvelous little paths going off into nowhere. And the *wind* – roaring like an ocean, choking us, making us pump like anything. Spent the first night at Princetown and had our first Devonshire Cream (food for the Gods!)."

Their second day found them at an inn that boasted being the second highest in England. It was on a 1,400-foot moor, with a fire in the living room that had been burning for 120 years. The girls wandered around the moor that afternoon, chatting with farmers who reminded them of Thomas Hardy's furze cutters and horse breeders.

After touring Exeter, where they partied at Captain Dutton's home and attended services at the cathedral, the women returned to Plymouth to clean up and rest. The next morning they took a train to Penzance and began a few days' exploration of the area. They ferried to the Scilly Isles for no reason other than that it was the end of the world and a marvellously romantic spot. They were enchanted by the ancient towns of Mousehole and Lamorna, the latter being a sudden surprise, deep down in an exotic valley, tropical in its luxuriance with palm trees, ferns, and gorgeous red and purple flowers – a sharp contrast to the bleak, windy, granite uplands. Lamorna Cove was the most splendid of all.

"I must live here some time," Catherine told Ellie over lunch in an old stone house by the sea. The restaurant owner kindly loaned the girls bathing suits for the afternoon, so they could enjoy the wild, rocky beach. Everywhere they went they met people who would advise them or drive them around to see the sights, invite them to tea or entertain them with tales of local history. Catherine described their Scilly Isles adventures to the last detail, including an encounter with bed bugs: "Kingman and I adjourned to new lodgings, having been bitten slightly but unmistakably the night before."

After leaving the Cornish coast they went to London for a reunion with several of their shipboard gentlemen friends, who showed them around. Captain Dutton took the travellers to tea "at the very most ultra hotel in London." Catherine was shocked at the way these Englishmen splurged, spending as much in one evening as she expected to in several months.

Shortly after their arrival in London, Ellie departed for Paris, leaving Catherine behind to explore further. Like many Americans on their first trip to Europe, Catherine was drawn to ancient artifacts. She visited eleventh-century Norman ruins in Kenilworth and climbed the spire of Coventry Cathedral on steps so worn that she was reminded of the tower, well, and stairs episode in Robert Louis Stevenson's novel *Kidnapped*.

It was fun to find places that triggered literary associations, rather like revisiting old friends. A half-timbered Elizabethan inn, filled with original furnishings and decorations, was so evocative of some of her favourite literature that Catherine described every detail to her parents – unaware that they were busy planning the construction of a new house in that same English-period style. They were looking forward to surprising their daughter with this news on her return. Jacob and Bertie could not have known that, by the end of Catherine's journey, she would be a very different person, with newly defined architectural tastes into which mock-Elizabethan clearly did not fit.

After a week Catherine decided to join Ellie in Paris. As the first member of her family to take an airplane, she sent home a colourful description of the experience, starting with the luxurious bus that collected her and six other passengers at the Hotel Victoria and drove them to Croydon Field. They boarded a twenty-passenger plane, furnished with comfortable wicker chairs, two abreast, separated by a very narrow aisle. The plane was glass all the way around, and little maps allowed the passengers to track the route.

After crossing the English Channel in only twenty minutes, the passengers peered out, trying to identify Amiens Cathedral, Crécy Woods, and old battlefields. The noise was so horrendous that ear plugs were provided and conversation was impossible. The motion did not bother Catherine, in spite of headwinds that slowed the flight from the usual 120 miles per hour to about 90, adding an hour to the trip. Individual spittoons were provided in case of motion illness. After three-and-a-half hours they arrived at Le Bourget Field outside Paris, where another beautifully appointed bus rolled them to town and the Hotel Edouard VII. From there a taxi took Catherine to Ellie's place on the other side of Paris, for a fare of five francs (about fifteen cents).

ELLIE KINGMAN (LEFT) AND CATHERINE IN PARIS, 1926

After a week [in London] Catherine decided to join Ellie in Paris.

The night of her arrival Catherine accompanied Ellie and two friends to the Opéra Comique to see *Manon*. The only seats left were the most expensive in the orchestra, at ninety-eight cents – but well worth it. Catherine was transfixed by the performance, and a lifelong affair with opera began. Although she had attended opera in New York, the voices and acting here were far superior, and she was inspired to discover the more complex pleasures of German operas by Wagner and Weber as well as Russian opera, ballet, and symphonic music. One afternoon Catherine attended a concert where a ten-year-old American violin virtuoso named Yehudi Menuhin brought down the house.

Paris was going to be an expensive proposition – this was clear to Catherine from the start. It didn't help that she was paying $2.40 per day at Ellie's pension. The accommodations were first rate, and the food was excellent, with the exception of the morning meal of croissants and Turkish coffee that struck the Americans as a rather odd breakfast.

Lunches were hearty and dinners delightful, served in a stately dining room where the table was set with pewter and fine china on a very chic red-and-white checkered tablecloth with matching napkins. This so impressed Catherine that she sent her mother a similar checkered tablecloth with matching napkins as a Christmas gift, with instructions to use these for guests instead of "ordinary" white linen. Aesthetically the girls had come a long way from Hacker's Hotel in Plymouth.

Catherine searched for less expensive rooms within a week, though she insisted on a place with a bathtub in a city where such amenities were not taken for granted. She had a penchant for cold morning baths, a habit that had amused and baffled the ship's stewards and the pensions' concierges. "I may be awfully fussy," she wrote, "but I do insist that there be a bathtub *somewhere* in the house."

After a few days she took a room in a tiny Left Bank apartment with a French family of three, believing this would be the best way to improve her French. In exchange for room and board, she would help with housework and be an occasional companion to their four-year-old girl. Although *Madame* was a doting host, introducing Catherine to some of the well-known sites and experiences of Paris such as the Arc de Triomphe, the Louvre, and a "pique-nique" at the Bois de Boulogne, the companion duties proved intolerable.

"If *only* I had stronger inclinations and sympathy for domesticity, or if only the four-year-old would stop hanging around me, I should say it was absolutely perfect," Catherine wrote home. "That awful spoiled child, either asked questions or cried *every minute of the day*, and loved me so much that I almost choked her ... Every morning I say to myself, 'I simply *won't* stand it – I'll spank her and leave.'"

Expressing gratitude to the French family, Catherine moved on to more practical accommodations in a large, comfortable, and cheap room at the Hôtel de Serbie on the Left Bank. She engaged a tutor, Mme Cosnard, who lived just around the corner, and fell into an enjoyable routine of studying for her daily French lessons, after which she would wander the streets of Paris practising her new vocabulary.

She embraced the Bohemian lifestyle of the Left Bank with enthusiasm and turned her nose up at the people living on the Right Bank. She was atypical for an American, her new French friends told her, because she loved beards and modern art. Once she posed for a young bearded artist who painted her hair green, much to her delight, but also gave her "perfectly *tremendous* legs." Another time, while taking an evening stroll in the rain, she tossed her soggy silver slippers into the Seine and continued barefoot, earning a round of applause from her companions.

LEFT BANK AND ITALY

The little Frenchmen are very energetic and hop all around,
or else do terrifying Tangos and Charlestons.

CATHERINE BAUER

Catherine crossed over to the Right Bank only when she had business at American Express, and then with disdain. She was disgusted to see "literally millions of people who trail around the Louvre and all those stupid dead places you just couldn't drag me, my dear," she pontificated to her diary. By contrast, she couldn't get enough of the grand Gothic architecture of Parisian churches. She wrote to her parents about an All Saints Day Mass she attended at Nôtre Dame de Paris, with the Cardinal of Paris presiding: "The Cathedral is *superb*. Really, I rather envy these Catholics the Faith that can build a thing like that. One can easily see, in the dim greenish light, looking up through the breath-taking chasm of the nave at the most glorious stained glass in the world, how it gets them so that nothing else under the sun matters."

AZAY - LE - RIDEAU

SKETCH BY CATHERINE

Catherine honed her drafting skill by keen observation.

Catherine and friends, including Ellie's concierge, took advantage of a few balmy days in November to go to Chartres. The cathedral "almost deserves a paragraph by itself," wrote the awestruck tourist. "It was just dusk and you can't *imagine* the first impression of that marvelously tall, slender, shadowy interior, with just a suggestion of light coming through the brilliant blues, purples, and reds in the windows (possibly the best in the world) – and no lights but about a dozen tall candles, standing in front of the famous Black Virgin in a chapel at the side and making the gargoyles and things around about look either alive or like ghosts." She was more passionate about the architecture of France than she had been even about the landscape of England.

Catherine made a point of visiting museums to enhance her education. The Musée Cluny, filled with art of the Middle Ages, including some of the most famous tapestries in the world, was the site of an embarrassing encounter. It had been raining, and Ellie was wearing oversized galoshes and Catherine a pair of ugly, old golf shoes. In the room displaying the unicorn tapestries, they crossed paths with a class of adolescent boys led by their teacher. As soon as the boys caught sight of the women's shoes, all decorum disintegrated. They abandoned their teacher and followed the two flustered Americans, shouting rude remarks and calling attention to their ridiculous footwear – effectively chasing them out of the museum. Now that the rain had stopped, they looked even more laughable and caused complete strangers to stop and stare at their feet. Catherine would turn this event, six months later, into an amusing story that she sold to the periodical *The Comet.*

In her museum travels Catherine found herself drawn more to modern than classical works. Rodin left her cold. Apart from *The Thinker*, Catherine found his sculptures "a little boring or sentimental or something." By contrast, she was swept away by the modernist works exhibited at the Salon d'Automne, which she visited in the company of new friends: Mme des Closets and her husband, a collector of modern tapestry who also happened to be a leader of the French *fascisti.* There were at least twenty rooms in the exhibition filled with modern furniture, lighting, decoration, paintings, sculpture, odds and ends of modern silverware, china, books, and even models of houses. "*Fascinating*," she wrote. "So different from the ordinary that they take your breath away – but entirely practical and very, very comfortable." The exhibit was a pivotal experience for Catherine: a turning away from the excesses of Victorian design toward something that struck her as fresh, exciting, and entirely correct for the times.

Taking advantage of a mild autumn weekend, the girls journeyed into the countryside with Ellie's French teacher, Mme Vielle, on the theory that "a little country and exercise and general loafing sets you up for another week or so of the educational." They stopped in Fleury because it was a beautiful French country village, with old stone houses, colourful roofs, and ancient cobblestone streets. On the way Mme Vielle took them to the studio of Fernand Léger, the prominent cubist painter. They found him an unexpectedly jolly little man who looked more like a golf player than a stereotypical artist. From Fleury they walked five kilometres along the edge of the forest of Fontainbleu to Barbizon, a little town made famous by

Millet, Courbet, Rosa Bonheur, and other artists. Another day they hiked along a fascinating little road through the forest to Fontainbleu.

Catherine was feeling more than a little guilty about having such a splendid time while her family was living in bleak Elizabeth, New Jersey, bogged down in their daily chores. Of course, they did not see things quite that way and scratched their heads on receiving a letter strongly urging them to drop everything and move to France. She argued that Jacob should retire early, and Betty and Louis should finish their schooling in Paris. "Father can fish in the Seine, and Mother and I can run around and look at things and ride bicycles, and Mother can learn to ride horses in the Bois de Boulogne – and you can all live for half as much as you do at home."

The pace of Catherine and Ellie's social life picked up following a reunion with some of their shipmates. Through them, they met many men who were happy to squire young American women to parties and dances. A wardrobe crisis ensued: Catherine's evening clothes began to show signs of wear by the beginning of winter, and a search through even the most affordable boutiques yielded nothing under $40 or $50. "They're all beaded, and I don't like them and one looks just like a piece of galvanized iron sprinkled with bits of broken glass," she wrote. In a sudden burst of creativity Catherine sketched what she considered the perfect dress and purchased some gorgeous white satin, black lace, snaps, belting, and other notions – all for $12. Her French tutor, Mme Cosnard, whom Catherine admired for her excellent taste, was stunned at the idea of a modern American girl making herself an evening dress in Paris.

The dress was finished (with the assistance of the tutor's maid) in time for a gala party celebrating Epiphany at the home of Mme Cosnard. What a party! Catherine was the only foreigner, and the others all knew each other well. "All the men were gallant and all the ladies gay, and there was a continual flow of wit and spirit. No one was ever bored – and yet, no one was ever boisterous. Everything is temperate in this country." She could not imagine American boys drinking so much champagne without becoming thoroughly intoxicated and behaving appallingly. But the French are always the same: gay, witty, and gallant, "never, never the least bit vulgar or nasty."

Her dress proved a great success, though she couldn't stop worrying it would fall apart at any moment. All eyes were on her when, following supper at one o'clock, she pulled a favour out of her *galleter* announcing that she would be crowned queen of the evening. She then crowned her king, and the two led a royal cotillion followed by singing and dancing until 4:30 a.m., when the party finally broke up. The next day Catherine was exhausted. "The little Frenchmen are very energetic and hop all around," she wrote, "or else do terrifying Tangos and Charlestons." She was generally taller than the men whom she found attractive, which made her feel uncomfortably big and awkward.

Among the shipmates whom Catherine befriended were a young American couple, Mr. and Mrs. Lockwood, who had come to Paris to study. He was a musician, and she was interested in stage design and costumes. They lived in a comfortable apartment on the Quay d'Orleans on the Seine island Île St. Louis. Catherine loved visiting with the Lockwoods at their home and happily obliged when they asked her to house-sit for a few weeks. They had just acquired a maid whom they did not wish to lose, but whom they did not want to leave alone in the apartment. Catherine would be doing them a favour if she lived there and let the woman look after her.

She checked out of her single room in the Hôtel de Serbie and moved into the Lockwoods' apartment. The timing (and living arrangements) could not have been better, since Catherine was planning a trip to Italy for the following month. An added bonus was the fascinating couple who lived next door, M. and Mme Sliwinsky. He was a well-known but poor Polish artist, and Madame was Russian. Both were short and stocky. They ran a little art and music shop to which they often invited Catherine. She was usually the only American among Poles, Austrians, Russians, French, Germans, and Italians. The others could speak at least four languages, had read everything worth reading in each of them, and were well versed in the arts. They were extraordinarily colourful yet polite people. One would come up to her, bow profoundly, and inquire, "May I have the honour of knowing what you think about the War Debt – or Theodore Dreiser, or American art, or Russian music?" Catherine's imaginative powers were challenged because she had no opinion at all on most of these matters but was obliged to produce one.

Catherine learned that M. Sliwinsky had degrees from German and French universities, had been in the Polish army for a good many years, and knew some of the most interesting people in England, France, and Germany. He had translated Chesterton, Wilde, and Stevenson into German and now ran this little shop in Paris. He usually had no money, and when he did, it would not last long because he would give it to one or another of his indigent artist friends hanging around the shop. They adored him, painted his picture, and played accompaniments for his Polish and German songs. There was always music. Sometimes an oversized Italian fellow would play opera while Sliwinsky sang, or a little bearded German would play a Bach duet with him. It was very gay and quite Bohemian, and of course no one ever bought anything.

One evening M. and Mme Sliwinsky invited Catherine to join them at a special concert given by their friend, Arthur Rubinstein, the most popular pianist in Paris at that time. The next day she was invited to call on Rubinstein with the Sliwinskys. "It was such fun," she told her parents. "He has a little salon in the Hotel Majestic, and it was full of well-known composers, two or three famous beauties, and so on. There were two Poles, a Russian woman, a Brazilian composer, a Greek, a Spaniard, and several French people. Rubinstein, who is a Polish Jew, talked to everyone in their own language, all at once, almost, and kept the whole room laughing and interested for more than an hour. An amazing personality."

Another evening at the Sliwinskys, Catherine befriended American caricaturist Adolph Dehn, whose drawings appeared in *Vanity Fair* and *The Dial,* and his wife, Thura, a Russian dancer and niece of Rasputin. She invited the Dehns for tea at her home the following night, and they all sat on the floor around the fireplace and ate with their fingers.

Dr. Whitelock, an Oxford surgeon whom Catherine had met on the ship, showed her an entirely different side of Paris. Passing through on his way to the Riviera shortly before Christmas, the thirty-five-year-old bachelor called and asked if she would accompany him on an afternoon stroll. While window shopping on the most exclusive shopping street, he turned to her and asked, "What shall I give you for Christmas?" Trying to think of something inexpensive and impersonal, Catherine replied casually, "Oh, you can get me a cigarette lighter if you want."

They continued walking until they reached Dunhill's. "It's a very snooty store and of course there were no prices on them," she wrote her parents. After some time they settled on a "pretty little one of blue enamel, plain and in good taste. *Then* when it was all wrapped up and in my bag I just barely heard the saleswoman murmur to the Doctor, 'one-thousand francs' (about $40)!!!! I don't suppose I've ever been in such a stew. *What* could I do? Of course if I'd yelled, then and there, the Doctor, being a perfect Englishman, would have been forced to make me take it – in a nice little bourgeois scene which he would have hated. I will say this for him, the expression on his face never changed an atom."

Once outside the shop, Catherine protested – to no avail. It was all she could do to keep her composure as they continued to stroll in the Bois de Boulogne. After a short time she told the doctor that she had an urgent errand and would meet him later. She rushed back to Dunhill's, told the clerk that she could not possibly accept such an expensive gift, and asked what the shop could do for her. The sympathetic clerk offered to return half the money if Catherine agreed to spend the balance on something else in the shop. "*So,* I picked out a stunning little pigskin bag (at the exorbitant price of $22), left the place, met Dr. W for tea, and simply made him take the rest of the money back." Catherine shuddered every time she looked at the bag for a long time afterward.

On his return from the Riviera, the doctor stopped in Paris for another visit with Catherine. In her letters she always referred to him either as the Doctor or more formally as Dr. Whitelock. She saved her most lavish praise for the restaurant meals they enjoyed together. "We had *such* a dinner at Lucas', which is *the* Epicurean place to eat here, and afterward we went to Apollo to dance." They danced late into the night. After seeing him off at the train station, she wrote: "He went back to England and Oxford and operations and hunting. He is really a most extraordinarily nice man – and if I had been in a marrying frame of mind, I should certainly have fallen in love with him. And I really think he felt the same way." Still smarting from her sister's angry response to the break-up of her engagement to handsome Doug Condie, she added, "Tell Betty, tho, that if I had been more 'responsive' I might even have had another chance."

As Christmas approached, Catherine became nostalgic for home. On receiving a note in French from Betty, she replied: "Crois-moi, mon noël n'aurait pas été complet sans ton cadeau. C'est absolument vrai." (Believe me, my Christmas would not have been complete without your present. That is absolutely true.) Impressed by Betty's fluency in French, Catherine urged her to keep up the correspondence, but made her promise not to show their letters to anyone who knew French well.

Teasing a little, she continued: "J'espère que tu ne sois pas fachée de moi parce que je n'ai pas épousé le capitaine ou le chirurgien anglais. Ne fais pas attention à çela. Peut être tous les deux seront encore ici quand *tu* viennes." (I hope that you are not angry with me because I have not married the captain or the English surgeon. Pay no attention to this. Perhaps both will be here again when *you* come.) Feeling lonely, and suffering more than a little anxiety about her future, Catherine wondered whether she should have pursued a romantic relationship with the doctor. "I only hope I shan't kick myself when I get back to America and can't find an interesting job and don't know any men at all," she confessed to her parents.

By February she was more than ready to leave Paris, where she felt her life had become purposeless and the experience was beginning to pall. She looked forward to Italy, where life would be equally without purpose but at least with new things to see. She was tired of dabbling and pined for a stronger focus. Perhaps she could find such a thing in the study of art, or architecture, or literature, she thought. Paris had given her something amorphous – something called *general appreciation*, which implied great variety without much depth.

During their travels in Europe, Catherine and Ellie took equal responsibility for setting itineraries. They were excellent travelling companions; both had enormous energy, they shared a love of nature and a common interest in art and architecture, and, best of all, they could laugh together. In the early winter of 1927, Ellie left Paris ahead of Catherine to meet her parents in Italy. She urged her friend to follow as soon as possible and to aim for a March reunion with the Kingman family in Naples. The plan suited Catherine well; she calculated that she had enough money to spend about two months in Italy before returning home from Naples in late April.

Catherine departed Paris at the end of February on an overnight train, amid much fanfare from her friends, who, full of wine and cognac, ran along the platform shouting farewells as the train pulled out of the station. Her first stop was Lucerne. As she stepped off the train platform and out of the station, she was enchanted by the sight of a little boy sitting on a curb, yodelling. Her short tour of Switzerland included rummaging about charming clock and toy shops, and ascending the Alps in a funicular. It did her good to inhale the crisp, clean, snowy mountain air.

By contrast, Milan was slushy, dark, and depressing. Catherine stayed there just long enough to attend *Aida* at La Scala, conducted by Toscanini, and to ascend the tower of the Duomo. The grim weather in Milan precluded a view beyond the roof statues, and she was happy to be back on the train, heading south, after an overnight stopover.

It was Catherine's habit to climb the highest tower in every city and village, for both the exercise and the splendid view. Once, just as she reached the highest platform of a church in a small Italian village, a giant bell started to clang less than three feet from her. "I all but turned ten backward somersaults down a few thousand feet," she wrote her parents. "Lucky it was three o'clock and not noon or I should have been deafened!"

After travelling alone for nearly a week, Catherine fled to Florence into the arms of her Vassar art instructor and his wife. Arthur McComb, an authority on Italian painting, was spending a year abroad with his wife, Constance, and their infant daughter. Both McCombs spoke Italian fluently and proved to be excellent guides. They ushered Catherine around museums, churches, palaces, monuments, and bridges, and made sure she had decent shelter and good meals. During that period she learned a good deal about Renaissance art and architecture from Arthur, who encouraged her to dip into his small library. Catherine toured many towns within a fifty-mile radius of Florence, some with the McCombs, others alone. Lucca was a highlight: the charming walled city, as yet unknown to tourists, was home to a number of small, simple Romanesque churches built in beautiful proportions out of black and white marble.

Catherine's trip south was documented in a series of twenty-two postcards. Numbers 10, 11, and 12 were devoted to a tour of Pisa and its Leaning Tower. She lunched at an unremarkable restaurant, filled with Italian businessmen. Seeking privacy, she took a table off to one side and busied herself with a glass of wine and a cigarette, avoiding the glances of the curious patrons. When she asked the waiter for her bill, the boy bowed in admiration and made her understand that the *signor* in the corner had paid her *conto*. Shocked and making a rapid compromise between Latin and French, she folded her arms across her chest and said sternly, "non e possible." The waiter blushed and disappeared into the kitchen. A furore ensued, which Catherine, unable to follow, ignored by staring at the wall clock until the manager came out. Having been overseas, he was sensitive to the cultural gap between American and Continental women and quickly agreed to let Catherine pay her own bill. He then escorted her to the door and invited her to return for a breakfast of ham and eggs.

In Livorno Catherine got her first glimpse of the Mediterranean. Summing up her impressions, she wrote: "Siena was delightful, with an interesting cathedral, very gay in white and dark green and rose marble – mostly *striped!*" San Gimignano was "the nicest and best preserved walled town in Italy, and Volterra probably the next." Catherine travelled through the hill towns by bus, agonizing around each hairpin curve, turns without so much as a small stone between the road and infinity.

Mussolini had already made an obvious mark on the cultural landscape. During the next two decades Catherine would become a staunch anti-fascist, but her first exposure to fascism prompted mixed feelings. "Mussolini has done the most extraordinary things with this rather languid, passive country," she wrote. "The papers are nothing but fascist propaganda and every move one makes is ordained or criticized by him. For instance, there *is no white bread* any more in the whole country – it's a law. There are no dining-and-dancing places any more – not even for the Americans. And one really doesn't have to tip." The last constraint was a relief after France, where even the smallest courtesy demanded payment.

Warm, soft spring was already in the air, and Catherine's heart melted. After a month in and around Florence she left by train for Capri, stopping in Rome to pick up Ellie Kingman and another school friend. On the way from Rome they rode in a third-class compartment with seven men, wine growers who shared their food with the Americans and passed bottles around. One young man, wearing a loud checkered suit and sporting a cane, sidled in beside Catherine. Like thousands of his countrymen, he had spent a few years in New York's Little Italy, learned some English, made some money, and returned home to "prestige and propagation." He turned to Catherine. "Gotta man?"

"No, unfortunately, not at the moment," was the reply she regretted instantly and proceeded to amend, describing her very jealous husband who had stayed behind in Florence.

"Capri is the *most* wonderful place in the world!" she wrote her family the day she arrived. The young women settled into a life of leisure, exploration, and decadence. As the weeks flew by they swam, climbed rocky bluffs, paddled skiffs into the grottos, read, and played bridge. They met a number of colourful characters whom Catherine, the extrovert, got to know well enough to include in stories she would later write under the pseudonym Cassidea for the Paris journal *The Comet*.

The women spent the month of April in a villa that they rented for $24. It was a two-story, white-washed, stuccoed cube with a façade entirely free of decorative elements, broken only by doors and windows. Buildings with these simple lines were being designed by architects in northern Europe who were in the process of creating a new kind of modern architecture. Catherine had not yet discovered this movement – one that she would soon champion – but she instinctively admired the utter simplicity of her little villa in Capri.

RIGHT BANK

We are America's most widely known, most peculiarly national, most exploited product. We are ... Les Jeunes Filles Americaines.

CATHERINE BAUER

Catherine fully expected to return to New York some time in May, but her plans changed when a cable arrived in Capri from the parents of her old college roommate, Fritz Goetzmann: "Would you be in France two months if we send Fritz early May?" She understood that Fritz would not be permitted to live in Paris without a companion known to her parents. The more she thought about it, the more she relished the idea of spending another few months in Paris. Defying her parents' wishes to have their daughter home by spring, she concentrated all her powers of persuasion and negotiation to win them over and, even trickier, to get them to send money.

"If I were a boy you would say 'Fine and dandy, just the thing,'" she wrote. "But I've had as good an education as a boy and more or less of a masculine point of view – so why not for me, too?" She insisted that Paris was the very best place for her to be, with its trove of modern art, modern literature, modern music – all the things that really interested her. If only her clothes weren't threadbare and her wallet almost empty! Catherine offered her parents a deal: if they would send her a clothing allowance now, she would not ask for more when she came home at the end of summer. Anyway, she argued, dresses and shoes could be bought much more inexpensively in Paris than in New York. And she could live very cheaply by sharing a room with Fritz.

The telegram from Fritz's parents triggered a surge of ideas and possibilities that captured Catherine's imagination. Now that she knew French well, she might be able to find work as a translator of French books and plays into English. She would apply for a position at the *Paris Herald* or perhaps at the English-language Shakespeare and Company book shop; her friend, M. Sliwinsky, had some contacts at both places and might be able to help.

Ellie and Catherine parted company on the morning of April 26, 1927 – Ellie joining her parents to tour southern Italy, Catherine boarding a train to Paris. The journey took four days, with nights spent sitting up in third-class carriages crowded with Italian labourers munching strong-smelling sandwiches and guzzling from vials of wine that they offered to share, but which she always declined. During a two-hour stopover in Rome, Catherine rushed to St. Peter's and quickly saw enough of its ornate architecture for her tastes. She allotted more time to Assisi and Perugia, where early Gothic architecture held far greater appeal. The Italian Renaissance did not please her, she decided, but Assisi's Giottos, frescoes, and Romanesque architecture were perfect.

Upon arriving on May Day, Catherine declared that she was "positively, sloppily sentimental" about springtime in Paris. Flush with the allowance cheque from her parents, plus a gift of cash from her grandmother, she rented a room and then set out to find work. Her first approach was to the local newspapers, to which she proposed to sell articles written during her year of travels. She found a ready market at the *Sunday Herald*, which bought a piece that she had titled "La Jeune Fille Americaine" and signed "One of Them" – choosing to remain anonymous. To her chagrin, the story ran under the headline "Some Trials of American Girls in Europe."[1]

"We are America's most widely known, most peculiarly national, most exploited product, recognized at a greater distance than a Ford. We are a Public Institution, a Society for the Amusement, Education, and Pecuniary Benefit of the European public, largely for the benefit of Mr. Europe," she wrote, going on to describe how, from the age of five, European boys look forward to the time they can make American girls fall for them. This is not because the girls are attractive, but for sport, like a rabbit hunt, claimed One of Them. For example, a young Italian man bragged that he had necked with a girl from every state but Nevada and was patiently returning to the same dance hall every day hoping to complete the series. By contrast, Mrs. Europe is critical of American girls because "we have such a strange and dangerous amount of liberty, we do not wear our clothes properly, we have a so much better time in their own country than they do, so we are quite unbearable." For the next few years Catherine often referred to herself as a Jeune Fille Americaine, which she contracted to JFA.

Although he liked her writing style, the editor of the *Sunday Herald* was unable to provide steady work. He gave Catherine an introduction to the publisher of *The Comet*, a new and short-lived English-language bimonthly magazine that initially struck Catherine as "sophisticated, rather like The New Yorker." *The Comet* immediately bought a story about Montparnasse and the Latin Quarter, apparently to benefit summer tourists. Adolph Dehn, the American artist she had met through the Sliwinskys, illustrated her story. The editors thought her work was excellent and were prepared to buy as much as she could write.

Each new story brought Catherine a little more money, but also a growing disillusionment about the quality of the magazine. They wanted humorous, slightly naughty, slangy, thrilling, and pseudo-sophisticated articles; at first these were fun to write, but the fun soon paled. She was happy to hide behind the pen name Cassidea, which she derived from her nickname Casey. "It's so easy to do junk for *The Comet* – but I hate it," she wrote her mother late in the summer.

One piece, titled "Such a Ridiculous Place, Capri," made fun of people whom she had genuinely liked. Using her unusual gift of observation, she took the liberty of combining characteristics of several people into buffoons to amuse *The Comet*'s readers. There was "Signora G," for example: "a Scotch English lady of indeterminate age, who married a Capri lawyer for her third husband. A large bass-voiced lady, who looks as if she might be a cross between a horse and a sentimental English bobby. It is said on Capri that once the signora Inglese was inadvertently arrested in Naples on suspicion of being a man dressed as a lady."[2]

Other work began to trickle in. An Italian poet and playwright asked Catherine to translate one of his plays from French into English, in the hope of selling it in Great Britain or the United States. Catherine persuaded three publishers to let her translate some modern French books in the hope that she could persuade American publishers to buy them.

One evening the Sliwinskys invited her to go dancing with them and a friend, the prominent modern architect Adolf Loos. Catherine jumped at the chance of meeting this "extraordinarily intelligent Viennese." At age sixty, he still loved to Charleston and left her quite exhausted. At the evening's end, she summoned all her nerve and asked Loos if he needed a "draftslady." Although he did not keep offices in Paris, he told her yes, he did happen to have some copywork for her.

Catherine arrived at his rooms promptly at nine the next morning. The work was simple enough, she wrote, "but the great man proved to be too affectionately inclined – so nothing could be done about it ... How very annoying and disillusioning – that brilliant and famous old men should have their little weaknesses!" Nevertheless, eight years later, in her first application for a Guggenheim grant, she would indicate that she had worked for Adolf Loos in Paris – his name carried weight and was certainly worth dropping. Catherine had read his famous essay "Ornament und Verbrechen" by that time, and she fully subscribed to his assertion that "Cultural evolution is the equivalent to the removal of ornament from articles in daily use. Ornament is wasted labor, hence wasted health ... it is also wasted material and all adds up to wasted capital."[3]

With no steady work, and reasoning that she could write stories just as easily on a trip as in Paris, Catherine decided to join Fritz on a six-day tour of Brittany. She wrapped her clothes in a large kerchief, stashed writing pad and pencils in her purse, and, with Fritz, boarded a train to Pontorson. From there, they walked the fifteen kilometres to Mont-Saint-Michel, where they toured the abbey and castle, then returned to the mainland just as the tide began to come in.

Sitting on the terrace of their inn, watching Mont-Saint-Michel become an island, they were soon joined by three young American men who were touring on bicycles. All were architects. Tommy Church would become a lifelong friend of Catherine's and many years later would be her colleague on the faculty of the University of California in Berkeley. Sterling Blaizey would be Catherine's beau for a short time that summer; the third man was a fellow Catherine vaguely remembered from her year at Cornell. Church and Blaizey were on travelling scholarships to study architecture in Europe.

The five Americans formed a little touring party, taking turns walking and riding bikes along the Brittany shore. Sometimes they hopped on local trains or on the backs of trucks to explore surrounding villages. In one town, where rooms were in short supply, they told a startled innkeeper that they were honeymooners and could therefore share a room. In another town they joined a party until 5:30 a.m. before trying in vain to find a room. They spent the remainder of that night in a hayloft, leaving their bikes and shoes outside. They awoke to find themselves surrounded by gawking, barefoot villagers (they had removed their *sabots* not to awaken the mysterious travellers). Eventually the Americans roused themselves and wandered down to the village pump, where, stripped to their essentials, they washed their faces and brushed their teeth under the admiring gaze of the entire village school. The women had peeled off their outer garments, which had become filthy from serving as towels after swims in streams. It had been nearly a week since they had properly bathed, but as Catherine blithely noted, "cleanliness is an acquired habit, not in the least necessary to personal happiness."

While frolicking with her new friends, Catherine paid close attention to the details of life and landscape in the villages they visited. Although each village had its own indigenous style, they were alike in their almost complete lack of amenities for comfort and privacy. The villagers were mostly stout, and women wore a variety of starched organdy caps, all of which Catherine duly recorded in her notebook for use in future articles. Indeed, the story of her trip to Brittany was snatched up by *The Comet* shortly after her return to Paris.

The Brittany article found its way to New Jersey, where it profoundly shocked the Bauers. Catherine was stunned by a bitter letter from her mother accusing her of being egotistical – writing reams about her own adventures while neglecting to inquire about the family's activities and well-being. As it happened, the Bauers were in the midst of constructing a new home. Money was tight, and Jacob and Bertie were starting to have second thoughts about the $100 allowance they'd just sent their ungrateful daughter. Catherine apologized and assured her family that she loved them more than ever. She was indeed very interested in their activities and attributed her neglect to a radical generational difference in letter-writing habits. "We have gone too far in fighting against sentimentality," she wrote. "If I had a husband and children and were away from them, I shouldn't dream of asking how they were or inquiring about the house. Also, I shouldn't in the least expect them to ask about my health. I suppose we're horrible egotists."

For the first time in many months, Catherine was beginning to feel grounded in Paris and was looking forward to a summer of serious writing. "I promise you one thing – by fall I shall know whether I can write or not," she tried to assure her parents. She was convinced that she had to remain in Europe in order to find herself, her true interests, and her abilities. If she were home, she would feel younger and would lose ground in her search for self: all the people she knew there were either her age and no more intelligent than she, or older and with different interests. "Here I am an adult," she explained. "I meet excellent people absolutely on their own ground and I feel as if I belonged. Good heavens, but I hope you understand."

One of these excellent people was a brilliant young Russian-French student of philosophy, Serge, with whom Catherine enjoyed hours of stimulating conversation. Often his ardent Communist friends joined them at the theatre after which they would retire to a bistro and argue the merits of the plays late into the night. Many years later these casual associations with Communist youths would return to haunt Catherine.

She was also spreading her wings in literary circles. In June the Sliwinskys introduced her to Sylvia Beach, the prominent English expatriate who ran the bookshop Shakespeare and Company; Beach also co-published James Joyce's *Ulysses*. Catherine hoped Beach would help her publish an article about an exciting new book, Virginia Woolf's *To the Lighthouse*. In her estimation, the novel achieved "the highest peak in the field of literature called the Stream of Consciousness School." Woolf's writing was less blatantly psychological than Proust's, argued Catherine, less self-conscious than James Joyce's, and infinitely more subtle than Dorothy Richardson's.

Having read several of Woolf's books, including *Night and Day* and *Jacob's Room,* Catherine wrote the author an eight-page fan letter. Woolf responded, but the correspondence lay dormant until 1939, when, on a professional visit to England, Catherine secured an invitation for tea. She found Woolf's attitudes toward the United States to be provincial. "Don't you *really* wish you were English, my deah?" Catherine was asked with honest amazement. The question was followed by, "Just what is a thesis?" A midwestern professor wanted to prove that Woolf's father was greater than Matthew Arnold, and she could not dissuade him. "It seems to be one of the greatest troubles with America," Woolf said of a proposed thesis on the subject.[4]

Although Sylvia Beach was interested in Catherine's work and may have helped her young friend find a market for the Woolf essay, there is no record of its publication. In the end, the Woolf encounter was chalked up to experience, and a rich one at that. Undaunted, Catherine moved on to a subject dearer to her heart: modern design. "No one in America knows anything about Modern Domestic Architecture," she wrote her parents as she embarked on an article on modern French domestic architecture, furniture, and decorative style. In it she would compare current American standards in building design with her observations at the *Exposition Internationale des Arts Décoratifs et Industriels Modernes* in Paris. It was eventually published to wide acclaim in *The New York Times Magazine*.

Sterling Blaizey, who had stayed in Paris following the Brittany adventure, escorted Catherine on a tour of modern buildings in Paris. Prominent architects, including Mallet-Stevens and Lurçat, opened their studios when they heard she was writing an article. By now she had mastered French, and the architects were enchanted by her forthright manner and sense of humour. She spent weeks taking copious notes and photographs; two photos, featuring the radical designs of Mallet-Stevens and Lurçat, were published along with the articles.

After Fritz returned to America in July, Catherine lived alone. Her parents, concerned about appearances, disapproved. "You needn't worry at all," she assured them. "I've never in my life led a more conventional life than at the moment. I do nothing but read and write and eat and walk, almost always alone." This monkish routine was reinforced when a wisdom tooth erupted and became abscessed, requiring daily visits to a dentist and severe restrictions to her diet and exercise. For several days she could eat only omelettes and drink only wine, and do nothing but read. "The growth of Wisdom is Difficult!" she moaned.

By midsummer a little community of ten Vassar women from the class of '26 had congregated in Paris. Although she enjoyed their high spirits – they laughed uproariously when they met, just as in school – Catherine felt she had outgrown this crowd and shunned their attempts to socialize with her. She preferred to spend weekends at the Sliwinskys' summer house among more interesting people: Poles and Russians immersing themselves in Western literature and philosophy; and Germans who persuaded Catherine that true modernity could only be found in their country and constantly urged her to learn German and go to Berlin and Munich if she wanted to see good modern art and architecture. Three years later she would follow their advice.

In August Parisians took to the streets in a furore over the execution of the anarchists Sacco and Vanzetti in the United States. The men had been falsely accused and sentenced to death for murdering a paymaster and his guard near Boston in 1920. In the summer of 1927, the Massachusetts Supreme Court upheld their conviction on appeal, even though another murderer had confessed the crime two years earlier. Catherine reported home that the mobs were "shouting à la college cheering: 'Sac-co-et-Van-zet-ti-liberez' – over and over again." She judged that mob psychology had taken over and most people probably did not have the slightest idea what it was all about. She expressed no personal view on this issue, nor had she taken a stance on fascism when she encountered it in Italy. She merely reported events as they occurred. Her opinions were reserved for art, architecture, and literature.

Catherine read one to two books a week and kept track of them in a small notebook listing titles, authors, characters, and brief summaries. During this period she discovered Waldo Frank, J. Middleton Murray, and Lewis Mumford, "who is excellent," she told her little book. She thought his *The Golden Day* contained very interesting explanations and criticism of pragmatism. She wrote:

> *Mr. Mumford seems to irritate me a little – as perhaps do all people who have given us a large amount of very good and well built-up information and their point of view – when we know that we are not well enough educated to be able to contradict even if we would. He puts me in my place. He makes me a little ashamed of not being interested in America as a separate cultural entity. He cares. Incomprehensible. Pragmatism is interesting. Its causes and*

effects are interesting – the machine and its ditto are also interesting. But
I don't care in the least if I am a transcendentalist, a pragmatist, an instru-
mentalist – or a pioneer. After all, if the nation lacks true culture – the only
actual conscious losers are people like Lewis Mumford who possesses culture
and also a missionary spirit. Why the devil should I pity my family and their
unopened volumes of Emerson? (or myself).

As an afterthought she added, "Must read Melville some time, Emerson
and *Sticks and Stones* by Mumford." Little could she know what lay ahead.

By the end of a long, hot summer Catherine had tired of Paris. This was
partly due to her chronic dental problems and partly to homesickness. The
Oxford doctor returned for a final dinner and a comedy club date. "He
asked me most politely to marry him, and I most politely replied that I was
awfully sorry but marriage didn't particularly interest me just now. So that
was that." On September 3, 1927, almost twelve months after she had left
New York City, Catherine departed from Southampton on a one-class ship
belonging to the Atlantic Transport Line.

New York

I am the Horrible Example of what a year abroad does to a
nice, impressionable young American girl.

CATHERINE BAUER

A self-confident, independent young woman was returning to New York.
Catherine had lived largely by her native wit, developing her social
instincts as she mingled with other young intellectuals who flocked to Paris
from all over Europe. Her gifts as a writer were confirmed that year: her
stories were bought as quickly as they were written. Paris would lie at the
centre of her affection for many years. The currents of European art and
architecture that she encountered would form a background against which
she would map the themes of her life.

It had been an extraordinary year for Catherine, whose life, until
September 1926, was governed by the well-established customs of politically conservative, middle-class America. Despite regular correspondence
with their daughter, Alberta and Jacob Bauer had no idea how deeply she
had changed in the year abroad. Had her mother accepted any of
Catherine's several invitations to join her in Europe, she might have been
more prepared for the firebrand who returned.

Bertie's greatest ambition for her daughter was for her to be settled in an
elegant home and married to someone like the Oxford doctor who had
squired her to Paris's best restaurants and theatres. Several Vassar women

who had spent the year in Europe actively looking for husbands were now "safely" married off – just two years after graduation. But Catherine was not to be courted. The stories she shared with her parents of her life on the Left Bank seemed strange and sinister to them, and the people she associated with there – the Sliwinskys and their coterie from many countries – seemed eccentric, even dangerous. But these people had opened doors for Catherine, leading to radical insights into the world of art and culture from which there would be no return.

Like any new convert, she was now extremely intolerant of the old order, which made her return home difficult for everyone. For one thing she hated the family's brand new mock-Tudor house at 722 Westminster Avenue, located in a more fashionable part of Elizabeth than their old home. Bertie and Jacob were stunned at their daughter's show of disdain, especially since they had employed an architect, a Cornell graduate whom Catherine had originally recommended for the job. They had been bursting with pride in their two-story house with its steeply pitched roof and half-timber façade. The ground floor held a spacious, rectangular living room bisected by a large stone fireplace and opening to a screened-in porch at one end. Behind the living room, facing the garden, were the kitchen, pantry, and dining room, opening onto a large patio covered by an awning. Upstairs were three bedrooms, two baths, and a tiny guest room built above the covered driveway. The guest room was reserved for Catherine. It would not do for more than a few days, she declared, and soon set out for New York City's Greenwich Village to find a more suitable dwelling.

In a satiric confessional piece for *Vanity Fair* titled "Thank God I'm a Decadent," Catherine attempted to capture the essence of her newly liberated self. She represented, she wrote, a horrible example of what can happen to an impressionable young American woman during a year abroad. A perfectly square girl who opposed makeup and dirty jokes, whose

BAUER FAMILY HOME, C. 1929

She hated the family's brand new mock-Tudor house at 722 Westminster Avenue.

greatest maidenly triumph was getting elected the funniest girl in camp for repeatedly falling into the lake, had been entirely transformed by Paris. She had become supercilious; a first-class dilettante so diversely and flippantly educated that everything under the sun, from Prize-fighting to Perversion, from the Lost Books of the Bible to Gertrude Stein's *Elucidation*, from the Sex-war in England to church-music of the Middle-Ages, from the subtleties of Perspective in the Parthenon to the love-life of Warren Gamaliel Harding, from Greuze to Man Ray, that *everything* then, should have its own particular prick, its own aura of amusing suggestion. "I refuse to know the fundamental facts. They might bother me."

She wanted to paint, write, play the mandolin, have children, be unfaithful to her husband, discuss the aesthetic satisfaction of grain elevators, or collect wax flowers – merely depending on whether she had oysters for lunch. She continued:

I have no Fundamental Female Urges which push me on regardless toward bigger and better races. (The definition of Decadent could be, I suppose, that person for whom Necessities are a Luxury – and vice versa.) And, I beg you, do not think that I have Missionary Spirit – that this article is educational propaganda because I want to make you just as happy as I am. Not in the least – to write for Vanity Fair is merely a decadent method of achieving the means to be a Bigger and Better Dilettante.

The article was signed Cassidea and, not surprisingly, was never published. Ironically, Catherine did come to be regarded as a dilettante by her colleagues years later, not for Cassidea's reasons, but for a life's work that was diverse and grew out of experience rather than formal education.

During the fall of 1927 the close bonds that held the Bauer family together were stretched thin. Enormous tension developed between Bertie and her eldest daughter, and for a time following Catherine's move to Greenwich Village, communication between the two all but ceased. In many ways Catherine missed the Sliwinskys more than her own family, and in moving to the Village she hoped to replace that bond. Cassidea's story reflected the credo of many young, aspiring artists, writers, and freethinkers who gravitated to the Village in those years – especially women who, like Catherine, arrived from affluent towns west of the Hudson River and from colleges like Vassar and Smith.

For nearly two decades the Village had been home to well-educated young women who sought equality with men and were willing to live a frugal life to gain it. The luxurious mansions that had housed Manhattan's upper class before the turn of the century had become run down and were now subdivided, often into cold-water flats. These were ideal accommodations for young men and women who lived hand-to-mouth, toting up debts at cafés where they met to hear and critique each other's stories and poetry.

It was the most benign form of poverty, sustained by wealthy socialites who were also drawn to these cafés and could be counted on to open their comfortable homes to gatherings, and even to pay off bad debts. The most promising writers found a ready market in magazines such as *The Dial, The Little Review,* and *The Masses.* Of course, mainstream publications such as *Vogue* and *Women's Journal* paid more, but did not carry the same cachet among the denizens of the Village.

By the time Catherine moved to the Village, women had made significant gains in their battle for equality with men. The institution of marriage was frowned upon, and a liberal attitude toward multiple sexual partners was in vogue. The women's suffrage movement, formerly centred in New York, was no longer relevant since women now had the vote. New battle lines were drawn at work, and a less strident approach was called for. Where ten years earlier women dressed outlandishly, cut their hair in mannish styles, and insisted on paying for their own meals and opening their own doors, Catherine's generation of liberated women favoured the kind of business attire and manners that would earn them respectable jobs at publishing houses or magazines.

The economy of 1927 was booming, and Catherine soon found work as the manager of pattern promotion for Butterick, which meant that she wrote blurbs on pattern covers. This lasted only a couple of months, however, as a corporate reorganization eliminated the job. She returned to magazine work and sold stories to *Vogue* and *Women's Journal,* which hired her for a while as an assistant editor. She tried her hand at other kinds of writing, including copy for ad agencies and travel brochures for the Cunard Shipping Line. But her real desire was to write about French architecture.

Drawing from her extensive Paris notes, Catherine assembled a comprehensive essay on modern architecture and, in the spring of 1928, submitted it to *The New York Times Magazine.* It was accepted – a remarkable feat for a twenty-three year old. Titled "Machine-Age Mansions for Ultra-Moderns" and subtitled "French Builders Apply Ideas of the Steel and Concrete Era in Domestic Architecture," the article featured her two photographs of family houses by Lurçat and Mallet-Stevens.

Catherine's intention was to educate American readers about the possibilities of modern architecture in residential structures, and she began with Le Corbusier's rhetorical question and answer: "What is a house? A house is a machine for living in." Noting that this notion of a machine-house "bumps hard even now against all our rosy ideals of 'homelike atmosphere,'" she went on to ask a question of her own: "Is a house a badge for social distinction, the proof of our taste in historic styles, or the one accomplished poem of our lives?"[5]

Her answer related modern architecture to current movements in art, such as cubism and futurism. She applauded the use of modern materials – concrete, steel, and glass – to create light and airy living spaces that afforded people great flexibility in organizing their dwellings. The arrival of these new materials spelled the end of brick and stone construction and the attendant compromises posed by massive support walls. Steel rendered these structural methods obsolete and unleashed the architectural imagination. Decorative elements now were embodied through textures, window arrangements, balconies, and colour, such as red tiled roofs. The new architecture flew in the face of the Beaux Arts' credo that corners must look solid. On the contrary, new buildings often featured windows that swept around corners.

Of the architects covered in her essay, Le Corbusier was given the most space. His sociological interests led him to design good and economic houses for the ordinary person, she argued. He proposed mass production of uniform elements that could be constructed easily, quickly, and cheaply. By raising the lowest floor off the ground, play areas and gardens could be incorporated. Roof gardens were installed on all his buildings. Le Corbusier's houses typically had long, unbroken walls, with long horizontal windows at either end, often embracing corners. These arrangements were more conducive to effective interior furnishing than dark corners and walls broken up by small windows. He was innovative in the use of built-in furniture and ramps instead of steps. Le Corbusier envisioned enormous blocks of apartment houses that might incorporate offices and shops on the lower floors, and connect to underground routes for transportation.

Lurçat, on the other hand, focused on single detached dwellings appropriate to middle-class needs. He emphasized uniformity in the elements of construction, but variety in plan, which resulted in an atmosphere of unity, convenience, and rational order. As this kind of construction was based on recent advances in engineering, Catherine wrote of the growing relationship between the two disciplines.

Le Corbusier characterized new houses as being "intelligent, cold, and calm." To this Catherine added "they may conceivably be good art because engineering is based entirely upon geometry." She pointed out that "geometrical perfection is the symbol of civilization pruned and carved out of the natural chaos. It is the primary justification for man's superiority complex."

Catherine postulated that the new dwellings were most suitable for unsentimental intellectuals who were not overly concerned about their living arrangements because they had better things to do with their time. By contrast, workers who function as cogs in machines all day take comfort from their cozy, over-furnished homes, filled with dusty knick-knacks. For the intellectual, a living machine is beautiful because it stems from pure intelligence and releases man for further intellectual effort.

She reached an interesting conclusion: America's unique natural resources, coupled with a system of government that empowers people to exploit those resources, result in terrific competition in which survival depends upon being more successful than the next person. During the work day, most people get ahead by being efficient. In their private lives, competition is banished and comfort embraced. "In the little worlds that people do more or less control, they do not live very differently from the way they might have lived long ago. With the addition of a few minor conveniences, houses are much the same as they were then."[6] The average American's sentimental desire for a home that is at once a hobby and a retreat precludes any general enthusiasm for a house-machine.

The article was very well received, causing many in New York's design intelligentsia to sit up and take notice of the young writer. Among them was Philip Johnson, an emerging champion of modern art who was being courted by Henry Russell Hitchcock to curate the Museum of Modern Art's first architecture show, scheduled to open in 1932. Clearly, this was no ordinary article but a ticket to the design community's elite seats. It also proved to be a remedy to heal the rift in Catherine's family, since her proud parents were overwhelmed with congratulations from friends and relatives.

Through her Village connections, Catherine met a typographer named Robert Josephy who shared her interest in architecture and whose work was influenced by the Bauhaus movement in Germany. Together they explored New York City, which Catherine found rather grim in comparison with Paris. The Chrysler and Empire State Buildings, two structures that vied at being the tallest buildings in the world, drew her fire. Fresh from France, where steel, glass, and reinforced concrete were used to great advantage, Catherine was disgusted with the current American skyscrapers, built with modern materials but cloaked in old-fashioned exteriors.

Like Adolph Loos, she believed that all the significant points of conventional architecture, such as cornices, pilasters, and mouldings, had no meaning in modern design. They were merely pasted on after buildings were finished: vestigial organs that served no purpose. The Woolworth building, the pride of New York, looked like a cathedral; Wall Street buildings were decorated with Tudor roses. On the other hand, Child's Restaurant, at 604 Fifth Avenue, won Catherine's admiration because of its simplicity and rounded glass block corners. It was one of the most controversial buildings in America.

Josephy, who did layout work for Harcourt Brace, helped Catherine obtain a job in the promotions department of the prestigious publishing house. Her brilliant conversation, wit, and good humour endeared her to her fellow workers, most of whom were older men. Through them she met poets, writers, and editors, including Viking Press editor Marshall Best, who, in turn, introduced her to his close friend Alice Decker.

Alice, a social worker and sculptor, was a consummate New Yorker who knew people in every walk of life. Catherine was enthralled, and a lifelong friendship was born – though it proved to be quite bumpy at times. For a short while the women shared a duplex apartment just north of the Village; Fritz Goetzmann joined them when she moved to New York. Shortly after Fritz arrived, however, Catherine moved out, preferring to live alone. During that period, Alice, inspired by Catherine's beauty, sculpted her head in clay and had it bronzed as a gift for her friend.

Alice introduced Catherine to her friends Malcolm Cowley, Kenneth Burke, and Matthew Josephson, publishers of a literary monthly magazine called *Broom*. Thirty-five years later Josephson would write a book, *Life Among the Surrealists*, in which Catherine (the pseudonymous Miss D.) was described as "handsome, vivacious and intellectual" – a free-living and free-loving woman who settled into a happy marriage and an illustrious career after having "lived in sin" for years.[7]

3

ROMANTIC YEARS (1930-33)

LEWIS MUMFORD

I am in love for the first time in my life and so proud of the amazing good taste of my instincts in their choice of a victim.

CATHERINE BAUER TO LEWIS MUMFORD

Catherine was happy to be working at Harcourt Brace, a bona fide publishing house, even though she was limited to writing promotional copy and occasional book-jacket notes for trade titles. Captivated by her keen intellect and knowledge of architecture, a young copy editor named Cap Pearce pointed her out to Lewis Mumford, one of the company's most respected authors. As it turned out, Mumford had already noticed the "new girl" working in a corner of the publisher's editorial room. At Pearce's urging, he invited her out to lunch.

CATHERINE IN THE LATE 1920S

Captivated by her keen intellect and knowledge of architecture, a young copy editor named Cap Pearce pointed her out to Lewis Mumford, one of the company's most respected authors.

Catherine was surprised by the attention of this handsome, urbane man who, at thirty-four, was ten years older than she. In Paris she had enjoyed reading Mumford's *The Golden Day* and recognized him as a towering intellect. Intimidated, she accepted the lunch invitation with apprehension and was fabricating an excuse to get out of it when a letter arrived:

Dear Miss Bauer:
We are never to meet at lunch! Fate, as they used to say in Victorian novels, has willed otherwise. I must run out of town next Monday; is your following Monday free – or what have you?

Regretfully,
apologetically,
yours,
Lewis Mumford

Lewis Mumford was one of America's great men of letters. "He supported himself entirely by his pen, producing a body of work almost unequaled in this century for its range and richness,"[1] wrote his biographer, Donald Miller, in *Lewis Mumford: A Life*. The biography aptly quoted Mumford's friend, Mark Van Doren, who called Mumford a master builder: "He builds cities, societies, civilizations, cultures – truly builds them, with the most durable stuff available to man: ideas."

Mumford credited the breakthrough in his emotional blockage and the release of his creative energies to his encounter with Catherine. "Who will be bold enough to estimate the energies that Catherine first released? NOT I! There's no one," he wrote in October 1971, on a visit to the Van Pelt Library at the University of Pennsylvania, where his papers are housed.

Immediately attracted to this tall, mustachioed man, Catherine resolved to be free for lunch the following Monday. It proved to be the start of an intensely passionate, intellectual, and occasionally ribald affair that would ebb and flow for years – resurrected even after Catherine's death in Mumford's writings. She was his muse, and he her mentor who, even after the romance waned, took his place among her many other distinguished friends. A year after they met, she wrote to him, "Art thou not the potter and I the clay?"

Their first lunch spilled long into the afternoon. They discussed *The Golden Day*, which, she confessed, had sparked her interest in returning to the United States from her year abroad. Enchanted, Mumford later wrote: "All that Pearce said about her intelligence is quite true. I cannot quite describe the candor and lucidity of her thought; the slight air of

LEWIS MUMFORD

Immediately attracted to this tall, mustachioed man, Catherine resolved to be free for lunch the following Monday ... A year after they met, she wrote to him, "Art thou not the potter and I the clay?"

hardness and cynicism that lies on top of it, or the warmth and subtlety of feeling that lies beneath."

During the next three months they occasionally met for lunch or dinner and usually discussed topics of common interest, such as literature and architecture. Lewis expanded her horizons beyond buildings and city blocks to the region. He told her about his eccentric friend Patrick Geddes, the Scottish biologist and seminal thinker on urban planning after whom his son, Geddes Mumford, was named; about Raymond Unwin, an English planner he admired; and about Ebenezer Howard, who inspired the Garden City movement in England. They roamed the streets of New York together as he gathered data for his latest manuscript, *The Brown Decades*.

One Saturday afternoon they visited the Havemayer Collection at the Metropolitan Museum of Art and discovered that their reactions were nearly identical. Over dinner at Child's Restaurant, their talk strayed onto intimate ground for the first time. Catherine felt she could let her guard down with Lewis, who demonstrated greater emotional maturity than any man she'd known. She confided that young men sometimes harried her by declaring that sexual intercourse was necessary for their health. As they considered themselves above resorting to prostitutes, they made demands upon her – and then made scenes when she refused. A few times she came close to marrying one or another, she told Lewis, but good sense always prevailed, and within weeks of breaking off such an affair she inevitably forgot all about the fellow. Sex was a pleasure but not central to her life, she said. Some men were so conscientious in their efforts to bring her to an orgasm that they took all the fun away. Her best lover was not even aware that a woman had orgasms.

Returning to Catherine's apartment after dinner, the pair suddenly became strangely remote. She complained of a sore throat and he of a "debility." Suddenly she withdrew into a shroud of indifference and announced that being with him was merely better than being alone. Lewis interpreted this turn of emotions as relief for his "lack of importunateness." It was an oddly embarrassing start to their romance. "A comedy of errors," Mumford commented much later. He was off-kilter that night, for a variety of good reasons.

He considered himself a devoted husband of nine years to Sophie Mumford, with whom he had a child. Yet he desired, and enjoyed, the company of other women. At the time he met Catherine, he had just ended a relationship in which he had experienced some impotence. And the day before the dinner at Child's, he had received a reproachful letter from another former lover. What he pined for, now, was freedom from these troublesome entanglements. The thought of entering into a new one made him suddenly morose. He wrote to her from his home later that night:

> *Whoops: Catherine, in a brief quarter of an hour you've managed to know me at my very worst … So if we see any more of each other, things are bound to get brighter and brighter. When I flirt with other people it is because I like them, and not because I am bored with Sophie; the other girls usually get the worst end of it and end by hating me. Be warned Catherine: perhaps you had better value me for my intellect and keep me at something more than arms length.*

Had Catherine heeded this warning, it would have drastically changed the story of her life – but she did not, and Lewis could not mask his powerful attraction. "It's only a few hours ago since you stopped calling me Mr. Mumford," he wrote, "and my inability to 'integrate' you in the rest of my high activities and plans is equaled only, no doubt, by your very warm desire to remain disintegrated." Lewis tried to explain the disastrous night away by saying he had a carbuncle that prevented amorous approaches, was suffering from inflamed tonsils, and, at the same time, was preoccupied by a book in progress. What he didn't mention was how her surprising pronouncements on sex over coffee at Child's had thrown him off.

While Mumford was drafting this letter, Catherine was scrawling a midnight confession to him. Unaccustomed to addressing him by his first name, she began:

> *Louis pardon me Lewis dear –*
> *You deserve an explanation, a week ago I had an abortion which very naturally put me hors de combat for two or three weeks. Now I do feel that it is not sheer rationalization to point out that one doesn't bring up such things in ordinary or architectural conversation. While I was embarrassedly trying to tell you all this, you with equal embarrassment were telling me the very thing that solved the whole situation except that I got more embarrassed because I realized that you had thought my apparent speechless agony was the bitter hurt of a wronged woman. And now pray God that I may be firmly hard boiled from this time on and let's have lunch together and begin from the beginning and court me all over again if you happen to feel this way. I do like you,*

> *Catherine*

Three weeks later Lewis helplessly admitted, "all my warnings to you, my dear, were only admonitions to myself." He could not wrest Catherine from his mind. Recuperating from a wound in his ribs "that would have made St. Sebastian proud," he hoped to meet her next Monday. "You have warned me how little people register on you when they're gone: so I am forearmed!"

He needn't have worried. Catherine was obsessed, and unafraid to admit it: "If you *would* like to go to bed with me, I wish to God you would some time, because I'd rather go to bed with you than with anyone else I know at the moment – And if you wouldn't, you'd better keep away from me, for I feel perfectly irresistible and very lusty."

"Your letter almost answered the six I hadn't written," Lewis replied. "Do you think you could have *kept* me out of your bed this last fortnight if I'd had half my usual energies?" Lewis assured Catherine that she was the nicest girl he had met in ten years. Her loveliness had a hundred forms, he said, and her body was none the worse for harbouring a fascinating mind.

As somewhat of a hypochondriac, Lewis often complained of a multitude of ailments, provoking Catherine's good-humoured ire. Longing now for physical closeness, she implored: "Please oh please don't have a carbuncle. Couldn't you have your tonsils out at the same time as treating the carbuncle? I am much more in love than – well, at least, than usual. I do enjoy you so because I have such an outrageously good opinion of myself when I am with you."

"From lover's compliments you must not endeavor to extract too much truth, my vain kitten," Lewis cautioned. "I could never have dreamed you, Catherine: but the totality of you is far nicer than anything I have dared to dream. I had just about given up the hope of ever finding an intellectual bedfellow: not that I want the intellect in bed, but that I rather like it when I wake up." He confessed to having difficulty making love to other women. They were all, in some way, physically unfortunate and their lovemaking inadequate. Many bordered too much on the compassionate. "Having now seen Paradise, even if I have not entered its rosy gate makes life very jolly."

Catherine grew coy and teased him by return mail. "He'll discover that I am not half as intelligent as he thinks I am," she wrote, "that my conversation is a trick, that I have a synthetic intellect, that I'm a show-off, that I am unsympathetic – and so on."

"What have I done to you darling," Lewis replied. "You are becoming humble too; now we both are. You may not know what that means, but I do: we are in love. You are on the downward path, dear: there's no stopping us." Here ended their verbal foreplay.

By the end of April Catherine embraced spring and life and the promise of love in utter jubilance – only to find her hero beset by melancholy. "Yesterday I felt like some deep sea monster, swimming under ten thousand pounds pressure at the bottom of a very black ocean, certain that

I should burst if I ever rose to the upper levels," he wrote. "I needed sleep but that oceanic blackness, that feeling that nothing could be worse finally brought its own relief." His wife was likely the source of his despair. He felt compelled to tell her about Catherine, and soon did. Fortunately for the lovers, Sophie accepted the news without apparent anger, freeing Lewis to indulge his passion for Catherine – to talk endlessly about art and architecture and literature, "and when we touch upon sex, it will not be in conversation." A few years later, when Sophie met Catherine by chance, Sophie admitted liking the woman she would have preferred to hate.

Lewis Mumford's lifelong passion for ideas about cities, architecture, and culture began when he was a child exploring the streets of New York City under the loving guidance of his grandfather. It was this passion, more than anything, that drew Catherine into her first complete surrender to love. She had known other amusing men, other attractive men, and other intelligent men, but Lewis was greater than the sum of all those. Were it not for Sophie, she would have sought his hand in marriage.

Her interest in architecture and regional planning flourished under Lewis's guidance, and she resolved to revisit Europe and see modern architecture with a new focus. Within a few weeks she took a leave of absence from Harcourt Brace, sublet her New York apartment from May 15 to August 15, and moved to Huntington, Long Island – not far from the Mumfords' Sunnyside residence. She paid one month's rent on a canvas cottage, after which she would depart for Europe. Her parents, persuaded by the merits of such a trip, loaned her the fare.

GERMANY

I almost decided, if things work out right, to be an architect after all.

CATHERINE BAUER TO LEWIS MUMFORD

Friends and family gave Catherine a grand send-off aboard the Scandinavian-American Liner SS *United States* on June 11, 1930. Lewis stayed home writing letters and imagining himself beside her at the ship's rail. He had provided her with a Memo on Introductions to many of the stellar architects he knew in Scandinavia, Germany, and Holland. The list included Walter Gropius, Erich Mendelsohn, and Walter Curt Behrendt in Berlin; Ernst May in Frankfurt; and Theo Wijdeveld in Amsterdam. He had also arranged for a bundle of books to be placed in her stateroom, including selections by Plato, Thomas Love Peacock, Walter Savage Landor, Henry James, and Mary Olivier.

Catherine's eye for detail alighted upon her fellow passengers, mostly

Danes whose demeanour and behaviour she recorded daily and compiled into a thirty-five page letter she mailed to Lewis at the end of the voyage. Her view of people was quite different from the first trip, perhaps because she was travelling alone, perhaps reflecting a new frame of mind. She described Danish men who ate themselves into a state of melancholic decay, and ladies who looked as if they might have been ornamental nurse-maids for provincial English families. Conversation with her shipmates was dull – largely postprandial discussion on the rate of exchange.

She described one maiden lady, swathed in great folds of black fabric, as an "admirably structured caryatid" for some lonely system of respectability. There were two Lithuanian priests "in the last stages of some complicated

CATHERINE LEAVES FOR EUROPE

Friends and family gave Catherine a grand send-off aboard the Scandinavian-American Liner SS *United States* on June 11, 1930. Lewis stayed home writing letters.

kind of decay often peering into dark corners, leaning helplessly toward each other as if they'd been hung for years on the same hook by the backs of their rusty coat collars. Their hands shook incessantly." The voyage had its rough spots, and one morning, having been the only person to eat a hearty breakfast, audacious enough to brag about it, Catherine was reduced to becoming publicly and copiously ill.

She befriended a young Danish woman, whose enlightenment Catherine attributed to having lived six years in the United States. Mrs. Ove Arup shared Catherine's fondness of the out-of-doors, and the two planned to take a few days' bike trip around Denmark in July, a trip that did not materialize. The young woman's husband was an engineer with aspirations of being a modern architect, she told Catherine. Indeed, Ove Arup would become one of the world's leading engineer-designers, responsible thirty years later for the concrete sails of the Sydney Opera House in Australia.

But Catherine's thoughts were mostly of Lewis. She had moments of anxiety about travelling alone and told Lewis she was unable to "contemplate even the next step without your stimulating (*and* disturbing, even at a distance of x thousand miles) catalytic effect." She felt as if she were made of wires and elastic, without tension and completely shapeless. The most she could hope for was equilibrium in tensile strength, derived from her association with him.

She was often overcome by loneliness and doubts about the purpose of her expedition, though usually a good meal and a dark beer restored her balance. She admitted to Lewis, after experiencing several episodes of "the most horrible melancholia," that she had never felt such loneliness in her life: "You may or may not fully appreciate what such a realization and admission would mean to one of my Spartan Education in individualism and self-sufficiency."

One day during the voyage, Catherine seized an opportunity to send Lewis a radiogram for one dollar – a good idea that backfired. It contained cryptic allusions to her bleak moods and "false bottoms," and was so muddled by the radio operator that Lewis struggled for hours to distil its meaning. Fearing that "false bottoms" meant Catherine was pregnant, he begged her to wire something plain and transmissible if she were ever caught with an embryo that he has fathered, something like: "The worst has happened, or hurrah for the three of us. Or, as Thomas Beer said when he dedicated Mark Hanna to me, 'now you are involved in the mess.'" Lewis missed her badly and berated himself for letting her leave, yet had not wanted to hold her back because "I was just bulldozed by your tradition of independence and my way of bossing and browbeating everybody and didn't want to begin with you. Oh what a fool I am."

Catherine disembarked in Oslo and was enchanted by the scenery and almost unimaginable midnight sun. Her introductions to Norwegian and, later, Swedish architects bore fruit, and she was guided and wined and dined until her head spun. She took hundreds of photographs, and her lexicon of significant artists' names grew so rapidly that she could barely keep track of them. There were Zorn, Lilljefors, and Milles. There was also Andersson, who thirty years earlier – during a crazed year, in Catherine's opinion – anticipated every trick in Picasso's bag. Ragnar Ostberg's architecture reminded her of Henry Hobson Richardson's shingled houses. An introduction to Stockholm's renowned City Architect, Sven Markelius, brought her into the company of Uno Ahren, a young architect working for the city. Ahren, whose command of English was excellent, was immediately taken by the attractive, lively young American woman and was happy to take the time to show her Stockholm.

To Lewis, she wrote: "I have no proper respect for the trackless distances between my little untrained intellect and yours – or that of the architects whom I approach so brazenly – that I have such a marvelously good time always." She did not lack the ability, or the confidence, to critically analyze all that she saw:

> *I think I could live in this city although it might be too coldly and*
> *efficiently well-managed. For a building to be erected it must be approved by*
> *a committee of the most eminent gentlemen in town as to color, and the*
> *windows and roof must be in direct line with all the other windows and roofs*
> *on the street. There is no place for a studio window. Swedes are just like the*
> *English without sentimentality – and just like the Americans without*
> *Romanticism, our most distinguishing feature.*

For the first time Catherine saw how architecture can express itself as a national style – for better or worse. A new library with pompous Egyptian doors made her laugh: it looked like a hatbox on top of a suitcase. A new tennis stadium, by contrast, struck her as an expression of pure functionalism: architecture used to its best possible advantage and properly finished in solid, brilliant colours.

After one week Catherine sailed to Copenhagen, where Mrs. Arup, her friend from the Atlantic crossing, guided her. She found it a charming and agreeable city albeit very dilapidated. The gardens were reminiscent of England. The variety of food and the decor of the dining tables were so impressive that she wondered how Danes who had migrated coped with the dullness of the American cuisine.

By now Catherine had great boxes of notes that she planned to condense into an article. Lewis, deeply impressed by her writing style, suggested she submit a proposal to the *New Freeman,* which frequently published letters from abroad. "You may or may not be an architect," he told her, "but heavens, even in the midst of being thrilled by the closeness of you, I was aware, like the young lady who noticed a systolic murmur in her lover's heart, that you are a writer."

On arriving in Berlin Catherine visited the American Express office to collect her mail and was greeted by a distressing piece of news from her employer. She and her boss in the trade books publicity department at Harcourt Brace had been fired in the course of internal reorganization. Although Mr. Harcourt extolled her virtues, he offered no assistance. Stunned, Catherine found herself torn out of the heady present and confronted by more practical questions about what she would do on her return from Europe. She might try advertising work, she thought, or another publishing house, or an editorial job with an architectural magazine. Teaching crossed her mind, but it was too late in July to apply for a job that would begin in September. After sleeping on the matter, she awoke refreshed and determined to turn this bad news to advantage. She would extend her travels in Europe, perhaps by a few months. She could manage on $75 per month and had $400 in her pocket plus an open return ticket. Lewis had contributed $100 to her education abroad and might be willing to send more. (He was, and sent another $100.)

Berlin, a city where nearly one-third of the population was foreign, felt comfortable to Catherine because, unlike in Scandinavia, she was not labelled American Tourist here. It was a city of extremes: good and bad, rich and poor, beautiful and ugly. She called it a city of haphazard disharmony, unlike the milder Scandinavian cities that seemed more like New York. Berlin's Baroque and Classic Revival architecture summoned visions of old-fashioned carved black-walnut coffins with cabriole curves. It was all dreadfully delicious.

She looked up the Behrendts from the list of people Lewis had recommended, and a lifelong friendship sprang from their first meeting. Catherine was delighted to be with folks who laughed at her jokes and then made better ones in return. Walter Behrendt had edited the modern architecture journal *Neubau* and had written significant books in the field. His wife, Lydia, an acclaimed concert pianist, suggested an itinerary through Germany that included big cities, such as Frankfurt, Nuremberg, and Stuttgart, as well as mountain villages near Munich.

Catherine left for Munich after a few days. There she found a room in a small *pension,* for 2.50 marks per day, with a landlady who was dismayed that someone with a German surname could not speak the language. The landlady prevailed upon a friend to tutor the American roomer, but Catherine was left after several sessions with little more than the ability to decline a few verbs. How might her life have unfolded, she wondered, had her ancestors remained in Germany? Her mother's sister, Aunt Clara, had told the children that their forebears were Gypsies. The notion appealed to Catherine, but was dispelled much later when her brother Louis, searching for his roots in Germany, discovered that their ancestors were farmers.

Munich's Deutsches Museum captivated Catherine's imagination. It was a technical museum that housed an elaborate nine-acre gallery devoted to mechanical and natural sciences. Catherine spent hours studying the scores of hands-on exhibits, all of which worked, to her amazement. Displays ranged from glass-blowing to early experiments with television and the latest means of pouring concrete. "Only Germany could produce anything so thorough and graphic and solidly instructive," she wrote her parents. Several years later she would recall this elaborate museum when she laid out plans for an exhibit at the New York World's Fair.

Catherine explored the Bavarian Alps for a few days of fresh air and exercise, taking along her photos in order to sort them out for an article. But she never got around to the sorting, losing herself instead in a long, despondent letter to Lewis from Gstadt am Chiemsee:

How would it be if we were comradely males, glad to get away together from the competitions and bitter compromises of the Battle of the Sexes? If we could – and enjoy ourselves – well, it would prove something, though on second thought I'm not exactly sure what – either that we should never see each other again or always should, I suppose. A reiterative worry came over me very suddenly and rather sickeningly when you said – and one could feel its importance – that you had failed to make me ecstatically in love with you. And then I realized for the first time that we might really be fundamentally incompatible after all. You could satisfy me, but that satisfaction might never be the rich, complete thing that your nature demands in response to itself. And so I couldn't be really satisfied either, women being what they are.

Before meeting Lewis she had enjoyed several agreeable but ultimately unimportant affairs, and had come to the reluctant conclusion that she was basically a cool, dispassionate person. But she still wrestled with this. "I don't *quite* believe it," she wrote. "I should so passionately hate to find that I really am just a tight little earth-bound rubber ball, bouncing meagerly – instead of a balloon capable of swelling and soaring and breaking away from its stake."

Prior to mailing the letter, Catherine hiked through a very dark and aromatic pine forest, then along a lake with the Alps in the distance, screaming camp-meeting hymns into the gale. Her head cleared, she returned to her writing table and added a postscript: she had almost decided, if things work out right, to be an architect. She would find a half-time job, live cheaply near Columbia University, and take afternoon and evening courses.

Lewis responded with three pages of musings. First he listed his own doubts about their love, then dismissed them. Believing that her letter stemmed from a wish to resume the strenuous "bachelor" life of an architectural student, he was prepared to modify their relationship according to her best interests. Because of his great love, he was equal to any situation that Catherine could devise, and he offered to remain in her life as a sympathetic critic and able teacher, if she really wished to cast their relationship as one of comradely males. "Permanence and solidity are my particular game," he wrote, "but why should a one-girl man turn Catherine into a one-man girl and divert all her talents into a biological career? Who said that she wanted permanence and biology?" This irony might not have escaped Catherine, but blinded by love she was deaf to his sophistry.

He assured her that he did not seek her out as erotic compensation for a man unsatisfied in his own bed. Sophie had just returned to him from her own solo trip to Europe, healthier and more confident, and more attractive than ever. She harboured quite a bit of jealousy toward Catherine, but managed to live with it, he noted. All of which only stirred up Catherine's own feelings of jealousy toward Sophie. At the same time, she found Mumford's letter encouraging – that he would truly accept her on her own terms. She would find out painfully that she was mistaken in this belief.

Alone in the Alps, Catherine wondered where this relationship would lead: she was in love with a man anchored to a wife and child in Amenia, New York. Later, in a more upbeat letter, she confessed: "I am in love for the first time in my life and so proud of the amazing good taste of my instincts in their choice of a victim that I can feel the beginnings of a real and honest self-confidence sprouting up to take the place of the brassy nerve which serves as a kind of martial law for a j.f.a. [jeune fille Americaine]. So you are forgiven for making a woman of me after all!"

After Munich came Stuttgart, where the experimental modern architecture excited Catherine. "Even if Van der Rohe's roofs *do* leak in winter – even if it *does* break dishes in a Corbusier basement when a man drops his shoe on the top floor – I don't give a damn – nobody ought to drop shoes anyway. It would be a serious reflection on the human race if people can't live comfortably in those swell houses." Introductions from the Behrendts led her to two young avant-garde architects, the Rasch brothers, who were happy to be Catherine's guides around Stuttgart. They plied her with information about their ideas and photos of their work when they discovered that she knew Mr. Mumford and was planning an article about architecture. They had in mind revolving houses with collapsible floors and moving partitions, and they hoped, within two years, to rebuild the United States along these lines. These young men, like many European designers, found American architecture to be mediocre at best. (Frank Lloyd Wright was excepted.) The Rasch brothers, aged twenty-seven and twenty-eight, were full of fun and adventure – and fine dancers too – so Catherine had a splendid time in Stuttgart.

Touring Stuttgart and Nuremberg, she became aware of good design in everyday objects. She suggested to Lewis that they start a *Werkbund* (workers' circle), not for the usual arts-and-crafts projects, but for the study of machines. She was fascinated to know more about the technologies that produced everything from pants to pencils: to discover their possibilities, push their limits, and sell designs for better machines to factories. Her hands were now itching to get at something raw and malleable. She decided that all civilized people ought to be able to cook, develop their own films, "and probably even take care of their own children (though there are still a few doubts on that question)."

On August 4, Catherine arrived in Frankfurt, the city she had come to Europe to see. Although she stayed only three days, it was long enough to be convinced that Frankfurt had the most exciting modern architecture anywhere. The weather was fine, and her spirits were so high the first morning that she wandered into the offices of the architectural magazine *Das Neue Frankfurt* without an introduction. A kind woman took the time to educate her about the latest plans for Frankfurt. Together, the two leafed through a special anniversary issue of the magazine showing maps, plans, and articles about everything that had been built in the city during the past five years. Best of all, she made an appointment for Catherine to meet architect Ernst May the next day.

Lewis had included May's name on his list, with a note saying he had studied city planning under Raymond Unwin in England, had "geist a-plenty," and was definitely worth meeting. She was lucky to be in Frankfurt now, just a few weeks before May would head to Russia, at the invitation of the Soviet government, to build as many brand-new complete towns as money would permit. He invited Catherine to his home – one of the most handsome modern houses she had ever seen.

The meeting with May was a pivotal experience in Catherine's self-education in architecture and planning. Although she had one year of formal training at Cornell, all her important teachers and mentors were professionals whom she sought out for inspiration and advice. Indeed, Lewis Mumford was her first professor, in the literal sense of the word. It was a title that he eschewed all his life, yet he might have made an exception for Catherine, who, as an astute student, brought him honour. Had she enrolled in one of his seminars at Dartmouth – which she couldn't have, it being a men's college – she'd have earned academic credit but might not have learned half as much. It was Lewis who made sure Catherine read the right books and met the right people. In Frankfurt, Ernst May was definitely the right man.

May steered her to the Nidda Valley developments at the outer edge of Frankfurt. Catherine was so impressed she ran around for hours snapping rolls of film and wearing out a new pair of heels. May persuaded her to return in September to attend a three-day course called "Frankfurter Kurse für Neues Bauen" (Frankfurt's Courses for New Construction) hosted by *Das Neue Frankfurt*. It would be her first professional architectural

CATHERINE AND ERNST MAY

The meeting with [Ernst] May was a pivotal experience in Catherine's self-education in architecture and planning.

meeting, and Catherine looked forward to the event because she was familiar with the names of most of the lecturers.

In the meantime she returned to Berlin. There she was fortunate to be guided around by a young English-speaking architect, Walter March, a friend of the Behrendts who had lived and worked in New York City. His father, Otto March, had been a leading Berlin architect and planner. The elder March, who died in 1913, helped organize a major exposition on city planning in Berlin in 1910 and had an influence on the innovative thinking of Ernst May. Walter's brother, Werner, was a respected architect practising in the capital.

After delivering a diatribe against New York's Chrysler Building at their first meeting, Catherine was terribly embarrassed to learn that Walter March had spent an entire year detailing Van Alen's sketch of the building. He must have excused her *faux pas* because he spent several days showing her the outside of historic architectural landmarks and several evenings showing her the inside of modern dance halls. After one such foray, exhausted from dancing until three in the morning, Catherine went home with Walter. Having stumbled over a rug and then kicked the dog in the dark, she took off her shoes – not to awaken his mother. She now found herself in a compromising position.

"Ladies who find themselves with their shoes off in gentlemen's rooms at three o'clock in the morning don't make scenes and slide down the banisters (which is what I really wanted to do) to Freedom and Solitude so that was that," she wrote Lewis. She spent the night with Walter.

The young man decided to advance his own education by joining Catherine on a small architectural tour of Germany. In addition to being translator, he was able to impart considerable technical and philosophical background as they toured Walter Gropius's Bauhaus in Dessau and Mies van der Rohe's buildings in Weimar. Catherine thought the Gropius settlement was excellent and learned that his houses were among the cheapest dwellings built in Germany. Each house had plenty of light, large balcony, central heating, and a good bathroom, and each was surrounded by a nice garden and spacious lawn. With Walter March's assistance, she was able to interview inhabitants, labourers, and their wives, all of whom took pride in their dwellings. Catherine told Lewis: "These laborers are most decidedly *not* bourgeois – they are really proud of modern architecture as something made *for them* and for a new order which belongs to them, instead of the hand-me-down, cast-off bourgeois houses they used to live in." To correct any notion that Bauhaus ideas prevailed, she pointed out that Dessau was "a nasty little town, with the Bauhaus quite artificially tacked on to one edge and generally unknown." Dessau also had miles of new construction, as ugly as anything that could be found in Pittsburgh.

In Leipzig Catherine and Walter visited a trade fair where she took samples of all sorts of new building materials. All the time she wished that Lewis and not Walter was at her side, except that his German proved to be very valuable. Lewis responded to her account of the March affair with characteristic wit: "I will still greet you sweetly, when you return home, provided you do not decide to switch your luck from an April fool to a March Herr."

Early in September Walter and Catherine joined 150 other students in Frankfurt's New Construction course. The only American enrolled, Catherine attended all the lectures and took every architectural tour offered. Visionary architects such as Mart Stam and Richard Neutra addressed the group. While Catherine admired the work of both men, she preferred Stam's personality (Neutra was self-centred and dull, she thought). Translations of lecture notes were usually provided to foreign students, and when they weren't Catherine relied upon her friend, Walter. She was most intrigued by the lectures on the Nidda Valley developments she had visited earlier. Later that year she would write an article for *Fortune* magazine describing her impressions of Römerstadt, the largest of the Nidda settlements:

Tiers of concrete and gardens curve beyond the sheep-dotted valley of the Nidda, each house with a garden, each apartment with a terrace, all half an hour from the city of half a million inhabitants. From Frankfurt there appeared a view of dazzling whiteness and the satisfactory geometry of clean lines, well-defined, largely conceived forms and simple surfaces occasionally curved to conform to the topography.[2]

The New Construction course covered the new *Siedlungen* (settlements) developed during the golden years of the Weimar Republic as part of a grand scheme of social reform following the devastating defeat of the First World War. A scheme of twenty-one settlements encompassing 15,500 units was made possible through the vision of Frankfurt's progressive mayor, Ludwig Landmann, and the skill of Ernst May, who was then chief architect and city planner. May had been charged with developing a new kind of housing around the outskirts of Frankfurt. A member of the avant-garde intellectual circle that advocated *neue Sachlichkeit* (new functionalism), he was in a unique position to put theory into practice: applying the English Garden City principles of satellite communities to the regeneration of Frankfurt's deteriorating city core. The inner city would be redistricted to its natural borders by "bedding expansion districts as separate settlement complexes in the open landscape."[3] The rapidly expanding municipal streetcar system would link these *Tochterstädte* (daughter cities) to metropolitan Frankfurt.

May commanded absolute power over Frankfurt's city planning and architecture during the late 1920s. Sometimes accused of being an aesthetic dictator, he was successful because Frankfurt's municipal socialism gave the city power over land development policies and control over land use. Exploring Römerstadt, Catherine learned about the power of public land ownership and the role that government can play in shaping the city. The Römerstadt development comprised 1,200 housing units on 116 acres of land at a density of 10.5 dwellings per acre, representing a bold housing initiative and its architectural resolution by local government. Located eight kilometres from the centre of Frankfurt, Römerstadt was built on municipal land and separated from the inner city by a permanent greenbelt devoted solely to recreational and educational uses. May and his colleagues believed the moral imperative that a healthy environment would shape the behaviour of its inhabitants. He is credited with creating a new comprehensive approach to housing and living: the old-style block plans were replaced by row houses oriented to the sun; living units and building materials were standardized and made interchangeable for purposes of economy.

Germany's substantial housing production between 1925 and 1930, during an economic depression, astonished Catherine. Four years later she summed up her impressions in her book *Modern Housing*. The new residential neighbourhoods represented "technically and aesthetically an entirely new method of approach and a body of ideas and experiments which no later housing can afford to ignore. Römerstadt did not mean the final fulfillment of the general longing for a new style – it only intended to be the true expression of architectural conviction formed from the living conditions of our times."[4]

The precepts that Catherine learned in the course, and the settlements that she saw, laid the foundation for housing principles she would espouse throughout her career. In Berlin she discovered a resonance of May's ideas in the work of Martin Wagner, another name on Lewis's list. Wagner also developed a comprehensive approach to planning and housing but differed with May about the "perfectibility of the modern city and its ordering according to rational, evolutionary principles."[5] Wagner believed the outward explosion of the metropolis was inevitable and viewed planning as ameliorative in its attempt to correct past mistakes. As a planning engineer, Wagner was concerned with the physical aspects of making the city work, here and now, whereas May, the architect, was more future oriented. Both men impressed upon Catherine their convictions that urban planning and housing can be used strategically to achieve social change. A decade later Catherine and Wagner would become faculty colleagues at Harvard.

This comprehensive approach to housing after the First World War grew out of the strength of individual German cities. Most had been independent entities long before the advent of nation-states. In medieval times the powers and responsibilities of German cities included public ownership of land and control over its use. This evolved into municipal management of public utilities in the nineteenth century, as well as the strategic practice of purchasing large tracts of fringe land in the path of expected urban expansion. Capital investment for social community purposes was a given. Inevitably, alliances were formed between municipal councils and groups of young architects and planners, who urged radical reforms in local housing and planning objectives.

The long history of municipal urban planning remained unbroken in Germany despite the loss of a war and legendary inflation. Housing projects built during the early 1920s by Socialist-led municipal councils demonstrated a commitment to immediate, locally relevant municipal land measures, shelter, and aid for co-operative societies. In Catherine's estimation Frankfurt provided "an excellent example of the far-sighted cooperative and well-organized municipal governments which, all over Germany, have successfully kept up the economic and social morale of the country in spite of the chaotic politics of the central government."[6]

Germany's postwar housing policy encouraged the expansion of local housing cooperatives and facilitated their access to public funds through *Hauszinssteuer* (house rent tax). The federal government levied a tax on all buildings erected before the war, taking advantage of inflation that practically cancelled the mortgages on all existing buildings, since they were payable in almost valueless currency. As a result, home owners enjoyed a windfall from the capital value of their buildings. A slogan ran, "House owners were the only war victors."

Each city received a fixed proportion of the tax raised within its limits, and each administered its tax revenues. The success of this strategy was reflected in nearly 1.5 million new dwellings erected in Germany between 1925 and 1930. Of these, 1 million units were aided directly by government financing, all of them benefiting from municipal land policies and public loans.

In most German cities, as a result, about one-quarter of the land base was municipally owned. (The city of Ulm was the most striking exception, owning 85 percent of its land.) Municipal land acquisition received a substantial boost from low land costs during the war. Berlin, for example, bought nearly 10,000 acres within its boundaries at an average price of five cents a square foot. Ultimately the city owned more than one-third of its area (78,000 acres) plus another 70,000 acres outside its boundaries. Catherine reported: "The city of Frankfurt now owns about half of the land necessary to the present scheme. In cases where speculation prices prevailed on land needed for immediate development, the properties were dispossessed by law at a price somewhat higher than the actual value of the land on the principle that expropriation is as justifiable in housing emergency as for railroads or waterways."[7]

Catherine left Germany after finishing the Frankfurt course, toting boxes of snapshots and notebooks filled with statistics. She stopped in Paris for a short reunion with her French friends, then went to Normandy for a week of relaxation with American friends. Her final weeks in Europe were spent in Holland visiting architects and observing their work. In Rotterdam she looked up J.J.P. Oud, a leading exponent of the *Neue Sachlichkeit*

CATHERINE IN GERMANY

Catherine left Germany after finishing the Frankfurt course, toting boxes of snapshots and notebooks filled with statistics.

movement that Catherine had learned about in Germany. Oud showed her a new development he had designed, which she had already read about in the architectural journal *Die Form*. She concluded that he was her favourite architect in Europe – both for his direct, informal manner and because he reminded her of Lewis Mumford.

INSTANT HOUSING EXPERT

Art in Industry must grow out of the best modern industrial method, and not be applied afterwards as apologetic camouflage.

CATHERINE BAUER

Catherine considered her little affair with Walter March quite meaning-less: a case of two young people spending ten days together in a balmy August, enjoying intellectual and aesthetic compatibility – entwined, but not in love. During this period Catherine's letters to Lewis Mumford were much lighter and more joyful than they had been while she was alone and given to brooding.

Lewis sensed the difference in her mood, and though he attempted to dismiss the situation with a clever pun, he was unable to brush it off entirely. Indeed, his feelings lay buried for more than two years before he allowed them to well up in a surge of self-pity. "I was on the point of living with her for good, marrying her, in the summer of 1930," runs a diary entry dated January 24, 1932. "She would also have to face the fact that her trivial affair in Germany with Walter March was what deflated my hopes and diverted my intentions. But it was Sophie who was faithful: and marriage, if it means anything, means that ultimate and rock bottom and infinite solidity."[8]

As Catherine's knowledge of architecture and planning deepened in the course of her travels, Lewis increasingly turned to her for advice. Often he sent her first drafts of his manuscripts, and she took the responsibility very seriously, sending the draft back with several typed pages charting annotations, paragraph by paragraph. For example, she corrected his assumption that concrete architecture was monochromatic, in the style of Gropius houses, citing Bruno Taut's use of riotous colours in his Berlin developments. As an ardent admirer of Lewis's writing style and breadth of knowledge, she would end her emendations with high praise and assurances that her suggestions could safely be ignored. Generally they were not.

Catherine returned home at the beginning of November aboard the *Nieuw Amsterdam* and lived for a short time with her family, now settled in

Princeton, New Jersey. Anxious to find a job in New York City, she took an inexpensive and rather shabby apartment on 48th Street west of Fifth Avenue, on a site designated for the future Radio City. Soon it would be torn down, and for the next two years she frequently moved, just ahead of the bulldozer, as Rockefeller Center grew around her.

Shortly after her return, Lewis took Catherine to a meeting of the Regional Planning Association of America (RPAA). The organization had been launched officially on April 18, 1923, by Clarence Stein, a leading New York architect. Its purpose was to study "man's physical environment as influenced by social, economic and aesthetic needs and the technical means of creating new environments serving these needs – with special emphasis on America and the future." The membership would include "architects, engineers, landscape architects, sociologists, economists, city officials, union leaders and writers."[9]

For several years before RPAA's founding, a group of friends had met informally to discuss issues concerning architecture, economics, and planned environments. Even after RPAA was officially launched, meetings continued on a mostly informal basis for the next ten years, usually at Stein's office or his elegant apartment overlooking Central Park. At certain intervals the group would retreat to the Hudson Guild Farm in New Jersey. The great Scottish urban philosopher Patrick Geddes attended its first weekend retreat at the farm and bestowed the imprimatur of the English Garden City philosophy.

The membership of RPAA never exceeded eighteen people, and the association never had a charter or bylaws. Three of its members – Clarence Stein; Benton MacKaye, an environmentalist who developed the idea for the Appalachian Trail; and Henry Wright, landscape architect and site planner – had worked for the federal government during the First World War, developing housing projects for defense workers. These three, along with Charles Whitaker, editor of the *Journal of the American Institute of Architects,* and his friend, Lewis Mumford, set the association's mandate: to build on the defense program's successes in order to create well-planned, harmonious American cities. "Mumford saw American architecture beset by one overriding problem: our best buildings were not complemented by intelligent community design," wrote his biographer, Donald Miller. "The result: isolated masterworks in the midst of spreading physical disorder. America would never have a distinguished architecture, as opposed to distinguished individual works of architecture, until our advances in design were incorporated in communal projects that restored a sense of orderly beauty and human scale to the city."[10] For Lewis, who became the group's chief spokesman, RPAA was a platform from which to bring a new regional order out of existing chaos.

Clarence Stein was a man of political acumen, leadership, and independent means; he headed the association and covered its operating costs. In
1923, Governor Al Smith appointed him to the chair of the New York State
Commission of Housing and Regional Planning, which afforded Stein and
his RPAA friends an opportunity to test their ideas. Upon assuming his
state position, Stein went to England to learn more about the applications
of Garden City principles. Like Lewis, he was influenced by Ebenezer
Howard's theories expressed in the little book *Garden Cities of Tomorrow,*
published in 1902. Drawing on the pioneering experiences of England and
Germany, Stein urged the government to assume responsibility for housing low-income families. This little group of idealistic intellectuals set the
stage for cataclysmic changes in attitudes toward human settlements in
the United States. It would take ten years and a devastating depression
before official circles would debate these issues in earnest.

After her recent visit to Germany, Catherine had much to report to
RPAA about government initiatives in planning and building. Her vitality
and intelligence coupled with her first-hand experience appealed to the
group, and they appointed her executive secretary. Her interest and
commitment were unparalleled, perhaps because she was the only
member of the association without a full-time job. (She was doing some
freelance work for Harcourt Brace and writing essays for the *Arts Weekly*.)

The only other female member of RPAA was Edith Elmer Wood, a Smith
alumna who had earned a doctorate in social work from Columbia
University in 1919 at the age of forty-eight, with a dissertation titled "The
Housing of the Unskilled Wage Earner." Dr. Wood had lived in Asia, Italy,
Switzerland, and Puerto Rico with her husband, a naval officer, and their
four children. In 1913 the Woods settled in Washington, DC, where Edith
went to work as an advocate for a cohesive housing policy and a vociferous
critic of disease-riddled alley dwellings.

With skills honed through decades of writing fiction, Dr. Edith Wood
emerged in the 1920s as a highly respected and oft-cited author of housing
criticism. Elaborating on research for her doctoral dissertation, she came
to the harsh discovery that one-third of the nation was ill-housed, ill-fed,
and ill-clothed. This became the rallying cry of the New Deal crusaders.
Catherine, who normally had no qualms about challenging experts, was
more than a little intimidated by Dr. Wood and was relieved to learn that
the distinguished woman rarely attended meetings. A warm friendship
developed later, based on mutual admiration. Catherine would celebrate
her friend's life in a touching commemoration read at Dr. Wood's memorial
service on May 9, 1945, at the Russell Sage Foundation.

After Europe the RPAA offered Catherine a new kind of learning
experience. She was able to discuss and dispute ideas with leaders in the

burgeoning field of regionalism and to envision a professional place for herself within the field. She now began to organize the previous summer's notes and photographs, with a view to submitting articles to the *New Republic*. One evening over cocktails with a friend, Viking Press editor Marshall Best, she learned of a competition sponsored by *Fortune* magazine for an essay about art in industry. That night she wrote to Lewis to find out if he knew about it. "That ought to be the easiest $1,500 you could ever make," she suggested, then added, "I'll find out about it. I suppose I should make a stab, but every decent thing I could possibly invent would really be yours (I cant remember disagreeing with you on a single point you have ever said or written on the subject) so it would be much better for you to win it." Alluding to their differences in style, she added, "Only if you use one 'swell' you must buy us a double blanket on the proceeds." Lewis was slow to respond, and Catherine decided she would enter the contest.

"I don't believe it but Mr. Bliven accepted that squib and I won the *Fortune* competition," she informed Lewis a month later, in a letter covered in drawings of birds, flowers, hearts, and a radiant sun. In a postscript she asked him not to mention the news to anyone, as it was not yet official. She did notify her parents, however, adding that the *New Republic* had also accepted an article of hers.

The *Fortune* award turned out to be $1,000, offered by Kaufmann Department Stores of Pittsburgh in celebration of the opening of a new first floor. It was for the best essay on "some particular phase of, or the general subject of, Art In Industry." Mr. Edgar Kaufmann, the man for whom Frank Lloyd Wright would soon build the Falling Water House, handed a smiling Catherine the cheque in his Pittsburgh store in May 1931 – the same month *Fortune* printed her article.

Her prize essay told the story of Römerstadt in a lucid style that would hold even the most casual reader. Based on Catherine's observations in Frankfurt during the summer of 1930, the article demonstrated how successful interactions of municipal initiative, social policy, and modern architecture benefit an entire community. Through public ownership of land, Römerstadt achieved neighbourhoods that integrated a variety of housing types, open spaces, and community facilities. Catherine argued that there is a significant lesson to be learned in the United States from the way in which Weimar Germany planned its housing. To support her argument, she listed four points: first, "a triumph of organization including far-sighted cooperation of all concerned"; second, "effective standardization [of planning, design, and construction] grows out of an intelligent acceptance of the means of production"; third, "the intelligent acceptance

CATHERINE ACCEPTING FORTUNE MAGAZINE AWARD

"I don't believe it … I won the Fortune competition …" Mr.
Edgar Kaufmann … handed a smiling Catherine the cheque in
his Pittsburgh store in May 1931 – the same month *Fortune*
printed her article.

of mass production"; and fourth, "excellent architecture, embodying a new building spirit, including a harmonious placing in the landscape." These points can only be brought to bear, she wrote, if public ownership of land is combined with appropriate social policies of local governments. The architecture in Römerstadt proved to Catherine that "art in industry must grow out of the best modern industrial method and not be applied afterwards as apologetic camouflage."[11]

The *Fortune* and *New Republic* articles had common themes. The *New Republic* piece was titled "The Americanization of Europe," and in it Catherine reviewed three architectural exhibits in New York City through the eyes of a modernist. The article began with her favourite *bête-noire*, the Chrysler Building, which she categorized as "advertising architecture." This was a building that can "make the public stare, gape, swoon, and glow with vicarious pride in record-breaking cost or height, but can't really give satisfaction – because it isn't architecture."[12]

By contrast she had high praise for an exhibit, held in a small space on Seventh Avenue, that displayed the work of a group calling itself Rejected Architects. Like the Impressionists of the last century, who rallied in the Salon des Refusées after being rejected by the Salon in Paris, these young architects were distinguished by having *not* been accepted into the annual Architectural League Show. The name they coined for their collection of designs and architectural models was International Style. Catherine quoted their catalogue: "The design depends primarily on the function which the building is to serve without consideration of traditional principles of symmetry. The style takes advantage of new principles of construction and new materials such as concrete, steel and glass." She added: "Real architecture is never competitive, it is the one art that must be a social expression – impersonal, anonymous, never by that specious conception of variety, which means 'one each' [or] samples."

Challenging the entire profession, Catherine continued: "The history of good building could, and should, be written without mentioning the name, habits or personal convictions of a single architect."[13] Years later she would still find herself defending such strong opinions, for which she was barely forgiven by her good friends in the profession – stars such as Frank Lloyd Wright, whom she later disputed on individualism in architecture, and Walter Gropius, as well as William Wurster, whom she eventually married.

In the *New Republic* essay she described the virtues of European modern architecture under a subheading, "Three Leaves from a Notebook," a tidy way to organize her notes from Germany, Holland, and France. A unifying theme was the irony of European admiration for American architecture, which is an architecture of the imagination, she maintained, given that most Europeans had not seen the sappy derivative structures built by Americans in search of a style. She applauded a Stuttgart house that had no identifiable style, "no indication of the wealth, social position or religious persuasion of the occupants. It looked like nothing at all. Nothing, that is, beyond an exceedingly handsome and practical place to live in, full of light air and space."[14] Germans walking by this building pointed it out as being an American house, a claim that sent Catherine's mind reeling back to the American houses she so despised: the French Renaissance on Fifth Avenue and Florentine Renaissance on Park; Tudor in Jackson Heights and Spanish on Long Island.

In Frankfurt, Germans credited the modern American assembly line with the mass-produced concrete and steel structures of Römerstadt. The only standardized steel-frame houses in the United States that Catherine could recall were made to look like log cabins. She argued that the only genuine American influence in Europe was derived from Frank Lloyd Wright's midwestern houses. European architects, trooping to America in search of The Master, were surprised to find that he was relatively unknown. Except for Wright's own writing in the *Architectural Record,* little had been published in English about his work, and no major commission had come his way.

CATHERINE, C. 1931

The *Fortune* award drove a wedge between Catherine and Lewis, who had entered the competition after all and must have considered it a blow to see his protégé beat him.

The *Fortune* award drove a wedge between Catherine and Lewis, who had entered the competition after all and must have considered it a blow to see her intellectual flowering with "pride and selflessness which would make the great abnegators of fiction seem ruthless ideologists."

Catherine was sceptical, detecting an echo of jealousy in his explicit denial. "There wasn't the faintest grain of jealousy in my feelings," he told her, "nothing more than a wisp of regret at not having my summer handsomely solved by the possession of an unexpected thousand dollars, and that had nothing to do with you."

Within a week of the prize announcement they spent a Saturday evening at her home that ended in tears and talk of terminating the relationship. Lewis became cold and analytical, Catherine hot and hysterical. It all turned around Sophie, whom he confessed he could not and would not leave. During their ten years of marriage they had forged a relationship that no one could break asunder, he declared, and walked out. Immediately after his departure Catherine smelled gas. The penthouse across the street suddenly burst into flames, as if kindled by Catherine's burning soul, and the neighbourhood let loose the city's most angry, destructive forces. The irony of these two calamities in such close proximity did not escape her.

Catherine's mood plunged to despair, and the days to come found her "weeping on Fifth Avenue and sobbing in art galleries." She received some consolation from her friend, photographer Alfred Stieglitz, who was empathetic without knowing the details. Sensing that her heart had been broken, he amused her with his own tales of love and anguish until his wife, Georgia O'Keeffe, walked in. Lewis was as shaken as Catherine by the painful evening. Upon reflection it was clear to him that "you and I are in each other irretrievably, for good and all." He was not yet prepared to face a future without Catherine.

She rallied her energy and focused on her RPAA work, resolved to make the most of her newfound media celebrity. She had become an instant housing expert. In May, Clarence Stein invited her to serve as his research assistant for a book on regionalism, for an hourly wage that would net her $25 a week. Catherine was a little hesitant about accepting the offer because she planned to write a similar book and wanted to protect her information. But she decided it would benefit her to work for Stein: she would learn research techniques and how to construct a full-length book. Her first assignment was to gather information about retail stores in shopping centres, and then to analyze the planning of a centre to the best advantage of the landlord, the retailer, and the consumer. She would use mail surveys and field observation in the first systematic analysis of shopping centres in the United States.

Stein persuaded Catherine to attend the Roundtable on Regionalism conference, sponsored by the Institute of Public Affairs at the University of Virginia in Charlottesville, July 1931. She arranged to be sent there as a correspondent by the *New Republic*. New York's Governor Franklin D. Roosevelt was the principal speaker. With an eye toward the White House, he waxed romantic on the theme of regional development, envisioning the blossoming of small, self-sustaining communities. Since the meeting was in the south, he proposed the establishment of a Tennessee Valley Authority.

Most members of RPAA attended the Roundtable, including Lewis, who was one of the main speakers. A young student of town planning, another protégé of his named Frederick (Fritz) Gutheim, also attended. He had met Lewis three years earlier at a series of lectures at the University of Wisconsin, where Gutheim, a student of medieval town planning, was assigned to be his chauffeur. They had become fast friends. Lewis had introduced Gutheim to Catherine the previous January at the New York Public Library, where the young man spent most of his working days. Gutheim and Catherine now met for the second time.

The conference proved to be sheer hell for both Lewis and Catherine: they had to observe strict decorum in public, which inevitably led to misunderstandings. Lewis was enraged when, after his lecture on the Monday morning, Catherine walked out of the room with Gutheim. Lewis looked for her in vain, even waited a while, but she did not return. She did not even slip him a note. Later that afternoon, returning to the campus from a formal lunch, Lewis observed Catherine and Gutheim playing tennis. Thinking that she had fallen in love with Gutheim, "life suddenly got dark and tasteless" for Lewis. Justifying his lack of faith in Catherine's devotion to him, he slipped her a bitter note: "I was once on an auto trip in England and saw two people fall in love even more quickly." She did not respond, confirming Lewis's fears. That night he "slept but two hours: all night I was in torture. My heart pounded violently and it worked my body into a fever." His only recourse, he decided, was to leave the conference early. He even considered skipping his Tuesday morning lecture, inventing an ill mother as excuse.

On waking Lewis decided to stay and give Catherine another chance. He would use his mother's illness if she showed no sign of remorse for having cut him so cruelly. Tuesday morning, unaware of Lewis's anger, Catherine stood waiting at the edge of a circle of people crowded around him following his lecture. Not daring to make eye contact, she decided to wait until he was alone before speaking to him, but Benton MacKaye suddenly took him by the elbow and led him off to lunch. Lewis passed her without a glance, and Catherine was devastated. She rushed to her room with a lump in her throat in order to collect herself before lunch. As she left her room she ran into Gutheim, who invited her to join him in another game of tennis. It was exactly what she needed to vent her frustration.

Lewis walked by while they volleyed, but was so deeply engrossed in

CATHERINE SITTING ON STEPS

Lewis passed her without a glance, and Catherine was devastated.

conversation that he didn't notice the players. Feeling considerably calmer after tennis, Catherine tried to locate Lewis at the club where he was to dine. Hoping to catch a moment alone with him, she was greeted instead with an icy stare. He was even more furious by now, having just gone to her room in a vain search. The next morning at breakfast Lewis avoided Catherine's eyes. She intended to leave the conference early, but instead stayed and wept much of the day, unable to concentrate on the proceedings. Wednesday evening at supper, puffy-eyed, she angled for a seat near Lewis. He ignored her, but she almost laughed when someone else addressed her as Mrs. Mumford.

"What was I to think," he wrote that evening, "but that you had wanted to avoid me yesterday? That made me resolve to report my mother much worse, which I did. I might still have left without lacerating you, but the glimpse of you and Gutheim disappearing over the hill. That upset me. I was black with jealousy."

Thursday morning, two days before the Roundtable ended, Lewis suddenly left the conference, and Catherine pressed a desperate note in his hand, fearful that he was trying to break away from her forever. She reaffirmed her love and expressed her desperate frustration of the past few days. Lewis was shocked to find Catherine so "unexpectedly desperate: so was I, too. The problem is to know when and how much to be jealous. Hadn't you the *faintest* notion of how much you were hurting me?" he wrote a few days later, oblivious to the pain he had inflicted. She responded with an apology: "It's taken almost a week for me to see my guilt" she wrote, admitting to having caused him "terrible hurt at not finding me in my room when you did come for me. Good Lord, can you ever forgive me?"

The air was cleared for the moment with declarations of rekindled love. Once again sure of her footing, Catherine understood that the nature of their relationship was dictated by Lewis's marital status and his role in the community. She deeply resented a situation that demanded him to initiate their meetings and forced her into a "feminine receptive role," but love overruled her reasoning and obliged her to accept humiliation.

Late in July Lewis emerged ecstatic from a seminar given by Carl Jung on his privately published talks. "I almost howled with delight, again and again, at finding that Jung and I had reached by different paths a very similar philosophy," he told Catherine. "Sections of my essay in Living Philosophies, might have been inserted in Jung's talks, and no one would have been the wiser." Jung asserted that man tells autobiographical lies because "he does not want to tell of the secret alliances, faux pas of his mind," explained Lewis. This "inferior side of his thinking" is unconscious in man just as sexuality is in woman. And as woman wields her power in sexuality, keeping secret its weak side, so man "centers his power in his thinking and holds it as a solid front against other men." Man, however, "can usually speak freely to a certain sort of woman." The two kinds of women are the mother and the hetaira, according to Jung – and to Mumford. The hetaira nurtures the inferior side of man's thinking, which she views as weak and helpless. Her role is to assist in the development of that side of man. Jung pointed out the paradox that "even a cocotte may sometimes know more about the spiritual growth of a man than his wife."

In a flash Lewis understood the nature of their relationship. Catherine was his hetaira. "You are the only one to whom I have ever shown the very first draft of anything I have written, the only one to whom I have completely let down my intellectual as well as my emotional barriers." Catherine understood and willingly accepted this role in Lewis's life. Once a young woman at Cornell, upon seeing Catherine eating an onion sandwich and smoking an English cigarette, told her she was the mistress type. Catherine was reminded of this casual observation now. Yes, she was his hetaira, but she wanted to be his wife.

That summer Catherine moved into Lewis's Sunnyside Gardens home while the Mumfords vacationed at their country house in Amenia, near Poughkeepsie. She took the opportunity to snoop through his cupboards and study his old photographs. He helped by suggesting places to look. Lewis never met her there, out of respect for Sophie, but they had several clandestine meetings in New York City hotels. When both lived in New

York they tried to meet every second day. Summer encounters were less frequent, but long letters bridged the gaps.

Sunnyside Gardens, in Queens, New York, was a planned community, designed and built by Clarence Stein and Henry Wright, and created by the City Housing Corporation of New York, a limited-dividend company. A champion of planned communities, Catherine now experienced one first-hand. In an effort to learn what home owners thought of the Sunnyside idea, she interviewed two couples who chose to buy there rather than in nearby Laurelton, which they found ugly despite its being highly touted in the American media. Laurelton was composed of monotonous rows of American Colonial, Spanish, and English period houses with well-appointed interiors. Both couples enjoyed the light and air of Sunnyside, but Catherine found it odd that neither commented on the carefully planned open spaces. The two wives found fault with Sunnyside's lack of interior comforts. They missed refrigerators, fold-up ironing boards, and laundry chutes.

All summer Catherine was immersed in research for Clarence Stein. She had hoped to glean some insights into regionalism at the Roundtable conference, but her volatile love life had intervened. By the middle of August, as the deadline loomed, she dipped into Lewis's home library.

EUROPE AND DARKNESS

*Don't you know that I care perhaps more about your work
than I do about you-personally-and-me?*
CATHERINE BAUER TO LEWIS MUMFORD

By the end of the summer Catherine had amassed thousands of pages of notes that needed to be organized. "Oh how I wish I had never started to do Research on Regionalism," she wrote to Lewis. "I'm completely lost. What ever made any of you think I *could* write 3,500 words about it anyway?" She was growing increasingly uneasy about many of the opinions she had voiced earlier, realizing only now, through intensive research, that many of them were premature if not entirely wrongheaded. She was gaining a new respect for hard facts and figures. "I love figures, it is the worst vice I have," she wrote later that fall. "I'll go and be a statistician for the Department of Commerce" she threatened Lewis, for whom charts and graphs were anathema. "Nothing under heaven is more restful."

After several months' work for Clarence Stein, Catherine had the confidence to write her own book, based on her experiences in Europe during the summer of 1930. She would have to return to Europe once more to consolidate her research and fill in some gaps. Besides, she desperately wanted to join Lewis on one leg of a European tour he had been planning, beginning in April 1932. Catherine offered to take care of their son, Geddes, while Sophie joined Lewis in Europe; then, upon Sophie's return, she would go over and join him for a time. Reality turned out to be different.

Catherine put her mind to finding ways of financing another trip to Europe. She was elated when Fritz Gutheim put her name forward for a three-month research contract with the Better Homes Bureau in Washington, DC, at $500 per month. Catherine reckoned this windfall would leave her at least $1,000 for next summer's trip. The offer seemed almost too good to be true, and unfortunately it was. The contract was withdrawn as abruptly as it had been tendered, and Catherine had to search out other funding sources. At Lewis's suggestion, and with encouragement from her RPAA colleagues, she wrote to the Guggenheim Foundation for a fellowship application for 1932. "I am a student and critic of modern architecture and town planning and I wish to do research for a history of domestic architecture," she explained.[15] The application deadline was November 1. Catherine's was submitted exactly one day late, then supplemented a week later with additional material and profuse apologies. Her "Concise Statement of Project" envisioned a book that would analyze the essential nature of architecture as social expression – as both symbol and stimulus in the coordination of society – and illustrate modern experiments in architectural aesthetics, housing sociology, and regional land economics.

Catherine hoped her command of languages would stand her in good stead with the review board: her French was excellent, her German was sufficient for research, and she could read some Italian. Her AB from Vassar College ought to impress, she thought, and her recent job history was respectable enough: advertising manager at Harcourt Brace for two-and-a-half years, and research assistant to Clarence Stein. Her list of references included the most prestigious architects and writers of the time, including Clarence Stein, Frank Lloyd Wright, Lewis Mumford, *New Republic* editor Bruce Bliven, German architect Walter Behrendt, Rotterdam City Architect J.J.P. Oud, and her former employer Alfred Harcourt.

Under the heading "Accomplishments," Catherine described her travels in Europe. During 1927-28, she wrote, her study had been centred on architecture and town planning, historical development, and modern experiment. She embroidered her connection with Adolf Loos, claiming she had worked in the Paris office of this "prominent modern Viennese architect for a very short time." She had returned to the United States with a clearly formulated professional interest in the problems of modern architecture. Her 1930 European journey was more focused on architecture than was her first trip, highlighted by interviews with some of the most important modern architects in Europe. She described the copious notes and photographs gathered on this second journey, leading to work for RPAA and Clarence Stein. She pointed out that her research for Stein on the planning of retail shopping centres was the only scientific effort of its kind ever made in America.

"For my own sake I must endeavor to bring all this material together – architectural aesthetic, building economics and planning sociology – in order to clarify my sense of the whole organism, and that, in so doing, I may reasonably hope to write a summary of specific trends and achievements today which will be not only an interesting and timely documentation of the material, but a clarification of the essential singleness of the problem, particularly for specialists in the field of planning."[16] Her list of publications contained seven articles on architecture, most notably her prize-winning *Fortune* essay. It was an impressive list for a twenty-six-year-old woman whose only formal education had been in English literature.

Under "Plans for Study," Catherine espoused the need for a book on modern architecture and the possible larger social significance – political, economic, aesthetic – of separate contemporary experiments in architecture and housing, town planning and zoning, regional planning, and land-use determination. In relating these elements to each other, her proposal broke radically with American tradition, which had treated each separately. She intended to link her European experience to the current needs of the United States:

> *Great architecture is the concrete expression of the common life, the working pattern, of a society. But there is no absolute precedence of cause and effect – and herein lies the only importance of writing about "modern architecture." Just as architecture may be the most significant monument to a society already coordinated, so the first instinct toward simplification and order may be given immediate and concrete satisfaction and symbolic form in planned building. And "modern architecture," by its very existence and use in public space, enriches and clarifies and gives further stimulus to the original instinct, and serves as a positive force working toward the new pattern of society.*[17]

Catherine was borrowing ideas from the Middle Ages, a radical notion in the United States of the 1930s. Her proposal referred to a period when architecture was a social work of art, when individual buildings existed primarily as parts of the whole, not as discrete expressions of individual personalities. Catherine's political bias echoed discussions with Mumford, Stein, and other members of RPAA:

Politically, at the moment, we are at least conscious of chaos. And the many manifestations of effort toward order and intelligent standardization and human clarity in the building and physical planning arts may well be considered the healthiest and most significant signs of the times. It seems to me highly important that such a work should be done at this time. Particularly in America and England, architects, landscape designers, town-planners, regionalists, land economists, sociologists, engineers, are all far too prone to treat their respective fields as almost entirely separate from each other. Over-specialization appears to have had a deadening effect on imagination, on the conception of any piece of work as an organic part of a necessarily ideal whole. [18]

She had so convinced herself of the merits of her application that it was a shock to receive a short notice of denial at the end of February 1932. Her application could not be granted, she was told, due to the limited funds available that year, and the large number of applicants. Henry Allen Moe, secretary of the Guggenheim Foundation, assured her that her application would be kept on file and encouraged her to try again. Indeed, in 1936 she would submit a stronger, better focused application (and without the misspellings and crossed-out words contained in the 1932 package), and this time she was successful.

Her affair with Lewis continued on its rocky course. An entry in his notes dated January 24, 1932, suggests that Catherine was "on the fringe of the picture" through the autumn of 1931, thanks to the lingering fallout of the Charlottesville disaster. He could not erase the memory of Catherine gallivanting with young Fritz. Through the fall Catherine and Lewis had been seeing each other only once every two or three weeks. She had been house-sitting for friends, as she had for the Mumfords during the summer, and the shabby surroundings of her rooms were not conducive to making love. This changed when she took her own apartment in the winter, and some of the old buoyancy returned to their relationship, though tension ran under the surface.

At a New Year's party Catherine told Lewis that her period had failed to come. One week later, the day after Lewis left for Dartmouth College, she had an abortion. "She bears it bravely" he wrote in his notes. They were once more passionately in love.

She bore it not only bravely, but with characteristic black humour, writing blow-by-blow notes to Lewis even as she lay recovering in the surgeon's living room one hour after the procedure. The surgeon supplied whiskey; she brought her notebook: "Five minutes of mounting agony, ten minutes when you know at least that it won't get any worse, finally that scraping sound which Dr. P. asks you to bear, then three swabs of iodine, an injection – and your parental responsibility is over." In the next room Dr. P.'s daughter was practising her scales "unmusically," and if that wasn't bad enough, on the other side of a screen next to Catherine lay another young patient accompanied by her mother. The empathetic older woman attempted to distract her daughter with a tale of her "sinus operation when they used a chisel and she felt pieces dropping on her tongue like stones."[19]

The doctor's mother, who spoke only Russian and Italian, ministered to Catherine with smelling salts and a damp towel, but could not understand her. One hour after surgery Catherine felt no pain but a great deal of hunger and thirst. Suddenly she remembered how to say "I am hungry" in Italian, followed by "si, si, si – Napoli e bella." These two phrases endeared her to the doctor's mother, who rushed out and brought her hot tea and some food. Refreshed, she took up her notebook once again and apologized to Lewis "for being so thoughtless yesterday afternoon" before he departed for Dartmouth to give a series of lectures. "I had seen how tired you were too and had groaned at the thought of the horrible 10 days you had ahead of you. *Do* take it as easily as you can."

Catherine's first stop after the doctor's apartment was a post office, to telegraph Lewis that all went well. Lewis replied that he found comfort in her telegram, then spent the rest of the evening "thinking about myself and pitying myself and I didn't remember you again until, after a long glass of hot gin and lemon juice at the Packard's house, I made my way back to the inn and crawled into bed. I am a sniveling, snuffling, coughing, wheezing, croaking caricature of my usual charming self."

Her ordeal would not be mentioned again. Two days after surgery, Catherine found herself at the Museum of Modern Art in the midst of a heated debate about naming the pending international show on modern architecture, which Philip Johnson would curate. There were at least thirty notables from all over the world arguing over each word in the title. "International" was controversial due to its global implication, as the exhibition dealt primarily with Europe and the United States. Catherine found the scene absurd and amusing. More than sixty years later Philip Johnson reflected on these discussions in a lecture he delivered in Berlin. The 1920s and '30s saw a flowering of utopias, he recalled. Many architects were convinced of the triumph of functionalism over monumentality. Housing the masses was such a significant target of modern architecture in many European countries that it led to the use of the currently maligned "International Style."

With the hope of a grant from the Guggenheim Foundation dashed, Catherine scrambled to raise money for her trip to Europe. Lewis would be of some help; the poet Archibald MacLeish, a special editor at *Fortune*, had offered him $1,000 to write a series of articles on economic and political aspects of European housing. He had already received a $1,000 Guggenheim fellowship for four months' research in Europe, and the additional sum from *Fortune* would enable him to bring Sophie and Catherine along, at different times. Lewis planned to rely on Catherine to do data collection and most of the writing for *Fortune*. He departed at the end of April.

Catherine persuaded MacLeish to pay her an additional $100 for a separate article on general land planning in the Ruhr. With less than a month to go before she would join Lewis in Europe, she had much to do. In a manner which would govern most of her life, she started each day with a long list, then inevitably got delayed on the first item and spent the rest of the day rearranging priorities until she collapsed in a state of utter frustration by evening, feeling she had accomplished nothing. Her archives are full of apologies to editors and colleagues for missing deadlines because she was over-committed. In the end, however, she always made good on her promises – if not always on time. Catherine was not as conscientious about keeping promises to herself, such as revisions to her own book or writing a second one. She simply could not find the time.

After Lewis sailed, Sophie mailed Catherine a cheque for $500 on behalf of her husband as an advance for the trip. Although the two women had not yet met, they had formed a tenuous relationship through their common love. They were quite jealous of each other, but through Lewis's skilful jockeying they also held each other in great respect. Above all else, Sophie wished to keep her small family intact. Above all else, Catherine was prepared to be with Lewis, albeit entirely on his terms.

With her departure date just three weeks away, Catherine pleaded with friends and family for loans. Her parents were in financial straits at the time, but much to her surprise and relief, her young brother offered a $500 loan from money that he had squirrelled away. She raised another $200 from friends. With the money in hand, Catherine suddenly became anxious about her qualifications for doing research. "If I am pretty green about the social, political and economic side of housing – I am just a complete blank about the technological aspects," she wrote Lewis. She sought guidance from Dr. Edith Elmer Wood, who was in a hospital recovering from surgery. Although flat on her back, she had enough energy to keep Catherine riveted for two hours.

Dr. Wood urged Catherine to start in Frankfurt and seek the counsel of Dr. Kampfmeyer before going anywhere else; he had the best grasp of the global European housing picture and would give her letters of introduction to key people in Germany and Scandinavia. The suggestion prompted a change in Catherine's itinerary, one that would take her through Germany, Scandinavia, England, France, the Netherlands, Austria, Switzerland, and Czechoslovakia. If she had time, she would add the Soviet Union.

She had intended to meet Lewis in Vienna on June 1 after travelling through Germany. Their plan was to spend short intervals of time together, then part periodically to pursue their own interests and meet again a few weeks later. Catherine wanted to introduce Lewis to "her Paris," hoping to find some old friends from her post-college year. Following Dr. Wood's advice, she started in Paris, then went to Frankfurt to begin the research. Accordingly, she invited Lewis to meet her two weeks earlier than planned, but left the final decision of meeting date and place to him. He was in Germany when her news arrived and opted for a meeting in Munich.

Four days before her departure, Catherine received a telephone call from a representative of the New Jersey Federation of Women's Clubs (NJFWC) announcing their decision to award her a fellowship of $1,000 for study in Europe. A series of happy accidents led to this welcome surprise. Catherine's mother, who actively participated in several women's organizations, had been heartily congratulated by the executive committee of the NJFWC upon her daughter's *Fortune* award. Bertie, in turn, kept them informed of Catherine's activities and publications. Upon rejection by the Guggenheim Foundation, Catherine notified the Federation of Women's Clubs that she was planning another trip to Europe to pursue research on regionalism. As it turned out, NJFWC had two subcommittees devoted to regional planning. It was a perfect fit, and Catherine was launched in style.

She met Lewis in Munich three weeks earlier than planned. The happy reunion turned tense within days; he was annoyed by her intrusion into his solitude, having enjoyed the freedom of roaming around cities, speaking with strangers on trains or in hotels, travelling entirely at his own pace. He was not prepared to accommodate another person's needs, and Catherine's were great. Despite lessons she had taken in New York, she was not fluent enough in German to conduct interviews or even intelligent conversations. This failure, coupled with insecurity about her ability to handle her new job, made her cranky and irritable.

After a testy time together she analyzed the situation: "I was totally incapable, unprepared and ridiculous in the role of Lady making a financial, economic, political, social and technological survey of housing in Europe. Not knowing German just seemed to touch it off, and make it impossible even to learn what to learn. Perhaps I *have* got an Expert complex." Characteristically she blamed herself for bringing about tension.

Lewis resented her desire to enjoy Europe in his company, at the expense of their housing mission. They travelled together from Munich to Vienna, separated briefly, met in Paris, which was an anticlimax, then continued to England, where they parted in surprisingly high spirits. Catherine flew to Amsterdam, where her serious work began early in July.

For three weeks she toured Holland, finding key people in each city to show her housing, provide her with city plans, financial statements, and aerial views of select neighbourhoods. She was tutored by leading Dutch architects, including J.J.P. Oud, whom she had met on her 1930 trip. They were happy to give her time, especially as they admired Lewis Mumford, and she, as his research associate, was a link to the great man. She was resourceful in begging or borrowing materials from unusual places, such as airline offices for aerial photographs. She purchased old prints of cities from antiquarian dealers and admired newly planned cities, still on the drawing boards. Catherine especially enjoyed Amsterdam and Rotterdam, which were harmonious in their layout with outlying towns that were also well planned. She was struck by signs of the English Arts and Crafts movement in Holland. Morris and Ruskin's influences were more visible in municipal equipment, such as garbage cans and letter boxes, than in their native England. Only The Hague disappointed her. It was dirty, noisy, and had no good restaurants; its beaches, she remarked, were even worse than Atlantic City.

On the way to Berlin, Catherine stopped in Kassel, where a remarkable new development called Randsiedlung had just been completed on the outer rim of the city. Rather than subsidizing construction companies to build housing for the unemployed residents of Randsiedlung, Kassel officials had contracted the people to construct their own homes. This struck Catherine as a progressive strategy for communities experiencing economic hardship. Officials in the *Bauamt* (municipal building department) were happy to give Catherine all the information she sought, and the Kassel visit went down in her notes as a favourite European stop.

Collecting facts in hot, stuffy Berlin proved a difficult job during the summer, especially with so many residents away on vacation. False leads, wrong addresses, and broken telephones hindered her progress. Catherine's spirits sank or soared with the contacts she made. She was such a gregarious person that a few days alone made her gloomy and suddenly doubtful about her abilities. During such periods she reviewed events that led to tension with Lewis – the petty squabbles and recriminations. He blamed her for being cold and indifferent, indeed turning her back on him at appointed meeting places. She countered by insisting she had looked everywhere for him, in vain. Such discussions became circular and led to bad feelings that Catherine usually managed to cast off when she was among people who interested her. But alone, in Berlin, they plagued her.

After a few morose days alone Catherine finally made contact with the people she had come to Berlin to meet: architects Walter Behrendt, Martin Wagner, and Hugo Häring. All were socialists, deeply involved in developing affordable, livable housing. Behrendt had written several studies for the *Reichsarbeitsministerium* (Department of Labour) that covered the labour, materials, and methods for everything from the latest kitchen design to complete structural and economic analyses of large settlements. Catherine hit upon a rich vein in making contact with these architect-planners: they gave her all she asked for, and more.

She was very impressed with Germany's highly organized municipal offices and well-articulated plans for future development. Yet she wrote to Lewis that she could not help but wonder "if there were any real hope for the Germany that we admire and find inspiring. The papers are full of awfulness – but on the surface everything looks the same." The very next morning she witnessed a parade of several thousand Nazis, just fifty yards from her window, followed by an enormous demonstration in the Wittenbergplatz.

"All the house-maids were running around with their heads off in enthusiastic excitement." Because of the sloppy decorum and lack of discipline among the marchers, who were either very young or very old, Catherine felt no personal danger. However, she pointed out, "there seemed to be no evidence of any clear-cut opposing faction on the fringes of the demonstration. At the proper moments in the discourse or singing, everyone either automatically raised his arm for the *Hoch!* or looked tolerant or just kept talking to his neighbor." A few days later Catherine poignantly observed to Lewis, "Did it ever occur to you, my darling love (as it did to me in these days) that *Europe itself*, at this moment and from the points of view from which we come to look at it, might well be blamed for our various neuroticisms, disillusions and distempers? It's not an ideal world for a romantic trip into the Present."

Walter Behrendt, she noticed, had become strangely tense since they had first met two years earlier. She did not know that he was Jewish. Indeed, Behrendt was soon forced to flee Nazi Germany, and with the aid of his friend, Lewis Mumford, he obtained a job at Dartmouth College. He died of heart disease in 1945. Martin Wagner also fled Nazi persecution for his strongly held socialist views and ended up teaching at Harvard, where he would work with Catherine.

Many days Catherine despaired of ever pulling together all the fragmented pieces of information she had been collecting. She did have moments of clarity. "I have suddenly had a few quite comforting and even exciting flashes," she wrote Lewis. "And more and more there is a conviction that, once the loose and messy figures are pulled into something sensible – something very real and sure will come up out of the morass of my own impressions and desires and likes and hates and hopes."

Eventually she collected enough data to write the first installment of the *Fortune* series. She was delighted to send Lewis thirty pages based on what she had learned in England. "The sheer weight of Achievement has made me dizzy," she told him. As a natural and fluent writer, Catherine enjoyed the process, though she belittled her effort: "The whole thing is patched together out of nothing – little odds and ends of hearsay and fact and fiction." Later Lewis rewrote large parts of the article, making it a truly collaborative piece of work – except that Catherine received no credit in the final copy. MacLeish was in no hurry to print the piece and gave Catherine permission to do the layout, which would include photographs and diagrams.

During that summer, Catherine and Lewis's relationship struck a reef. He cast blame on her, claiming that she should not have listened to Dr. Wood. Her return to Frankfurt was unnecessary, she did not need Dr. Kampfmeyer's introductions to people; the resulting change of her itinerary upset his own travel plans and made him irritable. The few letters that were not filled with petty arguments lacked all passion.

After Sophie joined him in Holland, Lewis realized that his allegiance belonged to her. He wrote to Catherine accordingly. Her response was a long, sad letter recalling her advice a year earlier, when she had suggested that Lewis spend a year abroad. She had written: "Mortgage your property. Borrow money. Make Sophie get a job. Tell all of us temporarily to go to hell. (Why not get a Guggenheim?) And discipline yourself to undisciplined exploration. The result might be poetry ... might be the book that will give the neotechnic age its real start ... might be anything. But that it would be something really magnificent I have no doubt whatsoever." Mumford revisited the letter in his archives on January 4, 1981, and wrote on the top left corner in a shaking hand "a beautiful suggestion that miscarried!"

In her unhappy letter she blamed herself for not heeding the "fine sensible letter I wrote you last year about how you simply *must* go to Europe *alone* and without strings of any kind. I was so noble then." She blamed herself for joining him and thereby creating burdensome strings. She regretted not listening to her emotions – she had had a foreboding that travelling with Lewis might be a mistake. She knew early on that she would not be able to concentrate on housing in his presence, but had lacked the mind, heart, and courage to air the issue. "I knew really, that I couldn't combine exacting research with what by its very nature had to be an

CATHERINE RELAXING NEAR LAKE

"I knew really, that I couldn't combine exacting research with what by its very nature had to be an extremely delicate and important and romantic journey with an absorbing lover."

extremely delicate and important and romantic journey with an absorbing lover." Added to these feelings were her "agonizing, bitterly selfish and hopeless jealousy of Sophie – and Geddes, and everything else in your life that I could never touch." Never before had she been in such an agony to possess something, completely and entirely, "for ever and ever, even if it killed both of us and everything we really liked or stood for."

Finally she confessed: "In my worst moments, architecture and housing and the whole texture of convictions and curiosities and desires and interests that had grown up in me in the past two or three years seemed to exist only in relation to you." She had sailed off to Europe nurturing an impossible dream of marrying Lewis and allowed herself to become "positively sentimental about the joys of settled married life and the horrors of loneliness and instability."

After this stormy catharsis Catherine regained her equilibrium. She would never allow herself to sink into such a desperate morass of self-pity and longing, she vowed. But she would allow herself to continue loving Lewis Mumford.

4

POLITICAL YEARS (1934-36)

JOURNALIST

*You transformed an insufferably smarty dilettante into a
good semblance of a serious and responsible worker,
with ... a passionate conviction of purpose that eclipses
everything else.*

CATHERINE BAUER TO LEWIS MUMFORD

As Catherine had predicted in the spring of 1931, Lewis's time
abroad led to a book that would give the neotechnic age its real start
– a book that would be something really magnificent. It would be
called *Technics and Civilization*. His biographer called it "the first full-scale
study in the English language of the rise of the machine in the modern
world and one of the first scholarly studies in any language to emphasize
the interplay of technology and the surrounding culture."[1]

Back in New York late in August, Catherine took a grimy apartment on
West 54th Street, where Lewis could come to visit. Their relationship was
back on a comfortable track, the tensions that haunted them that summer
having temporarily subsided. Catherine worked on the Vienna section of the
second article in Lewis's *Fortune* series while arranging the layout and
answering countless questions from the editors about the first article. She
dutifully deferred to Lewis as the final arbiter on proposed text changes. He
insisted that he would not consent to a single word change if they wanted
his signature on the article, "unless they catch me in a grammatical error."

Her mind became dizzy from German tongue twisters, as she pounded
on her typewriter "layer upon layer of words like Leistungsfahigkeit and
Stockwerksaufsetzungen." As recreation she toured Manhattan for signs of
new buildings. To her delight she discovered a partly filled reservoir at
Sixth Avenue and 81st Street, where twenty new dwellings were being
built by future inhabitants from odds and ends of bricks and stones left
over from a dam construction. Referring back to Kassel, she called it "our

Randsiedlung." She would photograph and weave it into an article when she had time.

Feeling particularly frisky one warm afternoon, she ended a letter to Lewis with the salutation "Fun and Friendliness," then added, "All right – but just so that the trustees of our correspondence won't think it a *little* mild, let's add Fun Fucking and Friendliness." Lewis was quick to concur. "Life in the morning," he wrote, "is surely to be preferred to Death in the Afternoon: and if our future biographer ... should have any doubts about our status or relationship, let's add, just to be provocatively explicit, FUCKING in the morning, too."

Catherine approached Clarence Stein for further part-time work in housing research. He wanted help on a new book about community planning, but she found it so prosaic and lustreless, without clearly defined points, that she refused to touch it. Stein was kind enough to find other work for her to do and hired her back on a part-time basis.

The *Fortune* articles took much longer than planned, and Lewis grew testy. Even though Catherine was very helpful in proofreading final copies and gathering all the extra information the editors wanted, she became his scapegoat. He charged her with trapping him into doing these articles so that she could join him in Europe. The extra writing demanded of him took time away from his book. She responded to his "torrential, daemonic discontent" with a cool "Shame Shame and For Shame ... Don't you know that I care perhaps more about your work than I do about you-personally-and-me? That I was much more passionately romantic about *your* trip than any sentimental yearning of my own at the moment?" In 1961 Lewis commented in the margin of the letter, "C's reproach was justified."

Toward the end of the year Catherine could look back with pride at all she had achieved. She had assisted in the preparation of the housing section of the landmark architectural show called "Modern Architecture: International Exhibition," which opened at the Museum of Modern Art on February 10, 1932. The same month *The Nation* carried her review of Edith Elmer Wood's latest book, *Recent Trends in American Housing*, which documented the deplorable living conditions of American workers. On March 2 the *New Republic* published "Are Good Houses Un-American?," her review of the MOMA exhibition in which she praised the show in all its aspects and promoted modern European housing. In the article she pointed out that luxurious private houses had much in common with subsidized houses because they had similar amenities: light, air, space, sun, colour, and form, and they were free from clutter. "Why are good houses un-American?" she asked. In the United States, "houses are things to look at, like amusements; or shown off as a possession or a literary symbol of culture; or lived in as a daily reminder of isolated personality in noble competition against the rest of the world; or merely a place to hang a hat, equipped with the latest gadget for hanging hats."[2]

Arts Weekly published many features and reviews carrying her byline. Among them was an article urging Americans to learn from postwar construction in England, Holland, and Germany. Catherine argued that the best planners and architects in these countries were employed to develop advanced, large-scale community planning techniques, such as dwellings oriented for sun and air, wide recreation areas, view space, mass-production methods, and elimination of through-traffic within the community. Another article, "Architecture in Philadelphia," was written when MOMA's modern architecture exhibition travelled to that city. Among exhibits added to localize the show for Philadelphia were plans for a new network of apartment buildings. They would be called Carl Mackley Houses in memory of a worker killed during a strike; the houses were designed by architects Kastner and Stonorov and built for the Federation of Full-Fashioned Hosiery Workers. Catherine bestowed her highest praise upon the project, comparing it with the best she had seen in Europe. Her enthusiasm foreshadowed her own headlong move into housing, which would begin with work for Stonorov.

She also gave a favourable *Arts Weekly* review to Brooklyn's new Marine Park and a photography show featuring Man Ray and Paul Strand. Her strongest condemnation was reserved for Vassar College's plans for a new gymnasium, designed by architects Allen and Collier. They had proposed a gym in the style of an English country house with farm outbuildings suggestive of Matthew Vassar's birthplace in Norfolk. Catherine decried the absurdity of housing a swimming pool, exercise facility, and dance rooms in a building designed to look like an old half-timbered inn with a fake chimney.

The first of the five *Fortune* articles on which Catherine and Lewis had laboured appeared in November 1932, under the title "European Housing: England."[3] Mumford got the byline, though the factual information and many of the illustrations and captions were Catherine's. Essentially the article described England's unprecedented housing production. Between the years 1919 and 1932, England built 1.8 million dwellings, of which 1 million were constructed for the lowest income group. In terms of quality and quantity, "it was perhaps the largest public achievement of any country in the world since the war."[4] The transformation of housing through nationwide subsidy represented "a Social Revolution, as deep and as bloodless as the Industrial Revolution in which, a century ago, [England] led the world."[5]

Lewis envisioned two Englands: the Black and the Green. Black England, now in decline, grew out of the industrial revolution and represented the worst degradation in housing. Green England was linked to the concepts of three men: Raymond Unwin, Barry Parker, and Ebenezer Howard. Thanks to their principles, England planned better houses and grouped them together in better communities. According to Lewis, modern housing in England rested on three pillars: the use of public credit; new building and planning techniques achieving better dwellings; and public subsides to ensure occupancy by low-income families. British postwar housing achievements were possible due to the influence of John Ruskin on the Victorian industrialists and of Patrick Geddes on Ebenezer Howard in correlating housing with town planning and industrial development. *Fortune*'s editors distanced themselves from Lewis's position on public subsidy in their introduction to the article: "America improved on England's industrialism and retains today a faith in private enterprise greater than that to be found in England – or any other country."[6]

The second article, "Machines for Living," appeared three months after the first.[7] Paraphrasing Le Corbusier's dictum, "A house is a machine to live in," Lewis described the remarkable housing achievements of Frankfurt, Rotterdam, Berlin, Vienna, and other European cities. "Functionalism as a guiding principle has taken hold of the design of a greater part of the new housing in Europe, and it is in the minimum house (for the lowest income classes) that its methods have become most clear and accurate."[8] In prose and pictures, the article introduced American readers – probably for the first time – to the experimental designs of Walter Gropius, Mies van der Rohe, J.J.P. Oud, Ernst May, Erich Mendelsohn, and Bruno Taut.

New housing forms were linked to social and political reform, and Frankfurt was cited as the best example of bold advances in coordinating building design with community design. At least twenty-four different kinds of houses were designed and built by the most eminent architects. Comprehensive site planning considered three factors to be equally important: innovative kitchen equipment, orientation toward the sun, and open space. For example, by orienting living rooms and gardens to the south, children and plants would be exposed to seven hundred extra sunlight hours per year. (The figures were lifted from Catherine's log book.)

"Taxes into Houses" was the title of the third article in the *Fortune* series, published in May 1933 under the heading "Housing Abroad: Subsidies."[9] Returning to many of the themes introduced in the first article on England, this one broadened the analysis with a balance sheet of the whole European housing movement. The European experience demonstrated that because private enterprise had failed to provide decent housing, the state must assume the obligation. Since 1919 more than 4.5 million dwellings had been erected with public funds or encouragement in Holland, Germany, France, England, and Austria. A chart of typical

European housing tabulated cost, finance, and rent in each country and made a strong case for public subsidies for low-income families. Assistance came in various forms, such as low interest rates, low amortization and depreciation rates, reduced land costs through the elimination of speculation, and low administration costs. Economies were also achieved through large-scale planning and construction.

Lewis concluded "by taking the community, instead of the individual house, as the unit of house production, European leaders have shown the way ... toward economic planning and construction to social integration and effective architectural design. This attack on the housing problem is the only one that includes the rationalization of *all* the factors involved. No sound housing policy can ignore it."[10] Such a radical perspective proved too much for the conservative magazine, and *Fortune* terminated the series. The editors believed that houses, like cars, ought to be manufactured through privately funded mass production. They held that state-subsidized housing was foreign to accepted American ideals, despite the fact that in the previous year President Hoover had established the Reconstruction Finance Corporation (RFC) to reduce unemployment in the construction industry. By 1933 President Roosevelt was using RFC to provide public construction funds and credit for the production of market housing, clearly identifying housing as an economic-industrial issue. *Fortune* had to accept such policy from Washington, but they didn't have to like it – or write about it.

Catherine felt deceived and betrayed by the termination of the series. She complained to Gutheim: "*Fortune*, the bitch, has just decided that what they really want was Lewis's personal impressions of architecture, the exact opposite of what they told us in writing last spring. I therefore had a harassed summer and am becoming an unbecoming housing expert for no apparent reason."[11] Nevertheless she had developed a substantial arsenal of analytical tools as an architectural design critic and was ready to begin work on a full-scale book.

Catherine was determined to use her wealth of data and photographic material to best advantage. Unlike Lewis, who barely dipped into her figures in passing, she would embark upon a mission that would take longer, and go deeper. Soon she would shake up the establishment with a book that was so well structured, clearly focused, and richly illustrated that all two thousand copies of the first edition would be sold out within two years. She would introduce Americans to the modern architecture of Gropius, Mies van der Rohe, Le Corbusier, and their colleagues in Holland, Scandinavia, and England, exploring ways in which the lessons of Europe could apply to North America.

Gradually Catherine's magazine articles and the material she collected for *Fortune* coalesced into a substantive manuscript. Its name, scope, and point of view were discussed at length with Lewis, Stein, and others. Everyone was convinced of the value and importance of such a book, but each offered different advice regarding target audience, content, and length. Lewis urged her to tackle it from her own point of view, distinct from his, and to set it within the framework of rapid urbanization in the late nineteenth century. Catherine settled on a formula whereby she would introduce herself to her readers as a "traveling student of modern housing ... as impressed with the international fellowship which exists in these matters as with the houses themselves."[12]

She was confident she could write a worthwhile book but still had to convince a publisher to take it on. Financial assistance of $1,000 was guaranteed from the Carnegie Corporation as soon as a publishing contract was signed, a qualification that worried Catherine. She was relatively unknown in the publishing world, and economic times were hard. Then serendipity played a hand.

In March 1933, Catherine spent a night in a hotel around the corner from the Boston offices of Houghton Mifflin. Without any introductions, but with nothing to lose, she took a chance and called on the editor, Ferris Greenslett. Fortunately he had read her prize-winning *Fortune* essay and had been impressed by her "lucid and vigorous presentation of first-hand material."[13] He easily persuaded Houghton Mifflin's executive committee of the merits of her proposed book at a time when the United States faced a critical housing shortage. Within two weeks Catherine had her publisher. They suggested a release in the fall of 1933, but she quickly applied for, and was granted, an extension to December 1934. It would be published with the imprint of Riverside Press, a subsidiary of the Houghton Mifflin Company, in Cambridge, Massachusetts.

The year 1933 found Catherine and Lewis deeply engrossed in their separate writing tasks – and actively involved in psychological combat. The previous autumn Lewis had resolved to give up all social commitments in order to devote himself entirely to his book. He continued to see and write to Catherine, but much less frequently than before. Catherine, now more on her own, met architects and planners through her work at Stein's office and her participation on various housing panels. Among her new circle was Oscar Stonorov, a gifted architect who, with his partner Alfred Kastner, designed the Carl Mackley Houses in Philadelphia.

Stonorov had been introduced to Catherine by Lewis a year earlier. Exactly her age, he was a debonair, good-humoured bachelor who sported a monocle and enjoyed flirting with attractive women. Catherine was often surrounded by serious, dull, older men, and she enjoyed the attentions of this fun-loving, extremely talented young man. Born in Frankfurt, Stonorov had studied art in Florence and architecture in Zurich before coming to the United States. He and Catherine had much to discuss.

By early March Lewis could not help but notice his friend's attraction to his lover and accused Catherine of shameless flirtation, predicting that their relationship would lead "to bed." She denied his charge as nonsense and accused him of reading far too much into innocent flirtation. Lewis would not be appeased. "If you have fallen out of love with me," he wrote, "if you feel only the staleness and sameness of our relationship, don't try to simplify matters too much by urging that you haven't actually fallen in love, perhaps, with someone else." Switching roles now from spurned lover to stern father, he pushed on. "My darling: these are hard things to think about: harder still to say. I am ruthless with you now, out of the fear given me by your letter, that you have not been ruthless with yourself, and do not know what you are doing and why you are doing it." He ended by vowing, "I love you," then made arrangements to see her the next day. He enclosed a few dollars, assuming she was low in cash.

Catherine's reply was cool. "You really have, as I feared, given the whole thing infinitely more scale and significance than it deserved. I did not feel any capacity or necessity for being unfaithful – nor yet any dissatisfaction or wearing out." She charged Lewis with being hurt out of all proportion and explained that the Stonorov situation grew out of her poor state of mind. "I am tired and nervous and depressed," she said, and saw in Stonorov "a tired business man's cocktail and chorus girl, only reversed for a tired business woman." She wasn't proud of herself – indeed, she admitted such an act was "much more immoral than if I simply went to bed with somebody out of sheer overflowing animal spirits. It is exactly the sort of thing that goes utterly counter to every moral and aesthetic precept that I possess so of course it always leaves me with a bad hang-over." Despite the disclaimer, Catherine admitted to Lewis the next day that she had always enjoyed flirting with other men, and always would.

Lewis apologized, in his fashion. "You had put me in the position of looking like some horrible combination of a psychoanalyst and a district attorney, trying to beat and bully out of you all your independence and self-respect and pride: so if you were a low creature and a miserable worm and a faithless sweetheart, I was miles and abysses lower than you because ... I was unmanly enough to drive home all the discrepancies between our two attitudes. You had hoped for sympathy met instead a monument of vindictiveness and self-righteousness."

He ascribed the profound change in their relationship to absorption with his book. Their summer in Europe had been bad because of it: when he wanted to make love, she talked of nothing but housing; when she cuddled up to him, his mind was on his book. Now he felt his book was "reaching out more tentacles, occupying more time, spreading to remoter and remoter layers of my mind." It was displacing her, in fact, though he was struggling not to let her go.

Her flirtations were proof to Lewis that she was no longer fully in love with him. He would have to court her all over again, to win back her love, but this would be impossible now because work on his book was too critical. Although his "every waking moment was clogged with thoughts and fears about us," he felt he was doing his best writing ever – and critics would later agree. *Technics and Civilization* proved to be his seminal book, but the creative process was exhausting, and the ongoing tension with Catherine didn't help. Eventually Lewis succumbed to a sore throat and fever.

Catherine was in no better shape, and in a face-to-face confrontation she finally told Lewis to go to the devil. She proclaimed that she preferred being herself – and having whoever came along – to denying herself just for him. That night she fired off an angry note:

> Is it so unnatural, no matter how absolutely all-important and all-absorbing a relationship may be, that in a passionate love-affair between two people in which you, the man, have gone home regularly after every encounter, punctually, to your wife and family and in which I, the girl, have never once been able to say: Come now, I want you today. – Let alone saying: Let us build a future on this splendid present. – Is it really so unnatural and shocking (though it be stupid, unreal, immoral and unsatisfactory) that I should sometimes find myself involved in other and temporary relationships – situations which I dominate, which I start and stop and could make anything I pleased of, and in which I call the tempo and vaguely, usually rather guiltily, derive a certain amount of comfort and satisfaction therefrom?

Within a few days Lewis was courting her again, but with a new ribald twist. He called Catherine "you doxy ... my Jezebel and my wench" in a letter that opened "Here is a kiss and a punch and a bite!" He also called her his "hussy." Had she been honest about her interest in others from the start, he equivocated, he would not have behaved in such a hollow, self-righteous fashion. He explained that his odious manners and pitiable attitude stemmed not from her willingness to make love to other people, but from her unwillingness to face it (or his unwillingness to understand it, he failed to add).

Upon cooling off, Catherine reflected that two forces governed their relationship. "One is that clean narrow break that ordinarily serves to maintain our separate identities and enable them to stimulate and enrich each other, and which demands of us, even in our moments of bright fusion, a certain delicate balance, an extra consciousness which makes the

CATHERINE SMILING WITH SMOKE

Within a few days Lewis was courting her again, but with a new ribald twist. He called Catherine "you doxy ... my Jezebel and my wench."

moments the more complete and satisfactory. But it also, when the pressure on some secret spring suddenly widens the crack to a roaring misty chasm, makes us not merely enemies, but much worse – complete strangers at opposite ends of the earth, mistaking even each other's signals of distress."

Their differences in temperament, background, and circumstance were to blame, she thought. "We do have to live in the Present. We have no Future. Our Present has been going on for a long time, and it may well continue for a very long time, perhaps for all of our lives, but – unless there is some terrific upheaval, which turns us into two quite different people – it will always be a Present."

Had she simply been a girl in love who wanted marriage, their relationship would have ended long ago. "But for one thing, I am your disciple and pupil and sometimes intellectual equal." The excitement she drew from the relationship was stronger now than ever, "opening up a whole new world of possibility, of responsibility, of large desire and of hopeful delight in my own capacities. And all of this was only aided and shaped and increased and sharpened and enriched by that very Present quality in our love ... And don't be an idiot! This has nothing whatsoever to do with your *work*. Your work is part of my life and our love, whether you want it to be or not." Having finally arrived at this realization, "that moment of knowledge, I have been more – and differently – conscious of other men." She thought she might never be married, but knew she would always be susceptible to the flattery, amusement, and physical powers of men.

"The whole thing is just simply your fault," she declared. "With all the power of which your mind and other implements are capable – you brute and you love. You turned an inhibited Narcissist into a fair approximation of a normal female, who wants not only to be married to *you* – but who even, in moments of weakness or defeat, has all too normal visions of the safe and secure marriage-mirage ... You transformed an insufferably smarty dilettante into a good semblance of a serious and responsible worker, with not only ideas and interests and receptivities and large desires but sometimes a passionate conviction of purpose that eclipses everything else."

Her six-page outburst ended on a positive note. "I have exciting work to do: And, if it is true that our love needs that, it is just as true that I need our love *for* that – more sharply, more *particularly*, do I need you as a lover and master, than as a husband. Thank you for *everything* you did to me. And: I love you, Lewis ... Will you go on with me?" She promised that when she was ready for marriage, she would make a clean break, "with no alibis, blame-shifting or nasty twittering evasions." She would keep that promise.

TRANSFORMATION

I was not made for the tragic role.
          CATHERINE BAUER TO LEWIS MUMFORD

Having vented her feelings for Lewis, Catherine was able to focus on her book. She now felt freer to seek advice from him, rather than sexual solace. He was not nearly so pleased with this turn of events. Although she had often voiced her opinion that serious work requires a certain physical withdrawal – "more flirting and less fucking," as she put it – he could not avoid the conclusion that this new stage of aloofness signalled the decay of their relationship. He was convinced another man had taken his place in her bed.

He proved to be not much help when she turned to him a few weeks later, in desperation. "I am having a momentary fit of stage-fright at confronting a thousand sheets of blank white paper," she wrote on April 4, 1933. "I need you most of all. Are there really 75,000 clear, concise, well-ordered, inspired words on European housing in this muddled, disorderly, rather weary mind?" In due course she drew up a working outline that she showed him. Confirming that her outline was both brilliant and distinguished, Lewis said that he had nothing to add, and besides, he had resolved to keep his hands off her book. He wanted her to "run your own race in your own way, without me plying the whip and holding on to the bridle."

The thought of the publisher's deadline coupled with the heat of an early New York summer drove Catherine into a "state of paralyzing inner conflict." She felt undisciplined, and in a letter to Lewis self-consciously divided herself into two halves. The masochistic half sneers and says: "Maybe you *can't* really do anything – maybe you can't think anything through – maybe your vanity has made you develop a fine surface semblance of thinking, feeling, doing. Maybe you've fooled everybody, including yourself. And *maybe* you don't really ever *want* to do anything." But the rational half "finds those maybes utterly ridiculous; knows I am intelligent, have things to say, like to work and would not enjoy life without problems to be solved."

Lewis countered with his own "mornings of sober agony over the first recalcitrant sections of the most difficult chapter of the most arduous book I have ever written." He made fun of her plight "as a housing expert and an authority and a stuffed shirt – or is it a stuffed chemise: dreadful thought! – for alas!, though when you met me I was concerned far more with letters and philosophy than with housing and architecture, I did, consciously or not, have something to do with your descent into statistics, figures, responsibilities, research, and communistic propaganda, and now that you are there, up to your neck in it, hating figures, hating housing, hating me, it is only too obvious that it was the last thing I had in heart or mind when we met." He went on, pen in cheek. "I reach for you and what do I touch? A housing expert. I call for you in the stillness of the night and what do I hear? The percentage of vacancies in Laubengang apartment houses as compared with cottages."

Catherine was indeed taken up with facts and figures about housing in Europe, and now also in the United States. As an expert, she was invited to give lectures to students at Bennington College and housers (people committed to improving access to shelter for the poor) in Atlantic City. At dinner parties with other housing experts, she encountered the stuffed shirts that Lewis derided. They were the people who would become her opponents in the fight for decent, affordable housing. In June 1933 the opposition was embodied in a Mr. Boyd of the New Jersey Housing League, who claimed that he, alone, knew all the answers. He thought that men like Clarence Stein and Frank Lloyd Wright had very few good ideas. Mr. Boyd struck deals with *real* banks and *real* big construction businesses to remodel old-law tenements so that they would bring in top dollars. The wonderful New Deal, he believed, ought to be broad in its housing program, but no one was entitled to have an opinion on housing unless he has had *real* practical experience (such as his).

Catherine travelled to the Midwest to learn more about American housing. She saw the blight of Pittsburgh and its antithesis, Milwaukee, where she could find no slums, vested interests, or smug capitalists like Mr. Boyd. Instead she found low land values, a Teutonically efficient sewage-disposal plant, the best city and county use-zoning (with admirable gardens and park systems), and what she considered to be the best transportation planning in America. No residences were higher than two stories. Unfortunately, however, nearly all of them were appalling duplex bungalows, divided by concrete pavement. English-type row houses were unacceptable here, she was told, because people refused to live with party walls.

The best architecture around Milwaukee was found in the clean, light, spacious factories built far from the city. They were well landscaped and set back from new boulevards. This arrangement ran counter to the garden city principle that placed work sites within easy reach of residences. By contrast, Rochester, Minnesota, combined working and living space that resulted in smoke and disorder, noise and confusion. The railroad ran right through the main streets, where there were no bridges, tunnels, or even safety hoardings. It was a grim town with buildings constructed of dark, crumbling bricks.

In her travels south Catherine encountered a remarkable experiment in public policy. Roosevelt's campaign promise of creating a system of dams in the valley of the Tennessee River came to fruition during his first hundred days in office. Fritz Gutheim, working at the Brookings Institute, alerted Catherine to the project's development potential. He was horrified to discover that a bill authorizing the Tennessee Valley Project had been passed by the House of Representatives with no mention of regional planning. Using the research facilities at Brookings, he developed a legislative draft for a regional planning program and persuaded Senator Joseph Norris to include it in his bill. Representative Lister Hill, the House sponsor, concurred; purely on the strength of the legislators' recommendation, the Senate passed the bill without subjecting it to hearings.

The members of the nearly defunct Regional Planning Association of America were mildly exercised over the Tennessee Valley project because Washington had failed to consult them. Only Benton MacKaye became actively involved on his own initiative. What was shaping up to be the nation's most ambitious planning project to date elicited nothing but a round of grumbling from RPAA, Catherine concluded. What bothered them was the appointment of a southern landscape architect as Director of Regional Planning and Housing for the Tennessee Valley Authority (TVA). The director's decision not to deliver a comprehensive plan for the valley in the immediate future – at least until the project was well under way – struck the northern planners as ludicrous. "I suppose [they are waiting until] they really have something to bite their teeth into, such as New York," Catherine sneered.

As originally conceived, model villages would be designed for TVA on the pattern of the earliest settlers' houses. Several hundred families would be brought down from the hills for a few years to work on one dam. They would be offered adult education classes and other amenities. Upon completion of each dam they would be sent back to the mountains, and another group would be brought down. This process would be repeated until all the dams were built.

No thought was given to how these "newly civilized" people would fare back in their cornfields, where even the market for moonshine was gone. Catherine deplored the lack of vision for such a vast, complex region. This was a missed opportunity to experiment with garden city concepts developed by Stein and Wright in the United States and already demonstrated in Europe, in the settlements described in her *Fortune* articles and which formed the heart of her book in progress. She bitterly concluded, "the only thing that any of [the government people] *really* wants is to keep the mountaineers quaint, dumb, inefficient, frustrated and *harmless*."

By the end of July Catherine was fully absorbed in her manuscript. The publisher sent her a mock-up of the book jacket featuring the Cologne Cathedral, which was highly inappropriate for a work on modern architecture. She disliked his choice of cover type; since her book would have a strong visual dimension, it was especially important that the cover be attractive. She also found the recommended title, "Modern Community Housing in Europe," too cumbersome and elected to call her book, simply, "Modern Housing."

Catherine's aloofness toward Lewis was turning into a morbid fatalism. She had not stopped loving him, but felt that in order to preserve their love she would need to further break from him or risk growing to hate him for his happy future with Sophie. She told him this, knowing he would misinterpret it as a lack of love. "You *are* just naturally a Demanding Male, and heaven forbid that you should *not* be – you could not have made me even into an independent Female if you hadn't been ... We can give each other so much this way, in some ways more than if I were essentially dependent on you. And I do love you."

Lewis's reaction was predictably melodramatic. To him this was an affirmation – not that they would part, but that they *had* parted:

Ours, whether you like it or not, has been a tragic relation: perhaps doubly tragic because at neither the beginning nor the end did you accept tragedy ... I really did not know tragedy in the classic sense, and now I do. The classic tragedy, as our teachers always explained it to us, was the fate of the strong and virtuous man, driven by external circumstances and by weaknesses in his own nature towards ends other than those he sought to encompass, driven there finally to his ruin. There has been more than a touch of the classic hero and heroine in each of us, my dearest: and ... I entirely agree with you that one cannot continue in that role forever, for one must finally come to some sort of resolution in the fifth act ... Well: our Fifth Act has been acted, and this is our Epilogue, with the lights up and the orchestra surreptitiously

tuning their instruments and the ladies fussing in the reticules – or is it
perhaps Faust Part Two: Act I: A Pleasant Landscape?[14]

Lewis was also stung. "I shall never, to my dying day, have the haziest notion as to what a Demanding Male is or why the Devil you think that I am one."

On Friday evening of Thanksgiving weekend, at a dinner party in the Central Park West penthouse apartment of Clarence Stein, Catherine met Sophie Mumford for the first time. Catherine charmed the guests, who included Benton MacKaye and the aging Raymond Unwin, but above all she charmed Sophie. "Drat your friend Catherine. I hate her," Sophie told Lewis afterwards, "because I really like her so much and I can understand why you do, too. There is something about the curve of her mouth and the delicacy of her neck that almost brings a lump in my throat." Lewis reported this to Catherine the next day. He, too, was charmed by Catherine that night as "six distinct images of falling in love with you" merged in his mind.

Catherine was devastated by the evening. Her charm must have emanated from stage fright upon meeting Sophie, and, like a seasoned actress, she rose to the occasion. In fact, she wrote to Lewis the next day, "I was sliding myself down into the lowest depths of bitterness, hatred and despair. Never, never again under any circumstances would I go any place with Sophie. There you were, perfectly happily married to a perfectly nice attractive girl who is undoubtedly the best wife you could have found, and there was I, about as important or suitable as part of your living edifice as a baroque reverse curve teetering on the top of an otherwise neat and functional dwelling."

Sophie Mumford and Catherine eventually became good friends. Sixty years after their first meeting, Mrs. Mumford recalled that she and Catherine were wearing the same dress the evening they met, though hers was red and Catherine's was green.

The new year found both Catherine and Lewis moving full-speed ahead on their manuscripts and still wildly vacillating in their relationship. Lewis eschewed all social obligations, while Catherine simply reduced hers. She needed some social contact to keep a certain equilibrium in her life. When she sank to the depths of despair, she sought the company of people who could distract and amuse her. She became a member of the Inner Council of the Housing Study Guild, a group that evolved out of RPAA and was beginning to attract people concerned about the sociology of housing.

The American housing situation was in crisis, with tens of thousands of people losing their homes each month to foreclosure. It was time for decisive political action, and the guild provided an interesting forum for the discussion of policy. Despite her protestations to the contrary, Catherine

SOPHIE MUMFORD

Sixty years after their first meeting, Sophie Mumford recalled that she and Catherine were wearing the same dress the evening they met, though hers was red and Catherine's was green.

was fascinated by the heated political arguments. Mumford was not inclined to give up time for this new organization, composed almost entirely of his friends, but Catherine reported the proceedings to him like a recording secretary; she wanted his feedback on the new ideas being floated. She noted with disgust the power struggles that emerge when a small group of stars convenes. Substantive discussion was too often derailed by dogmatism and hair-splitting, which made her impatient. Nevertheless the seeds of her political career were sown at these meetings.

Catherine quickly understood the difference between action and contemplation, and decisively placed her allegiance with the activists. Clarence Stein cautiously proposed sending experts around the country to learn from actual projects in other regions, as well as continuing research. Another leading light, Carol Aronovici, proposed establishing a university research centre to study housing. Catherine envisioned "all the architects retiring into a monastery to amuse themselves with the refinements of some abstruse and ever purer art until civilization shall have been reborn. My God, we don't need to *know* anything more about housing: we already know about ten times as much as they did or do in England or Germany or Holland."

Catherine observed that the lines were drawn between men of good will, who wanted to be useful even if they were hazy about housing technique, and men who wanted to hang on to the old ways. The latter would be "even more dangerous than at present if they understood the full implication of modern housing."

Stonorov was on the right track, Catherine told the Housing Study Guild. A man of action, he had gone directly to the Public Works Administration in Washington with elegant models and drawings to raise money for the Hosiery Workers' Carl Mackley Houses. "However opportunist and fancy, it may yet be the most productive," she told the group, "because it's the only way in which the technicians who know something can make a direct contact with the ultimate beneficiaries, without any lost intermediate motions in the morass of social workers, liberals, municipal politicians, saviors of real estate and philanthropical bank presidents." That is what men like Ernst May and Martin Wagner had done in Germany when they laid the foundations for postwar housing.

Using Weimar Germany as a model, Catherine suggested that perhaps the United States ought to work for a "permanent government fund for loans at low rates, without too many strings or too centralized control (and with some system of subsidies if possible)." She supported decentralization, in principle and theory, but had no faith in city governments that were dominated by real estate interests, as long as their financial structures were mixed up with speculative land values. The best thing that could happen under these circumstances, she believed, was municipal bankruptcy that would force changes to local government structure and taxation.

Catherine soon realized the importance of developing a radical housing program based on organized consumer demand. Although the senior members of the Housing Study Guild did not disagree with her point of view, they were unable to visualize how it could be achieved. She became part of a study group to suggest a viable program. Just as she stepped up her commitment to the guild's agenda, a job offer arrived from Charles Ascher on behalf of the Chicago-based National Association of Housing Officials (NAHO). She was flattered by the $2,500-per-year offer but shaken at the idea of leaping into a full-time job – and leaving New York to do so. The guild also wanted to hire her, for a much smaller wage, as secretary and acting head. Catherine rejected both offers. She needed work but wasn't at all certain what kind.

At this point Stonorov came to the rescue. Learning of the success of the Carl Mackley Houses in Philadelphia, workers in Paterson, New Jersey, asked him for help in developing a housing project of their own. With funds from the Civil Works Administration (CWA), he reasoned, Catherine could conduct a survey of the workers' needs similar to the one performed in Philadelphia. The job interested Catherine until she learned the details. She decided that the pay was too low and the responsibilities too great at a time when she still had her book to finish.

Later that spring, with her book ready for indexing, Catherine notified Stonorov that she was prepared to move on. He was delighted and introduced her to labour organizer John Edelman, who had participated in planning the Carl Mackley Houses as research director for the Hosiery Workers' Union. Edelman derived his interest in architecture from his father, architect John H. Edelmann, who in the 1870s had influenced the work of Louis Sullivan in linking architectural design with individual human creative potential. The senior Edelmann's ideals embodied a spectrum of social concerns, so it is not surprising that the son (who dropped one "n" from his surname) devoted his career to social reform. With one-quarter of the US labour force unemployed and banks foreclosing on defaulted mortgages, thousands of workers were evicted from homes into which they had sunk all their savings. Deeply moved by the resulting misery, Edelman resolved that labour unions must do something about housing these families, who were forced to live in hovels. Conveniently, he had many architect friends, including Oscar Stonorov, who were desperate for work during the depression years.

Stonorov and his partner, Kastner, a first-rate draftsman who had studied in Germany, obliged Edelman by producing a splendid model of a workers' housing project patterned on the German *Zeilenbau* (terrace housing). The 1933 National Industrial Recovery Act, which authorized the use of federal funds for low-income housing, had just been passed. Stonorov and Edelman went to Washington and persuaded Public Works administrator Robert Kohn to set aside $1 million for the proposed Carl Mackley Houses, to be built in the Juanita Park section of Philadelphia near the hosiery mills. To determine the precise housing needs of hosiery workers, interviews were conducted by Edelman's wife, Kate, and her friend, Betty Foster, daughter of a Main Line magnate and the future Mrs. Stonorov.

For the first time in the United States, good design was based on the social and economic survey model espoused in Catherine's *Modern Housing*. The result was a group of well-designed four-story buildings surrounded by greenery, with spacious living areas, a rooftop nursery school and laundry, and an outdoor swimming pool. This first federally funded housing project received so much favourable publicity that the architects and Edelman were inundated with requests for information from around the country. Catherine was hired to interpret the program. The Carl Mackley Houses would be featured in the 1936 show "Architecture in Government Housing" at New York City's Museum of Modern Art, curated by Ernestine Fantl, with a foreword to the catalogue by Catherine Bauer.

The project's only flaw was insufficient financing to ensure rents would be affordable to low-income workers. It was evident to everyone involved that outright subsidy rather than government loan was the prerequisite for affordability. Catherine's work with Stonorov and Edelman provided a turning point in her thinking. She finally understood that government subsidies for housing could only be obtained through explicit federal housing legislation.

Stonorov's career as an architect-activist remained tied to labour housing. Walter Reuther, the powerful president of the United Auto Workers Union, selected him as the UAW's architect in the 1960s, and they became close friends. With Reuther's White House connections, Stonorov was able to present creative policy initiatives, such as the Model City Program, to President Johnson in May 1965. The idea of constructing demonstration projects of experimental solutions in selected communities prior to launching national legislation had its start in discussions with Catherine. Tragically, Stonorov and Reuther were on a lobbying trip on behalf of housing programs in Detroit when their plane crashed in dense fog in 1970, killing them both.

When Catherine came to Philadelphia in the spring of 1933, Edelman was working on a survey of company towns in Pennsylvania and New Jersey, intending to create a workers' housing conference. He needed the endorsement of leaders at the American Federation of Labor (AFL), and Catherine was designated to secure their support. She was delighted to be in this arena, dealing with "labor skates" and far away from well-meaning social workers. One week after she began work, the Pennsylvania Federation of Labor established the Labor Housing Conference (LHC) to promote housing legislation, and Catherine became its executive secretary. She was thrilled to have the job, firmly believing "that there would never be a real housing movement until workers and consumers organized an effective demand: that housing is a major political issue or it is nothing."[15] One of her LHC tasks was to write a regular housing column in the union paper, the *Hosiery Worker*.

Spending time away from Lewis was the right medicine for both; they saw each other rarely but happily that spring. Then, in June, after a magnificent weekend with Lewis, Catherine admitted that she had gone to bed with Oscar Stonorov, just as she had admitted falling into bed with Walter March almost exactly four years earlier. She assured Lewis that it had not been planned, nor was it the result of "a sudden wave of uncontrollable passion." The two had simply fallen into bed together after an exhausting stretch of work in Meadville, where they had been spending sixteen-hour days meeting with labour groups. It was unsatisfying for both, Catherine insisted. She and Oscar were given to bickering, and she realized that no intimacy or companionship could ever develop between them. Two weeks later she spent a more pleasant Saturday night with

Oscar at Cape May, after a day's swimming. Still, Lewis remained her "darling," and she felt that nothing had changed.

Following this confession, Catherine's letters to Lewis returned to chatty descriptions of life on the Main Line of Philadelphia, where Stonorov's friends lived. Unable to reopen dialogue with a mute correspondent, she became a little flustered. "My dearest Lewis," she wrote at the end of a letter, "there is only one honest and passionate desire that I can find in myself in the midst of all this heat, worry, uncertainty, boredom, overwork, irritation, frustration and loneliness – and that is the desire to be with you. Won't you meet me somewhere?"

"I didn't," wrote Lewis at the bottom of the page when he reviewed this correspondence in 1962. For Lewis it was over. He charged her with faithlessness and treachery after a love that had spanned four and a half years. She countered that if he had demonstrated the slightest hint of regret about her moving to Philadelphia or her taking a job that was bound to separate them, she would have cancelled it all. But he had not and he could not; he was married to Sophie, and he could not take a stand that would have assumed the existence of a partnership between himself and Catherine. "Still," she wrote, "I cannot accept this as either real or final. You are the only real thing in my world, my darling, and when I am sane and in my right mind I would rather have one half or one quarter or one tenth of you than anything under heaven except the whole of you." Lewis's reply was a kindly and paternalistic review of their long association:

It is right and inevitable, my dearest, that we should both be agitated and numbed at times and resentful about each other, and regretful: but don't waste any emotional energy upon regretting the wrong things.

We have been parting for the last two years, and I have done nothing to prevent that from happening. Partly I couldn't if I had wanted to, and partly, because I loved you, I couldn't even want to. Our parting is a phase of your own growth. It began in that core of our lives, in the relation of our minds. It was an assertion – for your own identity as a thinking being.

If we were going to have any permanent life together it would have involved an intellectual surrender on both our parts: perhaps you sensed an unwillingness here on my part – although I was consciously looking in the other direction when we went to Europe and I soon, by the irritations and frustrations that attended our preparation of the articles on housing was conscious of a new unwillingness on your part.

I see this so clearly now: my very suggestion of the housing book to you was perhaps the thing that made it so difficult for you to tackle the subject. Very rightly, you dawdled over the subject, and sought new avenues wherewith to approach it, in order to escape my lead and my influence. Your whole work here was a growth out of the discipleship phase.

Thank god for that: you've been the only disciple who has shown the courage to throw me off and the capacity for further intellectual growth ... So here was the situation: for your own further intellectual development you had to throw off the bonds that once aided you here. As an alternative, you had to be free enough in your emotional life to establish fresh sexual relations with other people which might lead to your complete biological fulfillment. Both kinds of parting were necessary for your growth and your salvation: five years more of our relationship during the past year and you'd have been a savagely neurotic spinster.

Catherine referred to this letter, after so many angry ones, as "bringing back some sort of sanity with the mocking good sense of a Chekhov." Their correspondence continued in a more professional vein. Each turned to the other for opinions, interpretations, and ideas. Catherine sprinkled gossip among the labour news items. She was happy – a new woman, she said.

The contrast between my life at present and my life a year or so ago is fantastic: I seem, for the time being at least, to have made the complete swing from contemplation to action, from thinking to maneuvering, from intimacy to the easy, purely incidental comradeship of hundreds of people, from a few highly selective friendships with people of my own class, kind and purposes, to the systematic milking of "contacts" with everyone from Italian politicians to U.T.W. organizers and Washington bureaucrats. It's very dangerous: so easy to feel that this round of resolutions, committees, money-raising, etc. is really an accomplishment in itself. So natural to feel that you really know something better and clearer just because you can turn speeches on and off without batting an eye-lash.

By the end of September Catherine was truly on her feet again, proud of her successes at LHC, where she no longer felt in the shadow of Stonorov and Edelman. She would be able to use them rather than vice versa. However, her professional self-esteem did nothing to protect her from a sharp sting when she learned of Sophie's new pregnancy. That was the "final finality" to any hidden hopes that she might have harboured for a life with Lewis. He supplied the last words:

Catherine: we write elegies to each other: we talk about the dead. Let us bury the bodies of Lewis-and-Catherine: they moldered in the summer heat faster than I had counted on: by now they are too far gone even to interest medical students. Your letters are hollow ... Once I loved you and I valued our past. Another six months of this emptiness, and I should hate you just as passionately. Let us throw a few shovelsful of dirt on those dead selves: tell the sexton to stop tolling his hateful bell: have a final embrace, my darling, at the gates of the churchyard – and then part without a look behind. I can stand complete loneliness: but not this thin mockery of comradeship. It robs the past of its reality. Good-bye.

MODERN HOUSING

Modern Housing *remains the principal intellectual guide to the early public housing movement.*
                                        FREDERICK (FRITZ) GUTHEIM

By the summer of 1934 the manuscript for *Modern Housing* was out of Catherine's hands. It had been a long, arduous road along which she required and received much help from friends and colleagues. She had sought the advice of architects and planners at the projects she visited and had consulted with leading professionals in the emerging housing and planning movement in the United States. She had also drawn deeply on her 1932 experiences in Great Britain and continental Europe.

Her choice of the word "Modern" in the book's title expressed its multiple meanings: the functional forms of new buildings (modern architecture); the idea of advanced housing as a socioeconomic phenomenon worthy of public policy debate (modern politics); and the links to modernism in painting, sculpture, and music (modern art). The book was written in the fluent, conversational style of Catherine's letters and articles, making it a pleasure to read.

Modern Housing is divided into four major parts, each subdivided into several sections that are further broken down into bite-sized, often anecdotal vignettes. Scholar, student, or professional could nibble at special areas of interest for quick reference or consume the entire book and profit from its careful attention to detail. A comprehensive bibliography offered source materials to scholar and student, but Catherine's exhaustive research sufficed to satisfy the needs of most readers.

The first two parts of the book encompass the history and evolution of housing theory through the stories of some key players. The third part describes and analyzes housing and community achievements in important European centres. The fourth discusses applications of Europe's modern housing experiences to the United States. A detailed appendix lists national housing measures in Europe between 1850 and 1934. The last forty-eight pages are devoted to Catherine's photographs of old and new houses and to diagrams of European communities.

In her introductory note, Catherine defined modern housing as having certain qualities and embodying certain methods and purposes "which distinguish it sharply from the typical residential environment of the past century ... It is built for efficient use over a period of years, and is not built primarily for quick profits ... It is 'planned' and so it must be non-speculative [and] it fits into a neighborhood, designed and equipped as such ... One part is related to another part, and each part serves a predestined use." It also provides certain minimum amenities for every dwelling, she explains, "and will be available at a price which citizens of average income or less can afford."[16]

According to these definitions, hardly any modern housing existed in the United States at the time the book was written. European architects and planners were the pioneers who set the standards. England, Germany, Austria, and the Low Countries, with a combined population only slightly less than that of the United States, had 4.5 million such dwellings and about one-seventh of all families living in them. Catherine asserted that "modern European housing would be a tautological phrase: there is practically no modern housing outside Europe." This is because "Europe could no longer support the luxury of speculative, sub-standard, chaotic house construction ... Fortified by half a century of experiment and increasing dissatisfaction, Europe supplanted obsolete and wasteful nineteenth-century practices ... the land, construction, finance and management of low and medium-cost dwellings were removed from the speculative market: housing became a public utility."[17]

While she made no claim that Europe had solved all its problems, Catherine's research clearly showed that a new standard of human environment and a new technique for achieving it had been found on the Continent. Housing is linked to the political systems that produced it, she maintained, "Although it is not true that any socioeconomic order which could produce good housing would be *ipso facto* a good system, it is certainly true that any arrangement that cannot do so is a reactionary and anti-social one."[18]

Part One, "Nineteenth-Century Cities: A Record of Failure," addressed the historical need for radical change in public policies and private initiatives. Housing as a subject of systematic research is placed in the context of its time and society. "If individualism in the property sense was the dominant force of the nineteenth century, socialism was its great idea ... The vast bulk of construction [until the 1920s] was of a purely profit nature. But every real advance in both planning technique, housing standards and architectural design came from that small body of experiment which was removed from the speculative field."[19]

Part Two, "Gathering Forces," analyzed the antecedents of change and reform, including the proposals of Robert Owen and other Utopians; the writings of John Ruskin and Octavia Hill; and the paternalistic housing projects of Cadbury and Lever. A section entitled "Engels Versus the Housing Reformers" discussed his opposition to the reforms preached in the late nineteenth century by aristocratic reformers. "Engels," Catherine wrote, "showed how, by the very nature of the situation, upper-class reforms either accomplished exactly nothing or reached only the middle classes."[20] He argued that workers' wages must be lowered and their freedom must be limited when employers supply housing. Because overcrowded slums were a necessary condition of capitalist expansion, Engels was convinced that the housing problem would be taken care of through the redistribution of dwelling spaces after the revolution. Radicals of the day were opposed to any reform before the arrival of the "Future State." As this took longer than expected, Catherine wrote, radicals "began to promote trade-unions and other cooperative housing, and to urge municipal land-control policies and municipal house-construction. Indeed, they swung over so far from about 1900 onward that the majority of Social Democrats were hardly more than a left wing of the burgher reformers."[21]

Part Two also discussed methods by which municipal and state responsibilities for housing evolved in Germany and England. A new age emerged in the decade before the First World War, expressing increased concern for the human environment. Sentimental philanthropists began to merge their efforts with those of progressive bureaucrats, reformers, and revolutionists. Catherine revealed her aesthetic bias: "After a full century, during which even the houses of the rich have been inconvenient, ugly and uncomfortable, there were vague stirrings of revolt. Sun, air, cleanliness and order were beginning to come back over the threshold of consciousness."[22]

She attributed the stimulus for the housing movement to model houses exhibited at popular nineteenth-century international expositions. "The Paris Exhibition of 1900 had a complete block including exhibits from Belgium, Switzerland, England, Germany, Holland and France, just as 'modern' for their time as the Stuttgart Exhibition Housing of 1927. These activities were no longer confined to social theorists because architects, engineers and technicians were beginning to take part."[23]

The contributions of the great nineteenth-century construction engineers are documented, including: W.H. Lascelles, known for the cement slab process; Sir Joseph Paxton, whose Crystal Palace was built in London with cast-iron prefabrication construction; and the great M. Eiffel, whose tower looked down on the first International Housing Congress.

Catherine applauded the revival of traditional brick craftsmanship and simple cottage vernacular in England, along with the arts and crafts movement initiated by William Morris and championed by Raymond Unwin.

She ascribed the most significant step toward a housing movement before 1914 to the ideals of Ebenezer Howard's Garden Cities. He was neither a revolutionary nor a millionaire suffering pangs of conscience, nor a modern architect, wrote Catherine; he was a short-hand writer with a vision. On a visit to Chicago, Howard had seen the effects of the great fire, which led him to think about the possibility of creating entire new cities – whole and fresh from the bottom up, according to a rational plan. In 1899 the Garden City Association was formed in England, blossoming from theory to reality with the development of Letchworth. In several ways Letchworth embodied Howard's principles: building from the ground up; a location well away from congested areas (London); communal land ownership; and a buffer of permanent greenbelt surrounding the development.

Catherine also admired the Scottish scientist, Sir Patrick Geddes, whose broad interests led him to study the fields of sociology, economy, geography, city planning, and philosophy. She credited him with being the first man in the twentieth century to give a wholly new interpretation to the meaning of human environment. He placed housing within the larger physical framework of society, recognizing that a house is more than just private shelter: people use it to eat, work, socialize, and raise a family. Therefore a house becomes part of an expanding entity: a neighbourhood, a city, and a region.

Geddes was a proponent of "simultaneous thinking," which encompassed three poles: "Folk, Work, Place – Organism, Function, Environment."[24] He was a "prophet of the new science of planning," wrote Catherine, and as such stood in stark contrast to the self-serving industrial spirit of the nineteenth century, whose motto was "Exploit and get out." Geddes pioneered the technique and purpose of the regional survey: that a thorough understanding of resources and possibilities must precede any plan or action. "For the biologist, life is process," Geddes had written, "life is reaction ... of environment in action upon organism or organism in reaction upon environment."

Part Three, "Post-War Housing: Facts and Figures," used statistical analysis to document bureaucratic innovations that led to Europe's postwar housing achievements after a century of neglect in the production and distribution of shelter. A summary chart showed the quantitative success in most European countries. By 1930 more than 13 percent of people in England and Wales lived in state-aided housing. The comparable proportion for Holland was 15 percent and for Denmark 20 percent. Indeed, housing had become a public utility through a combination of public subsidies, grants, investment strategies, and community land ownership.

Part Four, "The Elements of Modern Housing," discussed ways in which affordable housing could be provided, while addressing the centuries-old problems of urban overcrowding and slums. This part of *Modern Housing* offered a consistent and tightly woven argument for government legislation and programs, contrasting the successes of Europe with the failures of North America. Catherine combined economic analysis with social values and stressed the need for architecture as a social art necessary to the provision of modern housing in the United States. Housing ought to become a public issue, worthy of the support of organized labour, architects, engineers – and especially consumers.

The keystone of the postwar housing movement in Europe was organized, well-informed consumer demand. The German trade unions were prepared to carry out large-scale programs with government aid. Labour and Social Democratic governments throughout Europe clearly represented a body of citizens who demanded a positive program of good housing. The lack of such demand, Catherine wrote, was the principal reason for the numerous obstacles to modern housing in the United States. Part Four concluded prophetically: "If only a small part of the vast energy which was once directed toward individual home ownership were now organized to demand a realistic program of modern housing, then there would be an American housing movement indeed." [25]

In her substantial appendix Catherine summarized, in image and word, Europe's national housing measures. Her photographs, with their succinct captions, caught the imaginations of planners, builders, architects, and administrators. The photographs were displayed in 1933 in Housing Study Guild's library in New York City, and became part of a major exhibition of the Museum of Modern Art in 1936. Many of her illustrations and charts found their way into books on housing, architecture, and public administration in the decades following the publication of *Modern Housing*.

The book was well received and generated many lively reviews in major newspapers and journals. Several critics used their reviews to advance their own beliefs about housing. "Catherine Bauer's authoritative study is as timely as this morning's newspaper," *New York Times* reviewer R.L. Duffus declared.[26] In a five-column spread that included three photographs, Duffus asserted that "the kind of quarters in which people live is almost the first index of the nature of a civilization," and went on to describe *Modern Housing* as a criticism of civilization as well as of houses. Americans would be interested in the book "because of what we have not done," he said, quoting Catherine: "Almost every dwelling put up since the war would have to be eliminated on the score of price alone, without even considering quality." Duffus applauded her criteria for modern hous- ing, including the context of a complete neighbourhood affording sunlight, pleasant outlook, adequate privacy, sanitary facilities, and children's play space – all available at an affordable price for mid- and low-income Americans. He agreed that good housing cannot be imposed from above, but must be effectively demanded by those who will directly benefit. He only demurred on her failure to provide a solution: "One puts down her book with its wealth of detail and its admirable pages of illustrations, with the feeling that she has stated a problem most effectively, but she has by no means solved it."

The Nation published a supportive review by Douglas Haskell, editor of *Architectural Forum*. He praised Catherine for avoiding "social-workerish" analysis, an unexpected blessing in a book on housing, in his estimation. He concurred with Duffus that it was a book for Americans since it was concerned with a great step in civilization that had left them out. While something phenomenal was occurring in Europe, little was accomplished in America. Haskell welcomed the emphasis on housing as distinct from houses, and found that even her technicalities make fascinating reading. He described Catherine as "a fresh writer giving us the first rounded account of a great decade of modern or nearly modern shelter that we need more of. We need new pioneers such as Unwin or Geddes tried in their time to be and we need them bigger and more daring."[27]

The *New Republic* featured Albert Mayer's unabashedly positive review. He thought the chapter on architecture was the best architectural criticism written in the country in recent years. "No one interested in housing can afford to miss this book," he wrote. "It combines the lucidity and raciness that interest the layman, with the completeness, grasp and thoroughness that the expert requires. It should alert technicians from their preoccupation with minutia and quicken them with new inspiration."[28] Mayer called for a cheap reprint of *Modern Housing* so that it could become required reading for college courses on current affairs and for adult education groups, including trade unions and cooperative societies. Although his suggestion never materialized, the hardcover edition did appear on college reading lists for the next three decades.

The *Saturday Review of Literature* printed Langdon Post's two-column review praising the book's social and economic analyses and the photographs with their descriptive captions. Post was Tenement House Commissioner in New York City and knew of Catherine through her magazine articles. Later, as field director of the US Housing Agency during the forties and fifties, he would work closely with her in California. In his review he concluded that Miss Bauer was contributing to the next act in the drama of the slums: their eradication. Although Post made a good point in connecting housing to slum clearance, he missed one of Catherine's central arguments: that housing ought to be built in locations best suited to the needs of the lowest income families, and not necessarily linked with slum clearance.

The only lukewarm reception came from the *New York Herald Tribune*. Albert Guerard, an architect and art historian, regarded *Modern Housing* as a sociological tract comparable to Lewis Mumford's approach to history. He appreciated Catherine's linking of art, economics, and technique as essentially civilized, but felt that in her ambitious synthesis the parts were better than the whole. He found her selected bibliography capricious. Like Duffus, he wanted a solution. "Granted that we should build," he wrote, "granted that we know how to build, the problem remains 'where?' On the very site of the old slums? On the outskirts of the city? In more distant garden suburbs? In new settlements altogether? Housing is determined by existing markets for goods and labor and by means of transportation." The choice of location was crucial. Guerard accused Catherine of trenchantly condemning the immediate past and possessing the verve of a reformer. He also charged her with being unscientific, and worse, unethical, because she irrevocably damned the nineteenth century.[29]

After sixty years the lessons in *Modern Housing* are still relevant. Today, as we review current solutions to housing needs, we can only lament that the book's proposals were insufficiently heeded in the decades since its publication. In 1995 Frankfurt's suburb, Römerstadt, celebrated its seventieth birthday in excellent health, having survived both war and depression. The aesthetics and layout of the settlement had stunned Catherine when she was young and inexperienced. She immediately understood and subsequently preached the possibilities derived from successful neighbourhood planning. The descendants of the original owners continue to occupy the terrace houses and tend their gardens. The greenbelt has remained verdant and is used all year round for recreation and community vegetable gardens. Similar settlements in other areas have fared equally well.

The last chapter of *Modern Housing* has yet to be written.

ACTIVIST

> *One of the first national housing bills was lobbied together*
> *by a pair of young architects and a pair of young researchers,*
> *man and girl, one of the sagas of the New Deal.*
>
> DOUGLAS HASKELL

Until the 1920s housing in the United States was a matter of affordability. With some local paternalistic exceptions, such as company towns, market forces determined the supply and regulated the demand for housing. Catherine's writing, particularly *Modern Housing,* brought her to the forefront of vocal advocates of national action to produce an equitable housing supply and concerted attacks on squalid slums. The pioneering activities of Catherine and her allies found a moderately supportive environment in Congress during Franklin Roosevelt's first term. At that time housing starts had fallen to an all-time low of 93,000, down 90 percent from 1925, and unemployment had peaked at nearly 25 percent. With the New Deal, Roosevelt's administration was committed to stimulating employment, and housing became a vehicle for fighting depression unemployment.

Poverty, some argued, could be solved by providing material needs, including housing, food, and clothing. Conventional wisdom held that unhealthy and dangerous inner city slums needed to be replaced by housing and related facilities built by the state on public account. In the United States, the demand for public action through legislation began with Jacob Riis's book *How the Other Half Lives*, published in 1890. While access to appropriate health, food, and clothing for the poor had improved substantially, affordable shelter in most cities continued to elude public action into the 1930s.

Historically, public initiatives in housing stemmed from outrage about the slums festering in the centres of America's major cities. Federal funds were provided for the first time in July 1892, when $20,000 was directed toward an investigation of slums in cities of 200,000 or more people. By 1908 Theodore Roosevelt established the President's Housing Commission to evaluate slum conditions. The commission recommended that slum properties be condemned and purchased by government loans in order to improve or replace them with inexpensive, livable dwellings available to the poor by rental or by purchase at low interest rates. These remedies were intended to relieve the overcrowded living conditions that promoted the spread of disease. The commission's initiative was stillborn.

In 1918 the first federal loans were offered to shipbuilding companies for housing their employees. That year the US Housing Corporation was established with federal funds to provide housing for war workers. More than five thousand single-family dwellings, apartments, dormitories, and hotels were constructed and, after the war, sold to private interests.

By the 1930s housing legislation was being proposed in response to the Great Depression. Measures now focused on housing as a means of employment. President Hoover convened the Conference on Home Building and Home Ownership and mandated it to find means "to take pressure off sound home mortgage lending institutions and permit them to recover; stimulate home construction and increase employment; prevent repetition of the mortgage industry's collapse in the face of economic difficulty; and to create a structure of the promotion of home ownership."[30]

No legislation resulted until the Emergency Relief and Construction Act

RÖMERSTADT

In 1995 Frankfurt's suburb, Römerstadt, celebrated its seventieth birthday in excellent health, having survived both war and depression. The aesthetics and layout of the settlement had stunned Catherine when she was young and inexperienced.

was passed in 1932 to provide loans to corporations established to provide housing for low-income families or to reconstruct slum areas. Only two loans emanated from the act, one to finance Knickerbocker Village in New York City, the other to finance rural homes in Kansas. The legislation hardly made any impact on the severe housing crisis within the nation's expanding community of impoverished citizens. Measures such as the creation of the Reconstruction Finance Corporation and the Federal Home Loan Bank System were passed to support faltering banks and loan institutions, while more and more people were stung by foreclosure – forced from their homes into untenable shelters.

Independently of the federal government, the Settlement House Movement responded to the growing need for shelter in New York City's East Side slums. Throughout the twenties the movement urged radical slum improvements and outright clearance. Among its leaders was Mary Kingsbury Simkhovitch, a Boston brahmin who personified the traditional volunteer settlement house worker. She was committed to clearing slums and improving living conditions for moral and health reasons. In 1931 Simkhovitch and her friend Helen Alfred, a social worker, founded the Public Housing Conference that advocated, for the first time in the United States, a program of long-range public housing. When it changed its name to the National Public Housing Conference (NPHC), the organization escalated the scope of its advocacy from New York City to the national level. The NPHC was committed to a frontal attack on the slums that it called "the greatest shame of our present civilization."

Catherine was sympathetic with the goals of NPHC and convinced that the drastically declining economic conditions demanded federal action. As executive secretary of the Labor Housing Conference (LHC), the lobby group launched in 1933 by the Pennsylvania Federation of Labor, she was positioned to fight for housing measures that were in the best interests of workers and consumers. Her resources were limited, to say the least. At the time, LHC was nothing more than letterhead, two filing cabinets, and a statement of policy headquartered in Stonorov's Philadelphia office. Stonorov and Edelman worked for the organization part time; Catherine was its only full-time employee.

Goaded by Stonorov and guided by Edelman, Catherine was determined to rise to the challenge. Although she had little experience in the political arena, she was convinced that LHC's mission was correctly grounded in the needs and desires of American workers. In order to successfully rally a unified labour force behind a specific piece of legislation, and to write legislation that fulfilled LHC's mission, she would have to take a crash course in government and union policy. Fortunately, Catherine was a good student.

A lively and intelligent speaker, she persuaded unions from Boston to Charleston, regardless of their political persuasions, to set up housing committees. She found that labour was both so angry and so hopeful that a totally unknown young woman could talk informally to a few labour mugs in any town, and a committee representing all the unions in that locality would be set up, eager to find out what this housing issue was all about and ready to carry the fight to the city, state, and national governments.

The Philadelphia Building Trades had so much faith in Catherine that they paid her LHC salary. She raised money from unions to begin the legislative push, and she lobbied Washington. "One of the first national housing bills was lobbied together by a pair of young architects and a pair of young researchers, man and girl, one of the sagas of the New Deal," wrote *Architectural Forum* editor Douglas Haskell in a 1965 tribute to Catherine after her death.[31]

By the early 1930s housing had been on various legislative agendas for forty-two years, with few results. Political action instigated by the Pennsylvania Federation of Labor was joined by organized labour in New Jersey, and the debates on housing in these two states rapidly grew to national proportions. In May 1934 the first National Housing bill was introduced to Congress with President Roosevelt's support, providing an opportunity for national debate on public policy and programs needed to curb the deepening economic depression. It was intended to be part of a comprehensive program to relieve unemployment and stimulate the release of private credit for housing investment through the banks. Upon enactment, the bill created a Federal Housing Administration, but fell far short of the demands of labour.

Prior to its enactment, Catherine responded to the bill in a brief to President Roosevelt on behalf of LHC, declaring "We represent the workers who need work building houses as well as the people who need better houses to live in. As both workers and people will live in houses, we (the labor movement) are amazed that the National Housing Bill in its present shape can be seriously presented as a constructive housing measure. If this bill is passed it will accomplish less than nothing towards the solution of the housing problem." She found that the issues raised by labour had been ignored or, worse, undermined and pointed out that "the housing problem as framed in the bill ... reflected the old methods of building dwellings for average citizens under 'prosperity conditions.' As consumers we pay too much for a low grade product. We were sold houses which today are not worth their back taxes, and we paid exorbitant rent for dwellings which menace the health and happiness of our families."[32]

The established process of house production was invidious because it encouraged waste of labour and materials, supported by speculative financing and abetted by high-pressure salesmanship. Labour was becoming increasingly dependent on luxury trade instead of a basic staple of production. The cost of labour began to represent a shrinking portion of the final building costs, which were escalating because of rising land costs driven by speculation.

The LHC's brief was intended to remind President Roosevelt that housing production had broken down because it was basically uneconomic and inefficient. Only through direct government intervention could the production of dwellings for low-income families be taken out of the exploitive, speculative field and transformed into a program that was planned, long-range, and realistic. Catherine wrote passionately on behalf of workers and consumers, charging that the bill before Congress reflected a conspiracy between organized real estate and banking interests to keep the housing movement as innocuous and impotent as possible. Taking a position that she would hold for life, she argued that production of adequate housing for those who needed it had to be treated separately from slum clearance. Her position opposed the reasoning of the settlement workers as articulated by NPHC.

Although the National Housing Act established a Federal Savings and Loan Insurance Corporation and a Federal Housing Administration to provide a uniform mortgage insurance system, it sidestepped the true socioeconomic issues of urban reconstruction through housing. Instead, the act enabled a hit-or-miss patchwork of privately financed construction, ignoring the necessity of planned, large-scale operations. The LHC concluded that the only choice was between a positive program of planned, nonprofit, modern, large-scale construction – or no construction at all. It demanded that Roosevelt give trade unions a chance to participate in planning and programming public housing.

Catherine made a strong plea for the common cause of labour and consumer in her attempts to bring together the many components of the labour movement directly involved in residential construction. A major player and ally in this endeavor was Ernest Bohn, city councillor and president of the National Association of Housing Officials (NAHO). During the next three years he would consult and guide Catherine in the push for federal initiatives. A warm friendship grew out of their collaboration.

In trying to build an effective coalition for housing legislation, Catherine proposed the formation of a presidential commission, modelled on the royal commissions on housing in England, to study the American housing problem. The real cost of speculative methods to owner or tenant and to city governments needed to be studied. Critical factors would be analyzed, including: unemployment in building and allied trades; real needs in relation to income; the effectiveness of national measures such as the National Housing Act, Federal Emergency Housing Corporation, and others; the experience of Europe as a model for the United States; and the legal, economic, and technical means necessary to solve the problems. Such an investigation had precedence in the current federal government's studies of production and distribution costs of electricity and other utilities. Bohn, a political realist, cautioned (correctly as it turned out) that this proposal for a commission was too ambitious, but he encouraged Catherine to continue building grassroots support on a city-by-city basis.

Throughout the summer of 1934 Catherine lobbied, talked, wrote, and cajoled whomever was capable of aiding LHC's program of housing reform. She was alarmed by an emerging tug-of-war between a centralized housing administration and community-based organizations. She feared the power of real estate interests to derail large-scale social housing production. And she was sceptical of the motivation of bureaucrats such as Harold Ickes, Secretary of the Department of the Interior, who had already staked his claim on housing to broaden his jurisdiction. Ickes wanted to centralize all federal housing under the Public Works Administration (PWA) in his department because of Washington's superior power of the purse. The LHC disagreed, and Catherine lobbied Congress for decentralization – to put program direction into the hands of suitable local agencies.

She tried to persuade Senator La Follette of Wisconsin that LHC, representing workers and consumers, understood the nature of the housing problem better than most so-called specialists in the private sector. Colonel Horatio Hackett, PWA Director of Housing in the Department of Interior, disagreed. He wanted "disinterested citizens" to serve on housing agencies, arguing that people who need better houses and labourers who need work building houses had no more logical right to representation than had contractors. His position angered Catherine. She responded that those who need better housing and those wishing to build it have a natural and mutual interest; both ought to be represented on local housing agencies. Consumer and producer must make common cause to ensure an effective and rapid solution to housing deficiencies. She told Hackett that "disinterested individuals" do not exist, in view of the highly organized real estate lobby opposed to government aid for housing as a public utility.

The National Housing Act of 1934, signed into Public Law 73-479, created the Federal Housing Administration (FHA), headed by a Federal Housing Administrator. The FHA was to establish programs, relieve unemployment, and stimulate the release of private credit for home repairs and construction. From the moment of its passage, organized labour opposed the act. John Locher, president of the Washington, DC, Building

Trades Council, summed up the flaws of FHA in a letter to Catherine more than a year later: "I do not know of a single job put up with Federal Housing Administration assistance where the prevailing wage rate was paid. At Colonial Village, the top was $0.70 per hour, or about half the prevailing rate. Moreover, they worked there 50 to 60 hours per week. By and large, the Federal Housing Administration works with the chiseling gyp-building contractor who could not compete with the better-class contractor if he had to pay fair wages. As for modernization, it has been done with transient unskilled labor, at $2 and $3 per week."[33]

With the passage of the National Housing Act of 1934, LHC's mandate as a political action group became more pressing. Labour across the country would have to unite behind attempts to promote more effective housing legislation. To that end Catherine focused her energy on expanding membership in LHC. The United Textile Workers of America made housing a priority at its convention, and the Labor Federation of North Carolina passed a comparable resolution. James L. McDevitt, Secretary of the Building Trades Council of Philadelphia, assisted Catherine in developing strategies to garner the support of national trade unions.

In January 1935, Catherine embarked upon a six-week tour of fourteen cities, a campaign that would be pivotal to LHC expansion. Having already made considerable progress in New Jersey and parts of New York State, she tackled Cleveland, where Bohn arranged a conference with officials of the Building Trades Council and the Central Labor Union. "You simply have to be around or else I'll be driven to look up an old flame, and you know how stupid that is,"[34] Catherine wrote Ernie Bohn, signalling the start of a new flirtation. As always, she arrived well prepared, with slides and photographs of European housing. To a gathering of about one hundred union members, Bohn introduced Catherine as a great author and secretary of the Labor Housing Conference. Their joint efforts gave considerable impetus to the labour housing movement; they persuaded unions, starting with the building trade workers, to establish housing committees and join LHC in support of a comprehensive national housing program.

Since LHC coffers were modest, Catherine's trip was subsidized by a $500 donation raised by Charney Vladeck, a New York City Housing Commissioner and manager of the *Jewish Daily Forward*. Hoping to save some money, she budgeted $6 a day (including rail fare) and stayed with college friends, whenever possible, or in cheap hotels. By now she was a compelling speaker who could persuade even the most cynical worker. In city after city she laid out programs for housing committees that would give them maximum coverage in the press while building political clout locally and in Washington. She distributed LHC literature at these meetings and usually fingered a member to stand up and propose that their group go on record as joining the conference.

In Cleveland the head of the Teamsters Union announced, "Whatever Ernie Bohn wants is okay with me, so let's give this little lady a hand."[35] Everywhere she went, friends in high places helped bring out the workers. She made such a mark in Chicago that the *Daily News* characterized her as "a little blonde girl with a great big brunette philosophy." This initially annoyed and later amused Catherine.

Returning to Minneapolis for the first time since Christmas of 1925, she stayed with her college friend Lib Melone, now married to Frederick Winston. Catherine seemed unchanged to Lib, and they enjoyed gossiping about old friends. But Catherine's reputation preceded her, and Lib's father warned his daughter "to watch out for this firebrand." He thought that she was out to make trouble for people in business. Lib took little notice of her father until she overheard Catherine speaking on the telephone to leaders of the truck drivers' union, calling them by their first names. She was startled by the familiarity and sudden change in Catherine's voice as she talked "man-to-man" with the tough labour leaders.

"Well, that was certainly the wildest $3^1/2$ days I have ever spent," Catherine wrote to her mother. "What with my old friends & their highly conservative husbands and fathers, & their innumerable children to be admired, and all the labor people in Minneapolis and St. Paul wanting to do something about housing right away, and getting a sort of Carte Blanche key-to-the-city card from the mayor & having a half an hour's chat with Governor Olson ... I had quite a time."[36]

To her distress Catherine sometimes found labour officials distrustful. They suspected that she represented Washington's FHA when, in fact, she had turned down an FHA job offer: her interest was more on the labour side of the housing problem than in housing per se. She understood their misgivings when she learned that FHA had made allocations for slum clearance in every city she visited, and no construction had yet begun. She found that the housing authorities of most cities were composed of indifferent citizens, rich enough not to be interested either in job opportunities or low-rent housing. Furthermore, prevailing construction wages of $50 per month, or $.38 per hour, totally undermined the confidence of the American labour movement in the New Deal. Eventually Catherine convinced labour leaders of her commitment and won the endorsement and support of most state federations of labour and central labour bodies.

Rapidly expanding her influence after the highly visible and politically rewarding trip through the Midwest, Catherine's focus shifted to the eastern states. She helped establish the Boston labour housing committee while promoting a statewide program through the Massachusetts Federation of Labor. The New Jersey Federation of Labor passed a strong set of resolutions that she had prepared. With pleasure and pride, she wrote to her friend Charlie Ascher at the Public Administration Clearing House in Chicago: "In Paterson and Camden, the local Labor Housing Committees are raising money, making surveys of the need, circulating questionnaires, getting ready to formulate a clear and concrete and informed set of demands."[37]

In his 1965 tribute to Catherine, Douglas Haskell wrote that she "was liked by the steel-helmeted shipyard workers of Camden with whom she had put in 16-hour working days. Of course, the top labor leaders whom she charmed and persuaded into making her a labor spokesman were tougher than these, as were the Congressmen and Senators. From the tough ones she always got respect."[38]

The trip across the country provided Catherine with some very important civic lessons. She talked with large numbers of city and town councillors. On April 24, 1936, she would testify at hearings of the Senate Committee on Education and Labor that there were at least a dozen states where it was illegal and unconstitutional to pass an enabling act for local housing authorities. This situation highlighted the urgency of federal intervention.

The lessons learned from her travels resulted in numerous long memoranda about building housing coalitions. The most thoughtfully delineated were written in January and March 1935, respectively. More than sixty years later, her words have remarkable applicability as both analyses and solutions for housing and neighbourhood crises. Both documents placed housing and planning in historical context, analyzed current needs, and prescribed solutions, lucidly and succinctly. Many of the ideas set forth in Catherine's documents found their way into legislation, starting with the 1937 Housing Act. Seeds for a federal Department of Housing and Urban Development (HUD) were planted in the second memo, only to sprout and mature thirty years later when the secretary of HUD attained Cabinet status.

5

LEGISLATIVE YEARS (1936-38)

ON THE MOVE

It's a long jump from a Radical Intellectual to a Labor Skate. My old Arty self of 1927-Paris would commit suicide at the spectacle – if she were not so thoroughly dead.
CATHERINE BAUER TO MARGARET POLLARD SMITH

The year 1935 found Catherine frantically busy on the lecture circuit, while producing endless memoranda on the small portable typewriter she carried wherever she went. The memos described her position on modern planned housing, and they were directed to labour officials, housing commissioners, and legislators she met during her travels in the United States. She regaled them with theories drawn from her European experiences and modified by American realities.

Communities are more than merely so many individual houses, built on so many lots, with so many feet of street, Catherine maintained. They should be *planned* as neighbourhood units that provide not only private family accommodations and garden space, but a system of streets, public open spaces, and recreation facilities, to prevent future blight. Houses ought to be grouped around an open space and turned away from road traffic. To accomplish all this, it is necessary, from the very outset, to consider not only the physical plan but also the system of tenure and administrative control. The family that buys or rents a home in such a neighbourhood is acquiring both an individual shelter and a share in the amenities and facilities of the entire community.

In order to keep the cost of the houses affordable for low-income families, Catherine stressed that finance charges must be kept at a minimum by creating projects as safe long-term investments, not for quick speculation. To protect those investments, the projects must be planned and administered so that no part can ever suffer blight or boom at the expense of the rest. In addition to laying out general principles, Catherine presented step-by-step development plans. She used as examples European terrace housing and American communities planned by Stein and Wright, such as Radburn, New Jersey; Sunnyside, New York; and Chatham Village, Pennsylvania.

Her most radical ideas about collective land ownership by local government came from England and Germany. She wrote that land for housing projects ought to be vested in semi-official corporations of a nonprofit public utility, or set up as limited-dividend ventures. Drawing upon Chatham Village, built by the Buhl Foundation in Pittsburgh, Catherine concluded that a foundation-based development can give better value for occupants' money in the long run, while securing the permanent amenity of the neighbourhood on a rental rather than ownership basis. She urged labour groups to support such cooperative developments with group ownership.

A sweeping memorandum written in March proposed the establishment of two permanent federal agencies with independent administrations. They would make modern housing affordable to American families unable to pay the price demanded by speculative private enterprise. The agencies would take advantage of modern planning and large-scale production techniques to benefit both builders and consumers. This approach would create immediate employment in the building and allied trades, and construct more houses for less money, thereby increasing real wages. It would put the housing industry, still smarting from the Depression, back on a stable production basis.

One of the proposed agencies was a Federal Housing Corporation (FHC), independent of any existing department and appointed by the President with congressional approval. The FHC would engage in large-scale construction of low-rent housing. The other agency was a Housing Bureau in the Department of Labour. The bureau would coordinate existing data on housing conditions, undertake new surveys, investigate any unreasonable rise in material prices due to monopoly practices, and disseminate relevant information.

The FHC would provide funds for housing construction by federal, state, and municipal authorities, including subsidies to offset low wages and unemployment. It would delegate operational activities to local housing agencies and assist responsible labour and consumer groups that were seeking housing for themselves. For example, the FHC could make loans on community housing projects up to 100 percent of costs, or turn over completed projects for administration to state or municipal housing authorities or responsible nonprofits. It could issue mortgage bonds, acquire land by purchase or condemnation, and subsidize interest payments on housing projects by congressional appropriation. The interest subsidy could vary from project to project according to local conditions.

Catherine's memo articulated specific policies for the FHC, many of which eventually found their way into the first federal housing act after much debate and compromise. Community housing projects needed to be planned as integrated units, she argued, large enough to constitute a neighbourhood taking advantage of large-scale economies. The land for these projects must remain in single ownership, either by federal corporation, local authority, or an organization representing tenants.

Slum clearance and low-income housing must be separate operations, she maintained. The determination of slum areas and their assemblage for clearance ought not to be a federal responsibility. Where local authorities desired, and in the interests of effective city planning, federally aided housing projects could be built on sites now occupied by substandard housing. Financing must be entirely separate from the cost-accounting of low-income housing, particularly if Congress provided specific appropriations to municipalities for slum clearance purposes. In light of the next fifty years' experience, her ideas were prophetic – foreshadowing the protracted debate over who would foot the bill for housing low-income families, slum clearance, and urban renewal.

Catherine suggested that the FHC provide steady employment at fair wages for low-wage earners and pay land prices no higher than justified by low-income housing use. This would eliminate blight rehabilitation of expensive land in city centres, where local authorities would have to bear the cost above use value for housing. The FHC ought to pay normal local taxes and commit itself to fair wages for all construction.

Since at least half the American population was unable to pay rent that covered upkeep, interest, amortization, and taxes on a decent new dwelling, some form of subsidy was necessary, Catherine insisted. But as wage rates, family incomes, and the cost of living were subject to wide fluctuation, it was more logical to provide interest subsidies that could be altered with changing conditions rather than grants to offset capital costs.

In a bid for consumer participation, she urged cooperation between the FHC and the community in deciding on the location, design, and administration of housing projects. Broad standards for space, equipment, and organization of construction would be a federal responsibility, but not standardization of local housing projects; these must be monitored by local architects.

Despite these rosy proposals, there were inevitable limitations to a housing program for which Catherine could find no solution. "No matter how ambitious or broadly conceived it may be, no housing program can be expected to cure all the economic ills of our society ..." she wrote. "Decent housing can be provided for families only if decent wages are paid, and adequate unemployment, health, and old age insurance established. Social insurance and housing are two arms of the same purpose. In the long run one cannot succeed without the other." The views expressed in these memoranda laid the basis for one side of the political struggle as housing became part of the emerging public welfare policies of Roosevelt's New Deal.

Catherine was chronically short of funds. Sometimes she had to dig into her own purse to make ends meet, and she often turned to friends for loans, which were always repaid. Appeals to large, powerful unions brought some welcome cash that dribbled rather than poured in. She found odd jobs to support herself as she continued campaigning for the Labor Housing Conference and for passage of housing legislation. The publicity of her six-week tour made her a sought-after speaker, and small honoraria helped pay for food and shelter.

Her schedule was hectic. In addition to her fame as advocate for the labour movement, Catherine was regarded as a connoisseur of good design in modern housing. One day she was invited to speak at the annual Fine Arts Conference in New Jersey, along with Columbia University professors of architecture Talbot Hamlin and Henry Wright. The next day she addressed the Federation of Architects, Engineers, Chemists, and Technicians on the subject of housing in America. A month later she spoke to the Family Society of Philadelphia on the subject of "Houses and People Who Live in Them." Having read her book, the chairman wrote: "We feel that you are the one person in the country who can describe that aspect of housing vividly." The same evening Catherine rushed to Washington to speak about high rents and low-rent housing before the Washington Central Labor Union and the District Department of the American Federation of Government Employees. That chairman declared: "No one else could speak with her authority on the problems of rents and low-cost housing."[1] Catherine urged the convening of a national housing conference of labour and consumer organizations and recommended including the teachers' union in a labour consortium on housing.

"The building trades people are pretty intelligent about [national housing legislation]," Catherine reported to Bohn after a regional labour conference, "and will, I think, take the initiative in setting up some kind of committee to urge collective action." She was often disappointed, however, at the blandness of union politics. "I had the feeling of having a heart to heart talk with a bunch of bankers ... I've been very respectable and haven't disgraced you by ranting or consorting with revolutionists!"[2]

Her financial situation worsened. "Things begin to shape up except for the little fact that I'm totally broke and don't know where I'm going to get any money for the next few weeks," she confided to Bohn on the way to

Philadelphia, "I don't know exactly where I will be staying yet [in Philadelphia], since bedbugs turned up at the last rooming house!"³ As a last resort she called upon earlier social connections. In Philadelphia she bunked with Dorothea De Schweinitz, a cousin of one of her Vassar instructors and a social worker with whom she had lived briefly when she first moved to Philadelphia. In New York she spent some weekends with the family of William Lescaze, a well-known architect with connections at the Museum of Modern Art.

Bohn's resources were also stretched, but his limitations were physical rather than financial. "I must say you've reached a pretty bad state when you look forward to a Sunday in a Pullman as a day of rest and refreshment, on your way to a social worker convention ..." Catherine sympathized. "You'll be losing your sense of humor and people will begin to whisper that you are taking this housing racket seriously. In any case my dear Ernesto Buonaparte, don't let any social workers do any case work on you."⁴

Catherine found her new life both exhilarating and exhausting. She wrote to her friend, Vassar English teacher Mrs. Margaret Smith: "I am having a very good time – although I am still astonished at the suddenness with which I seem to have changed my whole living pattern in the past year. Last spring I came down here, and ever since I've been tearing around making speeches (almost entirely to labor groups), organizing Committees, lobbying, etc. And believe me, it's a long jump from a Radical Intellectual to a Labor Skate ... all the way from thinking abstractly and in solitude to acting concretely en masse. My old Arty self of 1927-Paris would commit suicide at the spectacle – if she were not so thoroughly dead."⁵

Later that spring she accepted an appointment with the Department of Labor in Washington, DC, to set up a clearinghouse of information and promotion on housing for labour and consumer groups. The job bore the double benefit of providing a steady income as well as data and new connections to further her lobbying activities. She would earn $25 per day (up to ten days per month) and would be in an excellent position to meet key allies. One assignment was to organize a survey of living conditions in various types of small industrial communities. She planned to use the evidence yielded by this survey for her own political objectives.

On June 20, 1935, she reported to Dr. Isadore Lubin, commissioner for labour statistics in the Department of Labor, about the endorsements she was able to garner from federal agencies for the proposed survey. The strongest endorsement came from Charles W. Elliot II, executive director of the National Resources Committee, who promised close collaboration. The Central Statistical Board promised technical advice. Dr. Ernest Fisher, chief of Research and Statistics of the Federal Housing Administration, welcomed valuable data that might result from her research, and the

Resettlement Administration enthusiastically tied it in with their surveys of farming and industrial community needs.

A second assignment came from the National Resources Committee, predecessor of the National Resources Planning Board: to compile a list of knowledgeable and thoughtful people across the country who would help draft a chapter on housing for their national study on public works. She quickly produced an illustrious list of nearly one hundred professional and political heavyweights, supporters of public housing policies who could be persuaded to review relevant sections.

Another trip on behalf of LHC took Catherine through the Southeast, where she toured the Great Smoky Mountains and the developing Tennessee Valley dams. She had now been through the Midwest, New England, and the southeastern states and had "probably typed, spoken, argued and promoted this word 'housing' as many times as anyone in the country."[6]

While Catherine was beating the drum for a broad, new approach to housing legislation, Mary Simkhovitch and the National Public Housing Conference were promoting a more conservative program of federal housing subsidies for locally initiated projects. Simkhovitch persuaded Senator Robert Wagner of New York to introduce NPHC's drafted document as the first congressional public housing bill (S 2392) on March 26, 1935. The bill proposed the establishment of a Federal Housing Agency, responsible for a decentralized public program. The same bill (H.R. 6998) was introduced in the House of Representatives by Congressman Reuben T. Wood of Missouri, perpetuating provisions of the 1934 Housing Act under the jurisdiction of the Public Works Administration. The bill maintained a subsidy of 30 percent of the cost of labour and materials – too little to assure low-rent accommodation.

New York City Mayor Fiorello LaGuardia and others argued that instead of the subsidy there should be reduced interest payments on the loans made against housing projects. But NPHC was steadfast in its support of the bill, deeming it "wiser to cling to a good asset already in one's possession than to take a chance on securing support for a substitution, even should the latter promise to offer slightly reduced rental ... It is not often good tactics to swap horses in the middle of the stream."[7]

Senator Wagner's bill was an historic initiative, but Catherine and her LHC colleagues wanted a stronger and more explicit public policy commitment to housing poor people. As on previous occasions when LHC and NPHC pursued divergent strategies, LHC lobbyists drafted their own bill. Catherine, Oscar Stonorov, John Edelman, and Bill Jeanes, the first manager of the Carl Mackley Houses, cooked it up around Edelman's kitchen table one Sunday morning in April 1935. "I know a guy in

Washington who would introduce such a bill for us," Edelman told them, "the congressman from Pittsburgh, Henry Ellenbogen."[8]

CONGRESS

Sooner or later we may develop both a broad program of public housing, and real old age, unemployment and health insurance.

CATHERINE BAUER TO FATHER MOORE

With their working document in hand, the LHC team approached Henry Ellenbogen, a freshman in Congress. Edelman had met Ellenbogen while lobbying the state legislature in Harrisburg, Pennsylvania, on behalf of the labour movement. Born in Hungary, Ellenbogen had fled to the United States from Austria, where he had studied law. In Vienna he had become familiar with modern housing policies and projects, and took an immediate interest in LHC's draft bill. Ellenbogen was willing to sponsor the legislation, but pointed to a serious obstacle: he had not been a naturalized US citizen long enough to take his seat in Congress.

It would be a year before Ellenbogen had voting privileges in the House; in the meantime the Speaker assigned him a staff and office. This soon became Catherine's command post in the battle for housing legislation. It was a mutually ideal arrangement since Ellenbogen had plenty of time on his hands and was anxious to be identified with a leading social cause.

The Ellenbogen bill, HR 739, was introduced on April 10, 1935, and engaged Catherine in full-time intensive lobbying. The bill differed significantly from Senator Wagner's. It emphasized the need to stimulate the building trades, relieve unemployment, and provide new housing for the poor, whereas Wagner's bill stressed the physical dangers of unsanitary housing and the need to clear slums. The Ellenbogen bill proposed the establishment of limited-dividend companies and nonprofit housing agencies that would qualify for government funds on the same footing as public authorities. The Wagner bill retained the financial provisions in the PWA housing division, whereas Ellenbogen urged a subsidy for loan interest rates ranging from zero to the cost of the loan plus 1 percent. Another important difference concerned the administration of the proposed housing program. Ellenbogen, wishing to separate the new authority from the PWA, opted for an independent authority administered by a three-member board. He also called for a fair-wage guarantee on all housing projects.

Both bills were scheduled for congressional hearings starting June 4, 1935, which generated urgent discussions between NPHC and LHC to reach an acceptable compromise. Two competing bills would destroy the credibility of the whole process. Catherine attempted to head off a public fight by encouraging the acceptance of an integrated single bill before the House adjourned. She proposed a strategic meeting of Senator Wagner, Congressman Ellenbogen, and Charney Vladeck, who had worked with LaGuardia on New York City housing issues. Ellenbogen demurred, fearing a premature compromise, and the meeting did not take place.

During the hearings Catherine and Edelman, testified to the Wagner bill's deficiencies. It was embarrassing for Edelman who, though a labour man, had to testify against a bill introduced by Senator Wagner, another great friend of labour. Wagner tried to put them both at ease by inviting constructive criticism. Catherine agreed with the general objectives of the Wagner bill but held firm to her conviction that it was insufficiently broad to cope with the extraordinary scale of the housing problem. She advanced four major objections to the Wagner bill: (1) new housing construction would be limited to slum sites rather than new land; (2) construction would be restricted to municipal authorities, overlooking other forms of cooperative and nonprofit initiatives; (3) the lack of an appropriate corporate structure; and (4) the lack of minimal standards for government-sponsored housing.

She argued that the Ellenbogen bill was much more effective because it recognized that the real problem was not existing slums but the incapacity of private enterprise to meet the immediate need for new housing. Senator Wagner was clearly impressed by Catherine's succinct presentation and asked his legislative assistant, Leon Keyserling, to redraft the bill after Congress recessed and to consult Catherine in the process. Keyserling, who held a Harvard Law School degree, came to work for Wagner after postgraduate work in economics at Columbia University. At their first dinner meeting, he and Catherine got along like dog and cat, in the words of Edelman, though they eventually collaborated for the passage of the 1937 housing act and became lifelong friends.

The Senate hearings were held by the Committee on Education and Labor, which failed to report the bill out before Congress adjourned. The House also took no action on its bill, so both housing bills were doomed in 1935. The impasse prompted the Simkhovitch and Bauer groups to resume discussions in hopes of resolving their differences and submitting a joint bill in 1936. Senator Wagner let it be known that he was willing to introduce a new bill calling for a separate federal agency with general control over local governmental bodies that would not necessarily take direct title to land or buildings. Catherine, working with Keyserling again, pushed for seven specific provisions in the new bill:

- Responsibility for initiative and action would rest with local housing authorities.
- Every project would be large enough to require neighbourhood planning, community facilities, and approval within the context of local, regional, and metropolitan plans.
- Local housing authorities would have the power of eminent domain.
- All public-aided projects would pay full local taxes.
- Rents would remain affordable to those for whom the housing was intended.
- All public-aided housing would conform to established standards of planning, design, and equipment.
- Private agencies would be allowed to develop housing projects with federal funds, but on a strictly nonprofit basis.

Among other issues, this list became the basis of lengthy negotiations between NPHC and LHC. The differences between the two groups lay in their respective origins, practical experiences, and styles of negotiations. Mary Simkhovitch, who knew both President and Mrs. Roosevelt very well, spoke with vehemence and conviction about slum conditions. As a top-level civic leader, her primary interest was to improve social conditions. She and Helen Alfred, the social worker for whom housing was an ancillary concern, were regarded with some disdain by the professional housers.

Catherine, on the other hand, had become a well-regarded housing expert roughly half Simkhovitch's age. Another significant person in the discussions was Catherine's former colleague from the Regional Planning Association of America, Edith Elmer Wood, now vice president of NPHC. She considered slums "a national evil" and believed that "the physical, moral and economic health of the country was threatened by the slums' existence."[9]

Catherine deeply admired Dr. Wood's intellectual breadth and clarity. "Edith Elmer Wood never had a silly, weak, selfish, cynical or confused idea in her life and all her actions were direct and absolute expressions of her mind." She respected Wood's ability "to tackle a complicated problem seething with personalities and extraneous implications and boil it down to a sharp, incontrovertible decision based on an objective principle and commonsense."[10] Among her peers, Wood was considered the patron saint of public housing.

Catherine's opposition to tying low-income housing legislation to slum clearances set her apart from social workers and others focused on clearance. She believed that the housing movement provided an opportunity to apply modern analysis and design principles to the creation of new environments.[11] Federal legislation was the only means to generate sufficient funds to build large-scale housing enterprises for low-income families. Her experience in RPAA convinced her that housing had to be viewed as a citywide initiative within a regional planning framework. She had become critical of specialists, like social workers and architects, and considered them often naive about the broader political aspects of housing. Catherine had become a houser.

Progress demanded a change in attitude, away from beneficent bestowal by government or philanthropic foundations and toward the principle of entitlement. In August 1935, the first of two conferences of housers – representing a broad spectrum of viewpoints – convened in an effort to achieve some consensus on the proposed legislation. Ten people attended, representing the Labor Housing Conference, National Public Housing Conference, New York Housing Authority, and Housing Study Guild. Primed by her recent experiences with labour groups around the country, Catherine was the most politically astute person at the meeting. She stressed the need to increase the supply of housing for low-income families and argued that local group initiatives must be protected from the interests of the real estate industry and local politicians. The conference rapidly agreed to the urgent need: the establishment of a permanent federal housing program.

The second meeting occurred in October as part of a three-day session of the Joint National Conference on Housing in Washington. The keynote address was delivered by Frederick A. Delano, President Roosevelt's uncle. Catherine discussed acquisition of property, financing, and location of low-rent housing. Other topics included slum clearance, site planning standards, and federal government aid for home owners and tenants. A consensus for supporting legislative action was achieved.

Ellenbogen slightly revised his bill (now H.R. 8666) with Catherine's support. Keyserling had persuaded her that it was possible to frame the Wagner and Ellenbogen bills as complementary. She agreed that the proposed federal housing agency should have corporate form and was willing to give up the idea of an independent agency for a subsidiary of the Department of the Interior, as long as such a governing body could safeguard its independence within the department. She believed that rural housing needed special attention and deserved a separate section of the bill. Ellenbogen proposed a maximum of 45 percent capital grants toward construction, whereas she wanted 100 percent. Federally aided housing projects should pay full local taxes except where local legislation permitted exemption, she maintained. With a nod toward private enterprise, she argued that the bill should include aid to private construction as long as it met specific federal standards with no possible chance, ever, for speculative profits or exploitative rents. Federally subsidized housing, she said, should be reserved solely for tenants with income below a certain level.

Catherine's intense organizing activities were rewarded with an invitation to address the annual October convention of the American Federation of Labor in Atlantic City. The event overlapped with the National Conference on Housing, and she almost found herself in two places at once. Bohn, who was involved with the Washington conference, covered for her and offered reassurance as Catherine's health faltered under pressure. Shortly before the AFL convention Catherine wired Bohn, hoping he would join her: "Honorable the Bohn of contention Dear Sir Ernesto we await your message to us impatiently stop any friend of Catherine Bauer is worth a gold chair stop let me know your whereabouts I leave for Ambassador Hotel Atlantic City tonight and want to be able to bother you. Ekaterina."[12]

Too occupied by other obligations, Bohn did not respond. Catherine pressed on, this time a little more formally: "Having no concrete idea where you are exactly I nevertheless take this fling at asking if you would send some kind of a statement air mail to arrive not later than five Friday afternoon in order to make the morning papers and do wire me that you are coming fraternally, Catherine."[13] He went to Washington instead.

As it turned out, Catherine did not need Bohn's assistance at the AFL convention. Alone, she fared brilliantly and succeeded in persuading the powerful federation to establish a housing committee and adopt a strong resolution on a public housing program. Three major points of the resolution illustrate its strong support for a program that would protect labour:

Resolved, that in locating public-aided housing preference should be given to communities having a decent labor policy and offering a variety of employment opportunities, to avoid any extension of the feudal conditions now prevalent in one-industry towns; and that all public-aided housing must be built by labor working at union rates and under union conditions; and be it further

Resolved, that permanent Federal, state and local housing authorities, implemented with adequate funds and the power to acquire land and to construct and manage large-scale community housing projects, are the first requirements of an effective long-term program; and be it further

Resolved, that there must be a bona fide labor and consumer representation on all housing authorities, and that sponsoring and management committees of all specific projects must include a majority of representatives from groups for whom housing was intended.[14]

With AFL resolutions in hand, Catherine encouraged other labour groups to support the Ellenbogen bill and urged Senator Wagner to introduce more safeguards for labour in his original bill. In so doing, she won the support of legendary giants such as John L. Lewis of the United Mine Workers, M.H. Hedges of the International Brotherhood of Electrical Workers, and Walter Reuther of the United Auto Workers. She organized letter-writing campaigns by labour leaders in support of a new Wagner bill. The LHC became a clearinghouse of information about the progress of the new housing bill under consideration.

By the end of 1935 there was considerable nationwide support for permanent housing legislation. Catherine was hopeful that Wagner and Ellenbogen would soon get together on one good bill. The AFL's endorsement had increased the pressure on Senator Wagner to back a joint housing bill, but Catherine's optimism was ill founded. Although Senator Wagner was prepared to offer Congress a new draft, he stalled in order to win President Roosevelt's approval before submitting the bill.

By January 1936, it was obvious to Catherine she would have to broaden her horizons beyond the labour movement to find increased support for national housing legislation. She asked Father Moore, director of the Division of Social Services of the Catholic Charities of New York, to include housing and social security in a program of public lectures, citing the relationship between housing and social insurance in Europe. She wrote to Moore on January 11, 1936:

Sooner or later we may develop both a broad program of public housing, and real old age, unemployment and health insurance. How ought these two programs be geared to each other? What mutual effect will they, or could they, have? The European experience, where the direct tie-up between housing and insurance goes all the way back to Bismarck, would be very valuable in this connection. The scope and limitation of responsibility of each, in relation to the other, has always seemed an interesting and significant problem to me, and I have often thought that in many respects housing and physical planning are the logical positive factors without which no scheme of insurance can be thoroughly effective.[15]

LOBBYIST

[Our] houses are very bad they are dark, and they don't have any toilets.

A CITIZEN OF NEW JERSEY

Catherine continued to work with Congressman Ellenbogen, writing his speeches, letters, and memoranda, including one to President Roosevelt that

Ellenbogen submitted January 30, 1936. "Papa (FDR) apparently did read it," Catherine wrote to Charney Vladeck, "because he sent it down to the housing division of the PWA with a note asking for their comments." Colonel Horatio Hackett responded favourably to Ellenbogen's (Catherine's) message: "Your analysis is clear and convincing. I am in complete sympathy with the ideas expressed in your memorandum."[16]

On February 18, 1936, the LHC issued an edict to all Labor Housing Committees: "The danger is now that the sentiment for public low-rent housing will be diverted by the administration through pressure from the real estate and financial interests to a program that will *sound* like workers' housing but will in effect benefit only banks, private builders and non-union labor. The time has come when the frequent pledges of the Administration to develop a clear cut permanent national housing program designed to improve workers' living conditions and re-employ building workers at fair wages in productive work must be fulfilled."[17]

It was hoped that five points in Ellenbogen's bill would be incorporated in Wagner's bill:

- All public-aided housing project costs would be based on fair wage conditions.
- A permanent Federal Housing Authority would be established to make grants and loans to local housing authorities, build its own housing projects, and work directly with local labour.
- A clear-cut system of federal grants would be introduced.
- The program would not be limited to slum clearance, which would be a separate program.
- The program would be separate from FHA and other such agencies.[18]

The media picked up the "February 18th Resolution," as the five points came to be known, giving LHC excellent publicity in key newspapers such as the *Baltimore Sun* and *New York Times*. Catherine was now spurred to higher goals. At the suggestion of Ernie Bohn, she made arrangements for a half-hour talk with Eleanor Roosevelt, drawing on Mary Simkhovitch's friendship. The First Lady was impressed by Catherine's presentation and included a comment on the meeting in her nationally syndicated Washington *Daily News* column, "My Day," on February 27, 1936: "[A] very lean young woman who wanted to talk housing [and whose] general observations on the subject interested me greatly was the type of woman who would make a good public servant."[19] Catherine was disappointed that Mrs. Roosevelt agreed with everything she said and asked no additional questions. Mrs. Roosevelt also declined an invitation to attend opening ceremonies for a new housing project in Camden, New Jersey, in early March.

During the spring of 1936, the Wagner-Ellenbogen legislation found new momentum. Ensconced in Ellenbogen's congressional office, Catherine directed a cross-traffic of memoranda. To Bohn she sent a tentative draft of the bill. "It's written very broadly as you can see. It seems there would be two ways to write a Housing Bill: one as a definite program and statement of principle, and the other as a means of setting up a piece of machinery which would do anything you wanted it to provided you got the right fuel. This is sort of a blanket enabling act, with a mandate from Congress to produce something quickly."[20]

That summer Roosevelt appointed a Central Housing Committee to coordinate all federal housing activities. His uncle, Frederick Delano, a prominent architect with a conservative bent, became chairman. The committee membership included Hackett, Clas, and Peaslee of PWA's Housing Division, and representatives of the Resettlement Administration, National Resources Board, Farm Credit Administration, Federal Home Loan Bank Board, FHA, National Emergency Council, and Reconstruction Finance Corporation. The president had hoped that a coordinated federal housing policy would be articulated by this committee, resulting in a comprehensive housing bill that his administration could support. In fact, the members could not agree on the scope of the housing legislation.

Senator Wagner, stymied by the political pressures tugging at him, dragged his heels on the housing bill. Lobbyists and their backers in government grew impatient. Hackett, Ickes, and others considered the possibility of finding another senator to endorse a housing bill, and Hackett suggested Senator Lewis Schwellenbach of Washington.

"Really!" Catherine shot off to a colleague wryly, "Ellenbogen-Schwellenbach it's almost too much of a good thing." Keyserling tried to reassure Catherine that Senator Wagner would soon come through with a good bill. By mid-March, Catherine lamented that her little band of reformers had not stuck with the Ellenbogen formulation of the bill. Fortunately labour's commitment to a housing bill remained strong, as the creation of more than seventy local LHCs attested. "If it had not been for the sudden arrival of Labor on the scene," Catherine wrote to George Soule of the *New Republic*, "I am pretty well convinced that Wagner would have let the whole thing drop as quietly as possible."[21]

On March 19, 1936, the AFL Housing Committee, feeling the bill slip away, sent an urgent open letter to key individuals and organizations outlining possible actions for Congress. The first possibility was the establishment of a permanent national housing authority with all necessary powers to assist local agencies to carry out a long-term program of low-rent housing. Another possibility was the continuation of temporary federal public housing agencies, such as the PWA's Division of Housing and

Suburban Resettlement, but these had severe limitations. A third possibility would be to abandon any real low-rent housing program, extending instead the Federal Housing Act that gave government guarantees for work done by speculative builders. (This last option was a well-articulated argument against FHA, whose current mandate lent no assurance of low rents, high building standards, or decent wages.)

Attached to the letter was a copy of the AFL's February 18th Resolution. The recipients were urged to write or wire the President, Senator Wagner, and/or their own senators and representatives in support of the establishment of a national housing agency with a long-term, low-income housing policy.

Encouraged by labour's strong support and Keyserling's hands-on help, Senator Wagner began to prepare a new bill. Keyserling's aim was to revise the legislation to reflect LHC priorities; as the draft neared completion, he called a meeting of representatives of LHC, NPHC, and NAHO to review the major points. On March 29, Catherine sat up all night with Keyserling and others finalizing the bill. It retained the provision for an independent authority, with a five-member board that could include the Secretary of the Interior. This was the lobbyists' concession to strong pressure from Ickes for the housing authority to be set up within Interior. Wagner also leaned toward Interior, citing the President's reluctance to create a new, separate agency.

On April 3, 1936, Wagner introduced the Wagner-Ellenbogen Housing Bill to Congress. Catherine could not believe it was finally happening, having just spent two weeks "of the very fanciest finagling in every direction by fair means and foul in its support."[22] The bill retained almost all the provisions advocated by LHC. It established a US Housing Authority to carry out a comprehensive low-rent program. Although adequate funds were not appropriated under the legislation, the authority was granted the power to issue guaranteed bonds. Protesting the small appropriation, Catherine nevertheless asserted that "the bill is damn good since we wrote most of it."[23]

Slum clearance had been subordinated, as Catherine had hoped, and she was delighted that the bill gave the US Housing Authority power to construct demonstration projects when local authorities lacked funds or interest to do so. The debate on capital grants was settled with a 45 percent capital grant to be supplemented with a 55 percent loan at no interest. The bill also provided for large subsidies from the federal government with absolutely no requirements for locally financed subsidies.[24] Public housing societies run by low-income families – serving as project sponsors and lessees – would ensure cooperation between labour and consumer groups. These societies, Catherine wrote to Max Lerner at *The Nation* on April 5, "would also take the curse off federal ownership and administration in localities where there is no real local housing authority." Most rewarding of all, the bill called for an independent US Housing Authority with Harold Ickes as an *ex officio* member of a Housing Board.

The press responded positively to the bill, labelling it "mild" and "conservative," which surprised Catherine – she wondered whether they really understood its meaning – but nevertheless struck her as a good omen for its passage through Congress. A "radical" label would do no political good. Still, there was doubt that the bill would pass during the 1936 congressional session due to its late introduction. Passage depended on the President's endorsement and the bill's reception on Capitol Hill. Fearing the legislation might be gravely compromised in the process, Catherine launched an intensive three-month campaign to push it through Congress.

Labour was prepared to fight hard because its wage conditions had been met. The building trades even helped LHC with funds for the three-month campaign, which gathered momentum as LHC mailed copies of the bill and sample resolutions to union groups across the country, calling for resolutions in support of the bill. By late May, LHC had distributed about fifteen thousand copies of documents explaining the housing bill to its members. A massive mailing in support of the bill went out to all senators and congressmen.

The lobbyists received strong support from the National Council of Catholic Charities, which later sent its secretary, Dr. John O'Grady, to testify before the Senate hearings. Catholic charities made monetary contributions to the campaign.

The NPHC developed its own strategy, publishing an eight-point digest of the housing bill accompanied by "A Prayer for Slum Clearance," which it distributed to six thousand influential ministers in cities throughout the United States. They organized a letter-writing campaign in which slum residents wrote directly to Roosevelt attesting to their appalling living conditions. "[Our] houses ... are very bad," wrote J. Bruno of Paterson, New Jersey, "they are dark, and they don't have any toilets in the house, they are in the back yard, all I can afford to pay is $25.00 per month and we can't find a good house or flat for this. Senator Wagner's bill for housing will help us a lot. And we ask you to help us get decent living in Paterson. Thanking you for any help you can give us."[25]

The Housing Bill

*Low-cost housing is not synonymous with slum clearance.
I would almost be willing to say that they are mutually
contradictory ... Slum clearance with the taxpayer's money
is aid to the needy – aid to the needy mortgage holders of
tenements, but not aid to the needy home-seeker.*

Nathan Straus

Opponents of public housing gathered strength against the proposed housing act. The US Chamber of Commerce, the National Association of Real Estate Boards, the US Savings and Loan League, and the National Association of Retail Lumber Dealers joined in opposition. They viewed public housing as a threat to private enterprise that would lead to the eventual socialization of all residential real estate. Catherine found their opposition ironic; the real estate lobby had hardly existed during the early Depression when the building trade and real estate business "was flat on its back, but gradually fattened and strengthened due almost wholly to the *Federal public aid* provided it by FHA, HOLC, etc."[26]

On April 20, 1936, the Committee on Education and Labor of the US Senate convened hearings on "A Bill (S 4424) to provide financial assistance to the States and political subdivisions thereof for the elimination of unsafe and unsanitary housing conditions, for the development of decent, safe and sanitary dwellings for families of low income and for the reduction of unemployment and the stimulation of business activity, to create a United States Housing Authority, and for other purposes."[27] Senator David I. Walsh of Massachusetts presided.

It was Leon Keyserling's task to shepherd the bill through the Senate. With the help of Ernie Bohn, Catherine provided Keyserling with a list of "local government and housing authority officials strategically located from a political and geographical standpoint, and a few conservative business-men, industrialists and real estate men to endorse the bill. I am of course getting the building trades boys to line up a few material manufacturers and contractors."[28] In an April 9 telegram, she thanked Bohn for his "proper finger spitzen gefuehl" (intuition) and forwarded a list of those to be invited to the hearings, inviting comments and additions.

Catherine's friendship with Bohn grew as professional commitments brought them together with increased frequency. A Christmas present from Bohn was acknowledged a month late: "The bag is beautiful, how on earth did you have time to unearth something to fit my perverse and difficult taste so exactly? Most bags for me are too fussy or too small (I *do* have to carry a notebook and a fountain pen and other bric-a-brac even in evening clothes. Now don't protest – you're lucky that I manage to leave my brief-case at home). *So*, you'd better come back to Washington soon and I'll endeavor to stretch my credit to a new evening dress in the interim and we'll go places."[29]

The frequently suggestive tone of Catherine's letters drew a sombre response from Bohn, a confirmed bachelor who lived with his father during those years. They often dined and danced together, and at Catherine's suggestion had met in Paris for a few days during the summer of '36. They remained close friends until Catherine's death, which touched Bohn deeply. Throughout her life Catherine turned to Ernie Bohn for advice and counsel. A close friend and former disciple of Bohn's, Dr. Morton Schussheim, believes today that Bohn remained a bachelor because he could not have Catherine.

Robert Wagner was the first person to testify at the Senate hearings on behalf of his bill. He emphasized the economic benefits of a permanent federal housing program and linked high unemployment to the catastrophic decline in housing construction. He was convinced that the bill would "provide the most stabilizing and stimulating influence that could be devised."[30] During the seven days of hearings, the Senate heard from fifty-five people representing a broad spectrum of interests. Included were the three groups that had lobbied for the bill (LHC, NPHC, and NAHO), labour leaders, members of city councils, municipal housing authorities, and real estate associations. Sixty-five briefs were filed. Among them were fifteen from mayors of major US cities, including LaGuardia of New York.

As executive secretary of LHC, Catherine spoke persuasively on the fifth day of the hearings. Attesting to the solid support for LHC's program, she pointed to the seventy-five local labour housing committees in thirty-one states. She offered some amendments, including a request for greater appropriations (which would not be granted): "We feel, in view of the great shortage and the very bad housing conditions existing in this country today, which are growing steadily worse, that the actual provision which is in the bill should be increased to at least a $100 million, that the bond issue authorized for the first year should be increased to at least $250 million, and that the authorization for ensuing years should be increased in proportion." She also expressed strong support for the proposed housing authority's power to construct demonstration projects in cooperation with local groups, in view of the number of regions facing financial or statutory obstacles.

Nathan Straus, a member of the New York City Housing Authority and president of the Hillside Housing Corporation, one of the largest limited-dividend housing corporations in the US, spoke cogently both to the urgency of government intervention in the traditional domain of private enterprise and to the futility of coupling slum clearance with low-cost housing. "Whenever industry can take care of its own problems the Government should keep out," said Straus. "But whenever an industry is unable to cope with a situation which affects the lives and future of millions of people, then it becomes not only the right but the solemn duty of Government to step in."[31] His position on slum clearance was also clear. "Low-cost housing is not synonymous with slum clearance. I would almost be willing to say that they are mutually contradictory ... Slum clearance with the taxpayer's money is aid to the needy – aid to the needy mortgage holders of tenements, but not aid to the needy home-seeker."[32]

While progress toward passage of Wagner's bill was encouraging at the Senate, things were not going as well for Ellenbogen at the House. A major obstacle arose in the person of Representative Henry B. Steagall, chairman of the House Committee on Banking and Currency, who considered the bill socialistic and refused to hear it without explicit instructions from the President. Anxious to get the President and the House to act, Catherine continued to urge labour groups to press their congressmen to act. Senator Walsh was slow to report the bill out of his committee, even though he asserted that he was in favour of it. Once again, the pro-housing lobbyists were compelled to mount a massive campaign.

By the end of May the bill's supporters began to lose hope: Congress was anxious to adjourn in preparation for the forthcoming presidential elections. Active lobbying of congressmen and the President continued. Catherine told her union friends that "the President could change the whole picture in thirty seconds if he would make a statement – even a lukewarm one." But he remained silent. Catherine now applied enormous pressure on labour representatives in key states to introduce state legislature resolutions in support of the Wagner-Ellenbogen bill.

"Does this mean you don't need housing or construction?" she asked John Hickey of the Delaware State Federation of Labor, who appeared indifferent. Within twenty-four hours she received hearty endorsements from the Central Labor Union and Building Trades Council of Wilmington. She also persuaded Senator Wagner to introduce all the endorsements that LHC had collected into the Congressional Record of May 26. Finally, on June 1, the Senate committee reported out favourably on the bill, with minor changes. Catherine lamented that it was a week too late, as Congress was scheduled to recess during the Republican Convention from June 8 to 15. She attributed the advancement of the bill thus far to the quite remarkable last-minute endorsements by labour. By now even the Musicians International and the Typographers had joined in.

On June 17, after two days of floor debate, the Senate passed Wagner's bill. Congressman Ellenbogen did not fare as well. The House Banking and Currency Committee failed to act on his bill; consequently, when Congress adjourned on June 20, 1936, the Wagner-Ellenbogen bill was dead. "I only wish all our energy had been expended for some more fruitful purpose," Catherine lamented.

In her post-mortem analysis, she blamed the defeat on a multitude of factors. First was the President's irresponsible attitude toward the whole matter. Second were the people who wished to sabotage the bill for their own reasons – among them Ickes, who wanted the housing authority directly under his thumb in Interior, and members of the Treasury Department, the Federal Housing Administration, and the Central Housing Committee. (Ickes and FHA would later come around in favour of the bill.) She also pointed her finger at Senator Wagner for stalling after the failure of his 1935 initiative, which the lobbyists considered a weak effort reflecting the senator's failure to take housing seriously enough. Later, once Wagner understood the complexity of the issues, the whole campaign had to be relaunched from scratch. "Perhaps the most important thing accomplished in housing in this session was the education of Senator Wagner," Catherine concluded.[33]

But she reserved her harshest criticism for Congressman Henry Bascom Steagall of Alabama and his colleagues on the House Banking and Currency Committee.[34] Using a statement the President had made in April as an excuse – that the housing situation was a mess and nobody could get it together – Steagall had dug in his heels. This infuriated Catherine, who charged that the mess was in the President's mind and that he continued complaining about it even after his own advisers had publicly endorsed it. Congressman Ellenbogen had received considerable backing since first introducing his bill. Congressman Steagall and his associate, Congressman T. Allan Goldsborough, who was acting chairman of the committee during Steagall's absence, professed a particular hatred of Ellenbogen, in Catherine's opinion. Both men vowed that they would never report out the Ellenbogen bill and would not act until the Senate had voted on the Wagner bill. Catherine accused them of "anti-Semitism and political conservatism."[35] Ellenbogen was a young Hungarian Jew and exceptionally active in liberal causes, whereas Steagall and Goldsborough were "both reactionary southern aristocrats having very few liberal or labor constituents."[36] Support and opposition in the committee were along ideological lines, not party lines, she charged. These currents of personal animosity continued and ultimately led to a regrouping of forces, including the replacement of Ellenbogen's sponsorship of the bill in the next session of Congress.

The Housing Act

*We have, for too long, neglected the housing problem for all
our lower-income groups.*
President Franklin D. Roosevelt

Catherine was still new enough in the political arena to be devastated by
the death of the Wagner-Ellenbogen bill. Although she had mastered the
rhetoric of a "tough labor skate," she lacked the emotional armour of her
seasoned associates. She had entered the fray as a sheltered, intellectual
idealist whose political classroom was the coffee shops of downtown
Manhattan. Drained of energy and feeling very low, Catherine sought the
advice of a doctor, who warned her to take better care. "I guess I came as
near to a mild crack-up in the last week as I ever care to," she admitted.[37]

Condolences on the failure of the bill poured in from across the nation.
One letter was postmarked Bend, Oregon. It was from a new friend:
Robert Marshall, chief of recreation and lands for the United States Forest
Service. "I just read that your Housing Bill was tabled at the last moment.
I'm terribly sorry because you worked so damn hard and so well on it. It
seems as if any bill worked upon as you did on the Wagner-Ellenbogen Bill
ought to be passed by all that is either poetically or prosaically just."[38]

Marshall had recently been introduced to Catherine by Benton
MacKaye, an associate of hers from the Regional Planning Association of
America. He had been dazzled by the vivacious, independent Catherine
and concluded his letter with the humble hope of seeing her again some
time after her return from Europe. Although she may have hardly noticed
him at the time, Bob would become a valued friend during the next few
years, for two reasons: first, they shared a love of the wilderness; but more
importantly, his work had nothing to do with housing.

Bob Marshall inherited a love of botany, conservation, and civil liberties
from his father, Louis, a prominent lawyer and founder of the American
Jewish Committee. Like Catherine, Bob was a descendent of Bavarian
immigrants, but apart from their geographic origins the families had little
in common. Catherine's parents preferred to keep Jews at a distance, a
lesson she learned when they protested her brief summer romance with a
Jewish boy during her days as camp counsellor. By contrast, Catherine
admired and befriended many Jews.

Her second love in life, after housing, was nature. A good brisk hike
around a lake or in a forest always revived her when she was depressed or
exhausted, and Bob's devotion to wilderness conservancy interested her. A
man with several degrees in forestry, including a Ph.D. from Johns
Hopkins, he was one of four conservationists to found the American
Wilderness Society in 1935. MacKaye was another, and together they

drafted a platform for the society declaring "all we desire to save from invasion is that extremely minor fraction of outdoor America which yet remains free from mechanical sights and sounds and smells."[39] It would be a year before Catherine and Bob would correspond again.

Before embarking on the final push for the 1936 housing act, Catherine had decided to reapply for a Guggenheim fellowship. Three years after being rejected, she was confident that she was in a stronger position to receive the grant. This time her application was more focused. She planned to study "recent achievements and policies in housing, and city and regional planning in the U.S.S.R., with a brief survey of trends in the same field in certain other European countries."[40] She had published one book to high acclaim and now wished to elaborate upon her work with a year of travel and research. Catherine expected another book, perhaps a sequel to *Modern Housing,* to result from the experience.

"The time is ripe for a serious analysis and description of the achievements and policies of Soviet Russia in the field of housing," she wrote in her application, "and in the various aspects of physical and environmental planning which related directly to housing ... To my knowledge no general study or survey is available." Catherine explained that *Modern Housing* had dealt with one concise phase in the history of the housing movement from 1920 through 1932 – a chapter that was now all but closed. Russia would take its place in the next chapter.

Russian housing had passed through several distinct stages, as hundreds and thousands of dwellings were constructed and entire new cities developed. Initially German architects, planners, and technicians were imported. Later there was reaction against them and their severely utilitarian style. Catherine hoped to examine the important changes in administrative policies, from housing built and managed by the State to more effective, efficient, and economic management by tenant cooperatives. She expected that an analysis of the Russian situation might bear direct relation to current American problems. There were many people, she was certain, of varying political beliefs who would want to know what physical planning and housing might be like in the absence of private ownership.

Her list of references still included Lewis Mumford, but the others were dropped in favour of political associates from the recent legislative battle. She added Col. Horatio Hackett of PWA, Ernest Bohn, president of NAHO, and Charney Vladeck of the New York City Housing Authority. Her "Accomplishments" section now reflected a much more mature, self-confident applicant. Catherine had contributed substantively to the Museum of Modern Art's exhibition of modern architecture, resulting in a growing demand for her magazine articles. She had become a political activist in the emerging field of public housing policy. She had helped to build the Labor Housing Conference. Her application also recounted her participation in the legislative process.

On March 16, 1936, Catherine was notified that the Guggenheim Trustees were appointing her to a Fellowship of the Foundation, "to study recent developments in housing and city and regional planning in certain European countries." The fellowship was awarded for twelve months from a date to be determined, with a stipend of $2,000 and a stipulation "that she acquire a reasonably adequate knowledge of the Russian language prior to entering upon her Fellowship." Catherine was the first houser to win this prestigious award. She was delighted. "I cannot tell you with what pleasure and anticipation I accept the Fellowship"[41] began her reply. She promised to begin learning Russian after being freed from the hectic fight for housing legislation. Mr. Moe, the secretary of the foundation, gave her some latitude in commencing the fellowship, which allowed Catherine to bury herself in the fight for passage of the Housing Act until Congress adjourned. In its May issue, the prestigious journal *Architectural Record* carried news of the award along with a short biography and photo of a laughing Miss Catherine Bauer under the caption "Houser Wins Guggenheim Award."

Catherine relished the opportunity to get away from Washington. Now was the time to employ the Guggenheim fellowship and embark upon a European study tour. She turned over her LHC responsibilities to the AFL Housing Committee's Boris Shishkin, who had worked with her on the legislative campaign. On July 15, 1936, Catherine departed for Europe aboard the SS *Normandy*. She intended to review recent legislation in England, study housing in Scandinavia, and observe the urban planning achievements of the recent five-year plan in the Soviet Union. Her itinerary included a week in France, for old times' sake, followed by six weeks in Scandinavia and three months in the Soviet Union before returning to England.

Catherine hoped that Leon Keyserling would join her for part of the trip. Her close association with Keyserling while drafting the 1936 act had led to an intimate friendship and even, at times, to thoughts of marriage. At the age of thirty-one, she had a remarkable curriculum vitae but was all too aware of the social demerits of being single. Leon was a man of ideas, ideals, and, unlike Lewis Mumford, political action. For a while they lived in the same Washington boarding house with three other housing activists. Their correspondence from that period reveals a profound mutual intellectual respect, enhanced by a brief period of intimacy and complicated by occasional petty squabbling.

Keyserling saw her off with a heavy heart. "Seeing you go made me very

CATHERINE AND LEON KEYSERLING, MAY 1938

Her close association with [Leon] Keyserling while drafting the 1936 act had led to an intimate friendship and even, at times, to thoughts of marriage.

morose," he wrote to her, "not so much because it interrupted our being together, but because it symbolized the failure to carry through, the interruption in *media res,* that has become almost the imprimatur of my human dealings, you charitably call it waywardness. If I had gone and thrown myself freely into the jaunt, at least I could have garnered for my old age one complete remembrance of youth ... The ping pong tables on the boat were the last straw. I know that seeing them has made the destruction of my summer complete."

With concern for her well-being, he added, "Please, my dear, do remember that the last year has really been bad for you, and combine plain living with high thinking while abroad." Addressing his own conflicted feelings, Keyserling said:

> Our being separated will make it possible to do some thinking that otherwise would be honored in the breach. I feel that I must separate the novelty of our association from its essence, or I could never trust my own estimate of reality of the latter. And my thinking must be combined with action, with contact, with other people, else it will become mere ratiocination to which you know I have been prone. As for you, do not think of me at all, except enough to write me about four times a week; but if you can not abide by this

interdiction, then think about whether you really liked me, or just admired my action in the Housing Crisis of 1936.[42]

By the end of July Leon had received only one letter from Catherine. She abided by his interdiction, and he suffered for it. "This practically 100% estrangement is bad – very bad," he wrote in August. He became agitated when he learned that Catherine spent three days in Sweden with Ernie Bohn. "That little wizard has me worried. He saw through you so completely with respect to our (yours and mine) business engagements that the chill crept over me that he may have seen into me too, if not all the way through."[43]

Anxious for new experiences, Catherine made little time to write letters home. In Paris she stayed at the Hotel des Etats-Unis, near the opera, far from her old Left Bank residences. She immediately plunged into political research, visiting key people in the French labour movement, including M. Sellier, Minister of Public Health in the Labour government, who had long been a prominent figure in housing. She also spent a considerable amount of time with Marcel Lods, the best modern architect in Paris, she thought. He showed her Paris from the sky, out of his little private plane, and introduced her to his family.

Catherine left for Sweden toward the end of August to visit a trade union summer school called Brunnsvick, near Värmland. There she was invited by a charming old lady senator, Miss Hesselgren, to meet all the trade union leaders of the region. Catherine was impressed by this progressive and prosperous country with its almost complete absence of unemployment and serious poverty. Here, social insurance was efficient and housing excellent. She thought the Social-Democratic Party, Sweden's labour party, was very utopian and perhaps politically fragile.

Still tied to housing obligations at home, Catherine produced a Labor Housing Conference press release and a report for the AFL Housing Committee for their fall convention, while travelling in the north of Sweden. Her tour took her all the way to Lapland, where she hiked around clear lakes bordered by birch and pine forests that reminded her of Maine. She visited lumber mills, factories, housing sites, and called on local labour leaders who spoke English well and whom she found intelligent and helpful.

Catherine returned to the south of Sweden at the beginning of October to organize tours to Oslo and Copenhagen. Uno Ahren, her Stockholm guide in 1930, had moved to Gothenburg in 1934 to become chief of city planning, and she called on him there. Once again he acted as guide and arranged for her to present a series of lectures on the housing and labour situation in the United States. People filled union halls wishing to hear her speak. Catherine felt honoured when a group of Swedish architects

CATHERINE'S PHOTOS OF NEW BUILDINGS, CITÉ LA MUETTE,
FRANCE, JULY 1936

She also spent a considerable amount of time with Marcel
Lods, the best modern architect in Paris, she thought.

offered her $50 to lecture about Russian architecture during her return trip. She also spent a few happy weeks alone with Ahren, discussing life, architecture, and planning.

Toward the end of October, just as Catherine prepared to set out for the USSR, fate intervened. A cable came from Robert Kohn, an architect friend from RPAA days, now on the New York World's Fair Committee, with an urgent request: "Can you return now for six months work planning housing exhibit world's fair pay traveling expenses plus two thousand stop Guggenheim approve intermission cable address arslonga new york."

She wrote her parents, in disbelief. "I was sick in bed when it came and thought for a moment that I must be delirious." Bad weather and the pending new housing bill convinced Catherine to postpone her trip to Russia until the next summer. Two weeks later she sailed home, cabin class, aboard the SS *Gripsholm*.[44]

Catherine was determined to resume her research in Europe during the spring of 1937, a plan endorsed by the Guggenheim Foundation. For now she would concentrate on the World's Fair, preparing an exhibit called "The City of Tomorrow" for its shelter section. This would give form and content to a fully planned community in terms of social purpose and architecture – an enormous opportunity to produce in the United States the kind of full-scale exhibitions she had seen in Europe. She also drew on her participation in MOMA's architectural exhibitions by proposing a group of general exhibition buildings and a full-scale mini-neighbourhood on a ten-acre site. She planned to demonstrate the proper relationship of houses to each other, to the site, to the street, to recreational areas, and to non-residential buildings. The structures, equipment, and interior plans would be designed to meet the needs of different income groups and family sizes.

The site would be bounded by water, a highway, a main entrance, and a thoroughfare. The mini-neighbourhood would be composed of twenty-five to thirty-five dwellings grouped in clusters according to building types, price/rental ranges, and building materials. It would include a neighbourhood social centre and a nursery school for fair employees' children. The layout would include several cul-de-sacs, an underpass, walkways separate from roads, grouped garages, and dwellings properly oriented to sun and air. A row of flats suitable for low-income families, and furniture designed for low-cost mass production, would also be displayed.

The fair's administrators were not persuaded that the mini-neighbourhood would be cost effective or could be built on time. MOMA offered to conduct an architectural competition for those submitting designs for exhibition. Catherine welcomed the proposal but insisted on retaining the right of final decision when it came to integrating the fair's shelter exhibits with the museum's commitment to modern architecture. She proposed the novel idea of making and screening a movie on housing and planning, to pull the entire concept together. Fascinated by the idea of such a movie, Robert Kohn commissioned the production of a film called *The City*. Lewis Mumford wrote and narrated the script, Aaron Copland composed the music, and Pare Lorentz was cinematographer. *The City* was filmed in Greenbelt, Maryland, a planned community just completed by Roosevelt's Resettlement Administration. The film is all that survived of Catherine's ambitious plans.

By 1936 Catherine had been associated with MOMA for four years, beginning in February 1932, when she assisted in the preparation of the housing section of the historic architectural show "Modern Architecture: International Exhibition." Two years later, because of the popularity of *Modern Housing*, she was invited to participate in mounting a provocative show on modern architecture and progressive community planning, called "Art in Architecture." To her dismay she encountered a timid administration at the museum. There was considerable debate about the title of the show and some of its panel headings. Angered by what she felt was both a personal and professional affront, she fired off a letter to Philip Johnson, the show's curator. "If *planning for profit* or *for use* is too disturbing an idea for the bitches, what *can* you say? But really, if you cut too much of the point out, I just can't sign it – not so much on a personal score (I do need the money) but because of my present affiliations, and public pronouncements."[45] A compromise was reached between the affable curator and the angry consultant, to everyone's satisfaction.

In February 1936 Catherine was invited to serve on MOMA's Architectural Committee, where, for the next six years, she found a sympathetic platform for her aesthetic and social housing concerns. The committee saw housing as an opportunity to illustrate the design principles of architectural functionalism, and therefore was willing to expand the term *architecture* beyond its traditional limits of façades and individual buildings. Catherine regarded her participation on the MOMA committee as a chance to educate the public on the socioeconomic aspects of housing and community planning, coupled with the aesthetic principles of functionalism. Her opportunity came with the exhibition "Architecture in Government Housing" in the spring of 1936.

Although she was busy lobbying for the passage of the Housing Act at that time, Catherine took on the job of writing the foreword to the show's catalogue. The exhibition was significant because it linked the social concerns of modern architecture with a prestigious cultural institution. Catherine's foreword, "Pre-View ... or Post-Mortem?," was a manifesto for a federal public housing program. She emphasized that a housing movement ought to be judged by the houses it builds, not by its theories. The houses illustrated in the exhibit were all financed by PWA's Housing Division or the Resettlement Administration; all were built and planned within complete neighbourhood units. They were as different from the usual mode of residential construction as Chartres Cathedral is from a Roman temple. The exhibition provided an excellent opportunity to advance Catherine's case for low-income housing because people became enthusiastic when they saw good building design.

Shortly after Congress adjourned in 1936, a new effort for a 1937 housing campaign began to take shape. In June, before leaving for Europe, Catherine warned her colleagues that "the real-estate boys will almost certainly be smarter next year."[46] In her absence, leadership came from NPHC, which attempted to hold President Roosevelt to his October re-election campaign promise.

"We have, for too long, neglected the housing problem for all our lower-income groups," the president had said. "We have spent large sums of money on parks, on highways, on bridges, on museums ... But we have not yet begun adequately to spend money in order to help the families in the overcrowded sections of our cities ... Federal government will join with private capital in helping every American family ... We need action and more action to get better city housing."[47] Roosevelt was returned to power in November 1936 in one of the country's greatest electoral victories. His 1937 inaugural address challenged the nation to help "the tens of millions of its citizens who were denied the greater part of what the very lowest standards of today call the necessities of life. I see one-third of a nation ill-housed, ill-clad, ill-nourished."[48]

The rousing rhetoric stimulated the housers to regroup and push Senator Wagner for a new bill. Stung by his previous experience, the senator was now convinced that he had to get the President's unqualified endorsement for any housing bill before reintroducing it.

Although Catherine's full-time work with the World's Fair kept her in New York, she again coordinated the lobbying activities of LHC and NPHC. A Housing Legislation Information Office (HLIO) had been instituted late in the previous campaign to coordinate all lobbying efforts for the 1936 Housing Act. The office was reactivated shortly after the 74th Congress adjourned, in anticipation of a renewed battle in the 75th Congress. Initially Catherine participated only in strategy sessions, but she was quickly drawn into the fray and began commuting to Washington from New York twice a week.

By January 1937 she had launched a campaign of wires and letters to Senator Wagner and the President on the renewed housing bill. Catherine expected to spend at least one day a week in Washington once the new bill was introduced. Based on the 1936 hearings, the new legislation was drafted by Leon Keyserling together with Warren Vinton, a New Deal economist, and Coleman Woodbury, executive director of NAHO. Typically they would hold drafting meetings in Vinton's apartment above a French restaurant, to which they repaired for dinner before continuing work until the early morning hours. They kept in touch with Catherine by telephone and letter. The most important change in the 1937 bill was a provision by which federal capital grants would be made annually to local authorities at a fixed and uniform rate. A draft of the bill was printed early in February 1937, and Wagner sent copies to Roosevelt for his comments.

The Senator introduced the bill (S 1685) on February 24, 1937. On the same day, Congressman Henry Steagall introduced the same bill in the House (H.R. 5033). Although he had opposed legislation during the last session, Steagall responded to the President's pressure for a housing bill. He was chosen as co-sponsor for a number of pragmatic reasons. As chairman of the powerful House Banking and Currency Committee, he clearly was a source of political strength for the bill's passage. In addition to the strategic advantage of selecting a member of the conservative southern bloc, Catherine and her colleagues believed that anti-Semitism in the House motivated Wagner to drop Ellenbogen in favour of Steagall.

The LHC endorsed the 1937 bill and called for its immediate passage. But there was one more hurdle: though the President himself supported action, some of his cabinet and House Democrats had doubts. Secretary of the Treasury, Henry Morgenthau, a traditional conservative, objected to the financial provisions of the bill. On March 2, 1937, the President called a meeting at the White House of proponents and opponents, including Catherine. After a few opening remarks indicating his absolute commitment to an appropriate public housing bill, he asked the assembled to adjourn to the Cabinet Room and told them to "get together, boys, and resolve your differences."

Catherine later reported: "There were about twenty people, I guess, but the main issue was between the Senator [Wagner] and Henry Morgenthau, who found the 'annual contributions' formula pretty hard to take as a form of subsidy ... The three of us who were in the Senator's train were afraid that the Senator wouldn't be able to answer all the fine points and immediately started writing feverish notes to him. But the Senator brushed them aside without reading them, much to our chagrin. Instead, when Morgenthau was winding up, the Senator reached over and pulled his coat. 'Henry' he said ... 'for heavens sake sit down and stop worrying about your pocket book.'"[49] Wagner carried the day.

The LHC's major lobbying activity was pamphlets and press releases to build strong support for the bill within the labour movement. Catherine launched a barrage of memos, again enlisting the AFL Housing Committee to distribute them. Senate hearings began on April 14, again chaired by Senator Walsh of Massachusetts, who tried to limit discussion to changes and improvements in the bill since 1936. AFL President William Green, the first to testify, focused on labour support of the bill for urgent job creation. "In a very real sense," Green declared, "this bill is labor's bill ... Today labor stands as one in support of this bill ... This bill is bill number one in our legislative program."[50] Catherine followed him. She explained the differences between the financial provisions of the 1936 and 1937 bills, defended the provision for demonstration grants, and urged the immediate creation of local housing authorities.[51]

By the end of July the Senate committee reported the bill out, and lobbying took on increased intensity. Catherine returned to Washington to devote all her time to the campaign, commuting to New York for one or two days a week to finish up her work on the World's Fair. Her legislative focus was to ensure that the proposed Housing Authority would be an independent agency rather than a subdivision of the Department of the Interior under Harold Ickes, a formidable New Dealer. Catherine lobbied vigorously against Ickes's control, incurring his wrath. In his memoirs Ickes referred to Bauer as a "wild-eyed female who regarded herself as a housing expert." He regarded her as a troublemaker.[52] To increase their effectiveness, they set about flooding Congress with letters supporting passage of the bill, in hopes of pressuring Steagall into opening hearings as soon as possible. To engage Roosevelt, Catherine decided first to approach his wife. "Last year, when the situation on the Housing Bill was beginning to get complicated," she wrote Mrs. Roosevelt on June 15, "you were kind enough to spare me half an hour of your time and attention ... May we meet again?"[53] She thanked Mrs. Roosevelt for her past and present interest in housing, and for her active and very valuable assistance in these matters. The meeting was granted. As before, Mrs. Roosevelt listened sympathetically and promised her support. Of course Catherine did not disclose to the First Lady what she feared most about the President: that he was "keeping himself in a state of child-like innocence as to the nature of the problem" as a defense against trying to solve it. To her colleagues, Catherine confided her belief that the President had a "penchant for extemporaneous amateur policy-making."[54]

Senator Wagner approached the President directly and won his agreement that the bill should stand in its initial form. Roosevelt promised to throw his weight behind Wagner in urging Steagall to get things moving. Tensions mounted. Steagall was visited in his office by Keyserling, Bohn, and Catherine, who lost her patience with Steagall and declared that if something did not begin to happen in the House, the bill would be lost. "Well lady," Steagall retorted, obviously annoyed, "wouldn't that just be too bad."[55]

Under presidential pressure, Steagall finally held hearings from August 3 to August 6, with New York's Mayor LaGuardia the first to testify. The mayor was an eloquent advocate for federal public housing. He reminded committee members that he was one of their former colleagues. "Let us have the American people live up to the standards we boast about and sing about and write poetry about."[56]

While the House hearings continued, the Senate passed the bill on August 6 by a vote of sixty-four to sixteen. After considerable debate and further amendments, the bill was approved by the House Committee on August 16, and discussion moved to the floor of the House. Further amendments were offered, including one that allowed demolition of slums to be delayed in areas of acute housing shortage, which was accepted. Catherine and her allies were exhausted but pleased when the bill cleared Congress. Steagall supported the bill only because the President insisted. Representative Clyde Williams of Missouri summed up the feeling of the majority when he told the House: "We must recognize that there is a part of our population which can never be home owners and ... we must provide homes for such people through a public subsidy."[57] The House version of the bill was reconciled with the Senate's version, and the amended bill was passed by Congress on August 21, 1937, just before adjournment.

On September 1, Roosevelt signed the United States Housing Act of 1937 into law. With the President's signature a milestone in American social and political history was achieved. Upon the creation of the United States Housing Authority (USHA), Charles Abrams, who had abandoned his lucrative New York law practice to participate in the burgeoning national housing movement, immortalized Catherine's role in the bill's passage with a limerick:

There was a young lady named Bauer
Who resolved to help housing to flower
She fought and she battled
And couldn't be rattled
No power could cow her – this Bauer.[58]

THE UNITED STATES HOUSING AUTHORITY

Oh, for the good old days when all the housers of the country could comfortably hold their convention in a telephone booth.

ERNEST BOHN TO CATHERINE BAUER

One week after the enactment of the US Housing Act of 1937, Catherine wrote a piece in the *New Republic* calling it "the single most important left-wing bill passed in eight long months, a popular measure reminding the country that the last election was also a triumph of left over right. Its passage found democracy functioning rather better than usual in America."[59] However, she was left with a great discomfort at having abandoned Congressman Ellenbogen in her drive for political success.

"It still makes me squirm, we took the housing act away from Ellenbogen who deserved to get credit for it, and gave it to Steagall," she confessed to Mary Simkhovitch. "And yet we couldn't have got it through otherwise."[60] Coleman Woodbury, reflecting the perspective of the National Association of Housing Officials (NAHO), had another observation. With adjournment imminent, noted Woodbury, the congressmen thought it politic to endorse at least one act that Roosevelt supported. They had defeated his court-packing bill after bitter debate and were reluctant to return home without passing at least one piece of significant legislation.

The landmark act articulated the New Deal's commitment to housing as social and economic policy in the framework of national recovery. The stated purpose of the act was "to provide financial assistance to the States and political subdivisions thereof for the elimination of unsafe and unsanitary housing conditions, for the eradication of slums, for the provision of decent, safe and sanitary dwellings for families of low income, and for the reduction of unemployment and the stimulation of business activity, to create a United States Housing Authority, and for other purposes."

The act was also a declaration of new US policy "to promote the general welfare of the Nation by employing its funds and credit, as provided in this Act, to assist the several States and their political subdivisions to alleviate present and recurring unemployment and to remedy the unsafe and unsanitary housing conditions and the acute shortage of decent, safe and sanitary housings for families of low income, in rural or urban communities, that are injurious to the health, safety and morals of the citizens of the Nation."

It was immediately clear that the allocated funds were insufficient to carry out the act's mandate. Nine months later, in June 1938, Congress adopted amendments to increase USHA bond authorization from $500 million to $800 million for the following three years. Initially USHA was authorized to make $100 million available during the first year and $200 million each during the next two years. The proceeds of the bonds were to be available as interest-free loans to local housing authorities, to finance up to 90 percent of project costs. In addition, $20 million in contributions to local housing authorities, over three years, were raised to $28 million. The 1938 amendment removed the three-year provision and allocated all moneys immediately.

Catherine later asserted that many sections of the Housing Act of 1937 were borrowed from the English experience. She cited the substantial and clear-cut national subsidy (in the form of a contractual annual contribution) to insure rents low enough to re-house low-income families from bona fide slums. She also pointed to how the 1937 act provided for direct public construction and management of housing, which was seen as the only way the subsidy could achieve its purpose with maximum certainty and minimum cost to taxpayers. For the first time in American history, federal legislation defined families of low income and established an economic base for calculating low-rent housing. For the first time, also, there was a provision for decent, safe, and sanitary low-income housing, which could not be supplied by private enterprise. The act proclaimed a national housing policy with explicit federal subsidies. It established a national administration, while emphasizing local initiative and responsibility for meeting the needs of low-income families.

A major battle for housing legislation had been won, and Catherine's career would soon become tied to the expanding federal housing bureaucracy. To celebrate, she treated herself to a recreational tour of the western states by train. It would be only partly holiday, however, as she planned to devote several days to acquainting herself with local housing programs en route. Her first stop was Chicago, where NAHO friends showed her some of the city's projects, which ranged from excellent to deplorable. The worst had "dreadful Georgian details with a site plan which gives maximum frontage on highway and minimum on river."[61] The next few years would find USHA attempting to advance appropriate site planning, with virtually no success as legislators repeatedly refused to allocate sufficient funds.

Her next stop was Denver, where she was thrilled to see high mountains. There she explained details about the new housing bureaucracy to the Building Trades Convention and collected local statistical information to carry back to Washington. Escaping from the convention for a few days, Catherine rented a Chrysler roadster and drove to Boulder and into the wilderness area beyond. With only a typewriter to talk to, she hiked in Estes Park and Rocky Mountain National Park, and drove along back roads until she reached a dismal hotel, occupied mainly by prospectors. An easterner on her first trip west, she felt she was crossing a movie set.

Catherine's trip took her through small towns in Colorado where she met labour leaders and visited impressive Works Progress Administration ventures, including fairgrounds, zoos, and even a municipal golf clubhouse. In southwestern Colorado she was shown around by the local secretary of the United Mine Workers. He took her to mining communities where wages were reasonable but most houses had no sanitation or indoor water, though many boasted electric refrigerators. The next amendment to the United States Housing Act would address inadequate rural housing.

A bus took her to New Mexico: Taos, Santa Fe, and finally Albuquerque, where she joined Bob Marshall. Marshall had been among the first to congratulate Catherine on the passage of the Housing Act, writing her soon afterwards to relay best wishes along with a story. The day after Congress had adjourned, he had met Senator King of Washington on a train from Pittsburgh to Akron. Marshall sat down beside the senator hoping to persuade him "of the desirability of voting favorably for preserving the wilderness in southeastern Washington,"[62] but before launching his conservation pitch, he remarked, "You fellows certainly did a swell job in passing the Housing Act."

"I don't think so," shouted King, "I voted against it. It's Russian! It's German! It's socialistic! It penalizes every hard working, industrious, thrifty citizen for the sake of the lazy worthless, good-for-nothings who won't save up enough to build their own homes. The federal government has no business in housing. It has no business competing with private initiative. It's socialistic! This is a democracy but the socialists are trying to make it into a totalitarian state. If Wagner wants to be a socialist, why doesn't he go back to Germany where he came from?"

A young southerner sitting across the aisle joined in the tirade. "It's great to have a Senatuh with courage to speak out that way. I come from North Carolina where we have one of the few Senatuhs with courage like yours. We're all mahty proud of Senatuh Bailey."

King agreed. "Senator Bailey is one of the best men who's ever sat in the Senate. If all the senators were like Bailey, this country wouldn't be turning socialistic."[63] Marshall decided to drop the issue of the Washington wilderness, and, leaving the men to their discussion, headed for his sleeper.

Catherine and Marshall spent a week touring the Gila Wilderness, mostly on horseback, with a small group of rangers. Alarmed by the increasing damage to forests by private interests, Marshall wanted the federal government to buy and manage 80 percent of American forests then in private hands. "If private ownership leads to anti-social conditions and brings about undesirable results, there is no more reason why it shouldn't go by the boards than slavery went by the boards,"[64] argued Marshall.

He was regarded as a radical thinker, admired by many but castigated by some in high places. In 1939 New York Congressman Hamilton Fish accused him of being "the largest single contributor to a Communist veteran organization whose main purpose is to spread class hatred and propaganda for the destruction of American institutions." Refusing to be intimidated, Marshall shot back: "I've been out in the woods and up in the Arctic a good part of the past five years. It may be that the Bill of Rights was repealed without my hearing about it."[65] The charge against him grew out of a donation of $2,500 he made that year to the Workers' Alliance, a national union of WPA employees and the jobless. Their president, David Lasser, was later cross-examined by a House committee because he had visited Russia in 1937.[66]

While Catherine toured the West in the late summer of 1937, President Roosevelt appointed Nathan Straus administrator of the newly established USHA. Straus had headed the NYC Housing Authority and before that had served in the NY State Senate, where he authored legislation forbidding landlords from discriminating against families with children when leasing apartments. He was a seasoned politician and deeply committed to public housing in its evolving federal legislative framework. Both in Albany and New York City, he championed the housing needs of low-income families and stressed the distinction between low-cost housing – meaning poor or cheap construction – and adequate accommodation appropriate for families unable to pay market rents.

In spite of his background Catherine had some reservations. "I have sort of been holding my breath for the past two weeks," she confided to Ernie Bohn, "or I would have written you before. My opinion of the Housing Authority at the moment is pretty definitely OK. Nathan is clearly a stronger character than we had generally anticipated. If he gets into trouble it will be from impulsiveness rather than from stalling or weakness. The most amusing thing has been the vision of embarrassed intellectuals evading the responsibility that comes with reward. Nathan wanted me to set up and direct Public Relations and Education. I prefer to remain a consultant."[67] She added some in-house gossip. "Nathan also endeavored gracefully to bestow the Chief Counsel's job on a grateful Leon [Keyserling], but the latter has fussed around for two weeks without being able to decide (I think he'll take it though). Naturally Nathan is a little puzzled by it all. One of the most important things is that he has been acting in the best possible manner to win the loyalty of the HD [WPA's Housing Division] to himself rather than the Honorable Harold [Ickes]. His gestures of independence have been decisive, perhaps even too much so."[68]

Gradually Straus built a staff of experienced and loyal housers who had joined in the common struggle for federal legislation. During the next two years he gathered a team of social activists, seasoned lawyers, career public servants, and enthusiastic amateurs into the USHA's administration. Many were hesitant to trade independence for work implementing new programs in the federal bureaucracy. Catherine was among them, and initially consented to act as consultant only because Straus asked her to speak in New York and Cleveland on behalf of USHA. She doubted she would remain on staff for long. Other members of the team were Jacob Crane, Lee Johnson, Boris Shishkin, Warren Vinton, Leon Keyserling, and Robert Weaver. Weaver, who transferred to the USHA from the Department of Interior's housing program, would provide the major thread of continuity in public housing policy for the next thirty years. In 1964 he would become the first secretary of Housing and Urban Development (HUD), the successor to the USHA, and the first African-American to hold a cabinet post.

Catherine continued to turn to Bohn for advice on her career as she wrestled with the options of public service or an independent career as lobbyist for labour groups. "Did you hear how I have been loaded down with Research and Statistics? I need your advice being the only other person who appreciates the value of maintaining an amateur standing."[69] She often invited him to come to wherever she happened to be, to share ideas. Now it was to a party in Washington, later it would be San Francisco. In March 1938, she invited him to a party "in this sink of sin and statistics." When he failed to appear she wrote: "We missed you like anything. You were a big bum not to come. I needed you to keep me from worrying about whether we were getting siphoned or not. It was a good party though and you would have fallen for my kid sister who was quite the Belle. The housers really gave the impression of being very gay and cosmopolitan gentlemen, which probably took an enormous effort but had quite an effect on the out-of-town girls. When *are* you coming around?"[70] Despite her flirtations, Catherine regarded Bohn more as father/teacher than as friend/lover, and kept him at a distance by teasing him about her sister. Bohn's feelings for Catherine were carefully guarded, as he sensed she was mainly attracted to him for his intellect.

The USHA occupied itself in establishing criteria of reasonable housing, reflecting models of the Weimar Republic, while in Germany itself, Hitler busied himself with tearing asunder the hard-earned gains of the Social Democrats. Systematically he set out to destroy all traces of democracy at home, including the modern housing programs. Buoyed by his joyous reception in Austria when he annexed the country in March, Hitler turned his attention to Czechoslovakia. His plan was to destroy Czechoslovakia, the most democratic of European countries, by annexing the industrial

Sudeten region and returning its three million German-speaking citizens to their "rightful homeland." The fact that Sudetenland never was part of Germany (it had belonged to pre-war Austria) did not seem to trouble the western politicians – least of all Neville Chamberlain, who was eager to comply with Hitler's demands in order to avoid another world war.

Many intellectuals in the West took the position articulated by Winston Churchill in a press statement on September 21, 1938: "The partition of Czechoslovakia under pressure from England and France amounts to the complete surrender of the Western Democracies to the Nazi threat of force."[71]

Lewis Mumford was one of the most outspoken American opponents of compliance, and he lost many friends when he wrote of the inevitability of American involvement in another war. Catherine tended to side with Mumford, against the opinions of isolationists such as Frank Lloyd Wright, though she held no strong opinion until Chamberlain's capitulation on Czechoslovakia. Then she became alarmed. She wrote to her closest friend in Europe, Uno Ahren:

If only England had not played such a dirty game in Spain! And Austria – and now Czechoslovakia. Except for the Catholics, public opinion in this country is still very much in favour of the Government in Spain, even in spite of Franco's successes. And I haven't yet seen a paper which favored handing over the Sudetens to Germany. But if it comes to a real war – ???? I honestly don't know what I actually think myself. When even the threat of war brings all so-called democratic governments several steps nearer Fascism, one begins to count the price of a real war. I am pretty well convinced that Democracy as we know it would be gone forever. In Europe at least it seems to me one would have to accept the fact that some sort of super-nationalist Fascist interlude is unavoidable, before anything better can be hoped for. And can it be got through fast enough? On the other hand, just to let Germany go on and on – it's impossible! I wish I had more time to think these things out (imagine worrying about a definition of "substandard housing" in September 1938!!!) and I particularly wish I could talk it over with you."[72]

Indeed, substandard housing continued to absorb Catherine. Early that autumn she established USHA's Division of Research and Information and was asked to be its head. For the next eighteen months she gave up her cherished amateur status and plunged into a vortex of activities. "I have been in one continual state of harassment and worry over work and suffocation from the sheer weight of thousands of little silly administrative details," she told Ahren, full of anguish. "I still don't know whether it was really an unusually difficult job, or whether I am just congenitally unsuited for administrative work."

Catherine had been overwhelmed by the enormous task of hiring close to one hundred people, developing budgets, making organization charts for programs including housing surveys, analyzing proposed projects from the point of view of rents, incomes, and family size, doing background economic and social research, writing speeches, pamphlets, and publicity materials, and making models for study and exhibits. Such work would have been difficult enough outside the government, but the red tape in Washington was terrible: it took about three months to get a single job classified and a single person appointed.

Exhausted, Catherine rationalized her experience as valuable on grounds that every intellectual should have a good dose of bureaucratic responsibility. She was learning things about government that no outsider could possibly understand, and developed a genuine sympathy for the difficulties of public officials. She expected that her new insights would become an asset in her normal role of agitator and heckler.

At the USHA helm, Straus articulated initiatives that were welcomed by the housers. In an effort to cut costs and raise pride among user groups, for example, he urged that building and landscape maintenance be delegated to tenant families. On February 3, 1938, he addressed the Architectural League:

> If the open areas of a project are so arranged as to require maintenance by the management, it will be necessary to employ gardeners whose wages are paid out of rentals. The cost may run from 90 cents to $1.80 per month for the average tenant family. On the other hand, if the space is planned so that it can be allotted to the use of individual tenants, responsibility for maintenance is placed on them. We want to encourage pride of possession in those things of the home which are denied to families compelled to live in the slums. An hour or two a week spent on this maintenance by the tenants is healthful exercise, will tend to foster the pride of ownership, and will serve to keep down the rent.[73]

Straus was dismayed by the scarcity of active recreational opportunities and urged his staff to include open space in public housing projects. Believing that families ought to participate in sports rather than be spectators, he wanted basketball and tennis courts. He also asked for wading and swimming pools whose "location and design should be a matter of first consideration from the moment when the design of the project is first studied. Their large areas – for they should be large – can be used for sailing small boats as well as for wading and paddling."[74] As the nationwide network of local housing authorities developed, Straus continued to stress the importance of site planning and landscaping in order to secure a decent quality of life for low-income families.

On October 29, 1938, with an eye toward public relations, Straus directed Catherine to assemble a pictorial and graphic presentation. He wanted to mount a travelling exhibition of photographs and drawings representing the best in public housing. The Red Hook Housing Project in Brooklyn, built during Straus's tenure as head of the NYC Housing Authority, was selected on its architectural merits to demonstrate good design coupled with social value. Catherine recruited her old friend Ted Kautzky, a well-known delineator, to produce renderings and a model of the project, which housed 2,600 families. She commissioned a variety of visual presentations of USHA projects, including a model of a former slum site (based on WPA archival records and field inspection photographs) for a before-and-after comparison.

Straus believed that cooperation with WPA would be important because that agency was politically powerful and retained considerable housing responsibilities. Catherine agreed that WPA's housing surveys would be useful for the design and execution of projects. It was also hoped that WPA would provide USHA projects with art and sculpture to enhance public housing; it had already produced very effective posters and graphic material for other government agencies. "Why not for us?" Straus asked Catherine in a memo. He proposed a program of statuary to be sponsored by WPA, such as those placed around wading pools in Chicago's WPA housing projects. "Let us obtain similar statuary for our new projects in planning our swimming pools, they ought to be fitted into the surroundings and become an integral part of the original plan."[75] Straus reasoned that cooperation with WPA would save money for the USHA and create goodwill and mutual support in their next thrust for expanded legislation.

Catherine took it a step further. She envisioned working with WPA in four arenas. (1) Research: They would develop methods of effective housing surveys that were appropriate for a variety of local housing authorities; existing criteria for identifying substandard housing conditions were inadequate. (2) Information: They would disseminate nationwide materials such as annotated housing bibliographies that had been prepared in different localities. A comprehensive national bibliography would be created from local lists. (3) Education: WPA would provide posters and coloured broadsheets for use in schools and public buildings. A series of radio broadcasts on housing had been produced in New York City, and Catherine hoped to spread them to other cities. She also proposed that WPA's nursery school programs, adult education classes, and supervised play activities be incorporated in USHA housing projects. (4) Recreation: WPA labour might be used to build furniture for game rooms and playground equipment where project budgets were not able to shoulder the costs. By proposing these ideas, Catherine hoped to co-opt WPA's bureaucracy, which viewed the USHA as competing on its turf. She was attempting to lay the foundation for inter-agency cooperation in the field of housing; to this day, such cooperation remains a challenge to the integrated delivery of programs.

Her ideas were excellent, but moneys were lamentably short in spite of proposed cost-cutting devices. Early 1939 found Catherine once again in the role of political agitator attempting to shepherd a new amendment (S 591) to the US Housing Act of 1937 through the 76th Congress. The money allocated by the 1938 amendment was insufficient to cover the costs of Straus's programs, so he had returned to Congress for more. He now asked for authorization to raise an additional $800 million in bonds, and $45 million in grant contributions. The funds were to be put to several uses. One was to make up the difference between the rent needed to meet maintenance and operating costs, and the money that former slum dwellers were able to pay. Another was to meet new demands from cities in states where new local housing authorities were established after the act's passage; these states had not been covered in the original 1937 allocation.

A third goal of the amendment was to extend program benefits to low-income families in rural areas; $200 million was earmarked. Such an adjustment was necessary, according to the USHA, to acknowledge the contrasting needs of urban and rural families – the former being the chief beneficiaries of subsidies set out in the 1937 act. According to the original legislation, an agency that owned and operated its housing project would lose government subsidy if the project were sold to a third party. Also, families would have to vacate the premises when their income rose beyond a certain maximum. These provisions made sense in an urban setting in order to assure that housing would be maintained for families of low income. The rural situation was different. It was not reasonable to expect a farmer to move out of his farmhouse once his economic situation improved. It was proposed, therefore, that local agencies would use USHA contributions to enable farmers to buy their houses. As well, the amendment would waive the urban requirement of equivalent elimination of slum dwellings.

Catherine's experience of the protracted process of hearings in Congress had taught her to develop her own timetable. She believed that S 591 would pass, eventually, and with the Division of Research and Information in good shape she was able to turn her energies elsewhere.

Her personal relationships, for one thing, had become complicated. She had been involved with an engineer named Jacob (Jake) Crane since the previous December. In the fall of 1938 she wrote to Ahren about Jake, describing him as

one of the few "city planners" worth the name in the country. He is 46 and has been married three times. His first wife died, the other two were divorced, but he's made pretty much of a mess of all three marriages. He's Irish, and just as full of temperamental contradictions in his personal life as he is consistent and hard-boiled in his work. He is a sort of practical radical, but very much against any sort of fancy presumptuous intellectualism (which is good for me, as a matter of fact, and one of the things I like about him). He is in love with me all right, and would probably marry me in the long run, although he is very bitter about marriage and rather hates to get into it again. But – and here is something rather ironic when I think back to Gothenburg, and one of the reasons why I'm writing this all out in such detail – the one really big fundamental thing in Jake's life is his passionate attachment for his two boys, by his first wife. One is 16 and the other is 14, and they are splendid guys. They would always come first – or at least until the boys break away.[76]

Catherine had become spoiled by men who were able to shower their exclusive affections on her, without domestic expectation. "I don't have to get married," she rationalized to Ahren, "in fact there are lots of things against it. On the other hand, when one looks around at unmarried women of 40 and 50, it's pretty appalling. Something happens to them, regardless of whether they have had a good sex life or not. I guess most people need some sort of stable framework in their lives, in order to be complete and free for their real work."[77]

As long as she remained in Washington, Catherine would probably remain in love with Jake, she confessed to Ahren, even though Leon Keyserling would be the better man to marry. What should she do? She sought Ahren's advice on the condition that he *not* urge her to come to Sweden, because "if I did I'd probably just decide I wanted to marry *you* – and most of my present difficulties would just be repeated!"[78]

She was equally torn about her options in fieldwork. In early 1938 the Rockefeller Foundation had offered her a year's fellowship to drive around the country, study, and report on the housing situation. Although the idea appealed to her at the time, she had stayed in Washington to participate in the early stages of the USHA. In declining the Rockefeller grant, she bowed to pressure from colleagues who urged her to get over being an irresponsible intellectual and learn a little discipline.

In the spring of 1939 Catherine dropped the idea of asking for a new

Rockefeller grant and decided instead to complete her fieldwork for the Guggenheim fellowship, which had been interrupted in 1936 by the World's Fair. A visit to Scandinavia and Russia would be essential for the completion of the fellowship. She also had a political agenda. Catherine wanted to be in Stockholm on July 9 to attend a conference of the International Federation of Housing and Town Planning Organizations; her goal was primarily to get the German delegates thrown out. The German regime was systematically undermining the progressive housing programs of the Weimar period, the Nazis having politicized the housing movement through their method of delegate selection. This had to be

FRITZ AND POLLY GUTHEIM AND CATHERINE, SUMMER 1938

In early 1938 the Rockefeller Foundation had offered her a year's fellowship to drive around the country ... In declining the Rockefeller grant, she bowed to pressure from colleagues [including Fritz and Polly Gutheim] who urged her to get over being an irresponsible intellectual and learn a little discipline.

stopped. Catherine wanted to make certain that a decent program would be adopted for the following year's conference in Los Angeles.

Since the Senate had rapidly approved S 591, Catherine was confident the amendment would proceed smoothly through Congress with or without her presence in Washington. She booked a stateroom on the SS *Normandy* sailing June 28, 1939; half in jest, she invited Bohn to come along. When he declined, she invited him to come to Washington to attend the send-off party being given by the Vintons. She wanted to see him before her departure, but he declined this as well, explaining that he had to stay home to address an Ohio Real Estate Board convention on the subject of the amendment. "Really, it is getting impossible, and I think I'll just jump on the boat for Europe," he wrote Catherine. "I am sure that the struggle between Fascists and Communists cannot be half as bad as the struggle between USHA and local Authority bureaucracies."[79] Responding to a direct invitation from the Vintons, Bohn wired: "Unable to attend party tonight. Red tape, USHA's and mine, keeps me tied down. My love to our little girl ... My Gosh! Think of a Bauer leaving the country while the

Housing Bill is pending. Oh, for the good old days when all the housers of the country could comfortably hold their convention in a telephone booth."[80]

Catherine intended to stay in London for just a few days to revisit British housing, then depart for Stockholm. But her carefully planned program was torpedoed on the second night of her stay. Ernestine Fantl Carter, a friend from New York City's MOMA days, now married to a British architect, gave a dinner party to introduce Catherine to some of their friends. Shortly after midnight, Ernestine's brother-in-law drove Catherine back to her hotel in a raging storm. Suddenly a taxi spun around in front of them, and Carter jammed on his brakes to avoid a collision. The car skidded wildly and struck an oncoming truck, broadside. Catherine, sitting in the front seat, suffered gashes on her chin, forehead, and both shins, a torn lower lip, and, worst, the loss of three upper front teeth. Stitches were required for the gashes. "I was dripping blood and they put me in another car and took me to St. George's hospital," she wrote to her parents and Bohn. "How on earth I got banged on the forehead *and* the chin without even scratching my nose is hard to figure out."[81] Her good humour remained intact.

The hospital to which Catherine was delivered at 1:00 a.m. turned out to be more terrifying than the wounds. She was reminded of a morgue or cathedral crypt, and the young doctor who sewed her up did nothing to set her at ease. She was brought up to an overcrowded charity ward where a grim-looking woman laid a little bag of lavender, with a Bible attached, on her stomach.

Ernestine applied pressure to have her friend moved to one of the hospital's very few, very small private rooms and, after discussing the matters of plastic surgery and new teeth with the attending doctors, suggested to Catherine that she make do with temporary measures in England. After the swelling diminished, she could be fitted with a dental plate that would last until she returned home. Catherine fretted about the cost of dental restoration back in the States. "It's too bad I didn't get that traveler's insurance we were talking about," she told her parents.[82] The following November, in Washington, a highly regarded specialist would fix her up for $150.

News of the accident spread rapidly. Bohn expressed his sympathy in the words of a true houser: "I didn't quite realize how articulate housers could be until the news of your accident arrived here. So many nice things were said about you, and sincere concern over your welfare was expressed by everyone. This, you must admit is most unusual where a crusader is involved. Only too often, we have only fair-weather friends and at the end of the crusade we are remembered only by those we have opposed and they are, of course, forever against us."[83]

Catherine was disappointed:

I was hoping you would write me about everything, particularly my spiritual beauty, and that it won't be too bad once they get around to replacing my dazzling smile. Coleman Woodbury has been visiting me in the hospital. He looked to me more neurotic than ever. I keep feeling I ought to get out of bed and straighten something out for him. I wish I had been struck in Stockholm rather than here. The English and I don't understand each other. I have insulted all the doctors trying to make them explain what the hell they're up to. In dealing with a real professional gentleman in England you are expected to close your eyes and Believe.[84]

Bob Marshall was more romantic than Bohn. "Personally I don't care how good or bad a job the doctor did in sewing up the cuts on your face and lip," he wrote, "because scarred or unscarred, I'll still want to kiss you just as badly."

Feeling personally responsible for the accident, Ernestine became Catherine's handmaiden, spoiling her thoroughly until the patient became impatient to resume her journey. She insisted that Catherine spend three weeks recuperating at her home, after three weeks in the hospital. Now six weeks behind schedule, and having missed the Stockholm conference, Catherine was eager to see the north of England before proceeding to Sweden. She persuaded Ernestine to let her go. "I had a hectic two days in the north but 'did up' the housing in Leeds, Manchester and Liverpool," she wrote her parents.[85] "The general level of design is really quite a lot better in all three of these towns than London – 'dull but decent.'"

Back in Washington, Catherine's colleagues expected the amendment to the Housing Act to be adopted by Congress as easily as it had passed the Senate. In anticipation of success, they threw a party for Senator Wagner to acknowledge his steadfast support. "Think of it," Bohn reported to Catherine, "Morgenthau [Secretary of Treasury and an avowed conservative] attending a victory dinner for housing. You should have seen the gentleman squirm when Dorothy Schoell inadvertently started to talk to him about housing. He yelled out, 'Please lady, leave me alone. I am for housing, but I don't want anyone else to talk to me about it. Didn't I go out on a limb when I urged Congress to vote for the bill?'"[86]

The party was premature. The amendment failed the next day in the House, in spite of strong and eloquent support from members such as Sabath of Illinois, McCormack of Massachusetts, and Marcantonio of New York, a champion of slum dwellers. Opposition came not only from traditional conservative quarters who believed this was a socialist scheme, but from Democrats, including Albert Gore of Tennessee. He argued that the cost of sixty-year contracts with local housing authorities would be in the trillions of dollars. "My 18-months-old baby will be lucky to live to see one of these contracts consummated. It's ridiculous," declared the father of the future vice-president of the United States. Gore had done his homework when he told the House about a project, built at a cost of $6,710 per family unit, to re-house slum dwellers. There was no evidence, he said, that any slum dwellers had been re-housed in even one of these projects. He accused Straus of dealing in misinformation.

Indeed, Straus had not done his homework. At House hearings devoted to these projects he had been asked how many occupants came from the demolished slum areas.

"I do not know. I can find out. It is not very important," was Straus's reply.

"I thought it was important!" roared Gore.[87]

The House voted the bill down 192 to 169; 67 abstained. A bitter Keyserling charged that the amendment failed because it had been coupled with a Spending-Lending bill. He described the scene to Catherine:

The Housing Bill got held up in the House by as queer a co-operation of bungling and incapacity as ever you saw. We made every effort to have the Housing Bill brought up before the "Lending-Spending Bill," but the White House disagreed and all the leaders on the Hill were convinced that the Lending Bill could pass easily and that would make it easier for the Housing Bill, but that the Housing Bill if brought up first would lose by about 2 to 1. Well the Lending Bill was brought up and was denied a rule by a vote of 193 to 167, completely justifying our predictions. Then the leaders began insisting that the Housing Bill shall be held over until the next session. We finally got the White House to instruct the leaders to bring it up. It was brought up under more peculiar circumstances. The day before it was brought up the Chairman of the Rules Committee, Mr. Sabath of Illinois, and the House Majority Leader, Mr. Rayburn of Texas, issued statements to the press that the bill could not possibly pass. It didn't.[88]

Bohn was dejected. "All of us could have done more along the lines followed in support of the old Ellenbogen and Wagner bills. However, there is no use in my telling *you* the handicap one works under when one is a bureaucrat."[89] He told Catherine he had sent out some last-minute telegrams to all the Republican members of Congress, signing his own name and pointing out that housing was a nonpartisan matter that Republicans could well afford to support even if they were against Spending-Lending and the New Deal. "By the time we asked for their assistance, the cause was lost due to the opposition of both Democrats and Republicans to a Spending-Lending Bill."[90]

Devastated, Catherine blamed herself for not staying in Washington to lobby for the amendment. She continued her European tour, already a month behind schedule due to her hospitalization. In order to reach Moscow as soon as possible, she raced through Scandinavia, stopping in Gothenburg long enough to spend a weekend bicycling and swimming with Uno Ahren and his new wife, Kerstin. Much later Catherine learned that Kerstin had envied her ability to converse on technical matters with her husband. Prompted by the experience, Kerstin enrolled in a political science class where she was forced to deliver lectures. Feeling empowered and more of an intellectual equal of her husband, Kerstin confessed to Catherine: "I wish you were here to give me a bit of an inferiority complex occasionally. It is always good for me to be shaken up a bit by meeting swell people."[91]

Moscow was to be Catherine's base for a month-long tour of Russia, but fate intervened once again. She arrived in Moscow on September 1, the day Germany attacked Poland; England and France handed Hitler an ultimatum that led to the declaration of war two days later. The American ambassador informed Catherine she would have to leave the country immediately. Crushed at the thought of missing not only the Russian leg of her journey but Warsaw and Berlin as well, she decided to take a chance on being thrown out. Promising to maintain contact with Ambassador Steinhart, she managed to spend five days in Moscow and three in Leningrad before being pressed to leave.

CATHERINE, C. 1939

Bob Marshall wrote: "Personally I don't care how good or bad a job the doctor did in sewing up your face ... I still want to kiss you just as badly."

6

Transition Years (1939-42)

Urban Planner

"Functional design" (including the rationalization of site planning) has very largely been a reaction against the silliness and waste of the individualistic era.

Catherine Bauer

In one short week Catherine gathered some extraordinary impressions of Russia. Initially confounded by the strange language and alphabet, she was soon able to decipher "Academy of Architecture," "gastronomy, fruit and wine," and "Metropole," among other daily essentials, and felt at home. In her bewilderment she identified with the strangers who had come to North America's shores a generation earlier – the greenhorn immigrants who "felt lost when arriving in New York in the '90s."[1] Almost anywhere else in the world, the American tourist was considered special, but not in Russia, she noted, except "when the little girls in the street point enviously at my stockings, and the little boys tried to beg, borrow, or steal my fountain pen."[2]

She was struck by the sharp contrast between overwhelmingly large new buildings, most of them unfinished, and old dilapidated ones. Both Leningrad and Moscow were characterized by noise, dirt, and a retreating sea of slums. Moscow appeared to be a gigantic construction site where vast rows of new apartment blocks marched down endless streets, bulldozing ramshackle houses as they went. Thousands of dwellings were torn down despite a severe housing shortage, making way for "miles and miles of avenues and squares on the scale of the Place de la Concorde." Despite the social disruption, Catherine admired the design of the big, new apartment buildings, some of them as tall as twenty stories with "lifts, cross-ventilation, and only two apartments per floor." The apartments had three-metre-high ceilings and rooms that seemed bigger than their

American equivalents. Kitchen and bathroom equipment was modern and efficient.

Catherine was also impressed by the country's innovative financing. The capital cost of construction was written off as a public expenditure and rent was calculated as a flat 10 percent of the tenant's income. Rent bore no relation to construction cost. When Catherine asked "who gets the new dwellings?" the answer was "why, the best workers of course!" Her incredulity was countered with "and what would you do?"[3]

Construction progressed at a remarkable pace in response to urgent demand for more and better accommodation. Ingenious equipment, such as "fancy derricks, and all kinds of belts and conveyers" ensured that apartment buildings were completed within five or six months. In contrast to their functional interiors, the exterior appearances of buildings were "mostly pretty awful," with the exception of the new Lenin Library in Moscow. The exterior detailing of apartment blocks reflected a popular reaction against modern western design introduced by Le Corbusier. Catherine felt that the Russian resistance to modernism was a mark of due democratic process. Earlier buildings, designed under German and French influence, now looked very seedy; the recently imported German architects were far too academic and theoretical for modern Russian tastes; and Le Corbusier's severe style did nothing to soften the impact of the critical food and housing shortages of the last two decades – a period from which Russia was only beginning to emerge. What was called for was a grander, showier architectural style to reflect this age of optimism. In observing this, Catherine had a profound realization:

> *"Functional design" (including the rationalization of site planning) has very largely been a reaction against the silliness and waste of the individualistic era. We know we have plenty of resources, both materials and skills, but what we want to dramatize is that we know how to use them, simply and directly and efficiently. But that's not the way they feel in Russia at all. They haven't the least sentiment for anything "minimum." Quite the contrary. Circumstances may force them to pinch or scrape here and there but the* standard, *the working ideal, is always something super. It gives them a positive pleasure to waste space, and hang unnecessary trimmings on the outside of things.*[4]

In spite of their recent military alliance with Germany, Russians still harboured an anti-German bias. The most popular game at an amusement park consisted of throwing rings over caricatured heads of Hitler, Mussolini, and the Japanese Emperor. While most Russians held a cynical attitude toward all western politics, they were most critical of England and

Germany because they expected to have to fight them some day. Most agreed that in a bona fide war they would want Germany beaten, since that would produce a revolution in Germany. And if it looked as though Germany would win, the USSR would intervene, preferring that England and France not become fascist.

Catherine searched for signs of democracy without success, but she was somewhat encouraged at the absence of "the uncomfortable feeling of a Papa-and-Fuehrer complex, or a mystical religious subjection."[5] She saw that the USSR was on a war footing, prepared to vanquish the enemy, whoever it might be, by perfect coordination and ruthless discipline, and she wondered whether a great passive monster could be turned into a productive machine capable of producing a great modern civilization. She predicted that the USSR would survive in terms of production and distribution, but at the cost of freedom and social unity.

American engineers in Moscow assured her that the Soviets had mastered production processes, though results were often compromised by bungled maintenance and operation. This was best illustrated by the new Russian cars, which were almost always dented by bad driving and limped along on incompetent repairs.

Catherine identified two types of Americans stricken with a romantic fervour for Russia: the hard-boiled midwestern engineers, totally apolitical but very much at home in a frontier environment, and the "little Commie gals from the Bronx, who just adore the worst buildings and for whom the Revolution will henceforth mean Subway stations like Moscow's."[6]

She briefly visited Moscow's huge annual Agricultural Exposition where each Soviet republic filled a building with produce, artifacts, and other proofs of economic and social success. She was enchanted by the sight of thousands of peasants in their best finery, looking very proud and pleased with evident progress. Moscow's nightlife also intrigued her. She reported a midnight encounter at the famed Metropole Hotel with a self-styled composer who declared that "he loved to practice ze English, that he would pay for my drink, and what was my room number?"

The quality of services was grim. Waiters in the Intourist Hotels were dolts and incompetents, shops were dreary, dirty, crowded, and badly managed even though goods were abundant. Shortages of staff and floor space resulted in long waiting lines. The prohibition against photographing anything irritated Catherine, and she took fiendish pleasure in snapping forbidden pictures of a Youth Day parade, the Kremlin, Red Square, and the Moscow Hotel from the roof of the US embassy. She had them developed immediately and would smuggle them out of the country around her waist.

The embassy was suffering a bad case of jitters and was pressuring all

Americans to leave the country as quickly as possible. Ambassador Steinhart, a career diplomat, anticipated imminent Soviet encroachment into Poland. Catherine doubted this, "unless Russia could do it without any risk of getting into the war." She was not impressed by Steinhart whom she called a "petulant jackass – the worst guy imaginable to be in that job." Events proved Steinhart correct.

Under ambassadorial pressure, Catherine considered a trans-Siberian escape, via Vladivostok, but Intourist would not sell her a ticket on the Trans-Siberian Railway and refused to change her exit visa from west to east. Moscow fascinated her, and she considered "getting stuck in Russia for a year or more" should war engulf the USSR. She wanted to learn the language properly, and thought that a year or more of research and close observation would produce fascinating insights into housing, building, and planning under radically different circumstances.

But Steinhart prevailed, and Catherine flew back to Stockholm. The contrast was extraordinary. "It was a magnificent summer day and Stockholm looked like a glistening newly painted toy town – a progressive Montessori toy," she wrote in a letter to Jake Crane. Comparing Sweden with Russia was "comparing a beautiful little scientific experiment carried out under perfectly controlled laboratory conditions with an enormous crowd of people yelling in fifty different languages, milling around for all kinds of different purposes, with unimaginable ideas in their heads."[7]

In their own ways, both countries were pursuing material culture and general social welfare consistently and positively. Her Soviet Union adventure proved to be enormously stimulating but taxed her talent for arranging and rearranging plans at a moment's notice. She welcomed the dull routine that greeted her in Stockholm. She went to Gothenburg and persuaded the Ahren family to take a couple of days' walk in the country, to help her recover from Russia.

The end of September found a very disappointed Catherine aboard the *Kungsholm*. Once more fieldwork for her Guggenheim Foundation project had been interrupted. "Alas, if I had only been able to keep to my original schedule," she reported to foundation secretary Henry Moe, "I would have made that trip, arriving in Paris just about the day that they declared war! But the Gods were not with me, or at least they had their own plans."[8] She prevailed upon the board for an extension of the grant.

In October Catherine returned to Washington and resumed her USHA responsibilities. She was encouraged to share her newly acquired information in a series of public lectures, including an important talk at a conference of Ohio Housing Authorities in Cincinnati. Ernie Bohn had arranged the date, which included a formal dinner during opening ceremonies. "Does 'dinner' mean dinner dress?" she responded. "I have a very kitschy gold one which I would enjoy flashing in the provinces."[9]

Thanks to her lucid delivery and facility with numbers, the speech was an unqualified success. Catherine described Europe's housing movement during the years of 1919 to 1939 as representing concrete progress with a visible lasting achievement. "Whatever the future of liberal democratic governments may be, the achievements in housing must certainly be chalked up to its credit."[10] She cited England as Europe's most dramatic example in quantitative terms. Of the twelve million dwellings in England, four million had been built since 1919. This meant that one-third of all English families were living in comparatively new and modern housing:

Of the 4,000,000 new homes 2,900,000 were built by private enterprise, and are for the most part occupied by upper income families, but this leaves more than 1,100,000 new homes which were built by English local authorities, aided by the state under a plan similar to that of the USHA, and which are now let at low rents to low income families. In short "public housing." Almost one-tenth of all the families in England live in these houses and there are many places, big cities and rural districts alike, where as many as one-fifth of all the families live in public housing projects.[11]

The English rate of production was particularly significant because it had not been diminished by "feverish rearmament or the free market ideologies of England's conservative central government or its equally conservative local governments." During the twelve months preceding the outbreak of war, a record number of 102,000 low-rent homes were completed. This represented double the average production for the two decades between 1919 and 1939. By September 1939, 50,000 more low-rent homes were under construction.

Catherine berated her listeners. "Quantitatively, we have nothing to compare with this English achievement as yet. Our entire present program, which will have taken three years or so to carry out, will provide hardly more than 160,000 dwellings. The present rate of English public housing production, proportioned to our population, would mean a rate of more than 300,000 dwelling units per year in the United States."

She had less praise for the architectural aspects of England's new housing stock. It had "homespun virtues such as adequate space, light, air, solidity and bathrooms, but if you're looking for fresh ideas and design, look somewhere else. It is decent, but it is also rather dull." One exception was the experimental work of a group of modern architects who practised under the name of Tecton. Their apartment buildings stood out, in large part for their use of balconies. "Once we have satisfied ourselves that the maximum rock-bottom construction economies have been achieved," Catherine told the housing authorities, "it may be possible to permit ourselves the luxury of a few balconies!"

Typically English housing was being built in long rows of brick buildings with high space standards, both inside and out. Most units had three bedrooms with large windows, at a density of twelve houses per acre, something Catherine thought Americans ought to emulate. In Manchester and Leeds she had found large suburban communities that included highly subsidized low-rental units with special provisions for the elderly. There she encountered low-income tenants' associations for the first time and was impressed by their political prowess. They had a "salutary influence on the somewhat undemocratic management policies of most English authorities." Planning, she felt, was the major flaw in England during the interwar years. Slum clearance projects had not been considered (possibly because of the expense) and new housing had not been integrated with related social facilities.

Catherine also relayed to her audience the fresh ideas and good design she had found in Sweden. A ten-year residential building boom that rehoused about one-quarter of the population had produced well-designed structures with excellent layouts. In Sweden, Catherine was pleased to report, there was little contrast between public and private housing. During her trip in 1930 she had met young architects just out of school, many of whom were now in positions of authority. A very important point, which she frequently stressed, was that the best European architects were retained by local authorities to design public housing, whereas their American counterparts were mainly retained by the wealthy for their individual housing needs.

She credited the high quality of new housing in Sweden to "a firm base of municipal control of land development, including density, building heights, and site planning [thanks to municipal ownership of] all the vacant land ripe for development." With public land ownership, municipalities could determine the allocation of land, including which areas should be urbanized (and when), which reserved for agriculture, and which held as permanent open space. Sweden's public housing program was impressive because it was geared to large families with three or more children. Annual subsidies reflected the number of children in a family.

Middle-income Swedes were also accommodated by public housing policies, far better than were their American counterparts for whom virtually nothing new was being built. Swedish housing cooperatives were springing up thanks to public financing at low interest rates, the availability of municipal land at low prices, and public site planning.

Drawing frequently on her European experience, as she did in Cincinnati,

Catherine expanded her housing concerns to the larger urban community. From the very start of her participation in framing the 1937 Housing Act, Catherine had intended to go beyond the provision of shelter by encouraging neighbourhood planning and community services. Recognizing the act's shortcomings in this area, she lobbied for amendments to expand the federal housing initiative by establishing tools for controlling land use and construction on a regional basis. She continued to work for legislation, beyond the provision of housing, that would encourage balanced communities and neighbourhood planning.

A balanced community was one that provided shelter, play, and work for all families, regardless of income, within the context of a metropolitan planning and transportation system. Poor people needed more than a roof over their heads. To be successful, housing projects must be linked to community facilities: parks, playgrounds, social centres, clinics, and schools. Breadwinners needed easy access to their place of employment. Catherine was convinced that these changes could only be brought about by strong local planning programs, directed by professional staffs. She believed that federal housing legislation could be used to launch such local planning organizations.

Catherine's lobbying efforts for community planning bore fruit during the early 1940s when the pressure of war spawned federal incentives for land use planning. Historically, city planning had been entrusted to planning consultants, hired by agencies for specific municipal schemes that generally flowed from a "city-beautiful" format. There were few full-time municipal planners on staff, and they were usually attached to engineering departments or traffic and transportation divisions. During the 1930s, through conditional PWA or WPA grants, municipalities began to select public works projects within a planning framework. Under federal pressure, during and shortly after the Second World War, community planning gradually became institutionalized as part of local government.

Ironically, the Lanham Act of 1940, written by Democratic Representative Fritz Lanham of Texas – an opponent of public housing – proved to be a major catalyst for community planning in America. The act provided funds for construction of federally owned housing for wartime workers throughout the United States. Although the original legislation contained a provision against subsidies for low-income housing, a 1941 amendment provided the crucial bridge: Congress allocated $150 million for the construction of community facilities to supplement defense workers' dwellings, setting a significant precedent of government subsidies to communities, the benefits of which spilled far beyond the targeted population. Between 1941 and 1946, the Lanham Act funded the construction of 1,149 schools, 905 water and sewer facilities, 874 hospitals, 776 recreation facilities, 160 fire and police stations, 90 child care facilities, and 86 street and highway projects. Many projects required financial contributions from local government; upon completion, facilities reverted to municipalities.[12]

Mayors throughout the United States welcomed the new community-focused public works initiatives. Grant applications had to be submitted within a planning framework, and community participation was required. In fact, local planning was essential: building materials were strictly rationed by the US War Production Board, and the decision to build houses in a given community became a war decision. The result was an uneasy coalition between the War Production Board and the National Housing Administration in ensuring localities' commitment to planning for "better housing for better living through better neighborhoods, and to encourage them to think of total housing needs in an area, so that the parts of their local goals will fit together and make sense."[13]

Federal largesse was a welcome carrot for business leaders, real estate developers, and housing enthusiasts, all of whom gradually joined in promoting postwar planning. During wartime, municipal planning departments, operating under federal incentives, became integral parts of local governments. The Lanham Act encouraged Congress to underwrite the preparation and implementation of local plans directly. This led to the creation of a reservoir of detailed public works ready for postwar planning and construction.

The War Mobilization and Reconversion Act of 1944 extended temporary federal aid to local planning agencies. The act, terminated in 1947, attempted to ease the transition from a wartime to a peacetime economy by providing loans and some grants for "planning public works."[14] Between 1944 and 1947 Washington approved more than seven thousand applications for repayable planning advances, resulting in $61 million in loans to hundreds of communities. During 1946, market housing starts passed one million units, reaffirming a free market and private home ownership.

Local land use planning got another boost with the Highway Act of 1944, which provided $125 million over a three-year period to improve urban roadways. While federal funds had been used for highway construction since 1916, the 1944 act specifically provided money for "comprehensive surveys of traffic needs in urban areas, hitherto an almost untouched urban area."[15]

Further federal incentives for community planning included Federal Housing Agency (FHA) insured mortgages for veterans. President Truman's Veterans Administration enabled returning veterans to borrow the price of a future house with no down payment. The FHA-insured mortgages led to zoning and subdivision regulations that became common planning instruments throughout the urban US.

Full-time municipal planning staffs grew rapidly, leading to increased membership in professional organizations such as the American Society of Planning Officials (ASPO), the National Association of Housing Officials (NAHO), and the International City Managers Association, all headquartered in the same building in Chicago. Commitment to city planning and the increase in professional staffs was particularly evident in medium-sized towns. In 1941 the total expenditure on planning in the US, by towns with populations over 25,000, was $1.2 million; by 1948 comparable expenditures more than tripled to $3.8 million.[16] In 1940 San Francisco's planning department consisted of three people (including a stenographer) with a budget of $15,000; by 1948 the staff had grown to twenty-six with a budget of $300,000.[17]

Local planning, fully integrated into municipal administration, was further encouraged by programs emanating from the Wagner-Ellender-Taft (WET) Act of 1949. Federal support for local planning grew under the aegis of "intergovernmental relations" during the 1940s – the origins of what has been called the contemporary "grants economy." Federal intergovernmental grants-in-aid proved to be an effective means "to stimulate, support, or otherwise influence the policy decisions of other governments."[18] On state and local government levels, these grants-in-aid brought major changes in policies and priorities; through them the federal government exerted significant national influence on local urban affairs.

Catherine's vision of community and neighbourhood planning as a component of housing policy had been achieved. She understood the strategic importance of federal incentives in overcoming opposition to public housing by local real estate lobbies. She correctly predicted that these incentives would counteract opposition to public housing by realtors, chambers of commerce, and local building industries. For a while some of these groups formed local planning coalitions, ready to take advantage of federal dollars. They did not last long, however, because they failed to share a common ideology regarding federal funding for housing. Soon local support for federally funded public housing also declined, while the responsibility for land-use planning by local governments became firmly rooted within municipal administrations. The need for explicit subsidies on behalf of the poor would be repeatedly challenged throughout the next decades.

PROFESSOR

Miss Bauer became one of the first Americans to touch upon the connection between organized labor and low rent housing.

UNIVERSITY OF
CALIFORNIA BULLETIN

Toward the end of 1939 Catherine began to feel burnt out as a political insider in Washington. She confided to her good friend, Bob Marshall, that she was ready to pursue new directions, preferably at some distance from the capital. Between western wilderness trips, Marshall often visited Washington to report to his boss, Secretary of the Interior Harold Ickes. On these occasions, he would take Catherine out to dine and dance. She was able to relax with a man not obsessed by housing politics, and he saw in her "the perfect partner of the wilderness, appreciative and practical and always good natured." They were planning a trip together to the southeastern Utah desert before the year's end, but on November 11 a shocking note arrived from Leon Keyserling, informing Catherine that Marshall had died early that morning of a heart attack in a sleeper on the train between New York City and Washington. He was thirty-eight.

A condolence letter from Catherine's mother arrived two days after Marshall's death. "Father and I thought of you immediately," Bertie wrote, prompted by the obituary in the *New York Times*, "knowing what an awful shock it would be to you to lose such a great friend without any warning, so suddenly."[19] Her mother's instinct was correct – she was in shock. Catherine's letter home crossed her mother's. "I went out with him Thursday [the night before he left for New York] and expected to see him again yesterday, he seemed completely healthy as usual. It was really quite a bad shock."

In all her correspondence Catherine had never mentioned Marshall in terms of marriage. She seemed to be more drawn to older men, and he was wed to the wilderness. After leaving $3,000 in his will to a mountain guide, he divided his sizable estate into four parts. One-fourth was for the establishment of a trust to "safeguard and advance the cause of civil liberties in the United States."[20] Another quarter established a Wilderness Fund, from which the Wilderness Society received a generous endowment. The rest was left to his family. Catherine bid farewell to Marshall in a two-column letter published in the December 27 issue of the *New Republic*. Ten others, including Thomas and Catherine Blaisdell, co-signed the letter that clearly carried Catherine's stamp. "He would have deplored any time, space or energy devoted to a solemn eulogy," she wrote. "He would have advised his friends to take a thirty-mile walk, get dressed up and go dancing, or engage in a good rousing fight with the most obstructive stuffed shirt available."[21] In April Marshall's brother, James, offered Catherine a commission to write a biography. After seriously thinking about the idea for two months, she was forced to decline due to other commitments, but offered to work with another biographer. A wilderness region in South Dakota was named in Marshall's memory.

An invitation from Robert G. Sproul, president of the University of California in Berkeley, missed Catherine in Europe and finally reached her in Washington on her return late in 1939. The letter would radically change her life. "Last Sunday I found an old dead letter from the President of the University of California," she wrote to Ernie Bohn, "asking me to be a visiting lecturer in housing, apparently with about three hours work per week, and seemingly for the sum of $5,000 for six months. I haven't been able to think of any argument against it so perhaps you'd better wire me if you can think of any."[22] No objections surfaced, and she accepted the offer just before Christmas, taking a leave of absence from her job at the US Housing Authority. One last invitation to Bohn to come to Washington before her departure was greeted with a bon voyage note from Cleveland and a promise to visit her in California.

On Saturday, December 30, she set out in a bright red roadster convertible on a route that would take her through New Orleans and Austin, near the country she had explored with Marshall. She drove past swamps, mountains, rivers, decaying slums, agricultural co-ops, and horrible shack towns for migrant workers in California. Here and there she picked up companions who shared sightseeing and inspection tours of Farm Security housing projects and other recent planning achievements. She was stunned by the scenery, especially Death Valley, its "highness and lowness, heat and cold, dryness and wetness, roughness and flatness, bareness and luxuriance."[23] The trip was so splendid that Catherine resolved to spend a year, some time soon, just driving around. Upon arriving in the San Francisco Bay Area, she saw "swell redwood architecture without any Le Corbusier tour-de-forces," as she put it in a letter to Uno Ahren. "Had a first swim (naked, remembering Sweden) in the Pacific, and felt like a new person." To her parents, she wrote: "It's so bright and sunny that it makes you believe all the California promoters you have ever heard. Everything is bright green and lush and beautiful."

She reported to Keyserling on the many housing projects she saw en route – and on the local authorities who didn't mind telling her how disgusted they were with Washington bureaucrats. "Even the move to regional decentralization had not produced better projects or made local authorities happier with their role in the housing process."[24]

"Rosenberg Lecturer in the Public Social Services" stated the University of California press release announcing Catherine's appointment to the Department of Social Welfare. For the spring semester she would be taking the place of a Yugoslav academic, Andrija Stampar, who was called home at the outbreak of war in Europe. Within six months her title would change to Rosenberg Professor.

"Miss Bauer became one of the first Americans to touch upon the connection between organized labor and low rent housing," the release remarked. It described her travels in Europe, where she had learned about housing, modern architecture, and city planning, and her Guggenheim fellowship, the first ever awarded in the field of architecture or housing. It also embroidered her list of published books by adding three titles besides *Modern Housing*. She would offer two courses, one for "upper division and graduate students on the general problems of housing, and the second on housing policy, open to qualified graduate students."

Catherine doubted her competence in the face of this new challenge. The courses were too ambitious for an under-prepared, nonacademic person whose only experience lay in lobbying Congress and pushing labour leaders into action on housing. Her fears were unfounded, as this first foray into teaching proved to be a turning point in the life of a woman whose career was propelled forward by daunting challenges.

"I have always wanted to know California better," Catherine assured President Sproul, "and in particular wanted to view the current housing situation in America from the local point of view instead of from Washington." She added optimistically, "the preparation of lectures will force me to re-write my old book, something I could probably never achieve if I stay in Washington."[25]

She voiced some concerns to Sproul about her classes: Would they be small enough to run as a seminar? What would be the backgrounds of the students? Were fieldwork assignments possible? She hoped to engage students in practical studies and surveys that would be useful to local housing authorities in California. Anxious about the extent of housing material in the library, she submitted a list of new publications for her courses. Her questions foreshadowed the focus and style in which she would teach housing to students with broad backgrounds and varied interests. Fieldwork assignments leading to practical results would become a major teaching technique.

President Sproul handed Catherine's questions to Professor H.M. Cassidy, chairman of the Division of Social Welfare. He advised her that she would be offering a lecture course on "The Housing Movement" and a seminar on problems of housing policy. Fearing the class size could be up to two hundred students, she suggested: "It could be broken up into four-week units with six straight lectures during the first three weeks, followed by one week of group conferences. Each conference group should not be larger than about 25 and each student should be asked to come prepared on several concise topics for which systematic reading assignments would be made. Each conference hour could then be divided up among the different topics and one student asked to report on each for five minutes, followed by a discussion from the whole group acting as a panel."[26] Catherine intended to get students involved in the substance of housing by focusing their attention on solutions to specific problems. She restricted her seminar to twenty students with certain prerequisites; their challenge would be to cooperate with local housing authorities in the Bay region on course-related projects.

Cassidy's wife offered to scout out an appropriate vacant flat or bungalow for the new faculty member. "I would like to live out where there is space and a view," Catherine told her. "I have never been to Berkeley but assume there must be something to look at around there. Two rooms, kitchenette and bath is ample space."[27]

Professor Cassidy offered Catherine a teaching assistant. She asked for one with a background in economics rather than political science, but the most important qualification was a broad and realistic interest in social policies. She viewed housing as a complicated discipline, cutting across numerous fields. A teaching assistant with common sense and curiosity would be an asset.

From the outset of her academic career, Catherine made a habit of consulting many of her housing associates, such as Clarence Stein, of the Regional Planning Association of New York, Charles Abrams, who taught at the New School of Social Research, and Coleman Woodbury, NAHO's executive director. All were happy to offer assistance, and some, including Stein, sent volumes of lecture material from his own courses.[28] Over the next two decades, many of her associates and former allies in Washington appeared at her seminars as guest lecturers.

The beautiful, lively houser from the East was toasted almost nightly during her first ten days in the Bay Area. The difference between life in Washington and the new formalities of academia amused Catherine. She wrote a long letter to Keyserling describing her first impressions. Berkeley was "much more foreign than Sweden or even Russia. I have worn evening clothes Monday, Thursday, Friday and Saturday nights. The first night I was just dancing in San Francisco with housers. But the food was bona fide French and the nightclub atmosphere pure jaded New York. I dined informally but politely with four rather gay female professors and proceeded to a meeting of the Committee on Agricultural Labor, presided over by a crabby male professor (I foresee that The Women are going to be the best on the whole)."[29]

Soon afterwards she was escorted to a formal dinner party by "a refined, arty, fairyish, but up on things architectural professor who gave a course in Group Housing," she told Keyserling. "Full of rich people of a mildly Bohemian cast, including of all things, Tommy Church, whom I knew on a crazy bicycle trip in Brittany in 1927 and who is now *the* West Coast landscape architect with a snappy rich wife in Balenciaga clothes. (He used to be rather earnest and pathetic: it was the other guy I fell for on that expedition – but *he's* still a W.P.A. artist.)."

After dinner the party moved to an opening of a show of locally owned modern art at the San Francisco Museum. Catherine was impressed. No American city outside New York could make such a dazzling display of modern art, right out of its own overstuffed living rooms and closets. One evening was spent with "some very smart, sophisticated people who sounded progressive until you brought up something concrete, and then it was suddenly discovered that this or that lady was the scioness of the west coast lumber interests, and that one had been married to Hearst, and practically all of the men seemed to be lawyers who made their living by representing somebody against the NLRB [National Labor Relations Board]."

Her first Saturday night was the most interesting: a dinner party for eight female professors "whose average age was about 59." The party was held in Catherine's honour, and she observed to Keyserling that several of her hosts were "very distinguished in that saintly, female professor way, and I would say that practically all of them were extremely intelligent." A Sunday luncheon on January 21, 1940, was at the home of Alice Griffith, a member of the San Francisco Housing Commission. There Catherine met "Bill Wooster, the well known modern architect of these parts."[30]

Driven by terror about her courses and her lack of preparation, Catherine declined any more social invitations. She did not eschew outdoor activities, however, and often joined her students and other young faculty members on cycling tours to explore the rugged Pacific coast around Marin County. She was usually the only woman in the group, but easily kept up with the men and earned their respect when she dived, alone, into the icy Pacific. They could not know that she had taught swimming in frigid Maine lakes during her late teens – and enjoyed cold morning showers.

After living at the Women's Faculty Club for a couple of weeks, Catherine was delighted to move to 2525 Hill Court. She described to Keyserling

a perfect little house: near the campus but on the side of a mountain, with a view on three sides all over Berkeley and the Bay, and including living room, *bedroom, dining room, automatic furnace, terrace, garden, radio, an excellent economics library, rather nice old furniture (most of which I will move into the basement), a garage that I won't ever be able to drive into, real linen and sterling silver – all for $55 a month excluding utilities! If you come out I'll give you a dinner party – as I also inherited a maid with the house. So when will you come out?[31]*

CATHERINE, C. 1940

She often joined her students and other young faculty members on cycling tours to explore the rugged Pacific coast around Marin County.

This might have been a revisit to the wonderful apartment she had found in 1927 on Île Saint Louis in Paris, but for the maid, who soon revealed herself to be a tyrant. She prepared all the meals, but her rigid adherence to a strict dining schedule made Catherine's life impossible. The new professor often came home late, after student conferences or faculty meetings, to be greeted with a silent glare and a cold meal. Overcome by childish guilt she would virtually prostrate herself before the maid with apologies and promises that this would never happen again. Of course it often did, and Catherine soon found new, smaller accommodations at 1801 Highland Place, where she cooked for herself and kept her own hours.

In contrast to her lively social life, she found campus life at the University of California almost too serious. Academically and intellectually most students had unexpectedly high qualifications. Many were quite poor and, she reported, became interested in housing because of very bad campus housing conditions. On the other hand, faculty members were well-dressed, well-housed, and "well fed aristocrats, a contrast with Vassar."[32]

About one hundred students enrolled in Catherine's two-hour lecture course; for her seminar she selected twenty-three students from among three times as many applicants. Included were graduate students "and even some instructors from Public Health, Public Administration, Economics, Social Service, but just one lonely architect."[33] She missed Keyserling and begged him to "let me know you're still alive and remember me, so sit right down babee and write me. Washington seems awfully far away ... I seem to miss it and you."

Keyserling kept Catherine informed about the housing scene and Washington's social activities. He was pessimistic about resubmitting S 591 before Congress because, though "not very many people seem to be against housing, and there seem to be enough votes to pass the bill, nobody can do very much about getting anything started there. The Rules Committee cannot act until Steagall introduces a resolution and he has become invisible." Catherine's vitality and energy were badly missed. The Rules Committee was stalling because most of its members were against housing legislation. Keyserling believed that only pressure from the President could help a bill get through, but a presidential push "had reached about the same stage of development as Hitler's push against the Maginot Line."

Catherine's legendary energy failed her when it came to writing a second book, the promised result of her Guggenheim fellowship. Feeling somewhat guilty, she wrote to Henry Moe at the foundation and voiced her intention to revise *Modern Housing* in the near future, using material from her lecture course and the Guggenheim-funded travels in Europe. "It should reappear in fall," she wrote, "but it has been put off so often already that I hesitate to put it down in black and white now. Therefore my revised book can now really summarize 'The European Housing Movement 1920-1940,' certainly a major phenomenon of the between-war period."[34] The revisions and additions to *Modern Housing* never materialized.

In the spring of 1940 she turned her attention from national to regional matters by joining the California Housing Association (CHA). Gratified by this new focus, she would later resign her position at the USHA and concentrate entirely on regional planning. In the summer she drafted a circular, on CHA stationary, urging Congress to pass the amendment to the 1937 US Housing Act currently before the house for a second time. The amendment would provide increased funding for many key sections of the act and begin to address rural housing needs. She urged Keyserling to "wire the exact situation on S 591 re both normal and defense housing. Are any outside appropriations for defense housing feasible?"[35]

Keyserling replied that the House Banking and Currency Committee substituted its own bill "providing $5 million in annual contributions to release

$150 million unused loan funds. If passed this bill will provide funds for use for both normal and defense housing … While separate authorization for defense housing is possible, I don't think it advisable now, as approval of such authorization before action on S 591 is likely to be fatal to S 591."[36] Keyserling's prediction was correct. In a replay of the earlier scenario, S 591 was passed by the Senate and rejected by the House. And once again both Catherine and Keyserling experienced dismal defeat.

With her courses running smoothly, Catherine turned her attention back to the social scene. At dinners she was often seated next to the gentleman she met at Alice Griffith's luncheon. Tall, attractive, and articulate, the forty-five-year-old William Wilson Wurster was one of San Francisco's most eligible bachelors and the Bay Area's leading modern architect. He knew Catherine from the literature and was extremely interested in what she had to say about her experiences in Washington. He had recently completed the Valencia Gardens Housing Project, and this interested her. He, too, had spent a pivotal year in Europe after completing his studies.

In May Catherine's father died at the age of seventy-one. The last few years of Jacob Bauer's life had been especially difficult. Three years earlier he had suffered from a stroke that left him paralyzed and with impaired speech. He had been a staunch Republican who served his county and state well, both professionally and as an active citizen. As state highway engineer Jacob had provided well for his family. He looked forward to a rosy future during the late 1920s when he invested a substantial sum in a Florida land development scheme. Like so many other hopeful Americans, Bauer lost a small fortune during the Depression when his investment turned to mud.

During the Democratic sweep of 1932, the Republican governor of New Jersey lost his seat to a Democrat, and State Highways Engineer J.L. Bauer was soon drummed out of office. There were trumped up conflict-of-interest charges – Bauer was accused of using a state vehicle and chauffeur to drive his family – about which his son Louis still bristles. "I ordinarily hitch-hiked to school," said Louis, "but if father was going in early to work, I'd ride with him."[37] There were ugly hearings, and worse press releases, and Jacob did not have the stamina to fight back. Instead he opened a consulting practice as a civil engineer, but business never picked up and his fortune diminished.

Attempts to find work were repeatedly frustrated. The WPA took over jobs that might have been delegated to him. Even the Department of Sanitation refused to hire Jacob in spite of strong recommendations from two state senators. He continued to follow lead after lead, always hopeful for success, until he was felled by a massive stroke on May 14, 1940. During the last few years of her father's life, Catherine helped support her parents. After his death she continued to assist her mother until the death of her grandmother brought Bertie a small inheritance.

Jacob rarely, if ever, showered his children with affection, yet he became intimately involved in each of their lives. He celebrated their successes, sympathized with their pain, and protected their secrets so that each felt a genuine closeness to him. His son was the only offspring to follow in his footsteps, professionally and politically. Both daughters spun out of his political orbit, as they embraced social causes espoused by the Democratic Party. His counsel, often sought by Catherine, always focused on her best interest even if it conflicted with his ideology. When she wanted to visit Russia, he wished her bon voyage.

Her father's death came when Catherine was in the middle of her first teaching semester. She hurried home for the funeral, then rushed back to California. Upon learning of the death, Bill Wurster wrote Catherine a thoughtful letter of condolence, starting "Dear K.C." Bill had heard her family and close friends call her Casey and was trying it out. Catherine was different from the elegant women he squired to San Francisco's famous opera, and by the summer he had become quite infatuated. She enjoyed his company much the same as she had Ernie Bohn's. Toward the end of July, Bill began to press Catherine to spend more time with him. She was about to depart for a two-week inspection tour of the Farm Resettlement Administration (FRA) projects in the Columbia River Basin, as a special consultant to the USHA. Sensing his urgency, she invited him to join her for any part of the trip, and sent an itinerary. "I'll meet you in Seattle on Sunday August 11th or possibly Saturday evening. Or Monday or Tuesday, as I plan to stay around Seattle until Wednesday morning. So do come. [signed] yrs."[38]

Catherine also invited Ernie Bohn to join her on the portion of the tour, early in August, through Oregon, Washington, and Idaho. As usual Bohn's calendar had no room for her, so she promised to visit him later that summer on a trip east.

Departing on August 1, Catherine stopped first at Twin Falls, Idaho, where she met with staffers from the local housing authority. She then went to Boise to join Vernon DeMars, architect for FRA, his wife Betty, and some people from the Bureau of Reclamation on a two-day inspection of housing conditions around the huge Columbia Basin irrigation projects. There they found settlers living in one-room shacks with dirt floors and no indoor plumbing. These were not "bottom-level migrants, they [were the] 'successful' farmers, most of whom had a couple of thousand dollars capital to start with," an appalled Catherine wrote her mother.[39]

In Oregon's eastern mountains, Catherine and the DeMars took a little time out to hike and swim before driving west. They stopped in Walla

Walla and were very impressed by a superior Farm Security camp with wooden houses for a permanent labour force. Next they toured the region around the new Grand Coulee Dam, encompassing 1.2 million acres of newly irrigated land which, Catherine predicted, would eventually be some of the finest farming country in the United States. "The first big experiment in regional planning," she called it. "It is invaluable in dramatizing practically all of the problems of agricultural planning, standards of living, housing, city planning, etc. which we confront on a smaller scale all the time. Whenever I think of the destruction and waste of the war, the contrasting picture of positive possibility always seems to be the Grand Coulee project."[40]

On August 10 she wrote to her mother from the Olympic Hotel in Seattle, describing how Bill Wurster and possibly Tommy Church would meet her the next day; they would drive back to San Francisco together. Wurster, however, had other plans: he had no intention of inviting Church along on the trip. Instead he booked a flight to Seattle for August 12 – and a room at the Olympic. He alerted Catherine by telegram:

I send this to say the worst is upon you – I am to come up on Monday night, plane arriving at 11:49 [p.m.]. Damn this distance for I have lots to say to you and letters and telegrams are the bunk.

Yours,
Bill

With her itinerary as guide, Bill pursued Catherine by phone from Utah to Seattle. He finally reached her at the Olympic and confirmed his plans to fly up to Seattle. "And, let's get married immediately after I arrive," he said as he hung up. Known for his poise and rational behaviour, none who knew Wurster would characterize him as impulsive. Three months after the death of her father, Catherine, who had turned her back on countless proposals of marriage, briefly considered this offer from a man ten years older, and said yes.

CATHERINE,
c. 1942

With her itinerary
as guide, Bill
pursued Catherine
by phone from
Utah to Seattle.

MARRIAGE

*Here I am – Mrs. W. W. Wurster settled down once and for
all in San Francisco!*
CATHERINE BAUER WURSTER TO UNO AND KERSTIN AHREN

Vernon and Betty DeMars parted company with Catherine in Seattle after
their return from the Grand Coulee Dam. Bill Wurster arrived as expected,
and the next morning, as the DeMars drove down University Street, they
spotted the twosome walking hand-in-hand. Both couples waved eagerly,
and Vernon made a U-turn, stopping directly in front of them. He had
known Bill for some years and was surprised to discover that Bill also knew
Catherine. He was absolutely stunned when Bill announced "Catherine
and I have decided to get married this morning, how would you like to be
our witness."[41] Vernon invited his friends into the car, and the foursome
drove off in full hilarity in search of a Justice of the Peace. It was August
13, 1940.

Although Catherine was genuinely fond of Bill from the time they met at Miss Griffith's luncheon seven months earlier, there had been no hint of romance in their relationship prior to marriage. The wisdom of hindsight suggests that a prolonged romance might have been dashed against the rocks, as had happened in so many of Catherine's relationships. She had always been attracted to intellectually stimulating, witty men who challenged her ideas and were able to stand their ground. Some, like Lewis Mumford, were considerably older and offered guidance. Others, like Oscar Stonorov, were dapper, gifted designers and political activists. Most were physically attractive, like Doug Condie. Perhaps one reason romance never flourished with Ernie Bohn was his slightly overweight and dour appearance.

William Wurster, ten years her senior, seemed to embody the characteristics of all the men Catherine ever loved. Without time to weigh the pros and cons, she jumped into a union, much as she jumped into the Pacific Ocean: off the high rocks. "I don't remember actually deciding," Catherine later wrote to the Ahrens, "but somehow or other I did it. And we're both still wondering how we happened to have the sense to follow our instinct so clearly and decisively, so here I am – Mrs. W. W. Wurster settled down once and for all in San Francisco! Bill is a swell guy, he's a very good architect and just as absorbed in his work as I am in mine – which is fine."[42] Catherine trusted her intuition; it had served her well at most of the major turning points of her life. Bill would be her best friend for life.

Bill was born in Stockton, California, on October 20, 1895, to Maude Wilson Wurster of Maine, daughter of a Civil War veteran, and Frederick W. Wurster, son of a German immigrant who had crossed the Isthmus of Panama to reach California. Frederick's mother had arrived in California by way of Cape Horn. As president of the Bank of Stockton, Frederick Wurster provided a comfortable home for his family. Bill, called Wilson by his family and boyhood friends, immersed himself in architecture from an early age. During school vacations he worked as office boy for E.B. Brown, an architect with advanced ideas who designed indigenously Californian buildings adapted to the climate.[43]

After high school graduation, Bill studied architecture at the University of California under John Galen Howard, a pupil of prominent nineteenth-century Boston architect Henry Hobson Richardson. A prolonged illness and the First World War delayed graduation. After studying naval architecture and marine engineering, Bill shipped out to Hawaii and the Philippines as an engineer, then returned to UC Berkeley in 1919 to finish his degree in architecture. Upon graduating with highest honours, Bill worked in San Francisco for one year and Sacramento for two.

In 1922, after earning his licence to practise architecture, he made the Grand Tour of Europe for one year, studying the architecture of Italy, Spain, and France. In Paris the dashing young American met up with an English-speaking crowd, among them an architect named George Licht who ran the training atelier for the elite New York architectural firm of Delano and Aldrich. Bill had considered working in the New York area before returning to California, and Licht persuaded him to come to the Delano and Aldrich offices. William Adams Delano, Franklin Roosevelt's uncle, recognized Bill's talent and took such an interest in the young man that they formed a kind of father-son relationship. Delano helped to formulate Bill's architectural philosophy, and Bill became Delano's "boy Friday." Among other favours, Bill tutored Delano's son, Richard, before the boy went to Yale.

After a year in New York, Bill returned to Berkeley to open a small office in the Hotel Shattuck. There he worked for two years on a filtration plant for the East Bay Water Company. In 1926 he opened his first San Francisco office, where he primarily designed small houses. One year later he won first prize in a national competition for small house design, with the Gregory Farmhouse. It was a vacation house built in the Santa Cruz hills for Mrs. Sadie Gregory, mother of a classmate of Bill's and widow of a prominent corporate lawyer. She had wanted John Galen Howard, the man who had built her elegant Berkeley home on Greenwood Terrace many years earlier, but his designs were too elaborate for a country home. As a student at UC Berkeley, Bill had often visited the Greenwood Terrace home – the Gregory House, as he always called it – and dreamed of owning it himself one day.

Sadie Gregory wanted something simple and had the idea of asking her son's friend, Bill, what he could do. He obliged by designing a one-story L-shaped house, each room opening to the outside. A three-sided courtyard was formed by a small house attached to a three-story rectangular water tower, opposite the long wall of the main house. That water tower, shaped like a modern half-gallon milk carton, became the centrepiece of the compound.

Bill described such structures as "Large-Small Houses." In order to create a feeling of space, he raised ceilings and designed multipurpose rooms with large windows; the adjacent outdoor space was controlled with the judicious use of covered, partially glassed-in patios, exterior fireplaces, and gathering spaces for lounging and dining. His designs suited the benign California climate and lifestyle. Elegant simplicity was his hallmark. An exhibit called "Inside the Large Small House," originally mounted at MIT in 1993, opened at UC Berkeley's University Art Museum in 1995 to celebrate the centennial of the birth of William

Wilson Wurster, the man who created the College of Environmental Design and changed forever how architectural disciplines would be taught.

Donn Emmons, an employee of Bill's firm in 1940 and later a partner, recalled Catherine's chide: "You guys do houses that are expensive but look cheap."[44] Actually Catherine was one of Wurster's greatest fans. A badly yellowed and frayed sheet of paper extolling Bill's work was found among her papers. Bearing neither caption nor date, the paper was stored among congratulatory letters on their marriage and may have been written to introduce Bill to her friends:

I suppose more than anyone in the country he is actually doing what I have always screamed for – a natural unforced "vernacular," using all the things that come logically to hand, from big new ideas to sensible local materials and the particular needs and even style, honesty and not a trace of prima donna tour-de-force. I like his conception of the role of an architect as a good responsible imaginative craftsman (extending "craftsmanship" beyond materials to dealings with his office and his clients and the community at large) rather than a Messiah who Knows All ... In fact, the heart-warming thing about Bill's success is the extraordinary satisfaction his clients seem to take in their houses – the way they look, the way they work ... and not by any means just special people with intellectual "modern" tastes. I like the fact that, although they're "modern" in every detail ... they're essentially more a part of the local building tradition out here (which carries right along from the mining-town kind of functionalism through Willis Polk and Maybeck) and contemporary western living habits, than they are of the good old "international style." Bill would probably be doing much the same thing, if Le Corbusier, Gropius and even FLW had never existed.[45]

No one analyzing Bill's work has stated his gifts more succinctly than did his new wife shortly after marriage. It is likely that a common interest in planning had drawn Catherine and Bill together at dinner parties during the previous seven months. He had visited Europe in 1937 to look at modern housing projects in England, Frankfurt, and Scandinavia, unwittingly following Catherine's footsteps. Both attended the Paris Exposition that year. After his return to the Bay Area, he built the Valencia Gardens project in San Francisco (in association with Harry Thomson, Jr.) and Stern Hall, a women's dormitory at UC Berkeley (in association with Corbett and MacMurray). At the time of their wedding both projects were under construction.

News of the marriage spread rapidly on both coasts. Landscape architect, Fran Violich, a friend of both Wursters before they were married, remembers being amazed. He viewed Bill as a perennial bachelor, wed to his profession. Congratulations poured in from around the world. Catherine's family was delighted. "At long last I'm writing the letter that I've wished to write for years. Best wishes," wrote Catherine's Aunt Edna.

"Well, you could have knocked me over with a small housing pamphlet when I heard the news," Catherine's sister, Betty, wrote. "I was so excited that I rolled about the floor screaming with pleasure,"[46] added the sibling who had condemned Catherine to eternal spinsterhood fifteen years earlier when she broke up with Doug Condie. Upon receiving the news, Betty dusted off an old *Pencil Points* magazine featuring an article about Bill Wurster, with photographs of him in his studio, to show his new mother-in-law. Bertie Bauer was delighted and graciously welcomed Bill into the family.

Catherine's housing colleagues reacted with characteristic humour. "Condolences. Wurster never happened. Housing has been DeBauered," wired fellow houser Boris Shishkin from Washington. "Pandemonium reigns among large group of Washington admirers left without reason d'être by news of your infidelity," wired another. "And now I suppose you are going to stay in San Francisco forever," wrote Fritz Gutheim, in the only genuine expression of regret voiced by many of Catherine's former colleagues.[47] Ernie Bohn was most eloquent of all. "You are deserving of every bit of happiness that this cruel and uncivilized world is capable of giving you," he wrote. "All of your life you have been doing things for others and sacrificing your own rights for the good things of life. So here's to you and to him – may God bless you."[48]

Bill and Theodore Bernardi had become partners in 1934. At the time of his marriage, Bill's firm employed several young architects, among them his future partner, Donn Emmons. Emmons recalls Catherine's first visit to their office on the third floor of an old building:

> The first thing she said when she came in to the office, was: "what is this Mr. Wurster stuff?" (Bill had everybody calling him 'Mr. Wurster'). She said: "His name is Bill for Christ's sake!" Bill would have no women in the office, not even a secretary. In fact, we had a secretary two floors below. We had a hole in the floor and a cow bell. We'd write things out in long-hand, and drop them down through this hole. This nice old lady who did the typing would ring the cow bell and then we'd haul it back up. Shortly after Catherine came, Bill began to hire professional women.

Emmons believes that Catherine exerted a strong liberating influence on Bill. "She turned him around. Maybe he liked that because he certainly turned completely around in his aspects about things political and otherwise. The office became much more informal and relaxed, and people began calling him Bill. She gave him hell about his political leanings. He was a-political – she made a liberal out of him."[49]

Catherine and Bill Wurster moved into a small apartment at 2632-B Hyde Street near Fisherman's Wharf, with a sweeping view of San Francisco Bay. She was quickly embraced by Bill's circle of friends. Among the first were the Gregorys, whose "farmhouse" became a favourite weekend retreat for the newlyweds. Several friends were well-to-do social activists in the San Francisco Bay Area who shared Catherine's political passions. Many lived in elegant homes designed by Bill in the Pacific Heights district. Among them was Martha Gerbode, whom Catherine would dub "one of the best people in this city" when she later supported her application to work for the United Nations Relief and Rehabilitation Agency (UNRRA), under the direction of UC Berkeley's Dr. H.M. Cassidy, Catherine's former boss at the school of Social Welfare. Wife of a physician and heir to the Matson Line fortune and vast land holdings on Diamond Head in Hawaii, Martha Gerbode devoted her intelligence and wealth to social causes. Clarisse Stockholm, an old friend and mother-in-law of Gerbode's daughter, Marianna, told oral historian Harriet Nathan that it was Catherine who sparked Martha's interest in politics.[50]

"The downtrodden appealed to her," said Georgiana Stevens of Martha Gerbode; Georgiana was another proud owner of a Wurster house and a close friend of Catherine's. Drawn into in the movement by San Francisco housing activists Dorothy Erskine and Alice Griffith, Martha soon became a good friend of Catherine's. She devoted considerable time to the San Francisco Housing Association and later to the California Housing and Planning Association, and was an early and vociferous environmentalist who regularly went to Hawaii to lead the battle to save Diamond Head.

Another important friend was Elinor Heller, an active Democratic Party worker. Many years later, Heller would be the first woman on the Board of Regents of the University of California, appointed by Governor Edmund G. Brown to finish her late husband's term after his untimely death. Like Catherine's Vassar friends, these were well-educated, erudite, and affluent women who committed much time to social causes.

Global issues soon displaced social and professional preoccupations as the war in Europe made headlines in remote, idyllic San Francisco. The impact of the Blitzkrieg's inroads into US foreign and domestic policy occupied Catherine and her circle of friends. In May 1940 Kerstin Ahren had informed Catherine about the war's depressing impact on life in Scandinavia. Uno had become distant and brooding as he struggled to survive professionally while reporting for army duty under general mobilization. Before replying to Kerstin, Catherine immediately wrote to Dean Joseph Hudnut, at Harvard University's Graduate School of Design, urging him to bring Ahren out, but there were no openings. She let the issue drop in the face of more pressing matters in the summer and autumn of 1940. One year later she rediscovered Kerstin's letter at the bottom of a pile on her desk and responded with apologies in a four-page, single-spaced letter. Catherine was troubled by reactionary forces at home and poured out her fears:

> *Just thinking about anyone in Europe raises all those huge confusing questions – questions of what America ought to do ... Emotionally I still have many of the twinges of an isolationist. If we really get into the war (as we doubtlessly will), the dangers are enormous – of getting more and more under reactionary semi-Fascist domination ourselves, and then, assuming a complete Allied victory, of using our strength to prevent any fundamental solution of Europe's problems at the end. But I am now convinced that the alternative dangers are worse, for us as well as for everyone else. If Hitler can really finish off England and Africa, I wouldn't be at all surprised if South America were next.*
>
> *The red isolationists' notion that after Hitler wins there is bound to be a great left-wing revolution throughout Europe is just too romantic to swallow. The great Communist error all the way through, it seems to me, has been the failure to see that the Fascist idea itself has all the positive force of a revolution – making its gains just as much by conversion from within as by military force.*[51]

She urged Uno to get out of Sweden immediately by applying to Dean Hudnut for a job. Hudnut had been a colleague during her days at MOMA, and Catherine was confident that he would help a friend of hers. "Say that I suggested it. Emphasize your experience in site planning, your publications, anything about the relation of city planning to defense problems."[52]

Hearing of a new opening in City Planning at Harvard, Catherine pressed Hudnut to invite Ahren. With a faculty vacancy, and the expanding war in Europe, Catherine became more forceful. "I am not given to unqualified hyperbole, but I do believe that there may be no one in the world better qualified for the job," she told Hudnut. "He is the most enthusiastic, earnest, and engaging of the young modern architects in Scandinavia. He has done an outstanding job both technically and politically, but has somehow never lost that edge of intensity and philosophic freedom, anti-stuffed shirtness, and aesthetic concern that he always had. He has something entirely fresh to offer in the city planning field, not just from himself, but from his whole Swedish experience."[53]

Catherine's urgent plea fell upon deaf ears. With many foreigners already on the faculty – Gropius, Breuer, Wagner (from Germany), and Tunnard, an English landscape architect – Hudnut thought it bad policy to bring in another European. Indeed, he hired Professor G. Holmes Perkins, an American, in order to redress the social-geographic ethnic balance of the faculty. The Ahrens remained in Sweden, and their marriage ended up a wartime casualty: Uno and Kerstin separated soon after Armistice Day.

The attack on Pearl Harbor posed new challenges as well as opportunities for the Wursters. Bill accommodated his practice to the demands of an emerging war-driven economy. He designed the first pre-fabricated, demountable structures for defense workers in the Carquinez Heights section of Vallejo, and the Parker Houses in Sacramento – a total of five thousand buildings. As demands on his private practice diminished, he devoted time to postwar architectural and urban planning issues.

Bill and Catherine spent nearly as much time apart as they did together during the early years of marriage. Conferences and lecture tours took both of them away from home for extended periods. When Bill set out for New York, Catherine armed him with books to read on the long train ride east. Among them were her own manual, *A Citizen's Guide to Public Housing,* and Mumford's *The Culture of Cities.* Bill sent an admiring letter from the train, praising her lucidity and apologizing for his own "schoolboy outpourings – but the wonder of you being my wife grows and grows."[54]

"Not an intellectual," Catherine wrote of her husband in private notes. "And yet has very positive working and living philosophy (much more than most people whose medium is words and ideas.)" She thought of him as a man of contradictions: an outstanding rebel in architecture but, in a literal sense, a conservative, hating "everyone whose heart is destructive, whatever the form (more than I do who could easily fall into the revolutionist pattern because I am often attracted and stimulated by the ruthless)."[55]

She trusted his judgment and creative integrity more than her own, even in areas that were new to him yet were ones in which she had worked for years. By her standards, however, he neither spoke nor wrote well on general intellectual topics. Was she a snob? Perhaps. Certainly he could speak to students more directly than she could. Yet his verbal expressions seemed "formally uninteresting, even banal, while his basic principles are perfectly sound – probably more so than mine."

Bill's writing was indeed banal and rather dull in comparison with men like Mumford and Keyserling, who were extremely witty and eloquent. At dinner parties, conversation centred around Catherine, though guests remarked that whenever Bill spoke it was worthwhile to listen. Bill did find his voice. A few years later, Lloyd Rodwin, a student of Catherine's, and his young wife were invited to the Wurster home in Cambridge, Massachusetts. Before he got to know Bill well, Rodwin had thought of him as "Mr. Catherine Bauer." That evening he realized that Bill had panache embedded in a very strong personality. As Bill enthusiastically expounded upon a housing topic, Catherine interrupted.

"That's wrong."

Bill stood his ground. "No, that's not wrong."

"It's dead wrong," she insisted, heating up.

"No, it's not dead wrong," he replied, calmly.

"It *is* dead wrong, and I'll explain why," she persisted, ignoring their squirming guests.

At this point Bill turned to the Rodwins. "This doesn't happen very often," he said, "but when it does, the sparks fly." With that, they went after each other, hammer and tongs. The young couple found the scene daunting. They had not realized people could talk to each other that bluntly.[56]

SAN FRANCISCO

Is public housing really as popular with the people who need housing, as it ought to be? If not why not?
CATHERINE BAUER

San Francisco was among the world's great cities, in Catherine's judgment, but it was slum infested, with "the lousiest city planning commission west of the Mississippi."[57] Here she experienced the workings of a local housing authority for the first time, composed of dedicated (unpaid) citizens representing a cross-section of their communities. The authority, one of more than six hundred established across the country after the passage of the US Housing Act, was composed of college professors, businessmen, union officials, architects, lawyers, and "lady welfare experts."[58] Emotions were always immoderate: the housing movement was marked by violent opposition, resulting in bitter rows but also great enthusiasm.

The politics of housing continued to occupy Catherine as she submerged herself in the work of the California Housing Authority. In 1941 she helped to expand the California Housing Association into the California Housing and Planning Association (CHPA) and served as its vice-president for three years. The notion of joining planning with housing was still novel. "It is necessary to consider them both together," Catherine wrote, "because in two of the most urgent state-wide problems necessitating public education and action, they are practically inseparable. I refer to the rural shack-town problem which is equally a matter of housing and of county and regional planning – and the problem in defense areas, which has done more to make housers and planners realize at long last that they have a common cause, than any other single thing."[59]

The language of CHPA's mission statement was clearly Catherine's: "A non-profit organization in which Californians of various points of view work together to encourage intelligent public and private action for better housing, particularly for families of low income, and application of modern planning methods to all rural and urban areas of the state." CHPA Executive Director Ed Howden had attended her housing seminar at UC Berkeley.

Catherine's efforts at CHPA paralleled the work she had done in 1934 in Philadelphia, as secretary of the Labor Housing Conference (LHC). Unlike LHC, where she was sole staff member, CHPA was a statewide organization with a large membership. Her duties included organizing conferences and hearings, and publishing a monthly newsletter, *Agenda*, to which her many friends around the country were obliged to contribute. CHPA often joined the Western States Housing Authorities Association in declarations and conferences. During the first year three conferences were planned: on public housing; rural problems; and planning matters, including land-use control. A future conference would deal with private investment housing.

CATHERINE MEETING WITH CALIFORNIA COUNCIL TABLE

The politics of housing continued to occupy Catherine as she submerged herself in the work of the California Housing Authority.

As an officer of CHPA, Catherine again coaxed, coerced, and coached people on how to raise money to run local organizations, develop agendas for conferences, draw up guest lists, and devise ways to involve union personnel in applying pressure to affect favourable housing legislation at the city and state levels. She also smoothed the ruffled feathers of anxious members of local authorities.

Political activities were directed toward improving the appalling migrant towns and slums throughout the state. Now simply a consultant to the US Housing Authority, Catherine used those connections to further the cause of California housing and planning and, conversely, used her western experience to attempt to influence federal policy. Although a champion of decentralization, she worked hard to bring about an affiliation between disparate housing authorities scattered around the western region. They had much to learn from each other, but she was repeatedly frustrated by indifference and ignorance.

Catherine's life during her early married years was as frenetic as it had been during her time as a lobbyist. Her schedule in June 1941 was typical, beginning with three days in San Diego testifying before California Senator Tolan's hearings (organized by Catherine) on the social and economic consequences of wartime population growth. The day after the hearings, she flew to Spokane, Washington, as USHA representative at a number of governmental conferences on long-range planning of the Grand Coulee irrigation project. Two weeks later she would be back in Washington as USHA's representative on the Columbia Basin Irrigation Project.

The Washington State meetings were fraught with acrimonious debates among agricultural economists and government people, and Catherine was relieved to fly home after a week. But rest was not in the cards: she was greeted in San Francisco by two officials from San Diego who needed help putting together a visual show on defense housing. At the time she was writing an article for the *New Republic* about defense housing and planning, while also struggling to complete reports for the organizations she had represented at the Washington meetings. Catherine was always behind, and her reports typically began with apologies for being late, but they were always thorough, well organized, and well written.

Catherine advised Eliot F. Noyes, director of New York's MOMA, on a defense housing exhibition scheduled to open in 1942 and tour the country. She hoped the show would educate local officials and citizens on the qualitative and technical sides of housing by exhibiting excellent examples of revolutionary design, layout, and production methods; toward this end, she provided Noyes with examples of good and bad housing. "It seems to me that the role of the Museum is to strengthen the hand of that small group of people in every community who know and care about good modern architecture, up-to-date site planning, and adequate community facilities," she told Noyes.[60]

At home Catherine's desk was always blanketed with stacks of papers: letters, reports, bills, and "to do" lists that she would attend to in no particular order. When her desktop became overly cluttered, she piled papers on a nearby table; after that it was the floor. Eventually papers found their way into file drawers where they remained until her death. Catherine seemingly kept every scrap of paper that came her way. Bill, an orderly man, found her filing method chaotic and troubling. He coped by staying out of her office.

Catherine's grandmother had admonished her ten years earlier, when she was twenty-five, that she would soon be past child-bearing age. This warning played back now, but Catherine attempted to dismiss such thoughts as she and Bill raced around the country in pursuit of their separate missions. One year after marriage Catherine wrote a friend:

We still can't decide about children – though heaven knows we better do it pretty soon if we're going to. Every now and then I waver, but then on analysis it seems more like a good excuse to get out of the hectic round of meetings and such than any very gnawing maternal instinct. The main thing against it is the fact that I hate to think of having to run an Establishment with domestic responsibilities, noise and such all day long, and no hideaway where I can busily but quietly waste my time in the midst of a sea of papers, strengthened by the illusion that I'm "working."[61]

There was important work to be done. California's acute shortage of decent housing magnified the need for construction of defense housing as army bases mushroomed along the Pacific Coast. It was a fertile field in which Catherine's political and planning skills proved valuable. New federal policies and programs were needed, and she often returned to Washington, DC, to help promote amendments to various housing acts. On one trip she participated in the founding of the National Committee on the Housing Emergency, a citizens' group headed by Dorothy Rosenman, wife of prominent New York Judge Samuel Rosenman, a friend of public housing. It was to be a temporary organization for study and action on the housing needs of low-income families and of workers in defense industries throughout the United States. A watchdog committee, the committee included a broad range of national housing organizations – citizens' groups representing housing, labour, and welfare constituencies – but no government representation.

As western chairman of the committee, Catherine was responsible for selecting chairmen, vice-chairmen, and members for each state in her region. In California she persuaded her friends Alice Griffith and Martha Gerbode to join, and Helen Gahagan to become vice-chairman.[62] Catherine was able to complement her work on the committee by taking on the role of third vice-president of the National Public Housing Conference, an organization that paralleled the Housing Emergency Committee.

Had these organizations been around six years earlier, Catherine's lobbying efforts on behalf of the US Housing Act would have been much easier. Yet it was largely due to her efforts that the act had passed, making it possible for these and other groups to flourish. From the start she urged wartime planners to keep in mind postwar housing needs, and she hoped that the USHA, through local authorities, would coordinate planning for the thousands of families being relocated for the war effort. This, she

CATHERINE (LEFT) WITH BILL MALONE (DEMOCRATIC PARTY BOSS IN CALIFORNIA), HELEN GAHAGAN [DOUGLAS], AND JULIA PARTES, C. 1943

As western chairman of the committee, Catherine was responsible for selecting chairmen, vice-chairmen, and members for each state in her region. In California she persuaded Helen Gahagan to become vice-chairman.

reasoned, would hasten the establishment of new authorities around the country and provide for cohesive postwar planning.

The Lanham Act, though beneficial in many ways, also tended to fragment housing and land planning by dividing responsibilities among various government departments. To Interior went community planning, which included public spaces such as community centres, schools, shops, and recreation areas. To Defense went temporary or demountable housing for defense workers and military bases. The USHA continued to occupy itself with shelter for the poor, and Nathan Straus urged that war housing, under the Lanham Act, ought to be turned over to local housing authorities for administration during the war and for disposition afterwards.

Disgruntled letters from former USHA colleagues about bureaucratic hassles bolstered Catherine's decision to keep her distance from the capital. Straus, a well-liked gentleman, was criticized by his staff for ineffectual leadership. He wore kid gloves when boxing gloves might have been more appropriate in budget and planning negotiations.

By 1942 major reorganization had taken place among various agencies and authorities responsible for different aspects of housing. Under Roosevelt's Executive Order (No. 9070) of December 18, 1941, all the groups were consolidated into the National Housing Agency (NHA). The USHA became the Federal Public Housing Authority (FPHA), with Herbert Emmerich its first commissioner. He came to Washington from Chicago, where he had directed the Public Administration Clearing House that pioneered the training of local government officials. Emmerich had also helped establish housing authorities across the country.

Catherine and her old USHA colleagues welcomed the new commissioner. Since departing, she had kept a rather jaundiced eye on housing activities in Washington. Now, with the authority in capable hands, she issued an eleven-page document of proposals to the new commissioner. "Not that I can suggest any nostrums to make the public housing business as solid as public schools, safe as public parks, scientific as public health, or simple as public roads," she began her treatise, written from the perspective of a citizen living three thousand miles from the legislative hub. By drawing attention to local issues, Catherine hoped to affect the national scene. She raised topics of importance to the Association of Western States Housing Authorities and the CHPA. These included rural housing, urban redevelopment, and cooperative housing.[63]

As USHA's (now FPHA's) official representative on the Columbia Basin Joint Investigation team, Catherine urged the authority to develop postwar plans for new settlements within the basin. The Columbia Basin Irrigation Project was the largest enterprise of its kind in the world, affecting a projected population of 500,000, of which 5 to 8 percent would be farmers. Catherine saw it as a unique opportunity for the departments of Agriculture and Interior to work hand-in-hand with state and regional governments in developing new communities from the ground up.

A year earlier she had described the Columbia Basin project: "To USHA it means the one great opportunity to work out housing policies *not* merely as a remedy for past mistakes, but as a vital factor in creating a fresh *new* environment from the ground up, in which the mistakes can be prevented from being made."[64] She had spent many long hours compiling a sizable report proposing settlement plans to the committee overseeing the Columbia Basin Joint Investigations. Catherine found the subject fascinating because it posed every rural housing and planning problem in a most dramatic and inescapable form. Plans for the region were never actualized.

Although rural housing interested Catherine, her attention was centred mainly on the city. She dubbed the new term, urban redevelopment, "magical," and urged Herbert Emmerich to create a formula for coordinating public and private initiative within a sound comprehensive city plan. To Coleman Woodbury she wrote about really wanting "to do hard boiled research in this area on the Urban Redevelopment business."[65] She believed that large-scale private funding should be encouraged on an investment basis, along with essential government subsidies.

Her proposal to Emmerich raised a central question that still has currency more than five decades later: "Is public housing really as popular with the people who need housing, as it ought to be? If not, why not?" Too often the technical and architectural aspects of housing were not adequately considered, she argued. She then pointed out six major problems attached to public housing: grim appearance, wrong location, inadequate community facilities such as shops and transportation, overly rigid rules of eligibility, lack of real contact with groups who need rehousing, and a fatal charity smell surrounding public projects.

She suggested three broad remedies: increased tenant participation and responsibility in planning and management, reduced red tape on eligibility, and attention to aesthetics of the structures and surroundings. Technical staffs needed to be assigned to local regions to apply their ingenuity in meeting local conditions. Noting that the health and vitality of public housing varied enormously from one part of the country to another, she promoted the idea of identifying demonstration projects from which regional authorities could learn. Control would be at the local level while the national office would be responsible for providing technical assistance, stimulating innovative design, monitoring, and evaluating regional works.

Recalling the housing surveys she had encountered in Frankfurt, she urged that tenants in existing projects be surveyed about their likes and dislikes on issues ranging from design to maintenance. A performance analysis of their responses could then be broadcast throughout FPHA (formerly, NPHA) to form a basis for improved planning and building. Come west, she urged Emmerich, to see how the wartime housing experience could influence postwar national public housing policy. She praised Langdon Post, an ally in the legislative battles of the 1930s. Post now headed Region VII, the Western States Regional Housing Authority, and was a strong proponent of decentralization to local housing authorities. He was especially skilful at squashing well-organized opposition. Emmerich never made the trip.

During this period the leadership of the National Association of Housing Officials (NAHO) also underwent a major shift. Executive Director Coleman Woodbury, called to work in Washington, DC, was replaced by Dr. Charles Edward Winslow, formally head of a committee on housing hygiene. Catherine urged Dr. Winslow to turn NAHO into an action-oriented, lobbying organization. Rental housing was very much on her mind when she discussed rent control and rental subsidies with him. Defense workers' housing was under rent control by now, through an amendment to the Lanham Act. Why not low-income shelter? Catherine proposed.

The concept of shelter certificates was under consideration by NAHO and public housing advocates. Discussing the pros and cons with Winslow, Catherine could think of only one "pro" and a host of "cons." If shelter certificates were given directly to low-income families (like food stamps would be), they held the possible advantage of preventing the segregation of these families. On the negative side, shelter certificates would not increase the availability of appropriate accommodation for the poor. The administration and distribution of certificates would involve the private sector, and Catherine believed that low-income family housing ought to remain in public ownership with rents kept down by direct subsidy. Low-income families with shelter certificates would be able to occupy private projects where rents would be higher than in public housing. "Do we really want to pay more subsidy just to enable a low-income family to have a private landlord?" Catherine asked Winslow.[66] She believed that shelter certificates were based on a "filtering up" idea, where some very low-income families would have better quarters than many middle-income people. This made no sense, and Catherine sensed a plot.

She suspected that promoters of shelter certificates only wished to provide a barely adequate subsidy to enable the lowest income families to move into substandard or, at best, barely standard lower-middle-class homes. The real estate lobby welcomed certificates as an opportunity to unload poor-quality, often speculative housing. Poor people would displace existing residents, and large-scale private buildings or redevelopment programs would then be promoted – and subsidized for middle- and upper-income families. She failed to see the logic. "The one thing you can't be in a progressive, capitalist democracy past the frontier stage, is entirely logical."[67] Shelter certificates would release a flood of indiscriminate subsidies without targeting the needs of the poor, she warned. As it turned out, the floodgates would be opened shortly after the war when the battle for housing was waged between private interests (developers) and public interests (national and local governments).

There will always be a gap between the cost of housing for low-income families and their ability to pay for it, and subsidies will always be absolutely essential. In the 1940s expenditure for shelter was set at 20 percent of income (today it is 30 percent). For the impoverished consumer, not even 100 percent of income would necessarily provide adequate shelter as he or she juggled to pay for life's other necessities. The gap between costs and ability to pay required a subsidy that Catherine firmly believed should go directly to the consumer, not the producer. Part of the subsidy had to come from local sources in the form of exemption from land taxes. This was both workable and politically acceptable. She did concede that some form of controlled private management might be inevitable, but should be limited to cooperative ventures.

Leon Keyserling, now general counsel to FPHA, kept Catherine informed about proposed legislation that could be favourable to California. She heard that the federal government was contemplating a postwar program for large-scale urban, suburban, and rural redevelopment; she hoped the enabling legislation under consideration would be broad enough to meet any federal program, but specific enough to provide for local interests. In a letter to Keyserling in September 1942, Catherine asked whether the "power of eminent domain" could be legally extended to the acquisition of large-scale housing sites beyond explicit slums. She was hoping for a legal definition that would include housing for low- and middle-income families, so that projects could be built by both public and private enterprise. Catherine's thinking was modelled on comprehensively planned housing, based on sound public land policies that she had seen in prewar Europe.

On a personal note, she told Keyserling that wartime conditions had jeopardized architectural practice in California. "Bill, by the way, has just decided to close his office the first of the year and go to Harvard for a Master's in planning – unless some really useful war work suddenly appears I am pleased with the idea of a year in Cambridge."[68]

CATHERINE IN HER OFFICE

"I am pleased with the idea of a year in Cambridge."

7

ACADEMIC YEARS (1943-64)

CAMBRIDGE

*I do believe that the intellectuals always and continuously
need a check, above all when they're promoting policies
which affect the lives of everyone directly.*
CATHERINE BAUER TO LEWIS MUMFORD

Upon receiving an acceptance letter from Dean Hudnut at Harvard's
Graduate School of Design, Bill Wurster typed a characteristically
modest response. "Your generous greetings and offer of a
fellowship give such warmth of welcome that nothing I write will
adequately thank you," he wrote. "I look forward to February 1 with such
pleasure; mixed, I must confess, with the fear that I am embarking on a
course which may be way over my depth." Bill added a handwritten
postscript: "All this sounds so stilted – perhaps I can do a better job when
I see you."[1]

Catherine and Bill never enjoyed the luxury of a honeymoon away from
professional responsibilities. Two years after their wedding, still feeling
like a bride, Catherine told her friends that their drive east, coupled with
six months to a year in Cambridge, would constitute their long-awaited
honeymoon. "Most people go to Niagara Falls, we have chosen Cambridge,"
she said.

Upon arrival, Bill discovered that he was one of only two graduate
students in the newly revived Department of City and Regional Planning.
The other student was Martin Meyerson, half Bill's age and more than a
little in awe of his renowned classmate. Both men were medically unfit for
military service, and both went on to illustrious academic careers. Three
faculty members – John Gaus, Martin Wagner, and Christopher Tunnard
– were on deck to teach the two students, providing an unparalleled
student-to-teacher ratio. In an effort to even the playing field between Bill
and Meyerson, the faculty piled assignments upon the younger man.

Meyerson had studied classics and science at Columbia College and had intended to pursue a degree in architecture. Unemployed architects advised him against this during the Depression, so he went to Harvard to study engineering. There he became interested in regional development and switched courses. It was at Harvard that he encountered Catherine's writings, and was thrilled to meet the famed "Bauer-Wurster" woman in person. After one year at Harvard, Meyerson wanted field experience, as he found course work too theoretical. With introductions from Catherine to key housers in Chicago, including Herbert Emmerich, Meyerson packed up and found work as research assistant at the American Society of Planning Officials (ASPO) in Chicago. He and his wife, Margie, would return to Harvard in 1945 to work toward their master's degrees in city planning.

Joseph Hudnut created Harvard's Graduate School of Design (GSD) in 1936, encompassing architecture, landscape architecture, and city and regional planning. It was a pioneering concept: to offer students a carefully coordinated curriculum that would prepare them for thoughtful and cooperative practice in the design fields. Hudnut brought Walter Gropius, founder of the Bauhaus in Weimar and Dessau, to head the Department of Architecture in 1938; two years later Gropius brought Martin Wagner to teach city planning.

Professor Wagner was Bill's most demanding teacher. Catherine had met him in 1930 in Berlin where Wagner was *Stadtbaudirektor* (City Director of Planning and Construction). He had been among the first officials to spark her interest in the specific responsibilities shouldered by German city councils in producing and financing post-First World War housing for the lowest income groups. A tall, angular, and uncompromising man, he ran a tight ship in masterminding Berlin's public works program with particular emphasis on public housing. Wagner later applied this rigour to his teaching – intimidating and sometimes overwhelming his students.

An outspoken Social Democrat, Wagner was stripped of his title when Hitler assumed power. He then spent five years as the chief planner for Turkey's capital, Ankara, before joining Harvard's GSD faculty as associate professor of planning. For the next decade he exerted a profound impact on his students and on New England's planning profession. Wagner often held intractable convictions about planning and housing. In a letter to Bill after he left Harvard, Wagner wrote:

When you studied here I did not dare to tell you my real opinion on housing the people, especially not since I would then have lost the last remnants of confidence that your wife may have had in me. You know I revere her as the greatest houser of this country; but in one thing I cannot follow her and you and that is your belief in housing the lowest income classes. I think our past housing was – in principle – a complete failure. It was a wishy-washy policy that tried to ignore the whole capitalistic basis of our economics and to switch some kind of socialism into its cog-wheels. It did not work! As long as our municipalities depend so much upon property taxes, tax exemption, applied in a grand style, must run itself ad absurdum; and so must the application of much improved housing standards, because it is foolish if it is not linked to improved and secured income standards. I seriously think that there is no compromise possible between socialism and capitalism, and especially not in this country at the time being. We shall, therefore, have to compromise in ourselves and to improve drastically the capitalistic system by (a) fighting for a higher income of the people, (b) taking annually from the housing market the substandard dwellings, and (c) speeding up enormously the present "infiltration" procedure in housing, i.e., by shortening the life-time of the dwellings and by increasing the building activity. I cannot see any other solution of the housing problem in this country.[2]

The letter touched upon politically sensitive issues, challenging the capitalist system to adapt to socialist ideals. Catherine would struggle with this contradiction for years. Bill, son of a bank president and a Republican at heart, kept this letter perhaps because its political-philosophical perspective was so alien to his values. He maintained an openness to diverse opinions, a trait that would propel him into leadership in architectural education.

Throughout 1943 Bill was kept busy by the demands of graduate school. Catherine audited some of his courses, particularly enjoying a fiscal policy seminar at the Littauer School of Public Administration led by Alvin Hansen, whom Catherine considered theoretically sound but politically naive: "He has left housing and planning to Greer and I am still pretty anonymous in his class (which is fun). I'll wait till later to heckle him."[3]

Auditing these classes was the closest Catherine came to formal education in her chosen profession, which she was beginning to view more as planning than housing. Although Bill was enrolled in the city planning program, it was Catherine who became the bona fide planner and kept an eye on emerging legislation from that perspective. For example, Senate bill S 953, written to broaden the Housing Act of 1937, interested her because it dealt with the redevelopment of city land in central and suburban zones. Addressing her concerns about the bill to Cleveland lawyer Alfred Bettman, a specialist in land use planning and zoning who had taken issue with the bill, Catherine issued a broadside that she would articulate in various other venues over the coming years. While she applauded some aspects of the proposal, she found that it failed to define a policy for comprehensive land purchase for the central city, surrounding municipalities, and counties.

The bill focused on postwar construction at high levels of production, but did not link housing to urban planning. Catherine argued that any measure that provided substantial federal aid for urban planning and development must also protect the federal government's commitment to a comprehensive housing program. Because of local neglect, federal attention was required to address the needs of all income groups. What would become of the people moved from a blighted area once it had been acquired for redevelopment? Wholesale replacement of slum areas with buildings for higher income groups – or for nonresidential uses – without guaranteeing adequate rehousing of displaced families would create new slums and exacerbate blight.

S 953 also neglected administrative structure, in Catherine's opinion. She believed that the National Housing Authority should provide federal aid for planning and land purchase, but that local housing authorities should execute land acquisition. The bill stated that *municipalities* themselves would be eligible for aid because they possessed adequate authority to acquire real property, issue debentures, and enter into intergovernmental agreements. Local planning commissions, Catherine said, ought to implement master plans by acquiring and administering land.

She opposed the involvement of local real estate agencies, believing they would invariably dominate the redevelopment process from a purely land-market point of view. Alternatively, any local housing authority could be transformed into a land-and-housing authority, becoming a corporate instrument of local government with broad land-acquisition powers.

The bill did not survive congressional wrangling, though various components became building blocks for future legislation, including the 1949 Wagner-Ellender-Taft Act. Catherine's observations and criticism proved prophetic. Her ideas and words set the stage for a decade-long debate on how and when federal intervention would be welcome in housing and local planning. She envisaged the creation of a federal department, at cabinet level, that would encourage urban and metropolitan planning, and administer housing and public works in a manner similar to the Department of Agriculture's rural operations.

The war began to take its toll among people she knew. A British acquaintance, Barbara Clements, wrote in 1943 of the battlefield death of her nephew, a young man Catherine knew well. Clements also asked for help for a young stranger. "One of the men who came out of Spain, an Hungarian called Paul Partos, would like very much to be able to come to America," wrote Clements. "The problem and request are: he needs two sponsors, preferably people who would know him. If you feel you could act as one of the sponsors it would be very helpful."[4]

Partos, a radio engineer who had been living in Great Britain since the end of the Spanish Civil War, was in danger of being forced to leave. "He will not be well liked by the State Department," Clements warned Catherine. "As you must know, those men that escaped from Spain have all been branded as revolutionaries, and Paul has been a part of the Spanish Anarchist movement and is known to have so been by both the British and the U.S. side ... The thing is that you might be putting yourself in a very embarrassing position personally if you accepted the responsibility and as such I wanted to make it quite clear what his past record has been."[5]

It took Catherine less than a week to respond affirmatively on behalf of the political exile. "As for the Hungarian, of course I'll sponsor him," she replied. "Do I have to swear that I know him to be politically respectable by State Department standards? I can just say that I met him (in England in 1939) in a social way through a close personal friend and know that he could make a living and in general be a worthy citizen. I'd be glad to do it without further consideration."[6] Was this event a factor when the House Un-American Activities Committee deemed Catherine undesirable ten years later? One can only speculate, as the records on those hearings have never been fully opened.

One year later the large circle of friends was stunned by the combat death of Geddes Mumford, son of Sophie and Lewis, in northern Italy. Catherine had forged a special bond with the boy when he was very young, while his mother travelled by herself in Europe. She had offered to look after Geddes and urged Lewis to spend time alone with Sophie in Europe (an offer Lewis had not taken up). To his father's pleasure, Geddes had called Catherine "our friend." Now he was gone. Catherine found words of condolence when many others could not. "If some fantastic circumstances did confront Geddes, you can know that he was equipped with the only qualities that could bring him through, boldness and initiative. And that sense of adventure that he always emanated even when he was very small."

Lewis had been among the first intellectuals to argue fervently for American intervention to stop the spread of fascism in Europe. First Mussolini, then Franco increased his resolve, while other progressive thinkers argued for nonintervention. Once war began Mumford resigned from the editorial board of the *New Republic,* protesting the senior editors' cowardice in arguing for American restraint. Catherine had been uncertain, but respected Lewis's viewpoint. Now he had made the ultimate sacrifice. He coped by writing *Green Memories,* a heartfelt book about his relationship with his son.

Catherine's year in Cambridge was marked by frequent absences as she found opportunities to network with planners across the continent. In February 1943 she addressed the Ontario Association of Architects in Toronto on postwar housing needs and was amused by their high degree of formality, including toasts to King, Prime Minister, and Empire. Her honorarium of $50 was paid jointly by the OAA and the Canadian Broadcasting Corporation, which recorded her speech for future broadcasting. Three months later she received an income tax bill for $3.75 from Canada's Department of National Revenue. Always meticulous in financial matters she paid promptly, but soon received another bill.

Catherine fired back an angry note. "Now I have another bill, enclosed herewith, for the same $3.75 plus $4.13. I am returning it to ask you to send me a bill for the *total* sum owed to you, allowing for the $3.75 already paid. I will then remit the full amount in order not to drag this operation on throughout the year." It was, in fact, a full year, during which countless tax forms flew back and forth, before the matter was settled. Her income from the speech had been $50: $21.25 in Canadian dollars and the rest in US funds. "Must I pay Canadian as well as American income tax on this amount, and if so what is the Canadian rate and how is it arrived at?" she inquired. "Since my own work is almost entirely voluntary this year, and my income very low, I really must rebel if the net result of making a speech in a worthy cause is to pay the Canadian Government for the privilege."[7] In the end Catherine got a refund of $7.88 in Canadian cash. It was not unusual for her to be caught up in such minutiae, which might explain her failure to find time to work on a second book.

Bill made use of Catherine's absences to catch up on course work, but missed her badly. He had married relatively late in life and longed for a traditional hearth and home, even though he took pride in the professional demands upon his wife. Federal organizations, such as NAHO and NPHC, called her to Washington, and MOMA committee meetings took her regularly to New York. While she was away, Bill spent many dinner hours in philosophical discussion about architectural education with Dean Hudnut, a man he profoundly admired.

During their time together in Cambridge, Catherine and Bill took long bike and train rides. They explored New England villages from New Hampshire to the far corners of Maine, logging as much as five hundred miles in a month. Such activities were new to Bill and he loved them. During the summers he and Catherine returned to San Francisco. He would visit his architectural office, temporarily housed in a loft above Tommy Church's office. Bill's partner Theodore Bernardi shared the office with CHPA. Catherine often accompanied Bill, taking the opportunity to check up on CHPA business (it was floundering under the weak leadership of a man named McGrath). They would sometimes stay in the elegant Gerbode home in San Francisco or in the beautiful Berkeley home of Sadie Gregory. They talked about starting a family.

The first to learn of Catherine's pregnancy was her mother, in December 1943. It was to be kept a secret until the new year; the baby was due in July 1944. "I hope you will take life more easy and not rush about as you've been doing for years, for your own sake and for the child's future welfare," Bertie wrote.[8] This motherly advice would be honoured in the breach. Bertie was thrilled and could not keep the secret. Betty "danced mother right off her feet" when she got the news on Christmas Day.

Letters of joy, congratulations, and advice flew in from Washington and California friends as the news blazed across the country. Several friends either were expecting or had just given birth, and they offered useful suggestions to a woman who had never displayed the least interest in babies. The Wursters planned to be back in San Francisco by the end of April, after Bill finished his thesis. They planned to have the baby at Stanford Hospital.

Unfortunately the dream of motherhood became a nightmare in mid-February 1944, when Catherine lost her baby. "It does not bear thinking of you in a hospital, and all the shock and suffering and disappointment," wrote Sadie Gregory one month after applauding their "magnificent news." Catherine wrote to her mother on her return home from hospital: "I certainly proved to myself that I have no basic chemical necessity to have children. The periodic yowls on the maternity floor simply made me wonder what on earth I was doing there, instead of bursting into tears as I doubtless should have."[9] During the ten days following her miscarriage she turned out more published writing than she ever had managed in such a short period. A saddened Bill also buried himself in his work as he prepared for his Ph.D. orals, scheduled for later that month.

Shortly after passing his orals, Bill was approached by Professor F.J. Adams, head of the search committee at the Massachusetts Institute of Technology to see if he would be interested in becoming dean of architecture. By then his primary interests were education and national affairs. Bill was pleased with the offer, but he and Catherine left Cambridge for California at the end of March without replying to MIT's advances. He nursed the idea of heading the department of architecture at UC Berkeley.

Catherine and Bill were supremely happy to be back in San Francisco when a formal offer was tendered by MIT, without any strings or qualifications. UC Berkeley had not come up with the hoped-for appointment, and Bill agreed to begin his tenure as dean of the School of Architecture and City Planning at MIT in the winter of 1945. Catherine rationalized that life in Cambridge would be more conducive to her intellectual work than life in California, where she was distracted daily by political events. Bill continued to harbour the deep hope that one day he would return to the Bay Area as dean of architecture at UC Berkeley.

Shortly after returning to San Francisco, Catherine drove to Los Angeles to assess Baldwin Hills Village, a relatively unknown community housing project. "Baldwin Hills Village: Description and Appraisal" appeared in the September 1944 issue of *Pencil Points*. Catherine's article explored the project, whose layout and diversity of units reminded her of the best modern housing she had seen in Europe a decade earlier. Site planning and landscape details were exceptionally well designed for a dense neighbourhood. The article drew so much attention to this fine example of community development that students of planning made pilgrimages there for years afterwards. Catherine sent a copy of the article to Philip Johnson, her collaborator on several housing exhibitions at MOMA. He hailed it a journalistic masterpiece and urged her to write another book or, at the very least, more articles – her thinking was so clear and her style so colourful and apt.

Encouraged by favourable responses to the article, Catherine briefly considered writing a second edition of *Modern Housing*, but changed her mind. Her activities of the past decade had taught her much about urban planning, land use, the environment and, above all, the politics of social change. An entirely new book was in order. After considering titles such as "The Politics of Environment," or "Site, Shelter and Community," she settled on "The Politics of Planning: A Study of Land, Cities, and Housing in the U.S.A.," and cobbled together a two-page draft proposal. "Land is always planned, but by whom? for what purpose? how effectively?" she observed, under a preface titled "Land Plus Building Equals Environment. "(This book is not so much a history as an interpretation, pointed toward the decisions that confront us, of the social factors that have shaped our present environment.)"[10]

Catherine proposed four broad chapters. The first would replicate the successful format of *Modern Housing* by discussing historical patterns with emphasis on the framework of settlement and expansion. She would compare what she called "disciplined democracy" with "colonial feudalism," using examples from the mid-Atlantic and Hudson Valley regions. She would also contrast the settlement patterns of the New England community and southern plantation with California's Spanish mission.

The second chapter, titled "Against the Tide: Movements Popular and Otherwise," would explore the theme of "every man for himself." Catherine would compare the frontier homestead and its infinite quarter sections with "Boomtown" and its speculation, slums, and sterile skyscrapers. She envisioned the frontier homestead as a factory farm, whereas Boomtown represented an escape to the suburbs and metropolitan explosion.

The chapter would be further divided into two major sections. "Toward Regional Planning" would review environmental and regional development under the New Deal and focus on conservation, which Catherine defined as "the responsibility of owning a continent." Subheadings within the section covered issues of vital national importance that had been overshadowed by the war, including: national parks and wilderness; the Reclamation Act and planned resettlement, in which the Columbia Basin and California's Central Valley would be linked to the Tennessee Valley Authority and the Rural Rehabilitation and Farm Security Administrations; public power, the key to the pattern of production; metropolitan regionalism and the pioneers of urban wilderness, from Boston to Los Angeles; and, finally, a section called "Martyrdom of the Innocents," which would focus on regional and state planning and on the work of the National Resources Planning Board.

Chapter Two's other major section, "Toward Modern Cities and Houses," also contained numerous subsections, including: public health and welfare, and the need for new standards; the wartime housing experience, including home-front battles on certain basic principles; and outdoor living – "new habits, popular ideals and planned communities from Owen to Howard to Radburn and Greenbelt." Five subsections would be devoted to the US Housing Act of 1937; two others to Catherine's analysis of architecture and social class ("Modern Architecture: Snob Style toward a Fresh Vernacular" and "City Planning in Practice: Class Zoning to Embryonic Master Plans"). The final subsections would anticipate her future interests: "Tax Reform: Too Late or Too Early?" and "Metropolitan Government: Is It on Its Way?"

The third chapter, "Framework for the Future," would be based on the axiom that progress and prosperity require physical reorganization. It would address issues from micro to macro scale and pose the central question: "What do we really want?" The question would be answered in several sections comprising the core of the book. Her themes included: the significance of wartime migration; the conception of land as commodity versus public utility; regional planning on a human scale; the politics of neighbourhood protection; optimum versus minimum living standards; the US and world environment; the war between experts and people; and the dynamics of democratic reconstruction – initiative, decision, responsibility. One of these sections, "Housing: The Need Must Determine the Market," signalled a substantial shift in Catherine's thinking about public housing. The section on the US and world environment

("The Earth as a Place to Live On") anticipated the coming global preoccupation with environment and its universal implications.

The fourth chapter, "A Platform for Physical Reconstruction," had a geopolitical perspective that would cover land (from commodity to public utility), neighbourhood protection, and segregation versus community. The chapter would summarize the use of urban land, the necessity of planning its allocation, and the potential for innovative administrative decision making from neighbourhood to national levels.

Catherine circulated the two-page outline among her friends. None responded more enthusiastically than Lewis Mumford, who scribbled "First Rate" over the title page and endless notes throughout, transforming the draft into a battlefield of crisscrossing arrows and darts. Running out of space, Lewis expanded his comments into a three-page, single-spaced letter of encouragement, beginning with "the outline is magnificent and this is the very book you were born to write."[11]

Begin, Lewis exhorted her. "There is no reason why you shouldn't write a book that no one else will do for another generation and the sooner you get to work on it the better."[12] This was followed by a closely argued analysis starting with a suggestion of dropping "U.S.A." from her title. He questioned the word *planning,* believing it had become "a cuss word in many circles and is damned even before it is looked at," and suggested the word *environment* instead, but thought it clumsy, and decided to leave the whole title issue to the very end. In reference to the first chapter on historical patterns, he urged Catherine to distinguish between her proposed frameworks of expansion, which he called "a mechanical process," and "settlement," which he described as "an organic process."

Lewis urged Catherine to "do justice to the Mormons and particularly Brigham Young ... it would be helpful to show what a planned, intelligent settlement could accomplish, given the necessary social ideals, in the face of formidable natural obstacles." He also hoped that the book would deal with the broad conversion of the western frontier to urban settlements. To that end he encouraged Catherine to consult a colleague of his at Oberlin College "who knows more from a botanical and ecological standpoint than anyone else in the country."

Pragmatically, Lewis suggested that "a good writer's discipline" would be achieved if Catherine were to establish final conclusions before spending too much time on the preparatory work. He then waxed philosophical about "the nature of democratic decentralization and the relationship between the authority that is born of knowledge and skill, and the great mass of men who are affected by it," and warned "our abstract framework of responsible government whether in a trade union or a political state has no solid, concrete organs of expression, or at least not half enough of them:

voting and formal assent are often ways out of accepting personal responsibility instead of a way of asserting it."

Lewis recalled that he had meant to deal exhaustively with the content of politics in the third volume of his *Renewal of Life* series, but the pressure of the subject pushed it in a different direction. He regretted that he had not expanded on politics in *The Culture of Cities* and urged Catherine to tackle "the matter of democracy versus dictatorship, bureaucratic or military, smooth or rough." He saw "a danger in attributing some special powers to an amorphous or incoherent democracy as opposed to one in which there is a constant recruitment of talent. Jacksonian democracy is for me not democracy but a degenerate form of it: the essence of a real democracy is not lack of leadership but the presence of enough general intelligence and sense of citizenship to control and direct, to initiate and veto the proposals of the leaders." Lewis encouraged Catherine to hold an effective balance between the principle of authority and the principle of private judgment.

He apologized for getting so carried away from the core subject of her book, explaining that her outline had lit sparks that sent him off on impassioned musings. "Each of us has his own field, his own point of view, his own capacities." Referring to their earlier relationship for the first time in almost ten years, he wrote, "even in the first days I knew you, I recognized you were an enemy (temperament) quite as much as a friend: that is why I have learned so much from you ... Until people wanted better communities there was no sense in devising a means to their getting them. When I finally revise *The Culture of Cities* I shall devote a greater amount of space to the political instruments unless you doing *your* work makes any additions of mine superfluous."

Carefully choosing words from his rapturous letters of the past, he concluded, "Temperamental differences or no, the outline of your book tremendously excites me and I hope that the task will rouse you to your fullest efforts, and betray you into a few uplifting messianic words too."

Catherine had expressed some doubt about her ability to mount such an ambitious book. Lewis was not in the least taken in by the tactic of humility and asserted, harshly, that there was not a molecule of humility in her. Softening slightly, he urged her to learn to believe in herself if she was going to write a good book. He closed his analysis with admiration for the woman who had once been central to his life. "There is no one in America who could do it half so well or make such a positive contribution to fresh thinking, and what is more important perhaps, fresh acting. If you need any further bouquets, you will have to get them from Bill."[13]

Catherine was pleased with Lewis's letter and flattered by his praise. "It's just the boost I need and all the suggestions are exactly right. Curious that I left out the Mormons (I stopped off for several days in Utah a couple of years ago just to look at their village-farming pattern, and have been using it ever since to argue with the Columbia Basin powers)." In response to his political/philosophical peregrinations, she wrote: "It isn't that I believe that mass judgment is invariably better than that of the creative leaders. But I do believe that the intellectuals always and continuously need a *check*, above all when they're promoting policies which affect the lives of everyone directly." Catherine held the belief that "there are always several constructive courses possible – and the *right* one among them is the one that can best enlist popular support and understanding and responsible participation. (And conversely, any course that can't do that in the long run is probably wrong, no matter how it looks on paper). And to discover the positive path that *will* strike the spark is a fundamental and vital technique in itself – a technique which has been almost completely neglected by those very planners and philosophers who are intellectually most advanced."[14]

CATHERINE WITH BORIS SHISHKIN (LEFT) AND OSCAR STONOROV IN 1945

The Wursters and their friends [Boris Shishkin and Oscar Stonorov] entered into heated discussions about the best approach to postwar reconstruction in Europe.

Lewis offered such thoughtful counsel because he admired Catherine's gifts as a writer. "None could guess the scope of her sensibility and imagination as a writer who had not read the letters she wrote me, as a young woman," Mumford wrote to Frederic J. Osborn many years later.[15]

The acclaim from all who read Catherine's book outline ought to have encouraged her to begin writing. She did not, and the reasons remain a mystery. Although several publishers were interested in a second Catherine Bauer book, no manuscript appeared and no further drafts of this or any other book have come to light. Instead, over the next twenty years, her ideas and convictions – many of which found first expression in the book's outline – were framed and communicated to her students and the public through lectures and journal articles. Immediate social and political changes determined Catherine's priorities and preoccupations.

The Wursters and their friends entered into heated discussions about the best approach to postwar reconstruction in Europe. Some hoped to reestablish the professional organization, Congrès Internationaux d'Architecture Moderne (CIAM), founded in 1928. The CIAM had led the way during the prewar decade in housing and modern architecture in England and on the Continent. Several European architects in the United States – Gropius, Wagner, and Jose Luis Sert among them – saw in it a vehicle for postwar rebuilding.

Others, mostly Americans, expressed doubt about CIAM's continued viability. Harvard's Dean Hudnut led the oppositional group, arguing that CIAM belonged to the past, was too Eurocentric, and too biased toward modernist architecture. He favoured a newer organization – the American Society of Architects and Planners (ASAP) – to spearhead the postwar effort. In June 1944, Hudnut addressed a large audience at MOMA on the issue, but his presentation was flat and ultimately failed to move the audience, most of whom supported a rebirth of CIAM. Although she admired Hudnut, Catherine was among the CIAM supporters. The dialogue spawned by the debate served to promote discussion on the urgent need for thoughtful postwar reconstruction and housing. The CIAM forces continued to gain strength and eventually convened their first postwar congress in Bridgewater, England, in 1947.

On September 25, 1944, the Wursters loaded up their car for the long journey east. They stopped along the way at national parks (including Yellowstone), at architectural sites (including John Wellborn Root railroad station in La Crosse), and at private homes (their Madison friends, the Gauses, and relatives in Princeton). By Thanksgiving they had settled on Chestnut Street in Boston, as Bill prepared to take over the reins at MIT's School of Architecture. In January Catherine became pregnant. This time she waited two months to blast the news across the country. Her mother was the first to be notified. "I get shot with hormones twice a week and take all kinds of pills, and the doctor discovered that my blood is Rh negative, so poor Bill, who like all big strong husks practically swoons at the thought of blood, had to go and get his veins opened up too."[16] Catherine was sternly cautioned to avoid strenuous activities. Bicycle riding and swimming were prohibited, which made her truly "fair, fat and forty" by May 1945.[17]

It seemed the right time to buy a home, and impulsively the Wursters purchased the first property they saw, on Farwell Place in Cambridge. Many frustrating months elapsed before they could take possession of the place: the tenants refused to move until they found identical living quarters. This led to an embarrassing ordeal, with the tenants taking the Wursters to an Office of Price Administration hearing. The ruling favoured the Wursters but nevertheless garnered headlines in a local paper: "Housing Expert Caught in Own Noose." The location was perfect for the Wursters, between Catherine's Harvard and Bill's MIT.

THE HOUSE IN CAMBRIDGE

It seemed the right time to buy a home, and impulsively the Wursters purchased the first property they saw, on Farwell Place in Cambridge.

HARVARD

*A housing seminar can be most effective only when
the students represent widely differing viewpoints and
training, including the technical/aesthetic and
social/economic fields.*

CATHERINE BAUER

Sarah Louise Wurster was born on August 24, 1945, five weeks early. She
would be called Sadie after the Wursters' close friend, Sadie Gregory.
Another friend, Dorothy Liebes, a leading California artist, became Sadie's
godmother. "Congratulations on practically everything – your child and
your professorship at Harvard. She really is the sweetest little lamb I ever
saw,"[18] exulted the new godmother.

CATHERINE WITH BABY SADIE

Sarah Louise Wurster was born on
August 24, 1945, five weeks early.
She would be called Sadie after the
Wursters' close friend, Sadie Gregory.

Meanwhile the new mother was busily preparing to teach a housing
seminar at Harvard's Graduate School of Design. The early birth played
havoc with her preparation time, and with her plans to complete an article
called "Good Neighborhoods" for the *Annals of the American Academy of
Political and Social Science.* "Never ask a pregnant lady to do anything at
all," she had warned the editor, "elderly primiparas particularly should just
lie low before they lie in."[19] Three weeks after Sadie's birth Catherine
delivered the article with a note to the editor: "Sadie and I both feel fine
and now that this article is finally off my chest, I'll settle down to learning
how to prepare formulas, raise bubbles, and all the rest."

"Good Neighborhoods" was significant in that it foreshadowed a new
political direction for Catherine. She began looking beyond the housing
needs of the lowest third economic group, advocating a new civic

philosophy in planning neighbourhoods. Without a comprehensive plan, American cities would be compromised by social retrogression. "The trend towards segregation is one example of the kind of question we have neglected while we argued about cul-de-sacs," she wrote, arguing that planners and housers had ignored the critical questions of class and race relations in a democracy.[20] They had also overlooked the interplay between environmental patterns on one hand and increased leisure and minimum standards of economic security on the other.

Past generations of planners had fuelled the trend to segregation by promoting enormous one-class dormitories, separated from one another and from workplaces. She blamed "the zoners' feudal ideal of subdividing the city map into a series of standardized watertight compartments." She condemned early social workers for their paternalistic view of the underprivileged as a race apart. As a logical extension of such thinking, neighbourhoods might be designated as Negro low-rent areas or Jewish garden apartments or Anglo-Saxon estates or Italian truck gardens. "The truth is that isolation is as unhealthy and potentially disastrous at the neighborhood level as the national level."

Governmental paternalism was as hazardous to society as any private monopoly, warned Catherine, advocating citizen participation as the best tonic. Diversity was the key to healthy neighbourhoods, comprising a variety of people and offering a variety of services, including industrial. This would lead to a diversified tax base and broaden administrative responsibilities. "What must be assured is simply a degree of variety, a lack of exclusiveness, in short – a balance within the neighborhood as a whole." Her criticism was also directed at "distinguished academics" who equated neighbourhood planning with social stratification. She would become one of the first "distinguished academics" to advocate social action for a "balanced civilized life, a democratic life that nurtures and frees the individual while it respects the group."[21]

Catherine was able to finish her article and start planning her graduate housing seminar thanks to the help of Sadie's baby nurse, who had moved into the Wursters' crowded apartment. The course was originally scheduled for the GSD's 1945-46 academic year, to be offered within the Department of City Planning, but her pregnancy delayed its start to January 1946. Catherine welcomed the opportunity to influence future practitioners in her field, in contrast to the budding social workers she had taught at UC Berkeley.

The devastating social and economic consequences of the hungry '30s and brutal '40s had challenged the academic assumption that planning belonged to the architectural profession. Planners educated during the '20s and '30s were students of architecture, traditionally taught to design

CATHERINE, c. 1946

She would become one of the first "distinguished academics" to advocate social action for a "balanced civilized life, a democratic life that nurtures and frees the individual while it respects the group."

projects using brick and mortar. For the most part they had failed to anticipate the political, social, and economic consequences of their planning decisions. The fallout from the Second World War underscored the need for cooperation between design disciplines and social sciences, and for retooling educational curricula for postwar urban planning. For the first time in the United States, important questions were being raised: For whom, by whom, and by what means would the new world be planned? How would the university prepare students for action? Could planning be taught formally, or should it be learned through apprenticeship? Should professional planning practice stress physical, social, economic, or political issues?

The planning curriculum at Harvard sprang from a few courses offered in the 1920s under the direction of Professor Henry V. Hubbard in the Department of Landscape Architecture. Hubbard's retirement in 1944 occasioned a rethinking of the approach, and in 1945 the GSD's Dean Hudnut appointed G. Holmes Perkins – Gropius's teaching assistant at Harvard's School of Architecture before the war – to head up the school's new planning program. Perkins had spent the war years in Washington managing the complex process of allocating housing resources to urban communities reeling under the impact of wartime migrant workers. He had the right credentials and, equally important, he was an American. Hudnut wanted to balance his largely European faculty with some strong local talent. The Germans, in particular, were overrepresented on the GSD faculty, according to Hudnut, who resisted Gropius's push to add the painter Josef Albers to a roster that already included Marcel Breuer and Martin Wagner.

Perkins had proven his mettle as an agent of change when, as a student, he participated in a revolt against Beaux Arts training in architecture. "Without leadership or guidance we really did not know why we were revolting, but we were young and were searching for something better," Perkins recalls.[22] Now he was in a position to effect a substantive break with tradition. With Hudnut's support he reshaped the curriculum, offering students a wide range of courses leading to a Masters of City Planning.

Perkins created a faculty council composed of two geographers (Whittlesey and Ackerman), two political scientists (Gaus and Lambie), two economists (Harris and Abbot), a sociologist (Parsons), and an architect (Gropius). Together they developed a new curriculum for the education of professional planners. Students were sought with strong academic standing in the social sciences, life sciences, or design. Collaborative projects would be encouraged, drawing from all GSD departments: landscape architecture, city planning, and architecture. Students would also be credited for courses taken outside the school.

A major break with tradition was the creation of Planning I, a first-year joint studio course in architecture, landscape architecture, and city planning. Lectures in basic design, art history, and the history of the city were linked in the studio course's curriculum, with the goal of preparing students for collaborative approaches to solving common urban problems.

Perkins had met Catherine in Washington when both were involved in the debate on postwar housing. In May 1945, he invited her for lunch to outline his plans for a housing component to the GSD program. She was stunned when he ended the meal by inviting her to teach it, starting that fall. The timing was unthinkable, she said, given her condition. He was prepared to wait one semester for her, to which she replied that she would have to weigh the request. Bill had been making plans for a housing course at MIT, and she would not consider teaching in direct competition to his program. In this instance she deferred to Bill's wishes entirely. Fortunately, Bill sided with Perkins; "CBW," as she signed most letters and memoranda, now embarked on an academic career that lasted the rest of her life.

Catherine was fascinated by the seminar's possibilities and hoped to carry Perkins's notion of a cross-disciplinary student body further by enrolling students from other departments, perhaps even other colleges. At the University of California, she had given considerable thought to the creation of an effective curriculum and was pleased that she could test her ideas on planning students. To Perkins she wrote:

> *I am firmly convinced that a housing seminar can be most effective only when the students represent widely differing viewpoints and training, including particularly the technical/aesthetic and socio/economic fields. The problems cut across so many professional departments with almost equal emphasis that no one aspect can be handled successfully in practice without some positive discipline for breaking down some of the barricades that now isolate almost every profession, that it would probably be worth giving a course in it to a mixed group even if housing itself were not so important. Therefore I should like to urge that it be set up from the start to draw in Littauer [social sciences] students as well as architects.*[23]

Catherine's idea was radical: up to that time, no architectural or planning student enrolled in GSD would have taken courses at Littauer School. Nor would social sciences students have considered enrolling in GSD courses. She pushed her ideas further. How about bringing MIT students to Harvard to participate in her seminar?

> *So, presumptuous though it may be, the question that has been going through my head for the past ten days is: could there be any possibility at all of joint sponsorship for such a course, on a strictly temporary basis, by the School of Design, Littauer, and MIT? This may well be a screwy idea, entirely unworkable from anybody's point of view. The course might not fit at all into MIT's plans, and perhaps in any case this is getting too close to that husband-and-wife machine that Bill and I both loathe. And yet on the other hand it might be a chance to demonstrate that kind of institutional flexibility and coordination that could make Cambridge a natural center for all kinds and varieties of work in the broad field of social planning. And, as a purely one-term experiment, such a scheme would involve no future commitments by anyone.*[24]

During the next few months Catherine discussed her ideas with her husband and many of their friends. Perhaps spurred by these discussions, Bill broadened his own approach to the architectural and graduate school curricula at MIT, even as he made it clear that "Catherine and I want to operate on these matters of planning education entirely separately, for we feel so strongly that our own contentment, as well as the good we do in any cause, may depend on this approach."[25]

Carl Joachim Friedrich, an august political science professor at Littauer, shared ideas of approach and content with Catherine. He hoped some architecture and city planning students would attend his courses, and she wanted social science students in hers. He raised the possibility of a joint course on equal terms. "I'd really be tempted to try it," Catherine wrote to Perkins, "except that it would have to mean doubling the time and credits and there will unavoidably be students in each course who wouldn't need or want the other."[26] She would, however, encourage some of her students to take Friedrich's course and he sent some students to her. He devoted one of his weekend student "conferences" to housing in collaboration with Catherine.

Catherine was the first woman to serve on the GSD faculty. Her seminar, Housing 7, commenced in January 1946, though her appointment was not officially confirmed by the Fellows of Harvard College until June of that year. She taught housing in a community context: as an environment for living, with specific social, economic, and political goals. Her seminar focused on political action as it attempted to bring the social science and design disciplines together in a common cause.

Twenty-one students took Housing 7 for credit: six architects, seven regional planners, five political scientists, one sociologist, and two MIT planning students. There were ten auditors, including faculty members from Littauer and MIT's planning program. In her lectures she aimed less to impart information than to raise questions, clarify issues, and stimulate discussion. Two brief papers were required: a rough sketch of housing needs in the student's own community (aimed at familiarizing students with statistical sources and survey methods); and a summary of current issues in housing policy based on readings and discussion. Students were also required to write term papers on a topics of their own choosing. Much of Catherine's time was spent in individual conferences during which topics and approaches were discussed. Group topics were encouraged and several were undertaken.

Students were divided into three groups to work on joint projects. This was only marginally successful. "Of the three group studies," Catherine informed Perkins in her post-seminar critique, "the only one that could be called a successful group effort was that on [Planning] Standards by Davis, Oberlander and Olsen, i.e. two architects and a planner. The other two, involving cooperation between social science and technical students, were seriously hampered by the mechanical or temperamental difficulties of such collaboration."[27] Davis founded and still runs a major architectural and planning practice in New Orleans. Oberlander and Olsen pursued academic and professional careers for more than forty years.

To her profound regret, Catherine discovered that various professional neophytes regarded each other with very little interest and had little sense of the benefits of collaboration. She expressed her disappointment in the

May 1947 issue of the *Journal of Housing*: "If they are not tied together at university level, how can we expect the products of education do so once out in the world?"

Lloyd Rodwin, one of her Housing 7 students, remembers Catherine vividly. She did not present herself as a scholar (she once listed her profession as "reformer" when she registered at a hotel). Her lectures lacked the spark of political fervour, according to Rodwin, but she was always stimulating and unpredictable. With a vivacious persona, and a voice like Marlene Dietrich, she encouraged free-flowing discussions and taught by example and through dialogue. Never at a loss for facts, Catherine forced the students to think for themselves by posing difficult questions. She generated excitement by inviting eminent professionals to contribute to the class, then challenged the "experts" with questions that her intimidated students were reluctant to ask.

Housing 7 guests included Catherine's former professional associates and friends, including Warren Vinton, Herbert Emmerich, Ernest Bohn, Charles Ascher, Coleman Woodbury, Charles Abrams, and Lewis Mumford. Each made a provocative contribution and brought significant cross-disciplinary discussions to the seminar. She urged Leon Keyserling to come and discuss the national housing scene, specifically the broad purposes of S 1592, the future Wagner-Ellender-Taft Act under discussion in Congress. "My own students having by then enough background will want to haggle over specific aspects of housing policy."[28] Catherine taught Housing 7 for three years, using a similar format but refining the curriculum each term.

Her students and faculty colleagues loved her. Her office was always open to them for consultation. Talk sparkled in her presence, and she was fascinated by people's ideas and innovative minds. Catherine is remembered for her deep voice and lilting laughter that echoed through the corridors of GSD. Her flared skirts rustled as she walked in a broad stride, clicking along in low-heeled shoes. She would rush into the classroom carrying a full briefcase in one hand and balancing a stack of books under the other arm. After setting down her load she would invariably reach into her large, leather handbag for a cigarette and a small, portable ashtray with a lid.

Rodwin's first encounter with Catherine was interesting both in its historical content and in how it affected his career. Catherine was among the best informed housers in the country: she kept abreast of all the literature even remotely associated with the field. During the fall after Sadie's birth, she was able to catch up on stacks of reading. One day her eye fell upon an article titled "Garden Cities and the Metropolis" in the August 1945 issue of the *Journal of Land and Public Utility Economics* (later known as

CATHERINE WALKING, NOVEMBER 1949

Her students and faculty colleagues loved her. Her office was always open to them for consultation. Talk sparkled in her presence, and she was fascinated by people's ideas and innovative minds. Catherine is remembered for her deep voice and lilting laughter that echoed through the corridors of GSD.

Land Economics).[29] She noted with dismay that it criticized the Garden City concept espoused by the British urban theorist, Ebenezer Howard, in his 1898 book, *Garden Cities of Tomorrow* – a text she held dear. A lively, six-month long correspondence commenced between Catherine, the author, and eventually Lewis Mumford.

Catherine had applauded Ebenezer Howard's Garden City development in *Modern Housing* as "a town designed for healthy living and industry; of a size that makes possible a full measure of social life, but not larger; surrounded by a rural belt; the whole of the land being in public ownership or held in trust for the community. No tiny isolated colony ... but a complete working city whose estimated population was to be around thirty thousand."[30] The article debunking the Garden City idea was written by Lloyd Rodwin, an unknown graduate student and research assistant in the Department of Economics at the University of Wisconsin.

Rodwin had been a student of Charles Abrams at the New School of Social Research in New York. Abrams paved the way for his bright young student to attain a research appointment in land economics at the University of Wisconsin. There he enrolled in seminars offered by Leonard Salter and Catherine's friend, John M. Gaus. Rodwin's paper for Salter's seminar so impressed Gaus that he arranged to have it published.

A born and bred New Yorker who thought he understood the big city, Rodwin found Ebenezer Howard's ideas bizarre. In his article he disagreed with Howard and borrowed a quote from a Bauer article as evidence: "No general 'Back to the Land' movement can be part of a truly progressive postwar policy, in spite of the sentimental appeal such a program can always have in a country still nostalgic for its lost frontier."[31] Rodwin questioned Howard's promotion of healthy, modestly sized communities, each with its own land, surrounded by green areas beyond which other communities might be formed. In Rodwin's view, Howard had paid insufficient attention to the regions in which Garden Cities were to play their strategic roles. He challenged Howard's assumptions on issues of rural migration, population growth, industrial location, journey to work, comparative urban costs, and municipal government administration.

Howard had argued that best results would be achieved by starting a bold plan on comparatively virgin soil rather than by adapting old cities to new needs. "The major job of the future is that of improving the cities we have," Rodwin countered, "and of dealing with existing social, economic and political facts."[32] Howard had proposed that Garden Cities be planned and built without reference to special site advantages for industrial development. Rodwin considered this an error of judgment that ignored the importance of location. Although he demurred on Howard's notion of a close link between working and living, he warned of the consequences of restrictions of scale, variety of employment, and economic activities inherent in the size and location of a Garden City.

Rodwin conceded that some of Howard's ideals had some merit within the framework of modern urban planning. "Well integrated cities, planned land use, and controlled size and growth are recognized desiderata, [but] the weak points of the Garden City idea stem from its failure to comprehend many of the essential chores of the city. The wonder is that Howard, with his deep interest in moral well-being, formulated such a persuasive, even though partial, ideal."[33] In a word, Rodwin pronounced Howard's planning formulas simplistic: "The planning function has widened to include social, economic, as well as physical facts. He who would help build the city of tomorrow must reckon with ... jobs and security, homes and population trends, aesthetics and economics, politics and social drift." Rodwin concluded that Howard's inspirational message must be tempered by modern realities. "Prophets should never be taken too literally, especially by subsequent generations."[34]

Shortly after the article appeared, Rodwin got an urgent call from the journal's editor. "You'd better come down here quickly," she said, "we just received a six-page, type-written, single spaced letter from Catherine Bauer, raking you over the coals." After reading it Rodwin thought, "Lord Almighty, the first time I ever get anything published I get hit on the head as a dolt."

Catherine's angry letter demanded to know "who is this Rodwin and what's the basis of his assertions?" and added, "It's not often that you get a serious discussion on a subject like this, it's just a pity that it's wrong on so many counts." She eventually wrote a detailed response, published as "Garden Cities and the Metropolis: A Reply," that articulated the Garden City philosophy. It was, she wrote, based on the principle of a balanced environment, favourable to the family and designed on a human scale. "If England is ahead of us in urban planning and housing policy, isn't it partly because the revitalized Garden City movement helped to clarify and dramatize these basic modern principles?"[35] Catherine linked Howard's ideas to the American Garden Cities of Radburn and the Greenbelt towns. Rodwin's article gave Catherine the opportunity to air a pet philosophy in a journal of economics:

> *The phrase [Garden City] itself has been properly corrupted to signify nothing more than a segregated upper-class suburb of orderly, one-family homes ... The idea of planning and building a complete new self-contained city in virgin territory is so foreign to our current thinking that we do not even grasp the chance when it is handed to us on a platter – as it is, for instance, in the impending reclamation and settlement of the Columbia Basin in the Northwest ... There will be at least a quarter of a million people in a region where almost none live today. New towns of substantial size will spring up, in any case, to serve as market centers ... The federal government already controls water distribution, and is committed to buying up most of the land in the basin in advance of settlement. And yet, almost no one is seriously concerned with this opportunity to demonstrate a modern urban environment from the ground up.[36]*

Catherine welcomed a public debate on these important and timely issues. She shared Rodwin's opposition to a major US planning policy that would establish isolated, self-sufficient new municipalities of thirty thousand to fifty thousand people. Still, she asked, how many cities are even beginning to think in terms of drastically lowered densities in central areas? What metropolitan region has yet faced the need to prohibit fringe development and guide new building into satellite communities containing a healthy variety of people and a sensible balance of home and shops, work and play, building and open space? "It is too soon to bury the Garden City movement," she wrote.[37]

Three weeks later after Catherine's initial letter, Rodwin received a second summons from the editor who, this time, waved an even thicker envelope. "I don't know what you did," the editor said. "I got a 12-page, single-spaced letter from Lewis Mumford also raking you over the coals!" Stunned, Rodwin later turned to Professor Salter:

"I'm dead," he moaned.

"Boy, you're made," was Salter's prophetic reply.

Mumford took Rodwin to task much more sharply than Catherine had. His response came in the form of a short article, also entitled "Garden Cities and the Metropolis: A Reply."[38] He accused Rodwin of confusing three quite different processes: open order planning, population dispersal, and decentralization by urban reintegration. Calling this "growth by the Garden City method," Mumford addressed each of Rodwin's points, starting with a desirable size for a city. "Size when it reaches a certain limit is a radical defect for two reasons, first because it removes the possibility of maintaining a balanced environment, and second because the mere mechanical massing of population creates difficulties which can be overcome only by an undue expenditure of capital and income." Rodwin had criticized Letchworth, the first Garden City, for being unable to attract industry because it was too far from London. Mumford disagreed and argued that Rodwin had misinterpreted the Garden City idea, as "Howard's guiding idea was balance and completeness, not self-sufficiency."

Rodwin's assertion that "thinking, however imaginative, must reflect continuities not mutations if it is to find practical expression," earned a stinging rebuke from Mumford. He wondered whether Rodwin really believed this, because "if he did, by the same token people who sought to improve transportation should have devoted themselves to breeding faster horses rather than inventing railroads, motor cars or airplanes. Each of those inventions was a mutation, not a continuity."

Rodwin had touched upon the importance of "the journey to work" in relation to the scale and layout of Garden Cities, and had cited a recent publication, *Journey to Work,* by Kate Lipman, professor at the London School of Economics. In a letter to Catherine, Mumford rejected the book as "a fine example of pseudo-research, because the author accepts as a premise the very thing she should have investigated statistically, namely, the exact extent to which living in a big city actually gives one a choice of jobs throughout its area. That premise seemed so unchallengeable to her that she never bothered to check it up. Nothing she says has the faintest bearing on the Garden City and Rodwin was awfully confused to think that it had."[39] The chapter on "Social Cities" in Ebenezer Howard's book "attempts to show that the advantage of a single Garden City would be multiplied by having a circuit of Garden Cities with really rapid transportation between them."[40] Mumford judged that Rodwin probably failed to understand Howard because "no one can say that Howard ever wrote fancy English [and] it seems quite as easy to misunderstand Howard as it is to misunderstand me."

Flattered by this attention from two such prominent figures, and convinced that he could stand his ground, Rodwin issued strong rejoinders. He assured Catherine that he recognized the historic significance of the

Garden City movement and respected its American champions, including Mumford, Bauer, and Frank Lloyd Wright. Catherine had noted that "Mr. Rodwin rightly anticipates further inner migration, particularly from farms to towns, but for some curious reason finds this an argument *against* the feasibility of developing complete new cities." Rodwin was puzzled by this and by Catherine's conclusion that he opposed developing complete new cities. On the contrary, he thought he might have been too optimistic about the extent to which the useful elements in Howard's thinking have been incorporated in contemporary city planning. He based this assertion on the housing bill, then under consideration by Congress. "As for urban land policies being used as planning instruments, C. Bauer, I am sure, knows that if the Wagner-Ellender-Taft Bill ... is passed, municipalities will secure financial aid to purchase land in redevelopment areas and may, with suitable controls, resell or lease this land for use in accordance with the experimental urban redevelopment program."[41] It turned out to be an overly optimistic forecast.

In his rejoinder to Mumford, Rodwin paid tribute to Howard. "Where Howard anticipated vital currents, his ideas have excited men's minds and have possibilities for fulfillment. Where they are not well rooted his ideas forestall the attainment of his ultimate goal of a better way of living. Failure to sift the valid from the invalid may stultify his purposes."

This correspondence between Rodwin, Bauer, and Mumford was published and followed with interest by academicians. John Gaus, who had just moved to Harvard University, recommended Rodwin for a Littauer Fellowship. After the Rodwins settled in Cambridge, Gaus introduced them to Catherine and Bill, who soon embraced them in their circle of friends. With Catherine's encouragement, Rodwin pursued a Ph.D. in regional planning in the Graduate School of Design. Upon completing his dissertation, he expected to move back to the Midwest or to the west coast to teach, but the intervention of Catherine Wurster changed that. At her recommendation, Professor F.J. Adams, chairman of MIT's City Planning Department, offered Rodwin a teaching appointment. Rodwin believes Catherine was behind the offer. This became clear more than a decade later when she supported Rodwin's bid for a professorship. "I had recommended him for his original MIT appointment" she wrote in 1958; by then she was even more impressed by the scope and depth of Rodwin's work in planning.

Thus, an article written by a bright student in a specialized journal, read by a zealous woman housing expert in 1945, led to an illustrious academic career at MIT that would last for forty-five years and culminate in the prestigious Ford International Professorship.

During this busy period Catherine remained active in housing politics.

Encouraged by renowned visitors, her students wrote papers on issues regarding postwar housing. The classroom became an arena for lively discussions on what was going on in Washington. A general housing bill (S 1592) was under consideration "to establish a national housing policy and provide for its execution." Its preamble declared that residential construction and related community development must be encouraged to remedy the serious cumulative housing shortage, eliminate slums, and realize the goal of a decent home for every American family. The construction industry was expected to contribute toward an economy of full production and full employment.

The bill contained eleven titles; the second interested Catherine the most because it called for $25 million for local housing and planning studies in addition to $12.5 million to the National Housing Agency for research to reduce housing costs. Title IV dealt with land assembly and slum and blight clearance. It provided $500 million in one-time federal loans to be repaid with interest within five years, and $50 million a year for a five-year program of permanent loans to be amortized over forty-five years. The federal loans would cover only part of the project costs, with the remainder borrowed locally. It was assumed that this federal aid would stimulate $1.5 billion of land acquisition and preparation for redevelopment. Title VII provided federal contributions to localities for low-rent housing. Rents would be reduced to remain within the means of low-income families.

S 1592 generated predictable objections from the real estate lobby, which argued that short-term emergency measures were required for only returning veterans and displaced war workers. Re-using barracks and temporary wartime housing was more likely to solve the emergency than would permanent housing subsidies, they believed. Catherine protested. "The necessary emergency measures to overcome the evils caused by the war," she wrote, "must be combined simultaneously with S 1592 to remedy the evils which existed before the war and are still present, in order that the postwar housing program may be just and productive."[42]

She went further. "Is public housing necessary? Yes! Private enterprise cannot re-house families of the lowest income." The bill's goal of a decent home and suitable living environment for every American family could only be achieved with substantial public subsidies. These should be underwritten by the communities through local (not federal) capital financing, Catherine argued. S 1592 would enable the building of 125,000 low-rent public housing units annually over a four-year period for a total of half a million units. This was a conservative goal, she said, considering the widely acknowledged need for approximately 360,000 low-rent family dwellings per year for a ten-year period.[43]

Critics argued that S 1592 was a public housing bill in disguise. Catherine countered that the proposed public housing program was at most one-tenth of the total housing contemplated under the entire bill. "The annual amount of housing which the bill contemplates that *private enterprise* should be encouraged to provide – more than a million units a year – is about four times as much housing per year as private enterprise built on the average in the last ten years before the war. It is almost fantastic, therefore, to state that the bill stands in the way of private enterprise."[44]

Catherine saluted Title I under which the Federal Home Loan Bank Administration, the Federal Housing Administration and the Federal Public Housing Authority would be consolidated into the National Housing Agency (NHA). She pointed out that "both the Congress and the President can more effectively exercise the housing responsibilities if they can deal with one housing agency rather than with many."[45] During the war more than sixteen such agencies and programs were created. The postwar housing emergency required immediate coordination of federal initiatives. It was in the best interests of business and taxpayers to create one agency with a coherent policy and coordinated program.

Opposition to a single umbrella agency came from those opposed to public housing, as well as from the Washington bureaucracy that saw its own programs and powers threatened. But labour, consumer, and welfare groups, along with local public officials, recognized the importance of a single agency for postwar reconstruction.

Throughout 1946 Catherine continued her efforts to garner support for the passage of S 1592. More than sixty organizations endorsed the cause, including the American Federation of Labor, the American Veterans Committee, the Congress of Industrial Organizations, the Consumers Union, and a long list of national councils and associations dealing with professional and social concerns.

Opposition came from the National Association of Homebuilders of America, the National Association of Real Estate Boards, the National Savings and Loan League, the Mortgage Bankers Association of America, and the US Chamber of Commerce. The oppositional lobby succeeded in diluting the essence of the bill and weakening its administrative structure. It would be debated for three years before becoming the Wagner-Ellender-Taft Act, passed by the 81st Congress as the United States National Housing Act of 1949. The act's goal was a decent home and a suitable environment for every family; it also allocated resources for urban renewal. Colloquially known as the WET Act, the legislation would provide a framework for research and pragmatic education for a new generation of professional planners and housers.

Although Catherine's interests were focused on city planning, she had long understood the importance of addressing rural housing problems in the postwar United States. Perceiving the urgent need for reform in rural housing as a parallel to already articulated urban reforms, she persuaded GSD and Littauer to host a joint conference on the subject in the spring of 1946. Catherine opened the conference with an analysis of farm housing needs based on the 1940 US Census of Housing. "Of the 5.7 million farmers in the U.S. only 1.5 million were able to finance acceptable dwellings from farm employment alone, and 1 million from combined farm and off-farm employment." This meant, she noted, that 3.2 million people were unable to finance an acceptable dwelling costing somewhere around $2,700 in 1940. Over 95 percent of rural farm dwelling units were one-family, detached, and 60 percent of rural farm dwellings were twenty to forty years old or older in 1940.[46]

Catherine pointed out that 16 percent of farm families and 11 percent of rural non-farm families were living in overcrowded conditions in 1940. One-third of all farm dwellings were in need of major repairs, as were 20 percent of rural non-farm buildings; more than half of non-repairable farm dwellings were tenant occupied. Only 18 percent of farm dwellings and 56 percent of rural non-farm dwellings had in-house running water and flush toilets.

Based on these statistics, Catherine estimated that in 1946, 1.9 million farm families were living in dwellings that needed repair – and another 2.1 million farm family homes were beyond repair. She called for a rigorous analysis of rural housing needs and stressed the importance of a survey of farmers' attitudes in order to establish minimum standards for rural housing. The NHA ought to provide financial aid for housing to farm and non-farm communities, she argued.

In the fall of l946, when Sadie was a little over one year old, Catherine left her for the first time – in care of doting father, baby nurse, and housekeeper – to travel to Hastings, England, as a representative of the Federal Public Housing Authority to the 18th International Congress for Housing and Town Planning. Delegates numbering 1,257 came from twenty-three nations, eager to exchange ideas with other housers and planners at this first postwar meeting. Catherine renewed contact with people she had not seen since long before the war, among them Sir George Pepler, chairman of the congress; England's new minister of Town and Country Planning, Lewis Silkin; ministry employees William Holford, Jacqueline Tyrwhitt, and Gordon Stephenson; and Lewis Mumford's old confidant, Frederick Osborn. The Scandinavian contingent included people Catherine particularly cherished: Uno Ahren, Sven Markelius, and Steen Eiler Rasmussen. It was a stimulating meeting that rekindled Catherine's interest in matters abroad.

Her return to England shortly after the war was both heart-warming and shocking. Charred ruins were still visible. While walking beside a seemingly normal Georgian street façade, she suddenly saw the sky through the windows. "On the surface everybody is surprisingly normal," she wrote to Bill. However "underneath there are sudden flashes of tragedy and horror," as when a Dutch professor, "a charming sensitive man with lucid ideas about education, suddenly, with a queer smile on his face, shows you a photograph of his 2-year old child, laid out in a coffin, shot during a brawl among the 30 Nazis quartered in his small house throughout the war." The shock of the encounter, heightened by the thought of her own infant safely tucked in her crib at home, rendered Catherine virtually speechless moments later when Osborn asked her to say a few words. "I just couldn't pull myself together to do a decent job," she told Bill.[47]

The most important outcome of the Hastings Congress was a resolution urging the establishment of a permanent housing and planning unit within the United Nations. The resolution was adopted by the UN General Assembly in December based on the theory that there could never be true global peace until the wide gap in living conditions among various peoples was levelled. The resolution's execution was assigned to the Economic and Social Council.

Catherine was enthusiastic for international action. In her letter to Bill, she emphasized "you must absolutely come to the next conference, perhaps in Paris next year. It's a kind of duty, I think, a way in which we can make a not insubstantial contribution to international relations." They did not attend the next conference, but both became committed internationalists.

In a memo to the Social Science Section of UNESCO, written shortly after she returned from Europe, Catherine recounted her Hastings experience and itemized some of her major concerns. As an American visiting Europe, she recognized the universality of issues. Questions were the same everywhere: Should every family live in a private house with garden? How will we use increased leisure if we get it? Do we want more privacy or a more social life? What is a neighbourhood, what is a region? When is a city too big? What about the relation of home to workplace and open space?

All over the world there were specialists, she pointed out. Sociologists, economists, biologists, psychologists, political scientists, and others were studying family and community. All over the world there were people knowledgeable about welfare, education, labour, business, and politics. And all over the world there was a tendency toward academic expertise and professional specialization that made it difficult to fit the pieces of knowledge together into coherent programs and policy, and to develop working partnerships among people with different training and interests – which was, she wrote, the essence of the planning process. Catherine looked for an international organization with the broadest possible participation to tackle some of these basic questions. She suggested that it be attached to the Social Science section of UNESCO.

The following January she represented UNESCO at UN commission meetings at Lake Success, speaking for the United States in support of an international housing program. The UN eventually established a permanent housing agency that became the Center for Human Settlements, which has been responsible for many decades of housing and planning programs in developing countries. This period marked the beginning of Catherine's involvement with the UN and other international organizations.

She returned from Hastings with a new understanding of the state of European education and research in housing. Schools in England, suffering from postwar staff and resource shortages, were no better than Harvard or MIT. She was now more convinced than ever that, in the wake of the war – with its wholesale urban destruction in Europe and its unprecedented population dislocation – a new generation of young planners was called for, capable of understanding the complex needs of the postwar city. None of the schools abroad offered a suitable curriculum for modern urban planners, one that balanced physical and social sciences.

In February 1947 Catherine became pregnant again. "How swell ... let's hope it's twins," wrote Dorothy Liebes when she got the news. Everyone agreed that Sadie needed a companion. "If there is anything at all in eugenics, you and Bill ought to set a record for standards," wrote the proud godmother. The pregnancy was difficult, and in July Catherine had a miscarriage. She was saddened, but grateful for what she had. "It certainly makes Sadie herself more miraculous," she wrote to Dorothy, adding "the only thing lower than a miscarriage case in a proud maternity hospital is a miscarriage that happens to a 42 year old intellectual who gets occasional mail and phone calls addressed to *Miss* Bauer." As a daughter of two very busy parents, Sadie might have enjoyed the company of a sibling, but there would be none.

Catherine kept an active interest in Democratic Party politics. "Dig up a more inspiring candidate than Truman," she wrote a friend in the California delegation to the 1948 party convention. "The more I think of it the more I am convinced that the whole future of the Democratic Party depends on it."[48] She considered Eisenhower but found him less liberal than Truman and equally unsophisticated on international matters. Henry Wallace was too far to the left. Paul Douglas appealed to her as the best potential leader, yet she didn't expect he could win in 1948. "Truman can't win either. A

CATHERINE AND SADIE

Everyone agreed that Sadie needed a companion. "If there is anything at all in eugenics, you and Bill ought to set a record for standards."

Democratic administration just isn't in the cards until 1952, except via some Eisenhower miracle."

The issue was leadership. "People aren't going to feel any more personal confidence in [Dewey and Warren] as leaders in the most dangerous era of all time than they have in Truman," she wrote. They will "want someone who at least looks a little idealistic and large spirited, someone who seems to have some bona fide knowledge and convictions about the world at large and America's role in it, and that won't be Truman. And if you stick with Papa you're going to hand that kind of leadership to Wallace and the fellow-travelers by default, purely out of fear of war, if nothing else." Catherine felt that many Wallace supporters could be persuaded to switch to Paul Douglas "particularly the labor-skates who have never been very sure. Their endorsement of Truman is entirely meaningless unless they do more work than they seem likely to at present." She hoped Douglas's fresh face would be "a good shot in the arm for the Democrats right now, even in *this* election, particularly against that peanut-face which even his supporters must be sick of. I doubt if he could win but I bet Douglas could make a better showing than Truman." Catherine was among the many Americans proven wrong by Harry S. Truman's victory.

Catherine also followed local congressional elections. She was sceptical about her representative, John F. Kennedy, who had given a campaign talk on foreign policy that almost made her work night and day for anybody else, not a Catholic, she told a friend. Her prognosis was wrong again. She could not know, then, that she would be invited by this congressman in October 1960, to attend a conference in Pittsburgh to help him learn about the problems of slums and urban blight, as he prepared to become US President. She would be one of several illustrious delegates including

Mayors Wagner of New York and Daley of Chicago, and Roosevelt's public housing commissioner, Philip Klutznick.

After five years at MIT, Bill Wurster's dream of returning to the San Francisco Bay Area became a reality with his appointment as Dean of the School of Architecture at the University of California in Berkeley. Catherine welcomed the news for two reasons. She was eager to return to the Bay Area, and she had viewed the leadership at the Berkeley school as weak. In 1942 she had fingered her friend Walter Behrendt, an exile from Hitler's Berlin, for a possible position at UC Berkeley's School of Architecture. "It really is ironic," she had written to the Behrendts, "that this should be such a lousy school, dead and small-minded without a single strong person attached to it, in the middle of the healthiest area architecturally speaking in the country. The trouble is it needs a complete upheaval not just one man."[49] Behrendt died of heart disease in 1945. The man to bring about change, if not a complete upheaval, would be her husband.

Catherine welcomed the move but her colleagues and friends in Cambridge were crushed. A dozen of her devoted admirers assembled a "Last Supper for Catherine Bauer and The Twelve Housing Apostles." Among them were professors and deans from Harvard and MIT, members of the Massachusetts State Housing Board, and the Massachusetts Housing Council, which Catherine was instrumental in establishing. She was saluted in poetic parodies, none more poignant than a verse Dean Hudnut dedicated to Caterina Bauer:

Oh California! Golden State!
What is this greed insatiate?

Shame on you! In your bursting store
You've half the nation's names and more.
One half our olives, half our gas
And all of Hollywood, alas.
You have the best part of our coast
The biggest trees, the biggest boast
You have Bette Davis and the view
From Telegraph Hill. You have the U-
Niversity of Berkeley too.

Oh California! Have a heart!
You have enough in gain and dower
Don't be a pig, leave us our gem
Leave us our Caterina Bauer.

Berkeley

*Any country can count itself fortunate to have one
Catherine Bauer.*

Nathan Straus

In preparation for their departure from Cambridge, the Wursters purchased a green jeepster convertible. They built a little play platform over the rear seat for Sadie, who was nearly five, and spent one month travelling south and west. They visited family and friends along the way and stopped at attractions like Oak Creek Canyon in Arizona.

Describing herself as "a housewife with overdue deadlines,"[50] Catherine planned ahead by hiring a housekeeper before leaving for San Francisco. Fortunately the woman who had worked for several years for Catherine's sister, Betty Mock, was now available. Thelma Redd had elected to stay in the North with her daughter, Shirley, when the Mocks moved to Tennessee. Thelma was a nurturing African-American woman who possessed the kind of spirit of adventure and intelligence that appealed to Catherine. The two families moved to California together and proved a

BILL, SADIE, AND CATHERINE IN CAMBRIDGE, 1950

In preparation for their departure from Cambridge, the Wursters purchased a green jeepster convertible. They built a little play platform over the rear seat for Sadie, who was nearly five, and spent one month travelling south and west.

perfect match for one another. Bill, who had longed for a second child, developed a special fondness for young Shirley. When he travelled during the next few years, his letters home expressed paternal concern for her well-being and intellectual development. (He would have been proud to know that today Shirley is president of a college in Georgia.)

During their first few months in the Bay Area, the Wursters sublet a number of apartments. Among them was the Hyde Street flat belonging to Betsey and Tommy Church, who were away for a month. Catherine loved the flat and welcomed an offer to stay in the "demi-blighted" Hyde Street neighbourhood, which boasted colourful shops, restaurants, and mixed-income neighbours ranging from Irish workers to professors and prelates. The next move was to Berkeley, for Bill's sake. On Buena Vista Way they found a small, slightly rundown Maybeck-designed house with a good view. Although Bill fixed it up, the enlarged family (including Thelma and Shirley) found themselves cramped, and the following year they moved to a larger house on nearby Le Roy Street. Only then were they able to take their belongings out of storage and properly set up house.

Since moving to Berkeley they had their eyes on Bill's beloved "Gregory House," the large Greenwood Terrace property situated on a hilly acre overlooking San Francisco Bay. Owned by their friend Sadie Gregory, the house was currently occupied by a tenant. The Wursters envisioned leasing it while building their own home on one of the property's adjacent lots. In 1953 the tenant died, and the Wursters purchased the Gregory property, situated above idyllic Greenwood Commons and surrounded by old trees. They never did build their own family home; rather, Catherine and Bill lived out their lives in what by now was an old, rambling house. Bill and some colleagues subdivided the land around the commons for elegant architect-designed houses.

"It's really a ratty old redwood number, vast (4,000 square feet) and beautiful in its way," Catherine said of her new home. She called it "one of the original Bay Area Style monuments." Bill had wanted it since he was a student, and Catherine said it was all right with her though she might have preferred one of his simple houses. Eventually she got one, in the form of a beautiful beach house retreat, one of the first weekend cottages to be built on a sand spit called Sea Drift, north of Stinson Beach, near the base of Mount Tamalpais in Marin County. The Wursters would fondly refer to it as "the camp."

Sadie grew up in the Greenwood Terrace home, surrounded by furnishings designed by many of Bill's modern architect friends. Bill was also a great collector. "They had pairs of everything," one visitor recalls. There were two Alvo Aalto chairs and two by Saarinen, in addition to a long, white couch in the big living room. Naguchi floor lamps did little to illuminate the tree-encircled home.

It was a perfect home for entertaining, whether the guest list was sixty strong or an intimate half-dozen. Visitors would drive along a gravel carriage path, past a small coach house, and park facing the south side of the house below the living room windows. They would be greeted by their hosts as they ascended a few steps to a large, flat terrace bordered by clusters of shrubs and large, earthen pots of flowers. On fine evenings, drinks and hors d'oeuvres would be served outside where guests admired the setting sun behind Golden Gate. A leaded glass door led into a formal entrance hall running north and south between a spacious dining wing at the north end, and a living room wing at the south. Windows lined the western wall of the entrance hall, leading into a cozy library. Warmed by a fireplace, the library served as Bill's study and gathering place for small groups of friends. On cool evenings, large groups congregated in the living room for drinks and conversation before dinner. Behind the dining room was an enormous kitchen with pantry and laundry. Between the kitchen and living room was Catherine's study, a large space perhaps intended as a playroom, with a ping-pong table in the centre. She spent nearly all of her time at home working in this study, the ping-pong table perennially stacked to overflowing with papers and memorabilia. On the desk sat her Olivetti, and beside the desk stood an enormous paper basket purchased in Chinatown.

Two staircases, invisible from the entrance hall, led to the second floor: one to a small wing where Thelma and Shirley lived, the other to the Wursters' bedrooms. The main staircase was behind a door that opened out of the wooden panelling from the entry hall; the other was accessed from the kitchen. The second story, built after the lower portion was completed, resembled a rabbit warren, its rooms opening to a narrow corridor that wound around to form a bridge between an original addition and a later one. Catherine and Bill had separate bedrooms because their sleep-wake cycles differed. Bill was usually in bed by 9:00 p.m.; Catherine did some of her most creative thinking between 8:00 p.m. and midnight.

When the Wursters were alone they followed an immutable daily routine. Bill gently woke his wife in the morning, and the day's work ended with drinks in front of the library fireplace at 6:00 p.m., followed by dinner at 7:00. Sadie sipped ginger ale while her parents had cocktails. Events of the day were discussed during this hour, so by the time they sat down for dinner not much was left to say. Thelma prepared dinner five nights a week and never got used to the speed with which her carefully prepared meals were consumed. Shortly after dinner Bill would settle back into the library with a book, Sadie would head upstairs to finish her homework and

Catherine would return to her study. Thursdays and Sundays Catherine reluctantly donned an apron and cooked. Although she had boasted to her mother of her newly developed culinary skills, kitchen work never held much appeal for her and, with Bill's tacit approval, she happily left most such chores to others.

It was Thelma who usually prepared the food for the Wursters' elegant dinner parties. Sometimes Sadie and Shirley helped serve. Occasionally caterers prepared and served food under Thelma's watchful eye. Catherine did not believe in cutting flowers (she thought it cruel) and decorated her table with bowls of fruit or arrangements of beautiful stones. The hosts sat at either end of a long table, and guests often included luminaries from the world of politics, architecture, and planning, among them Adlai Stevenson, Walter Gropius, and Lewis Mumford. Guest-list regulars were "UC Brass," as Bill called them: President and Mrs. Clark Kerr, Chancellor and Mrs. Glenn Seaborg, Vice-Chancellor and Mrs. Edward Strong. Menu notes and thank-you letters, now yellowed, attest to the care taken with every detail. For example, Catherine wrote that Ernest Weissmann of the UN "prefers scotch to bourbon and his native slivovitz, and don't forget cheese, peanuts and radishes."

Dinner conversation often revolved around Catherine who was renowned as a hostess capable of discussing anything with anyone, from world affairs, to music, art, architecture, and literature. Bill was quieter but when he spoke he commanded attention. Generous in praise for those he admired and tolerant of those he did not, Bill provided a salve in the wake of his wife's occasional outbursts. She tended to be most vociferous when disagreeing with him, for which she once earned her mother's reprimand. "Keep your disagreements private," Bertie instructed her daughter. Catherine agreed to try.

Such altercations were rare because the Wursters counted themselves best friends. Their private relationship was characterized by easy words and good humour, Catherine's effusive personality complementing Bill's quiet demeanour. When Catherine was away for three months in India, Bill became withdrawn. "The days are so long [without her]," Thelma pined, "as Mrs. Wurster is like eight people."[51]

The Gregory House, as the Wursters continued to call it, served as a meeting place away from campus for faculty members of the departments of planning and architecture. People from all walks of life felt welcome there, with one small qualification (often printed on invitations): stiletto heels were not to be worn in the house out of respect for the beautiful wooden floors.

Formerly an avid athlete capable of hiking or cycling many miles and of swimming in ice-cold water, Catherine now kept fit by hosting a "Monday

Muscle Group" in her home. Thelma took part, along with a few neighbouring women. Catherine and Thelma also enjoyed walks around nearby Tilden Park, to commune with nature while sharing intimate conversation. For the most part, however, walks were a means of getting from one place to another. With her broad stride and rapid pace, Catherine tended to leave companions behind, forging purposefully forward, head down, arms swinging – unless she was toting heavy bags. Catherine enticed her more sedentary husband outdoors in the summers, embarking on two-week camping trips to the high Sierras.

Within a year of arriving in Berkeley, Catherine was appointed part-time lecturer at the University of California's Department of City and Regional Planning. She was the first woman on faculty and, though operating cautiously from the wings, she had a remarkable impact on curriculum and student recruitment. The planning department was composed of people with strong opinions, and though Catherine was never one to equivocate, she proved to be a natural conciliator. As such she became a key figure in the sometimes acrimonious debate on what was then Bill's pet project: the gathering of three Berkeley departments under the roof of a single new college.

This had been Bill's mission since assuming the office of Dean of Architecture, and it was no mere organizational challenge. His desire was to recast the mould for the study of architecture – to bring practical relevance to what he believed was an overly academic institution. At that time architecture was taught in UC's College of Architecture, landscape architecture was offered in the Department of Agriculture, and planning was linked to Graduate Studies. Bill's experience as a student at Harvard's Graduate School of Design had convinced him of the benefits of an

CATHERINE, C. 1952

Within a year of arriving in Berkeley, Catherine was appointed part-time lecturer at the University of California's Department of City and Regional Planning. She was the first woman on faculty and, though operating cautiously from the wings, she had a remarkable impact on curriculum and student recruitment.

integrated faculty. A timely letter from his mentor, Walter Gropius, written as the distinguished man approached the end of his academic career, inspired the new dean to pursue his goal:

Though my hair is graying more and more every day, I develop more and more into a rebel. I have become more and more critical as to our educational methods because I think that there is something basically wrong in our much too intellectually emphasized society. I cannot help feeling that a university is the wrong framework for our highly practical profession which, besides its important philosophical background, should after all deal with building. Where do our boys learn building? After they have rubbed the school benches, they go right away into offices and do not see building. So we still remain in the mind of the people a luxury profession to be called in when there is extra money to adorn buildings. Our profession has not been able yet to make it understood among the population that we are indispensable for the building effort of the nation. For that, I think, we have to educate the next generation, and it is pretty hard to do this within the intellectual framework of the university.[52]

Catherine certainly subscribed to Gropius's dictum that students should "deal with *building*" – in other words, should learn by doing. But unlike Gropius she was convinced that this kind of learning could occur within the framework of a university. Since 1940, when she had been hired as a Rosenberg Lecturer at the UC School of Social Welfare, she had been a part-time but fully engrossed teacher. She had meticulously prepared each lecture, along with reading lists and mid-term and final exams. Her first course, Social Welfare 190, consisted of thirty lectures, each one formulated as a Socratic question. "Why is Housing important to individual, family, and community?" was her first lecture. The last one of the semester asked, "What fruits should we expect of the housing movement in the next 10 years?"[53]

Her ambitious reading list for SW 190 included *Modern Housing,* her 1932 *Fortune* article, Mumford's *The Culture of Cities,* Edith Elmer Wood's 1931 book, *Recent Trends in American Housing,* and the National Resources Committee's report, *Our Cities.*[54] The mid-term exam allowed students to pick two out of four questions. Most students selected: "If you were a social worker or architect or building trade worker or business man, why would you be interested in housing and what would you do about it?" The least popular question was: "What features of the European housing experience, 1919-1939, can be most helpful in the development of a successful housing movement in America?"[55] The final exam contained five questions covering national and local issues, from "Describe the

CATHERINE IN THE CLASSROOM

Catherine certainly subscribed to
Gropius's dictum that students should
"deal with *building*" – in other words,
should learn by doing.

functions of the two principal Federal housing agencies" to "Evaluate Holly
Court [a local housing project] in terms of community planning."[56]

Over the years Catherine's teaching style evolved toward a more
democratic model, allowing her to improvise on lectures and her students
to teach one another. By 1955, in her introductory course for City and
Regional Planning 222, lectures were held to a minimum. Students were
expected to do self-directed reading and gather information about the
historical development of housing policy. Instead of discussing "Recent
Trends ..." which was central to her first course, she now challenged
students to think laterally: "How important is housing anyway? ... Initially
it was a physical welfare issue, now it is a social and economic one....
Initially the public's interest [focused] on housing results, now on housing
as an economic-political process."[57]

During the 1950s the American economy hit its stride. Housing starts
reached 1.9 million units, with an average 1.5 million for the decade. The
premise of CRP 222 was that modern city planning grew out of efforts to
solve housing problems. The course's main focus was the development of
housing policy in Europe before and after the Second World War, though
Catherine ventured deeply into history texts to track the dynamic
movement in legal and economic aspects of housing – as far back as 1851,
when Lord Shaftesbury introduced health and housing reform in England.
She continued to assign *Modern Housing* and *The Culture of Cities* but
now included examples from California by bringing regional housing
practitioners into her classroom.

Catherine never offered CRP 222 the same way twice. Over time her
presentations became even more informal and anecdotal. She came to
prefer seminars over lectures as she guided graduate students preparing
for careers in both the public and private sectors. Her students left the
classroom to attend public hearings, pore over official reports, and
interview civic officials. They then converted concepts into action by

making recommendations on real challenges posed by the urban renewal program that was disrupting Bay Area neighbourhoods.

Meanwhile, Bill struggled long and hard to create consensus on his new interdisciplinary college. It took eight years to iron out organizational wrinkles and arrive at an appropriate name, one that would describe the college's mission yet denote equality among the three disciplines. In 1958 the College of Environmental Design was officially launched, with the full blessing of Bill's longtime supporter, Chancellor Clark Kerr.

Kerr, who became president of the entire UC system in 1959, would work closely with Wurster and Regent Don McLaughlin on a new plan to expand the campus. To Kerr, initially, Catherine was simply Bill's wife, but soon the two became friends. "I would have known her, whether or not she was married to Bill, just because she was a very energetic, innovative, quite an unusual person," Kerr recalls.[58] Planning Professor Emeritus Don Foley, an urban sociologist on the planning faculty, concurs. "I both loved and respected her as a close colleague," says Foley, "but I was so much in awe of her that I felt like a little hick from the country." Her years of experience in New York and Washington had brought her close to most of the important thinkers and doers of the day in housing and planning. As Foley put it, she was a "bridger who felt equally at home with design people and social science people."[59]

Since her Harvard days, Catherine had been committed to multidisciplinary education, and this she brought to the Department of City and Regional Planning. She broadened the discussion of curriculum and teaching to reflect the changing needs of postwar urban United States. To Clark Kerr she was an elemental force that was central, not to the administration, but to the orientation of the department. Catherine was both an intellectual power and an active presence: she had ideas and she expressed them. "I certainly knew what her ideas were, directly from her, without having to go through administrative processes," recalls Kerr. "She was more interested in results than going through the niceties of all the bureaucratic steps."

From the start, Catherine helped bring new professors to the department, largely from the social sciences. Don Foley had joined the faculty in 1953 at Catherine's urging, with the expectation that he would bridge the gap between physical planning and social consequences, in the manner of Robert Merton of Columbia University. Much later, economists Bill Wheaton and Jack Dyckman joined the faculty with Catherine's encouragement. "When they came in," Kerr says, "I thought the level of the department made a quantum leap forward. They were all on the Catherine Bauer model. It became a centre of intellectual activity. Almost overnight, my impression was, we became one of the top places in the country."

Not everyone agreed. Jack Kent, then head of the planning department, remains sceptical to this day about the value of interdisciplinary hirings. "We never should have done that because we had strong social science departments on the campus, available to us in the planning department," says Kent. "You cannot introduce the whole university into the department, because you might not get the strongest people. We made that mistake, but I went along with it."[60]

Initially Catherine found strong support for her ideas among the core of professors, including Kent, Francis Violich, Vernon DeMars, and Mel Webber. The group spanned the range of environmental concerns, from architecture to planning to landscape, and became the foundation for the emerging College of Environmental Design (CED). Violich remembers lengthy debates on departmental minutiae and philosophical concerns. Central to these discussions was the place of the social sciences in relation to planning, and the role of the department in the unfolding local politics in Berkeley and the Bay Area. Catherine believed in John Muir's concept – "Everything is hitched to everything else" – and that planning needed to be taught in the context of social-political change. As the CED evolved, Webber sided with Catherine's concept of the centrality of social sciences and the necessity of teaching the social and economic consequences of planning. Kerr concurred. Enrolment doubled, then tripled; it grew too rapidly for some of the faculty but, according to Kerr, "it was hot and going well and I let them run fast."

Her friends applauded Catherine's activism and her nonconformist image (she was often seen driving her green jeepster, roof down, through the Berkeley hills). But her daughter was often embarrassed, as are many pre-adolescent children of flamboyant parents. Sadie's discomfort was heightened by her mother's rather stiff reception of her young friends. Sadie attended Anna Head School, an exclusive private girls' school on par with Vail-Deane, the school her mother had attended. Unlike Bertie Bauer, who had been intimately involved with her daughter's schooling and social life, Catherine remained on the periphery of Sadie's. Although committed to providing the best possible education for her daughter, she had no interest in participating in classroom activities or the PTA. Nor did she handle behaviour issues with confidence. Often she consulted friends for parenting tips and counted on Thelma to mark relevant pages in Gessell and Ilg's book on child development. In her role as mother, Catherine lacked the convictions she displayed in her professional life. That is, until her loyalty to her country was publicly challenged.

Soon after the Wursters had settled in Berkeley, they were drawn into a raging controversy concerning the "Oath of Allegiance for Civil Defense Workers (Public Employees)." In June 1949, the UC Board of Regents had asked the faculty to sign a non-Communist oath. Most did willingly, but a few refused and the regents had lacked leverage to enforce compliance. In 1950, at the insistence of Regent John Francis Neylan, and with the support of Regent Goodwin Knight, who was then California's lieutenant governor, the Board of Regents passed a new measure with teeth, over Governor Earl Warren's opposition. The resolution of April 21, 1950, demanded proof of allegiance from all faculty and staff; it passed with the overwhelming support of the academic senate. All American citizens employed by the university had to swear that they had never belonged to the Communist Party or its affiliates. The "Loyalty Oath" took the form of a statement signed upon acceptance or renewal of appointment, with the understanding that his or her job would be in jeopardy if a person refused. The statement included the following provision:

> *Having taken the constitutional oath of office required of public officials of the State of California, I hereby formally acknowledge my acceptance of the position and salary named, and also state that I am not a member of the Communist Party or any other organization which advocates the overthrow of the government by force or violence, and that I have no commitments in conflict with my responsibilities with respect to impartial scholarship and free pursuit of truth. I understand that the foregoing statement is a condition of my employment and a consideration of payment of my salary.*[61]

The regents instructed the university's controller to "secure said signatures to said Oath or Affirmation" by October 3, 1950. All academic and administrative university personnel had thirty days, "but not later than November 2, 1950," to comply. Those objecting could take their case to a special Academic Senate Committee on Privilege and Tenure.

Of the university's 256 nonacademic employees, 157 refused to sign the new contract and were fired. Seventy-four were rehired almost immediately. Sixty-two academic senate members were fired and then reappointed after faculty committee hearings. One month later the special committee was disbanded by the regents, who deemed it a disservice to the signers to forgive "a few" conscientious objectors. In fact, the committee had heard the pleas of *many* objectors.

Dean Wurster signed. So did Catherine and most of the nearly 1,500 faculty members who simply wanted to teach and not become martyred in a battle of political principle. A few refused, and the campus became so bitterly divided that forty-five years later, those who had the courage to refuse to sign the oath still bristle about the majority who went along. Jack

Kent supported his father-in-law, Edward C. Tolman, chairman of the Department of Psychology, who had harnessed a group of non-signers in a campus-wide protest against the Loyalty Oath. On June 29, 1950, Tolman presented three points:

What my untrammeled conscience tells me is: (1) that War or no War, the application of what-to-date is still a political test of employment at this University, with its attendant probability of accusations of guilt by association, is a basic threat to the American Way – to that very way for which, if there is to be a war, we supposedly would be fighting; (2) that a Board of Regents, which first imposes and then repudiates its own "Compromise," is not a Board of Regents whose governance of this University can be trusted; and (3) that a University Administration which is so weak, or so unwilling, that it cannot impose its own purpose against that of such a Board is an Administration which bodes ill for the future of this University as a truly great and liberal educational institution (and not as just a mere appendage of the Armed Forces.)[62]

The faculty had earlier agreed that Communists should not be hired by the university and therefore the new demand was both redundant and insulting. Having made his points, Tolman emphasized that all those who would persist in not signing should be perfectly aware that they were likely to be fired and then smeared by the press. "Since mine was the opening gun which started the oath controversy, I have during the succeeding months suffered increasing feelings of responsibility for fear that I may have encouraged other members of the faculty to jeopardize themselves and their families in a way in which I was not jeopardizing myself or my family," stated Tolman. "I am to retire in three years ... therefore, can indulge in the sin of self-righteousness and in the luxury of untrammeled conscience." Wishing to avoid any hint of pressure, he concluded, "I am going to remain a non-signer, [and] I wish to indicate that I, on my part, will continue to feel friendship and respect for any others of you whose circumstances or whose reasoning makes it seem desirable and right to you that you should sign."[63] Today the non-signers are viewed as heroes.

Eighteen faculty members, including Tolman, were fired after submitting the following resolutions to the Board of Regents:

Our objections to the so-called Loyalty Oath, and to the new contract, have always been based on our conviction that the University must uphold the personal freedom and integrity of the scholar and the individual and must maintain the operating autonomy of the Faculty and of the President in matters of Faculty appointment and dismissal. As academic teachers we have

opposed demands made on us by the Board of Regents of the University
which seemed to us in conflict with this conviction.

On the other hand, we are fully aware of our duty to give all assurances
which our country may require from us in connection with work to be done
in a national emergency. As far as the University may become involved in
such work, we stand ready to fulfill any conditions laid down for it by the
Government.[64]

The eighteen professors took their case to the Third District Court of Appeals on September 14, 1950. It would be seven months before a decision was handed down, on April 6, 1951, finding the Loyalty Oath in violation of the state constitution. The court ruled that "no one can be subjected, as a condition of holding office, to any test of political or religious beliefs, other than this pledge to support the Constitution of the United States and of the State." The court found that a constitutional pledge demonstrated the highest loyalty and "the exacting of any other test of loyalty would be antithetical to the concept of fundamental freedom."[65] The Board of Regents was ordered to rehire those who had been dismissed.

During this period the university suffered untold damage as a result of boycotts by several professional organizations. The American Psychological Association and the mathematics association refused to recommend people to the campus. Classes were cancelled when teaching positions remained unfilled. In time, old wounds began to heal. In March 1959, Professors Edward Tolman and Albert Elkus, another non-signer, were awarded honorary degrees at the UC Berkeley convocation. Bill reported the event to Catherine, who was in India: "All of us felt ground was gained in righting the great wrong of the loyalty oath."

The oath crisis occurred during a growing national fear of "un-American" activities following the Second World War, when the Soviet Union's expanding influence in eastern Europe was seen as a direct threat to the United States and its allies. Spearheaded by Senator Joseph McCarthy in Washington and State Senator Jack B. Tenney in California, the federal government became involved in hunting out organizations and prominent people presumed to be involved in subversive activities that threatened the integrity of the nation.

In California, the State Senate Fact-Finding Committee on Un-American Activities held public hearings in 1949 on the grounds that "these are yet times of public danger. Subversive persons and groups are endangering our domestic unity so as to leave us unprepared to resist attack from without or within." The Tenney Committee, as it was known, resolved to investigate hundreds of illustrious citizens accused of "being members of organizations who have as their objectives ... the overthrow of the government of the State of California or of the United States by force and violence."[66] Many of the country's most prominent actors, writers, playwrights, politicians, theologians, artists, and musicians were listed in one of the committee's report, including Frank Sinatra, Pearl S. Buck, Lillian Hellman, Helen Gahagan Douglas, Catherine Bauer, Reinhold Niebuhr, Lewis Mumford, Rockwell Kent, and Paul Robeson – all individuals, the report said, who "followed or appeased some of the Communist Party line over a long period of time." The report recommended an investigation that would lead to "prompt and consistent law enforcement against subversive activity."[67]

Altogether, the Tenney Committee printed about a dozen reports, ranging between four hundred and over seven hundred pages in length, with lists of what they called "subversive publications and organizations," along with the names of hundreds of subscribers and members.[68] Printed between red covers, probably an allusion to the political tone of their target, the alphabetical listings resembled small-town telephone books.

The *New York Times*, in its lead editorial of October 8, 1950, castigated municipalities across the land for passing ordinances that would either run local Communists out of town or require them to register with the police. "Some of these laws are masterpieces of loose thinking," the editorial observed, citing an ordinance in Birmingham, Alabama, that would run out of town not only Communists but also persons who "shall be found in any non-public place in voluntary association or communication with a member of the Communist Party." Not only was it unlikely that many Communists would be caught by such ordinances, but the measures could actually do harm by weakening respect for the country's most fundamental institutions. Urging local communities to stay out of national policy issues, the editorial concluded: "It is doubtful that good purposes can be served by piecemeal efforts on a small and ineffective scale."[69]

During this very disturbing period Catherine welcomed invitations to leave the Bay Area and visit new planning schools in Seattle and Vancouver. Canada offered a welcome relief from the witch-hunt atmosphere at home. The newly created Community and Regional Planning program at the University of British Columbia (UBC) and several Vancouver civic organizations were anxious to hear her views on Washington's housing and planning initiatives, particularly in light of her involvement with the Wagner-Ellender-Taft Act.

Early in April 1951, Catherine spent three days in Vancouver, beginning with a civic luncheon hosted by the mayor and city council and attended by the American consul. Radio interviews followed. The second day was hosted by Vancouver's Junior League, the University Women's Club, and the Community Arts Council. The evening belonged to the Architectural

Institute of British Columbia. The third day was set aside for the chief purpose of her visit – a noon-hour lecture at UBC on "Housing and Community Planning," followed by discussions with members of the School of Social Work, architects, and planners. UBC published Catherine's lectures, and the weekend was applauded as a huge success by almost all participants.

Catherine had a different impression. Her Vancouver hosts had run her ragged. "Four speeches a day for three days!" she wrote to her sister Betty. "And when they found that I was a little irritated by the schedule they reacted by saying 'Oh it will just be a little informal group you don't have to prepare a thing' and then I'd find that I was confronting either the Mayor and all the Aldermen, or all the University bigwigs, and was obviously expected to sell them the whole works on housing and planning – not forgetting every special Vancouver angle – at one gasp, along with achieving the usual high British standard of form, literacy, wit, and good taste." She bravely pulled through because "they do feel removed from the world and are grateful for outside attention, and because our rather off-hand slapdash vernacular American way of orating (which I perforce rather cartooned) tends to amuse them. It's astonishing, with their extreme American-Frontier geography and economy, that their culture is still so extraordinarily British."[70]

Catherine admired the magnificent, uncluttered scenery of the Northwest and was fascinated by fish hatcheries "where they dump millions of tiny salmon into the river in spring who then come back and hop up the ladder full sized to produce more babies the next year. Probably the most conclusive argument for home and neighborhood attachment extant."[71]

While she was in Canada, the Court of Appeals' ruling came down forcing the University of California to rehire the non-signers. "We don't think the Regents will appeal it as there have been a couple of changes on the Board," she told Betty. "Maybe – just maybe – this is a turning point in our national and local hysteria. To realize how bad we are it's worth while to spend a few days in a British Dominion."[72] In fact the regents did appeal and the case was ruled unconstitutional by California's Supreme Court in October 1952. California's Levering Act, in place then, nevertheless demanded that state employees swear loyalty. The national air of suspicion gradually began to ebb after 1955 with the demise of McCarthyism.

Bill Wurster, who had reluctantly signed the Loyalty Oath in order to continue his work at the university, breathed a sigh of relief when it was found unconstitutional. He was stunned, therefore, when his firm, Wurster, Bernardi, and Emmons, which had enjoyed government commissions to build army, navy, and air force installations in the West, received a letter dated January 9, 1953, from the Office of the Provost Marshall General on behalf of the Army-Navy-Air Force Personnel Security Board. The board denied him and his firm any further contracts and terminated one under construction. His security clearance, which had been granted by the Strategic Air Command on October 17, 1951, was revoked because Wurster was accused of belonging to organizations friendly to the American Communist Party or its many associate groups.

After consulting his attorney, Frank Newman, Bill mounted a strong counterattack. He had never been a member of, and indeed had never heard of most of the "Communist" organizations to which he allegedly belonged. The National Council of American-Soviet Friendship was the only one that rang a bell. Near the end of the Second World War, under the auspices of that organization, he had joined a group of twenty American architects in a discussion of possibly preparing an exhibition of American architecture, housing, and city planning for distribution throughout eastern Europe.

Bill suspected that the Security Board was concerned not with him but with "my closest associate, my wife Catherine Bauer." In his reply to the board, he asserted "she, like me, has never knowingly supported or worked with a Communist front organization and is very strongly opposed to Communist doctrine and tactics."[73] He pleaded with the board to review its decision and assured it of his fullest cooperation. Bill's suspicion was confirmed six months later when a letter from the board, dated August 7, 1953, stated that he "currently maintains a close continuing association with a person who has engaged in activities or associations which are Communist or fronts therefor, namely Catherine B. Wurster, wife."[74]

Having failed to protest the inclusion of her name in the Tenney Committee reports, Catherine was forced to spend an entire year defending her own and her husband's integrity in order to save his career. Writing to lawyer Newman on August 9, she expressed deep regret over having ignored the "Tenney Committee guck." She carefully assembled detailed arguments against the unsubstantiated accusations "that my past activities and associations were a major factor in denying my husband access to classified material and thus cutting off the work of his office for the Department of Defense."[75]

She appeared before the Army-Navy-Airforce Personnel Security Board on August 26, 1953. No longer the firebrand lobbyist who had argued successfully in the 1930s for bipartisan housing legislation on behalf of the unemployed and workers, she was now a sombre fighter for her own survival. At the top of her typed testimony she wrote a message to herself: *"Talk slowly"* – the only time such a cautionary note ever appeared on Catherine's speeches. She was not now fighting for a future when even the poorest people would be entitled to a decent life, but was reflecting on a past when it had been safe to join with like-minded people in a common mission.

Her presentation, consisting of twenty double-spaced typewritten pages, covered her personal and professional life. She spoke of her commitment to improving housing in the United States. "For the past 23 years – first, last, and all the time – I have been a housing expert, hence in part a housing politician." Catherine understood that "housing is a controversial subject" but as a "reformer" she always represented positive viewpoints on housing needs and progress. Although she had survived powerful opposition, years of advocating for change had not prepared her for unexpected attacks of this magnitude, where her very integrity was challenged. "When you are on the firing line on a hot issue for almost a quarter of a century, you are likely to become a controversial person yourself."[76] Her only political objective had always been for progress "in the USA, towards slum clearance and decent housing, based on the absolute undeviating faith in our democratic form of government, the best and only system for making real social progress."

Catherine was stunned by the accusation that she belonged to nine blacklisted organizations. Two were unknown to her. Far from joining the Progressive Citizens of America, she had spoken out against them. She had never belonged to the American League for Peace and Democracy, though she admitted supporting its precursor, the American League Against War and Fascism, in the mid-1930s after she had witnessed Nazi demonstrations in Germany. She had not joined but delivered one talk each to: the California Labor School (in 1944); the California Youth Legislature (as Rosenberg Lecturer in 1940); and the Federation of Architects, Engineers, Chemists and Technicians (FAECT), which ran a technical school. The FAECT was identified by the House Un-American Activities Committee as "Soviet Firsters [who] follow the party line." She had addressed them as a faculty member of UC Berkeley and on behalf of the US Housing Authority as director of research and information.

In 1935 Catherine had briefly belonged to the League of Women Shoppers in order to rally consumer groups behind housing. She had also belonged to the National Citizens Political Action Committee as a Democrat, during the early stages of the 1944 presidential campaign, to garner independent support for Roosevelt and to collect housing data for the national campaign office. Her political participation was always for "clear cut and wholly non-subversive reasons, mostly as a housing expert."[77] Catherine thought back to the days when some of her friends on Paris's Left Bank had argued for the Communist Party line. Yet there is no evidence that these youthful associations were discovered by the vigilant members of the State Senate Fact-Finding Committee on Un-American Activities in California.

Catherine thought it important to clarify "one aspect of my life – and my husband's – namely our relationship to each other: all friends agree we are exceptionally close and enjoy a happy personal and family relationship based on much common ground ... We share our outside working lives as well as our family to an unusual degree ... We are always interested in each other's ideas and activities and therefore know what the other is doing or thinking."[78]

In conclusion she firmly declared "it is absolutely clear that I never engaged in activities that are communist or fronts thereof ... Your letter of August 7 is either an attack on my basic loyalty to this country and its institutions or it has no meaning whatsoever. It is unreasonable that my record of consistent loyalty, entirely open and public throughout, should cause my husband to be put in a position of distrust which endangers his magnificent professional and personal career. It is unreasonable, it is unfair, and I hope it will be righted."[79]

The committee had done its homework, and so had Catherine. To her submission she attached letters of support from significant professional colleagues, including Lee Johnson, executive vice-president of the National Housing Conference, an old friend and fellow housing warrior. She underlined Johnson's statement that "Catherine always represented almost exactly the same viewpoint re housing policy as the late (Republican) Senator Taft, indeed the very last public speech Taft made paid tribute to Catherine's analysis and insight in American housing."[80]

Leon Keyserling, chairman of the Council of Economic Advisors under Truman, provided a five-page sworn statement. He recalled their joint work in support of Senator Wagner's public housing legislation and characterized her trustworthiness as "absolute." He called William Wurster "a fine and loyal American citizen of distinction with integrity that is unimpeachable and his loyalty to his country is absolute."[81]

Support also came from Nathan Straus, first administrator of the US Housing Authority and Catherine's boss in Washington. "To Whom It May Concern: Miss Bauer brilliantly justified the confidence I placed in her ... I feel personally very much indebted to Mrs. Wurster for what was achieved during the years 1937-1942 by USHA ... The people of the United States owe her a debt for what she has done to inculcate understanding of the evil effects of bad housing, and the beneficial effects of replacing slums with livable low-rent homes ... Any country can count itself fortunate to have had one Catherine Bauer."[82] Ernest J. Bohn, director of Cleveland's Metropolitan Housing Authority, and Henry C. Bates, chairman of the housing committee of the American Federation of Labor, both longtime friends of Catherine's, also submitted strong letters of support.[83]

Catherine was cleared of all charges. Her loyalty seemed to be reestablished beyond reasonable doubt, but Bill Wurster's office was never again awarded a federal government contract. In 1962 Catherine's clearance to attend a White House conference was subjected to bureaucratic delay. Organized by Robert Weaver, the USHA's new head, and his assistant, Morton Schussheim, the conference was supposed to bring together prominent people in the field of housing. Schussheim was shocked to receive a raw FBI file on Catherine Bauer stating that she was involved in a number left-wing organizations. Other notables, such as Charles Abrams, also had questionable FBI files. Schussheim was strong enough to call the information "rot" and go on record saying "I know these people and I know they are not disloyal to this country and they are coming to our conference." He obtained their clearance, and thus the witch hunt officially ended for Catherine.

Hurting from the accusations launched against her by the Security Board, Catherine attempted to help others who were smeared, including European friends who were barred from travel or immigration to the United States. One was Gordon Stephenson, a distinguished British academician. Through Bill's initiative in 1953, Stephenson was offered a position as visiting professor at UC Berkeley for a year, to be followed by a permanent appointment as professor of city and regional planning at MIT. Catherine had met him in 1936 during his study tour of the United States, when she advised him to observe the consequences of regional planning by the Tennessee Valley Authority. They had met again at the Hastings Congress when Stephenson was Lever Professor of Civic Design at

BILL AND CATHERINE AT AIA CONVENTION IN YOSEMITE

Catherine was cleared of all charges. Her loyalty seemed to be reestablished beyond reasonable doubt, but Bill Wurster's office was never again awarded a federal government contract.

Liverpool University. Before that, as a senior civil servant in the Ministry of Town and Country Planning, he was responsible for Britain's postwar "New Towns" program, including the development of Stevenage New Town, the first example of the country's planned urban decentralization. During the 1930s Stephenson had travelled in the Soviet Union. Subsequently he had lectured and written extensively about planning in the USSR, all of which was held against him when he applied for the US immigration permit in order to begin teaching at Berkeley. Stephenson describes his encounter with McCarthyism in his memoir, *On a Human Scale: A Life in City Design*.[84]

Having resigned from the University of Liverpool in anticipation of assuming the American positions, Stephenson, without a US permit, found himself suspended in mid-air. Outraged by the injustice, Catherine brokered a solution through her friend, Canada's leading houser, Humphrey Carver. The University of Toronto invited Stephenson to teach in its new urban planning program. MIT would continue to press his case, to no avail. Professor Stephenson settled in Canada, where his impact on planning education was substantial. He taught there until 1960, when he moved to Western Australia. Catherine's intervention proved strategic to Stephenson's personal and professional life, and by supporting him she also assisted the University of Toronto's struggling planning program. In his memoir Stephenson applauded Catherine Bauer as "perhaps the brightest star who 'graduated' from the Regional Planning Association of America with a greater understanding of the human side of housing and planning than any other person I have ever met."[85] On a personal note, he credits Catherine as his "philosopher guide" in planning; *Modern Housing*, wrote Stephenson, "is one of the best books I have ever read ... It is ranked with the best of Mumford."[86]

GLOBAL VISION

The international scene ... should offer as piquant a frontier to the Bauer pioneers as housing did in 1933.
CHARLES ABRAMS TO CATHERINE BAUER

Shortly after the defense department hearings ended in the summer of 1953, Catherine and Bill headed to Lake Tahoe for a much needed rest at the home of their friends, Elinor and Edward Heller. A prominent investment banker, Heller had purchased the waterfront property on Crystal Bay in 1950. Bill designed a magnificent vacation house on their private beach. The house fitted so well into its surroundings that Bill patted himself on the back. "You'd never know an architect had been here," he told Catherine. Heller was the only member of the Board of Regents of the University of California to oppose the Loyalty Oath. Catherine's successful testimony was reason to celebrate, and they could not have found a more beautiful spot to relax and put the political nightmare behind them.

Bill had known the Hellers since the early 1930s and became close friends after marrying Catherine. The friendship grew during the war; Edward spent his army years stationed in Boston, and by a delightful coincidence the couples were neighbours in Cambridge. The Hellers' son, Alfred, remembers admiring Catherine from the time he was a high school freshman in Cambridge. He was so inspired by her intelligence and outlook that she became his mentor.

Conversation was always more stimulating when the Wursters were on hand, with discussions ranging from architecture and planning to current events. Alfred fondly recalls their many visits to Lake Tahoe: Catherine swimming far out in the ice-cold lake with strong, broad strokes, and Bill watching her from the shore (he could be talked into joining her but preferred not to). While Bill and the Hellers enjoyed their armchair perspective, she and Alfred often hiked the nearby Sierra trails. Catherine was clearly very fond of this bright young man who would devote much of his life to preserving California's endangered natural resources. Perhaps Alfred reminded her of Bob Marshall, founder of the American Wilderness Society, who had died tragically fourteen years earlier on the eve of a trip they had planned together to the Southwest. She had been looking for a way out of the Washington bureaucracy at that time, and the trip might have entirely changed the trajectory of her life. Like Marshall, Alfred Heller was descended from a liberal, socially committed, politically active Jewish family.

A few years later Alfred conceived the idea of starting an organization committed to conservation in state planning. He asked Catherine to come aboard as a founder, and she consented during a period when she turned down most demands on her time. In 1960 the illustrious team of William Matson Roth, Catherine Bauer Wurster, and Alfred E. Heller gave birth to California Tomorrow: a nonprofit, educational organization whose mission was to safeguard the beauty and productivity of the state. On Catherine's recommendation, Samuel E. Wood was appointed executive director.

Catherine felt an urgency to protect natural resources for future generations, and she was often asked to write or speak on related subjects. In 1960, UC Berkeley President Clark Kerr put her name forward to draft a paper on the physical environment for the President's Commission on National Goals. "Yes, Ike!" she wrote a friend. "But it's 'nonpartisan' and carefully being kept out of the presidential campaign." Many oldtime friends also served on Eisenhower's commission, including Ernie Bohn, Bob Weaver, and Douglas Haskell. Although the "National Goals" were modest, extending a mere ten years into the future, Catherine embraced the challenge with the same passion she had always invested in her work. To her lifelong pursuits of a better future for housing, neighbourhoods, and communities she now added a larger goal: the earth.

Catherine devoted so much time to the paper that she declined an invitation from Jacqueline Kennedy to participate in a meeting of the Women's Committee for the New Frontier to be held at the Kennedy home. It was election year; JFK had Catherine's support, but she felt she could do more for the environment than for the presidential race. She was diligent about collecting information and typed nearly identical letters to a score of experts around the world. "I am drafting a paper on the Physical Environment for the Commission on National Goals," she wrote to Wilfred Owen of the Brookings Institution, "and as this plunges me into the transportation field, I need some help. Our affluence is wonderful, but if we really want to achieve a better environment, we may have to learn how to balance our expenditures a little more carefully in terms of necessary costs and real benefits. This could mean encouraging a development pattern that wouldn't require an even longer and more costly journey to work."[87] A similar letter went to the Air Pollution Control Officer in Los Angeles with questions related to his work, and to the head of a mobile home manufacturers' association about trends in mobile housing and family sizes. Another went to Sweden for data about its national policy on the environment. Catherine's research for the paper was both exhaustive and exhausting, and the final product was well received.

In 1963 Alfred Heller asked Catherine to critique a draft of a book he was co-authoring with Samuel Wood entitled *The Phantom Cities of California*. After reading the draft carefully, she wrote out a few recommendations that prompted the authors to recast the book entirely "because she was right," Alfred recalls. It was a significant and far-reaching book, the first to warn Californians of the postwar hazards that overdevelopment posed to agricultural land, and the first to flag the dangers of freeway expansion.

Throughout the 1950s and '60s Catherine continued to pursue her many priorities: teaching, attending campus meetings, conducting research, writing articles, giving public lectures, and entertaining at home. She wrote a substantial piece for the housing section of the *Encyclopedia Britannica*, which required periodic revisions. Nine years after her death, the 1973 edition of the encyclopedia still carried her column, "Housing: A Perspective."

She earned a reputation as an outspoken lecturer and addressed a different audience almost every month, somewhere in the United States. In one keynote speech, delivered to a joint conference of Canadian and American city planners at Niagara Falls, she exhorted listeners to look beyond politics to the communities where they intend to work, to be part of a team of citizens and experts, and to raise questions. She urged them to consider racial integration, economic integration, sanitary housing, traffic patterns, and the needs of inner-city children. In Berkeley she addressed citizens at the First Congregational Church, raising similar issues and pressing them to become involved.

In 1961 she spoke at the North Western Assembly at Yakima, Washington, on the challenge of urban growth in the western states. "Can we learn to do it right the *first* time?" she asked. "The eastern states had to cope with redoing: rehabilitating old, badly planned cities, burdened by built-in evils left over from the nineteenth century. We in the West must learn to cope with growth," she warned. "We spend billions of dollars on reform, but only pennies to avoid the evil in the first place. We do not lack public power," she argued, "just the will to use it."

Since the early 1950s Catherine had been using every opportunity to hammer away at growing environmental abuses, and her polemics were by now well honed. In an address to the American Wilderness Society in San Francisco in 1961, she chose the topic "The Urban Octopus" and posed the question: "How can our conflicting demands on wilderness be resolved?"[88] She made a pitch for planning – "the process of figuring out how conflicting demands can best be reconciled in the general interest" – and urged "single-minded wilderness zealots" to channel their efforts into effective programs at the state level by cooperating with planners in the urban, recreational, and resource fields. The California State Planning Act of 1959, not yet implemented, would provide a framework for such action, establishing a comprehensive plan for the location of major public and private works and facilities.

At the Chrysler Center Auditorium in Anaheim, Catherine gave the first lecture in the 1963 Chancellor's Lecture Series on "The Urban Explosion." By then, California had become the most populous state with nearly 15 million of its 17 million people living in metropolitan areas – more than half of them south of the Tehachipis. She warned of the inevitable conflicts that would result if nothing were done to curtail trends in large-lot zoning, freeway development, and the random mushrooming of factories and shopping centres. One foreseeable result, she predicted, was "scatteration" caused by land speculation, where small, specialized communities would grow in isolation to one another – with no identity or visible boundaries. These small enclaves would sharpen social divisions by age, race, and income, Catherine cautioned. Work-to-home distances would increase, requiring more freeways. Inevitable tax-base inequities would lead to unequal services. Without adequate controls, practically all buildable land would be used or cut up in Orange County by the year 1980, its residents beset by severe air and water pollution.

Recalling the greenbelts around the planned communities of prewar Europe, Catherine offered two solutions: conservation of open land and natural beauty, and more compact urban development. Only stringent planning policies can effectively save natural resources whose fate can no longer be left to accident or market forces, she argued.

As in the classroom, Catherine favoured the Socratic method, posing questions to direct her audiences toward answers. "Can cities compete with suburbia for family living?" she asked an Oakland Junior League luncheon in 1964. Her own belief was that a vital future for cities depended on refocusing development in core areas, not lifeless suburbs. "Are we really social isolationists rather than cosmopolitans?"

Until the war California had seen itself as a kind of spacious haven for the rich and retired. Continuing to promote such a false mythology was both foolish and dangerous, said Catherine. The "Cottager's Prayer" was California's death wish:

We thank the Lord that by Thy grace
Thou brought us to this lovely place,
But now, dear Lord, we only pray
Thou wilt all others keep away.

"This is a vain prayer in California, and I fear we'll have to ask the Lord for something quite different if we are going to solve our future problems of urban growth."[89] Appropriate planning included recreational, educational, and residential uses for the rich and poor, people of all races, children and seniors, handicapped and agile – in short, for a broad diversity. This would only be achieved by a meeting of minds, a union of experts with potential users. She appealed to her listeners' logic and decency, challenged their selfishness and, finally, harangued against abusive, self-serving, short-sighted planning. Catherine was an excellent speaker, and she filled the halls. For the most part, people nodded in agreement but pursued agendas set by real estate interests.

One Berkeley campus event Catherine rarely missed was the Little Thinkers' luncheon meeting every Friday at noon at the UC Men's Faculty Club, attended by faculty members at large. She often arrived late, preferred to sit by the door smoking her cigarettes, and always had something to say. Junior faculty deeply appreciated Catherine's encouragement – a relief from the usual dog-eat-dog atmosphere of competitive academics. Don Foley remembers her positive attitude toward projects he and his colleagues brought to her attention. Typically she would mull over one, look up, and say, "I think we ought to try it."

Catherine's seminars in the Department of City and Regional Planning attracted a broad spectrum of students from design disciplines and social and life sciences. The idea of bringing students of various disciplines together was novel at UC during the 1950s. Questions were fielded during informal encounters after class, in the corridor or by appointment in her office. Her office door was always open for consultation on personal and professional matters, though students seeking advice were often sent back to the library to discover answers for themselves. She insisted the college library holdings be kept up to date because she was convinced that in the marketplace of ideas, people learn most from their own research.

In November 1954 Catherine submitted an ambitious proposal to her friend Paul Ylvisaker, program director at the Ford Foundation, for an intercampus research project between UC Los Angeles and UC Berkeley focused on planning issues in southwest California. She envisaged the collaboration of a broad spectrum of academics and students in sociology, demography, economics, ecology, political science, and planning. The southwest, which was poor in natural resources, had recently come under considerable pressure from urbanization due to a surge of immigration. Catherine proposed that teams of researchers study intercultural tensions and economic consequences of the region's changing demography.[90]

There was no precedent for interinstitutional research, and her proposal was viewed as too ambitious by both the Ford Foundation and UC faculty. But Catherine persevered, carving up the project into more digestible components. A study titled "Urban Expansion and Community Structure in California" was submitted to the Ford Foundation's Resources For the Future (RFF), promising a critical analysis of recent trends, their causes and effects, and alternative policies for development. This too would fail to garner financial support.

Denials of grant applications were disheartening. "Perhaps this will finally push me back into the Ivory Tower," Catherine had written her longtime friend, Charlie Abrams, after being turned down by the Russell Sage Foundation some years earlier, "where all you have to do is have some ideas of your own, run down to the library now and then, and put the results on little pieces of paper."[91] Abrams was a New York lawyer who specialized in urban land and housing law. Early in his career he had written a seminal text, *Revolution in Land*, while pursuing various housing crusades in the wake of the Housing Act of 1937. He had just finished editing the proceedings of the United Nation's first symposium on land problems when Catherine's note arrived. "The best laid planners are mice not men," he replied, disgusted by the planners. "None have any ideas of their own – people simply copy from one country to another. What is good for England is good for India."[92] Abrams encouraged Catherine to broaden her vision beyond the United States to the United Nations. And so the seeds of global research were planted in her mind.

Catherine's persistence eventually paid off. In 1956 her department was awarded a $10,000 grant from the University of California to study the "Rural-Urban Frontier: a key area for intensive research on resource and development problems." The study's purpose was to define basic issues and interrelated problems and to suggest a pilot program of related area studies. The notion that rapidly increasing urban populations were imposing pressures on natural resources was new. Catherine argued that even in wild areas, hundreds of miles from metropolitan centres, conflicting demands on land and water for economic production, conservation, and recreation were a reflection of urban growth – particularly in California.

The study brought together a number of Berkeley faculty members: Albert Lepawsky from political science, Baldwin Woods from economics, and Don Foley and Mel Webber from Catherine's department. Her proposal, to "discover some alternative models for resource development programs in the Western States," was written for intercampus and interdisciplinary groups. Catherine predicted that research and teaching facilities in the separate institutions would be strengthened by collaboration as various disciplines became more refined.

With another team of colleagues, and the university's support, Catherine asked RFF for a grant to develop an "analytic approach to the spatial structures of metropolitan areas." This would become a building block in her ambitious southwest California study, serving to "describe, evaluate and measure alternative spatial arrangements of economic and cultural activities within metropolitan areas." It would deliver predictive results and lead to alternative metropolitan spatial and administrative forms "representing different combinations of population densities, transportation systems, topographic situations and different distributions of activities."[93] With RFF's award of $10,000, Catherine's own research program was finally launched.

At Abrams' suggestion, in the spring of 1952 Catherine contacted Ernest Weissmann, chief of the Housing and Town and Country Planning Section of the UN Department of Social Affairs. She had met him when both worked for the 1939 World's Fair in New York; Weissmann had come from Dubrovnik to design and build the Yugoslav Pavilion. Delighted to renew contact with Catherine, he immediately invited her to make suggestions on a report prepared for publication by his office on the applicability of cooperative housing to less developed countries. In the spring of 1955 she wrote a comprehensive report for the UN's *Town and Country Planning Bulletin*, titled "Planning the Neighborhood." The article achieved wide circulation, and Weissmann later asked her to expand it by adding non-American examples. By now Catherine was convinced that successful planning had to extend beyond the arbitrary limits of neighbourhoods and municipalities. The region, she argued, was the logical framework for physical, social, and economic conditions to merge geographically and conceptually.

A small UN contract in 1956 spurred Catherine to write a paper called "Economic Development and Urban Living Conditions" for Weissmann. At his request she later revised that article to produce "The Regional Pattern of Urbanization: A Tool for Social Progress" for the first UN Asian Regional Planning Seminar held in Tokyo in 1958. Her message was that the goals for regional planning were social and political stability.

Abrams was delighted by Catherine's interest in the UN. "I find myself talking more and more about the international scene which should offer as piquant a frontier to the Bauer pioneers as housing did in 1933. In fact it is very odd that we got into federal housing on the basis of what foreign countries were doing, and now foreign countries are looking to America to find out how they should do things."[94]

Catherine thought she had left the politics of housing behind when a surprise announcement arrived from the National Association of Housing and Redevelopment Officials hailing her selection, in 1954, for its highest award. "Individual Achievement During the Pioneering Past" was granted for outstanding pioneering work in housing. Although "delighted beyond words," she informed the president of NAHRO that she was reluctant to accept the honour "in view of the small contribution I have made to housing and redevelopment progress in recent years."[95] She also lacked funds for a trip to the Philadelphia meeting and suggested, therefore, that the organization bestow its honour upon Dorothy Montgomery, who lived and worked in Philadelphia.

The NAHRO turned a deaf ear to her protest and awarded the citation in absentia. It heralded Catherine's "twenty years of clear foresight and dedicated conviction as philosopher, author, speaker, teacher, and organizer for legislative action in the housing and community rebuilding movement" and applauded her for "recognizing – twenty years ago – the need for new housing design and appropriate legislation, [for] awakening citizenry and an informed electorate, [and for] initiating and executing community rebuilding programs lodged firmly in local institutions."[96]

Five years later she was voted honorary member of the American Institute of Planning for her pioneering work in planning during the 1930s and '40s. Catherine was proud to accept this honour. At the ceremony she emphasized the necessity of strong national and local leadership, urging continued cooperation among labour, consumer, welfare, and minority groups to achieve lasting housing improvement. Fortunately, these awards came to Catherine before she published an article generally critical of the housing movement.

In 1965, after her death, the American Society of Planning Officials offered Catherine its highest honour by awarding her the ASPO Silver Medal "for leadership and contribution to the advancement of planning." In 1988 the American Institute of Certified Planners (AICP) posthumously confirmed Catherine as a "pioneer in American planning." At that time, Professor Eugenie Birch, a member of AICP's planning landmarks jury, called Catherine a "Cassandra-like figure" and identified here as a "pioneer in her efforts to make the planning profession more conscious of power and citizen needs."[97]

At the start of her professional career, Catherine had characterized herself as a houser and might have added lobbyist. Later she became a planner; by now she was a full-fledged academic. That she always favoured the title "planner" was made clear in an outraged letter to Douglas Haskell, editor of *Architectural Forum*. Upon receiving an offer from *AF*'s business manager for a 50 percent reduction on her subscription by virtue of being "a professor of engineering," she shot back: "If you want to get subscriptions from planners, this is the wrong approach. We're quite jealous of the fact that planning is not only a separate profession but a *major* one ... If there is any jurisdictional dispute it's only because many engineers, architects, and public administration people are trying to act like 'planners.' If you want a generic term that will please people, use 'planner' *not* 'engineer.'"[98]

Much as Catherine preferred to look toward the future, the past held its grip on her, and in 1956 she was asked to provide a critical assessment of the current status of public housing for the May 1957 issue of *Architectural Forum*. "The Dreary Deadlock of Public Housing" provoked heated reactions. Fortunately, she was safely in Bangkok when the article appeared because it left many of her former housing allies fuming.

Dorothy Gazzolo, a colleague of Catherine's and editor of the *Journal of Housing* at NAHRO, felt betrayed by the *AF* piece. "Public housing was having a pretty hard time," recalls Gazzolo. "She wasn't helping us very much with that article. She didn't know the pain that was going on. It was a real blow."[99] Some housers went farther, accusing Catherine of abandoning her housing principles as she strived for prominence among the academic planning elite.

In the article Catherine contended that after twenty years public housing "still drags along in a kind of limbo, continuously controversial, not

dead but never more than half alive." The Housing Act of 1937 was suffering from "a case of premature ossification." The real estate lobby deserved
some blame for keeping public housing officials on the defensive, creating
a climate of fear in which administrators became excessively cautious,
rigid, and lacking in creative initiative. Their program was not popular, she
declared, because "life in the usual public housing project is not the way
most American families want to live. Nor does it reflect accepted values as
to the way people should live." The weaknesses were in part inherent in
the physical design of the high-density, high-rise buildings, where interior
space was deficient and there was no private outdoor space. Such standardized housing inevitably became stamped by the same "charity stigma"
that was attached to veterans' hospitals and orphan asylums.

While praising the success of mixed racial occupancy policies in
northern projects, Catherine lamented the lack of progress in slum
clearance despite lip service by policy makers during the decades since
the 1937 housing act. "Even after a long period of high prosperity slums
still exist and there are as many unsanitary, congested, and dilapidated
homes in the U.S. as there were in the middle of the depression."
Catherine pointed out that prosperity made "the continuance of slum
living conditions less excusable, the need for effective solutions more
urgent."

Her argument for slum clearance was the same as it had been in the
1930s: slum re-housing should be established as an independently funded
program with its own legislation, separate from any other housing policies.
It is the fact of *subsidy*, not of geography, that ought to unite these
initiatives, she thought. Public housing in the central areas cannot be
separated from FHA-financed, mortgage-supported single-family housing
in the suburbs. "We now have a proliferation of special-purpose local
agencies concerned with slums and low income housing, but without
responsibility or influence for the rest of the housing market, particularly
not at the metropolitan level." The result: fragmented policies and
fractured administration at federal and local levels. Urban housing
operates as one integrated market, she wrote, and government should have
assumed the responsibility for developing integrated policies.

To her regret, planners had been blindly following the British Garden
City plans, modified by the Bauhaus. "We embraced too wholeheartedly
functionalist and collectivist architectural theories that tended to ignore
certain subtler esthetic values and basic social needs," Catherine wrote.
While experimentation along these lines was healthy, she now realized it
was a mistake to combine policy and practice in "rigid formulas that
prevented further experimentation." If the principles imported from
Britain had been properly adapted and humanized for the American

market, rather than rigidly applied, the undesirable "beehive type of community life" might have been avoided.

Catherine proposed two solutions: (1) greater flexibility in housing policies, with programs based on local needs, and (2) a greater variety of housing choice, including location, dwelling type, and neighbourhood. While freedom and flexibility are probably the hardest things to achieve with public policy, she wrote, it should not be beyond the American genius to invent and perfect policies and instruments that strive for economic equity and social justice.

Catherine's plea for a comprehensive slum-clearance plan resonated among reform-minded planners across the country, particularly in New York City. Under the aegis of urban renewal, Robert Moses, then head of New York's Housing Authority, was engaged in slum clearance of the worst kind: urban removal, not renewal. To make space for Lincoln Center, Shea Stadium, the UN headquarters, and other public landmarks, Moses sanctioned the eviction of close to a quarter of a million residents. In a 1954 study, NYC's Planning Commission condemned Moses for creating large-scale population displacement unlike any previous population movement in the city's history. In so doing, they wrote, he was "solidifying existing ghettoization of New York – dividing up its residents by color and income."[100] Although his biographer, Robert Caro, would later characterize Moses as the "greatest builder in the history of America, perhaps in the history of the world," few in the planning community agreed. Certainly Catherine and her husband did not. Bill had dubbed Moses "that fascist-minded, power-mad person" after reading a *New York Times* article in which Moses attacked foreigners and Lewis Mumford. It did not surprise the Wursters that Moses went on to exploit the urban renewal platform to impose elitist values at the expense of neighbourhoods and closely knit communities.

THE METROPOLITAN FUTURE

I hate ruins. Love, Sadie.

SADIE WURSTER

By 1956 both Catherine and Bill were ready for a major break from work. Catherine took the initiative to plan a family trip to the Middle East, Asia, and Europe, roughly plotting their route based on a list of professional introductions supplied by Ernest Weissmann, Lewis Mumford, and others. Sadie would come along, though they knew it might be stressful to accommodate the needs of an eleven-year-old who would prefer to be cavorting with friends. The global tour would ultimately go down as one of the major events in the Wurster family's history, an opportunity to discover together the art of living, building, and surviving in foreign cultures.

The transition was made easy for Catherine when her friend and fellow houser, Coleman Woodbury, former executive director of NAHRO, offered to assume her teaching obligations at the University of California for the year. It helped, too, that Coleman and his wife, Josephine, agreed to move into the Wursters' home. Catherine sent the Woodburys a five-page, single-spaced letter with detailed instructions ranging from the care of their two dogs and jeepster to kitchen maintenance and refuse collection. "I really intended to write up something for your/my seminar," she added almost as an afterthought, "but finally decided there wasn't much point. I've given it differently different years. I honestly think it will be best for you to do it in your own way ... However you tackle it, it will have more substance than what I've been doing." She had come a long way from her early obsession with classroom detail.

The Wursters embarked in relaxed good humour, their itinerary set only in broad strokes. They wanted to see, hear, and experience as much as possible and be open to change their plans as opportunities arose. Bill kept a diary and Catherine recorded the trip on two cameras: a Roliflex for black and white, and a Canon for colour. Bill reported to his office each week, and his partners posted business updates to major cities on the itinerary.

Departing San Francisco and moving westward around the world, the Wursters visited twenty-five countries and slept in eighty-two different beds over the seven-month journey. They tarried here, rushed there – seven weeks in India, forty-five minutes in Monaco. Flooded by impressions gleaned from covering so much territory in such a short time, the Wursters were able to see dramatic links between places and communities. Bill would later gather his impressions, as much for himself as for his readers, in an article called "Row House Vernacular and High Style Monument," published in the August 1958 issue of *Architectural Record*. The article describes and compares the architecture observed as the family meandered through Europe, Asia, and the Middle East. Catherine provided excellent photographs for *AR* and went on to produce her own article with photos for the March 1959 issue of *Sunset*, featuring "The Gardens of Isfahan and Shiraz." Characteristically, her piece focused more on cityscapes than on the land, though it placed the wonderful gardens in an interesting historical context. Together the Wursters wrote an article for *Perspecta* 5, the Yale architectural journal. Titled "Indian Vernacular Architecture: Wai and Cochin," their piece featured some of Catherine's best close-up photos.

In a lecture called "Across Asia with an Architect," delivered at the Fine Arts Museum of San Francisco shortly after her return, Catherine would note: "I was more and more *particularly* glad I had married an architect."

Bill helped her see houses in a new way and reinforced the notion that internationalism in architecture was not invented by New York's Museum of Modern Art in 1932. He pointed out that architecture had always been international in that all great styles were derived from religious, military, and cultural influences. Everyday buildings serving similar conditions produced similar results, he said, no matter where they are built. And the universality of wood construction reinforced the congruity. Wood is wood, wherever it is found. "A house is a house whether in Katmandu or Liverpool," concluded Catherine. Together they discovered that Victorian architecture might have been an import from the Empire to Great Britain, rather than the commonly accepted reverse. "Victorianism" might have been a reaction of the Western mind to the gorgeous tumble of forms it encountered in the East, she mused.

It was sometimes difficult for Sadie to cope with the professional fixations of her travelling parents. After visiting Angkor Wat in north-western Cambodia, she wrote identical postcards to her friends with the message "I HATE RUINS. Love, Sadie." From Bangkok she wrote a hopeful postcard: "No more trips to boring ruins. Love, Sadie." Her parents experienced frustrations of a different sort. "After three months of travel we propose a traveler's formula," Bill wrote his partners. "Let us call x the amount of time available for a place. It should be divided as follows: $^1/_3x$ for making endless arrangements for hotels, plane, train, and auto schedules, entrance visas, exist visas, money exchange, etc. $^1/_3x$ for sight seeing, and $^1/_3x$ for time in which to recuperate and perhaps even to think." The last third was the hardest to come by, but Bill forced himself to make time for weekly typewritten reports to his partners, Theodore Bernardi and Donn Emmons. The reports would serve as background for the Wursters' articles and talks.

The travellers followed traditional tourist routes but were also able to see more than most visitors thanks to the guidance of colleagues and former students who joined them. In Bangkok, Catherine met a university professor who had taken her Housing 7 seminar at Harvard. He was keen to return to the United States for further studies and enlisted Catherine's support on his fellowship application. She was happy to oblige, as she did for many former students.

Like most tourists they were thrilled by the sight of great Asian temples and palaces, but were equally moved by life on the streets – the daily traditions of eating, shopping, and social intercourse. They noticed a split "between high style and vernacular and the latter's neglect by modern architects, particularly in Asia in respect to housing."[101] Japanese villages appeared romantic, beautiful, irregular, and picturesque. By contrast, Chinese villages (outside Hong Kong) had an architectural plainness to

BILL, CATHERINE, AND SADIE IN MACAU

It was sometimes difficult for Sadie to cope with the professional fixations of her travelling parents ... From Bangkok she wrote a hopeful postcard: "No more trips to boring ruins. Love, Sadie."

which the Wursters could relate. Some villages were walled, while others were in open country and consisted of brick row houses with decorated doors facing fields. Typically five hundred or so people lived in each village.

The tiny city of Macau, near Hong Kong, enchanted all three Wursters. The sixteenth-century Portuguese settlement had hardly changed since its inception. With only four hundred cars for the 200,000 residents in a two-and-a-half-square-mile enclave, pedicabs were Macau's main form of transportation. Catherine and Bill enjoyed being swept along the beautiful waterfront *Avenida* in a rickshaw with Sadie gliding beside them on bicycle.

Bill's interest in architectural form and style was balanced by Catherine's curiosity about people, their customs, and cultural heritage. The family sometimes encountered alarming contradictions. Kerala in southeastern India reminded them of California. Cut off by mountains, the region had a unique climate and was the most densely populated, most Christian, and most literate state in India. It was also the first place in India to elect a Communist-controlled legislature. This event exercised both the national press and the Wursters, who hoped it would awaken the rest of India to the dangers of unemployment, absentee land ownership, and the corruption of Indian National Congress party officials.

They made a stop at a museum designed by Le Corbusier in the western city of Ahmadabad. Although it offered a wonderful pool that provided welcome respite from the sun, the treeless site was a disappointment. Too much unassigned open space in the hot, dry, and windy climate created a dusty disincentive for visitors to linger or residents to pause and chat, remarked Catherine. But Bill liked much of what he saw in Ahmadabad. "Here we were in a great working town in which leadership had brought things into focus so there were some great things happening in the architectural world," he wrote to his partners. "It is just what *is not* happening in San Francisco where decisions are being made by people of limited vision." His words were echoes of Catherine's impressions upon returning to New York from Frankfurt's Römerstadt in 1930.

Chandigarh, the new capital of Punjab, boasted Le Corbusier's beautiful new High Courts building. Bill observed that its rough concrete exterior and rough lighting were appropriate for the climate, where the more typical painted plaster surfaces crumbled and looked shabby after one year.

Bill and Catherine compared what they saw with familiar places in Europe and North America. They were reminded of the Tahoe region as they explored the valley cradling Katmandu. In 1957 only one rough road joined India to Nepal, and they hoped that automobiles would be kept off the handsome, narrow local streets. "We spend millions to make pedestrian malls in America but here they have always been, if only they can be preserved," observed Bill.

The journey ended in Great Britain after a few days' stopover in Scandinavia and the Netherlands, where travelling was easy and predictable. Catherine had most of her black and white film developed along the way, but saved the colour rolls for Rotterdam because the Dutch had a reputation for fine work. The only time her family saw her cry was when she learned that almost one hundred rolls had been ruined when someone turned on the wrong light in the darkroom. She was not consoled by the photo shop's offer of two rolls for every one spoiled.

Back in Berkeley, Catherine carefully prepared her lectures and seminars, using examples from recent observations and inviting new Asian friends to address her students. The Wurster guest list now included people from Asia and the UN.

Her professional interest turned to India, and Catherine soon decided to return there for more serious research. In 1958 she received $2,500 from UC's Institute of International Studies "to explore the question of urban living standards and minimum improvement costs under Indian social-economic conditions, in relation to the scale and pattern of future urban development."[102] The Ford Foundation, which was running several major projects in India, had advanced the funds through the university on the understanding that Catherine would return to stage a seminar on urbanization in India. Another Ford grant went to the architecture department for a survey and exhibit on architectural design in India, for which Catherine would collect additional data during her travels.

The date of departure, January 12, 1959, found Catherine barely ready. Last minute directives to Bill and Thelma regarding Sadie's schedules and Bill's professional entertainment protocols were written en route and delivered by mail. All three missed Catherine terribly but, by their own accounts, managed very well during her absence. Catherine had cleared her study for the first time in years, allowing Sadie, Shirley, and their friends to move in and, finally, to use the ping-pong table for its intended purpose. Sadie wrote to Catherine of the hilarious times she, Shirley, and Thelma had on the ice rink, where the girls had an advantage over the older woman because they were taking dancing lessons. Sadie prepared occasional meals for her grateful "pop" and joined him, sometimes grudgingly, at countless luncheons and dinners with their many friends. His busy schedule worried her, and Sadie attempted to make their home life cozy by playing his favourite records. From his letters Catherine detected the flowering of a special bond between father and daughter. He heaped praise on Sadie, pronouncing her to be like Catherine in so many ways.

Catherine had planned a three-month "freelance trip," with no rigid itinerary. Israel was her first stop, and despite a limited three-day visit she managed to take away strong impressions of the young nation. "You have been doing the only bona fide regional planning in the world," she later wrote her Tel Aviv host, Ariel Sharon, director of planning for the State of Israel. She was fascinated by the great diversity of the Israeli people, with their cultural differences "far more dramatically visible than the religious unity that brought them there."[103] Also intriguing was the way the state succeeded in absorbing waves of immigrants on a thin sliver of arable land between the Mediterranean Sea and Jordan.

During her whirlwind tour of Israel, Catherine was introduced to regional planning on a national scale. She observed how the settlement philosophy of Walter Christaller, Germany's leading theoretical geographer, was being applied. He envisaged a hexagonal pattern of service centres comprising a hierarchy of services and distribution facilities around regional centres of fifty thousand people. Each centre, or city, would serve a network of market towns of five to ten thousand inhabitants, spaced five to ten miles apart. Guided by Artur Glikson, architect and head of the planning department of the Ministry of Labor's Housing Division, Catherine saw Christaller's theories manifested in the Lakish region between Tel Aviv and Beer Sheva. Kiryat Gat was the urban centre, a brand new city struggling to provide regional services such as banking, higher education, hospital facilities, and industrial employment. Kiryat Gat depended on surrounding market towns to provide local services including shops, schools, clinics, and repair of agricultural equipment. Here was a dramatic example of the kind of regional planning so badly needed in areas of rapid growth in poor and crowded developing countries, Catherine thought. She took the diagrams and maps Glikson gave her of Lakish to her next stop, India.

On January 25 Catherine arrived in New Delhi where she contacted government planner Tarlock Singh, who helped her line up people and places to see across the country. In the weeks ahead she would visit Ahmadabad, with side trips to Rajkot, Baroda, Anand, Bombay and surroundings, Pune, Bangalore, Coimbatore, Madras, Calcutta, Kharagpur, and Jamshedpur. Transportation was tricky: roads were bad and train routes indirect because the railroad gauge varied from place to place. Much time was spent making travel arrangements, mostly for flights.

India was engaged in the experimental development of "Industrial Estates," some of which Catherine had the chance to visit. It was a program to promote industrial and market research and training in small, mostly rural regions such as Rajkot, once a princely seat renowned for metal crafts. Investments in electricity, sewage and plumbing, railroad sidings for product distribution, roadways, and workers' low-cost housing were putting Rajkot on the map as a manufacturing centre for metal products like ball bearings and heel tips. New industrial communities across India were receiving funds from international organizations, including the Ford Foundation, Stanford Research Institute, the World Bank, and the World Health Organization (WHO). However, the international planning community was by no means unanimous in supporting the program; some claimed the development came at the expense of large urban areas such as Calcutta.

Since independence in 1947, extraordinary social and political turmoil had engulfed urban India. At that time, Calcutta, a Bengali city of 3.7 million inhabitants, was the economic capital of British India. Its major industries of jute and engineering were reasonably healthy and productive, albeit largely for the benefit of the British who dominated ownership and management. But Calcutta was also the economic and cultural capital of India and would remain so throughout the 1960s, before bowing to Bombay.

Arthur T. Row, professor of City Planning at Yale and a former student of Catherine's Housing 7 class at Harvard, was seconded to the Ford Foundation as staff director of planning for the Calcutta program. His report, "An Evaluation of the Calcutta Planning and Development Project," describes the situation that Catherine encountered. Between 1947 and 1959, he observed, Calcutta had more than doubled its population, presiding over an enormous hinterland of 250,000 square miles and a population of 100 million. "Its food supplies and its raw jute were provided by the lowlands of East Bengal, its coal and iron ore by the plains of West Bengal and the uplands of Bihar, its labor by these three provinces as well as Orissa, Assam, and the United Provinces."[104] The city was horribly congested, half of it without sanitary sewers and potable water. Virtually no new capital investment had been made in infrastructure since the beginning of the Second World War; prior to the war, improvements had been largely limited to the city's European section.

Independence resulted in a truncated economy from which Calcutta never recovered. East Bengal, the primary source of Calcutta's intellectual and political leadership, agricultural wealth, food, and raw materials for major industries, was lopped off some thirty miles from Calcutta's eastern boundary and became part of East Pakistan (later Bangladesh). The Hindu refugee stream flowing westward into Calcutta grossly outnumbered the counterflowing Muslim stream eastward. By 1949 the city, bursting at the seams, exploded in the worst communal riots in its history.

In 1959 a team of four WHO professionals was invited by the state's chief minister, Dr. B.C. Roy, to study sanitary conditions in the State of West Bengal. Their report was devastating. "In India the region of endemic cholera falls within the State of Bengal with its nucleus in Greater Calcutta and dominantly in the bustee population, ill provided with even elementary sanitary facilities. The cholera situation has great significance not only to West Bengal and all of India, but to the world at large."[105] They found that "hardly any aspect of community development is keeping pace with the growth of Calcutta's population or with the requirements of its hinterland. Overcrowding, degradation of housing, health hazards, primitive water supplies, lack of space for new industries, traffic bottlenecks, power shortage, and a still unsolved refugee problem – are all increasing the cost of moving goods and of providing the many services that a growing industrial region demands of its metropolis." The World Bank added that failure to solve Calcutta's problems would impede economic growth in India's most rapidly expanding industrial region. These were desperate cries to the world for help.

But Calcutta was also a vigorous and vibrant city. Its metropolitan district stretched forty miles along both banks of the broad, muddy Hooghly river. In some places the built-up area was less than a mile wide, in others three to four miles. The city centre had a contemporary business district. Old British areas, characterized by wide streets and rectangular city blocks, once boasted elegant palaces that were now being replaced by high-rise luxury apartments.

It was a city of enormous contrasts, little understood by the New Delhi government and even less by the world. A university enrolled more than 150,000 students, while 700,000 children did not attend school at all. Calcutta had an open and politically democratic society, but political parties and their factions battled more frequently on the street than at the polling booths. Nehru had declared Calcutta's problems a national concern and allocated ten *crores* for its "Third Development Plan." One *crore* equalled 10 million rupees; thus Nehru allocated 100 million rupees, which represented a shortfall of at least 100 *crores* in terms of Calcutta's dire need.

The Ford Foundation, which had assisted the Indian government in preparing a master plan for Greater Delhi, now turned to Calcutta. Dr. Roy approached Douglas Ensminger, the Foundation's representative in India, along with Edward (Ned) Echeverria, chief physical planner of the Delhi project. Roy warned the two planners that "unless some bold steps are soon taken Calcutta will be lost to the Communists."[106] Ensminger persuaded the foundation's Overseas Development Division that Calcutta presented "the greatest urban problem in the world [and] must be tackled." The division's response: "We are well aware of the effects on the rest of India and Asia of what happens to Calcutta."[107] Foundation staff then explored financial support with the World Bank and the US State Department, while Ensminger and Roy talked to Nehru. Ensminger also consulted the US ambassador to India and World Bank personnel. They secured millions of dollars in promises from all these sources combined and millions more from the Indian and West Bengal governments.

The Ford Foundation believed the project could have a significant bearing on the development of the Ganges industrial basin. It could also provide a better understanding of the processes of rapid urbanization in developing countries, for which Calcutta would provide "the first (as well as the biggest and best) laboratory." To ensure a high level of commitment to this long-range study, the Ford Foundation sponsored the establishment of a consortium of US universities, including MIT, Harvard, University of Pennsylvania, and UC Berkeley. The foundation's role would be to provide technical experts, arrange for services from the participating universities, and underwrite expenses up to $1 million. Through a special fund, the UN would finance the preparation of plans for water supply, drainage, and sanitation. All this would be coordinated under the aegis of an aid organization: the Calcutta Metropolitan Planning Organization (CMPO).

The challenges facing Calcutta were grist for the Bauer mill: an opportunity for Catherine to test her planning credo ("Decentralize!") and to stretch her new professional direction. After returning to Berkeley, she would become a consultant to the Ford Foundation on the Calcutta Planning and Development Project.

During her stay in Calcutta, Catherine absorbed the character of old neighbourhoods aboard a tricycle-taxi and by walking. On a road leading out of the city was the Indian Statistical Institute (ISI), directed by an irascible economist, Mr. Mahalanobis. He was an avowed Communist who had alienated most of the American consultants in Calcutta with his tirades against the US and for China. As a consequence his work, which deserved recognition, was ignored. Consummate diplomat that she was, Catherine disarmed Mahalanobis's anti-West passion by hearing him out, then focusing on his useful knowledge. She won his trust and was invited to spend a week observing the work of ISI.

The institute, housed in a mansion from the Tagore era, fascinated her. Computers whirred in one corner, village industry experiments in another, and social scientists went about their business – working on all kinds of projects in a lively, experimental, and thoroughly unbureaucratic atmosphere. Mahalanobis was one of the ablest and most powerful men in India, Catherine wrote to Paul Ylvisaker and Ned Echeverria, and his ISI was probably the best and most influential research group in the country, running the government's sample surveys. The two men remained sceptical.

Upon returning from India, Catherine found herself drained. For the first time in her life she was unable to rally the legendary energy or muster the will to write her report on India for the Ford Foundation. She was chided by her physician for harbouring unrealistic expectations. After all, at the age of fifty-four Catherine might reasonably expect to slow down. The doctor's advice did not sit well, and further visits and laboratory tests confirmed hypothyroidism. Catherine was prescribed medication that boosted her energy only enough to make her acutely aware of how far behind she had fallen in her professional obligations. She began to rethink the thrust of her life.

Up to now public speaking had been a high priority, and she endeavoured to accept dates, given adequate warning. No sooner had she returned from India than the invitations began to pour in. Her status as a member of the Democratic Party Advisory Committee on Urban and Suburban Problems made her a popular draw at the podium. Leon Keyserling's wife, Mary, invited her to address a luncheon of the Women's National Democratic Club in Washington in January 1960. "I'd *love* to," replied Catherine, but would not commit herself as she had promised to participate in an as-yet-unscheduled meeting of the Yale Architecture-Planning Visiting Committee. Mary did not let her off the hook, offering instead to shift an impressive roster of February speakers (among them, Paul Butler and Chester Bowles) back to January so as to accommodate Catherine. At the same time, she was invited to give a speech at the White House Conference on Children and Youth at the end of March. These were tempting offers, but they arrived at a time when her energy was waning and her guilt mounting over the Calcutta report and the Ford-sponsored conference on Indian urbanization.

On January 2, 1960, Catherine stepped on the brakes. "No," she wrote to the White House conference, and "no" to Mary Keyserling. To her regret she had to honour the Yale commitment. "One thing I should have done long ago," she told Mary, "is get out of the Institutional Life, and just do free-lance writing. I don't really enjoy teaching." She hoped to write a book on the architecture of the firm Wurster, Bernardi, and Emmons, preferably in collaboration with Bill. Charles Scribner's Sons had expressed interest. Perhaps they would write it in three years when Bill planned to retire. Noting the dearth of good books on Asian cities, she thought this too would be a worthwhile project for the two of them.

Even as she vowed to refocus on writing, Catherine became embroiled in lobbying for grants to study California's development problems. She was running at cross purposes, launching new research initiatives while wondering "if academic research *can* really be made useful at all."[108] She also became involved in establishing the Institute of Urban and Regional Development at UC Berkeley, and looked to President Clark Kerr for support. Catherine argued that Berkeley's Department of City and Regional Planning was probably tops in the country and must be equipped to address challenging questions about the future of California's environment.

CATHERINE AT PODIUM

Her status as a member of the Democratic Party Advisory Committee on Urban and Suburban Problems made her a popular draw at the podium.

By March 1961, two years after her return from India, Catherine had gathered the strength to write a detailed report to Echeverria and Ylvisaker at the Ford Foundation, recommending an appropriate course of action for Calcutta, because she vehemently opposed the "ad hoc Metropolitan Plan" proposed by the Calcutta Metropolitan Planning Organization. She argued that such a general plan would treat the urban area as an island, paying little attention to the national or regional interrelationships so important to a developing country with limited resources. Furthermore, the Calcutta plan should not be based on western models and assumptions, as the Delhi plan had been. An eastern plan needed to bring the appropriate set of social and civic standards into its own complex physical scheme. She pointed out that in American and European communities, underlying assumptions and standards were usually quite well understood and widely accepted. In western plans, for example, it was implicit that minimum physical standards of housing and services were desirable and feasible, that growth trends could readily be projected, and that the established economic base would continue to provide increased employment and adequate tax resources with little direct public intervention beyond zoning and services. In contrast, developing countries had yet to clarify their viable urban standards.

In her Calcutta report Catherine asked questions that were not addressed by the Delhi planners: Could India afford an overhead investment of 2500 rupees (or even Rs 250) per capita for the next 100 million urbanites? Would Calcutta have to take care of 20 or 30 million people, or could economic opportunities be provided elsewhere to divert such a flood? What was the optimum pattern from the viewpoint of social conditions, overhead costs, and maximum productivity in variable local situations?

The Delhi planners had neither time, resources, nor even instructions to do the research required to find real answers to these and other questions. They merely made assumptions on their own, which may or may not have been correct. Catherine charged that the Delhi plan was based on hunches with little real knowledge about critical issues such as suitable housing standards and industrial location criteria. Once carried out, the hunches would be tested and adjustments could be made. But this would take time, and Calcutta, in a state of emergency, could not wait for answers. Besides, to Catherine the government program in Greater Delhi looked confused.

Calcutta had certain advantages over Delhi, she pointed out. It was located entirely within the powerful state of West Bengal, which already made many key decisions and expenditures in the metropolitan area; the state was directly involved in important programs of resource, rural, industrial, and urban development elsewhere in West Bengal, which would have implications for Calcutta's future. Although the state government did not address locational planning, it was engaged in responsible, economically well-developed, statewide budgetary planning as an integral part of the national planning process.

Catherine proposed that Calcutta planners reverse the general planning processes applied to Delhi. She recommended seven steps to developing a pragmatic scheme, based on an understanding of the entire region's real problems – and basic planning criteria:

1 The State of West Bengal should assume direct responsibility for all emergency programs, creating a WPA-style body that combined planning, research, and field operations and avoided the bureaucratic difficulties of acting through existing ministries. State responsibility and strong local administration would be *sine qua non* for all international aid. Outside pressures should *not* encourage the creation of some temporary ad hoc agency at the metropolitan level.

2 The whole state should be a field laboratory in which improvement and development programs were organized and analyzed. This would allow for the immediate betterment of both physical conditions and employment, and contribute to basic knowledge and future planning criteria with respect to: (a) urban physical standards, including housing; (b) industrial and employment location; and (c) optimum urban and regional development patterns. With Calcutta, the Damedor Valley, and some very underdeveloped areas, West Bengal offered one of the most significant test cases for regional development in all of India.

3 An immediate program for improved housing, urban sanitation, and transportation should be designed, using scientific work already available for field testing. The program would include a range of systematic experiments and provide a testing ground for future development policy. Thus, 5 million rupees spent on housing construction, with a small fraction for research, would contribute to the tested knowledge of better alternatives. Rural community development programs might be tied to this as there was a continuum of problems from village to congested city, and experience at one level might offer leads for another.

4 The National Planning Commission should work with West Bengal's economic planners to develop hypotheses about monetary and other resources, such as foreign aid, likely to be available for urban overhead investments directed toward the next 5 to 10 million urbanites in the

region. This would provide a framework for economizing efforts and for a tentative determination of feasible future standards and expenditures. It could also provide a tie-in between statewide and local budgeting and planning.

5 A program should be organized to stimulate new productive enterprise and employment opportunities for Calcutta and other communities in West Bengal. This would be planned and tested on an experimental basis, serving the dual purposes of relieving current needs and gaining more knowledge of locational economics.

6 Present and potential overhead costs should be analyzed in different types of urban communities, including Calcutta, its environs, and more isolated areas. This could be set up as a permanent operation where data from research, experiments, and experience would be continuously gathered.

7 The intensive groundwork of the first six steps would lead to the possibility of creating effective machinery to prepare comprehensive, general, long-term plans of various types, including a statewide plan for urban-industrial development related to economic policy and available resources, a metropolitan plan for the Calcutta area, a regional plan for West Bengal, and a metropolitan plan for Durgapur, another West Bengali city.[109]

Catherine recommended incentives to promote industrial development in a variety of locations. These included favourable tax and credit policies, the provision of utilities and transportation, and the development of better housing and cultural facilities. Programs would be illuminated by systematic research on recent trends in industrial location and by private and public decisions that shaped these trends. Data for this research was available in the Sample Survey cards at the ISI and in the considerable experience with Industrial Estates. The educated unemployed, who presented an extremely urgent problem in Calcutta, needed special incentives to start up businesses or to engage in teaching and other professional services in outlying communities.

The report was not well received by Ylvisaker and Echeverria. Despite being longtime admirers of Catherine, they now accused her of being one of the old guard: an obsolete decentrist. She countered by pointing out that the situation in India was fundamentally different from that in the United States and urged them to have a talk "with that old devil, Mahalanobis," who had his finger on the pulse of the region and could provide useful information.[110] In the end, her report to the Ford Foundation was ignored.

Little progress was made by international planners over the ensuing years, concluded a report by the Ford's own man in Calcutta, Arthur Row. The CMPO remained in place, headed by Lt. Gen. D.R. Chakravarti, who was also director of health services for the government of West Bengal. Chakravarti had little time to coordinate CMPO, and friction arose between Ford Foundation advisors and CMPO staff over slow progress and political skirmishes between state and city governments. In 1962 the foundation replaced its on-site advisors with two leading lights in urban renewal from Pennsylvania. They argued for a long-term interdisciplinary team instead of short-term consultants. Moneys originally promised by USAID and the World Bank for infrastructure (including an emergency water supply system) were not forthcoming. Conversations about international assistance were carried on for ten years to no avail.

Eventually the number of Ford participants would increase to seventeen, excluding Ensminger and Echeverria who turned to other pursuits. In early 1969, CMPO staff drew up a 21 Point Program delineating Calcutta's problems and offering the first strategic ideas toward their alleviation. The West Bengal government established a Town and Country Planning Branch of its State Development and Planning Department; CMPO operated within the branch, but not before conditions in Calcutta became truly dismal.

Catherine had witnessed a dire emergency in Calcutta in 1959. What would she have thought, ten years later, when information was still being gathered, with no remedial action taken? Would Calcutta's modern history have been different had her advice been heeded? And would it even have been possible to heed her advice, given the region's political crosswinds?

DEATH

Her works are people, students, ideas that have shaped institutions, vital courses which, but for her counsel, might have strayed.

DOUGLAS HASKELL

Catherine still had to make good on the promise to the Ford Foundation and UC's Institute of International Studies to deliver a seminar based on her travels in India. The event was scheduled for June 26 to July 1, 1960, and the weeks preceding it found her in a frenzy unequalled since her lobbying days in the mid-1930s. Besides assembling material for her

CATHERINE , C. 1960

Catherine still had to make good on the promise to the Ford Foundation to deliver a seminar based on her travels in India.

contribution to the seminar, there were long-overdue book reviews and articles to write, classes to prepare, and meetings to attend.

The seminar, "Urbanization in India: Urban Trends and Problems in a Developing Country," was the first such gathering of Indian and American experts. Sponsored by the University of California, with aid from the Ford Foundation, it was launched with a Sunday afternoon tour of the Berkeley campus, followed by refreshments at the Wursters' home. The real business began early Monday morning at the Claremont Hotel in Berkeley.

Thirty-three people, about half from India, attended to hear twenty-eight papers. Among them were planners, geographers, sociologists, population experts, anthropologists, political scientists, and statisticians. Papers ranged from the general ("Urbanization in India: Past and Future") to the specific ("The Impact of Urban Society upon Village Life"). Catherine's topic was "Urban Living Conditions, Overhead Costs, and the Development Pattern." A book of the seminar proceedings, which included most of the papers, was edited by Roy Turner, a planning specialist on leave from the University of Chicago to work in international population and urban research at UC. Titled *India's Urban Future,* Turner's book was published by the University of California Press in 1962 and served as a useful text. "The character of the seminar," Turner wrote, "may be taken as evidence of the desire, the energy, and the ability, on the part of those responsible to tackle heroically the challenges offered by a coming urban population growth of unprecedented scale."

The seminar brought together at least a dozen different kinds of "experts" who normally never met, Catherine observed to Jean Joyce, a Ford Foundation employee in Delhi. "Heaven knows nothing was solved, but it did open up and sharpen a whole universe of rising issues." In short, it was a success.

Soon after the event Bill Wurster went to the hospital for a routine

CATHERINE,
BILL, AND SADIE
AT HOME

The seminar
was launched
with a Sunday
afternoon tour
of the Berkeley
campus, followed
by refreshments
at the Wursters'
home.

prostatectomy. An enlarged prostate had been troubling him for some time but was ignored as he pursued what he considered to be more pressing matters. Such stoicism was not new; Bill had been suffering quietly for years from arthritis in various joints, complicated recently by gout. Remarkably, he was able to tolerate the additional discomfort of a hypertrophied prostate when he journeyed to Brazil in the spring of 1960, as a consultant on the proposed plan for its new federal capital, Brasilia. He knew surgery would be imperative on his return, but delayed taking action until after Catherine's India seminar. Perhaps he waited too long, perhaps his other ailments complicated the situation. In any case, what had been planned as a standard prostate operation became a major crisis. Bill lost so much blood that he needed seven replacement units. He spent a month in hospital and then slowly recovered his strength at home, nursed by the three women in his life: his wife, his daughter, and their longtime housekeeper, Thelma. Taking so many weeks away from work stressed Bill, who was now balancing three hats on his graying head. In addition to being senior partner in a busy architectural practice and dean of a major university department, he headed a new campus planning committee for UC President Clark Kerr.

After the seminar's successful conclusion, Catherine was free to tackle two other major projects. First she would wrap up her report on the physical environment for the President's Commission on National Goals, then turn her attention to the launching of the long-awaited Institute of

Urban and Regional Development. Upon receiving the first draft of her report at the end of September, the President's Commission advised her to amplify and clarify every point (or so it seemed to Catherine), cover a few more, such as water and economic base – and cut out three thousand words. Although she was frustrated and angered at having to "sweat through" a second draft, she conceded it was much better than the first. This time she showed her revision to Clark Kerr, who had recommended her to the commission, before sending it to Washington. He applauded her work.

The birth of the Institute for Urban and Regional Development (IURD) entailed a difficult, decade-long labour. The IURD's purpose was to strengthen research in planning, and its realization required the support of many sceptics within the Berkeley campus community. Although a member of an intramural steering committee of six professors, Catherine seemed to have the most active hand in the institute's establishment and was its biggest booster. Early in 1960 she became restless and began to fire off memos seeking support from key administrators, including Kerr. "A suitable research program and agency is the primary need of our Department, in terms of both professional training and service to the State,"[111] she wrote him in February that year. To her, the institute represented a vital expression of professional and civic leadership on planning and development issues within the Bay Area.

She called in credit and worked her professional network to the fullest. She pleaded with Jack Kent, her department chairman, to lobby both Harmer Davis of UC's Institute for Traffic and Transportation Engineering, and Kerr, whose support remained uncertain. Catherine seemed to think that the head of the steering committee, Sherman Maisel, was not forceful enough in promoting the institute and the kinds of problems it would tackle. "Forgive me if I seem so emotional about all this," she told Kent. "I only wish I knew why it bothers me so much. Maybe it's just personal pique and frustration."[112]

In May she penned a "personal and private" letter to Kerr, urging action. It begins diplomatically, thanking him for his support in recommending her for the National Goals commission, after which she again launched the institute missile. "I keep wondering about the future program of the Department of City and Regional Planning [DCRP] in relation to the University and the State," she wrote. "In view of your interest in the physical environment and your apparent confidence in me, here are some frank opinions." She pointed out that DCRP was on a par with similar departments at MIT, Harvard, Penn, and North Carolina (the only other state university), all of which had established strong research agencies in recent years. Such agencies served to enrich university faculty and staff, and to provide Ph.D. programs. She warned that "we must rapidly fall behind unless we can soon do likewise," arguing that this would be the only way that the complicated problems of physical planning and development (so important in California) could receive adequate attention. The need had been recognized in Sacramento and throughout the university. "But we cannot take any steps until the proposals have been fully discussed and cleared with you, in their various State-wide aspects."[113]

Perusing the Annual Report of the Survey Research Center for 1959-60, Catherine was dismayed to find no mention of DCRP, even though the department had engaged in specific projects with the centre and had provided faculty consultants to its advisory committee. This clearly indicated that DCRP's social scientists were not taken seriously. The only remedy for such an omission, in Catherine's opinion, was a strong director for the institute, one respected by key social scientists. The School of Social Welfare *was* mentioned in the annual report, and she urged Kent to hold a strategy session with the school's dean, Milton Chernin, who had made social welfare respectable to academic social scientists, and social scientists useful to social welfare practitioners. Chernin urged Kent to identify a potential institute director as soon as possible. He must be highly respectable and a bona fide empire builder, said Chernin, and ought to become a full DCRP professor. Catherine agreed, and offered her own part-time professorship if it would help. Once again she proved to be a relentless lobbyist, capable of creative and shrewd means to her end.

The final straw came when a promising young UC graduate in political science sought Catherine's advice on where to pursue a Ph.D. in planning for underdeveloped countries – and there was no place for him in the College of Environmental Design. She pointed him eastward, and he was accepted everywhere he applied. MIT offered the young man a fellowship, and Penn offered free tuition and a research grant in their Institute of Urban Studies. UC lost a potential star. Catherine sent an urgent memo to fellow faculty members Kent, Foley, and Webber, who also edited the *Journal of Planning*: "Maybe we should consider putting our Ph.D. program in the mill along with the Institute."

The search for a director was launched. Catherine put forward thirteen names, headed by leaders in the field of policy-oriented research: Martin Meyerson, director of the Joint Center for Urban Studies of MIT-Harvard and professor of city planning at Harvard (he had been Catherine's student in the Housing 7 seminar and, before, Bill's sole classmate at Harvard); Dr. Harvey Perloff, director of Regional Studies for RFF and member of the Committee of Nine for the Alliance for Progress; William L.C. Wheaton, director of the Institute for Urban Studies and professor of city planning at the University of Pennsylvania; Paul Ylvisaker, public affairs director at the Ford Foundation; and John W. Dyckman of the Department of City Planning at Penn.

Catherine championed William Wheaton, whom she met during her Cambridge years when he was housing expediter at the Federal Housing Agency in Washington. Impressed by his sharp intellect, she had persuaded Wheaton to complete a Ph.D. in planning at Harvard, where he eventually became an associate professor under G. Holmes Perkins. When Perkins became dean of the College of Fine Arts at Penn, Wheaton joined him as a professor of planning. His strong social science background influenced student admission criteria and broadened the curriculum. Later he became the first director of the Institute for Urban Studies.

Wheaton was well regarded by eastern foundations and able "to run with the research charge," Catherine observed. But she feared the deeply rooted easterner would never consider moving. (She did not know then that personal considerations made the West very appealing to him.) To tempt Wheaton, she let him know that he would be offered a free hand to launch and develop a multifaceted research institute, independent but linked to the planning department. Early in 1963 he beat Charles Abrams to the appointment of US delegate to the UN's Economic and Social Council for housing and related issues. Catherine was worried that he may not have time for a new institute; under the strain of Bill's poor health, her written pleas resonated with urgency. "Please come and take on the Director of the Institute," she begged Wheaton. "The game is killing me ... with no one to talk to." She knew that more than anyone, he could create a unique team capable of raising the quality of education and thus return planning at UC Berkeley to the top of the profession.

On September 22, 1962, the Office of Public Information of the University of California announced an intensified three-pronged attack on the problems of urban and regional growth with the creation of broad-based new research units on the Berkeley campus designed to give both faculty members and advanced graduate students improved facilities and support. "This action," President Kerr exulted, "will enable the University to join even more fully than it has in the past in the urgent task of keeping our cities livable and of helping them further to fulfil their historic civilizing role." Chancellor Edward Strong applauded the decision because the Institute of Urban and Regional Development would attract to the campus substantial federal, foundation, and private funds to underwrite a wide range of urban and regional studies.

Chancellor Strong told the press that the need for the institute had been felt for more than a decade. It would coordinate and support the work of some 110 faculty members from more than fifteen of Berkeley's departments and units, all of whom were actively engaged in urban studies. The institute would comprise three main branches: a Center for Research in Real Estate and Urban Economics; a new Center for Planning and Development Research, focusing on physical problems of urban growth; and a Center for Research in Urban Social Organization, which would launch special projects dealing with social welfare, criminology, sociology, education, public health, geography, law, and architecture.

William Wheaton was announced as the institute's first director in June 1963. Catherine's hand in his appointment was clear. She had arranged private meetings for him with Kerr and Strong. The entire selection committee, enormously impressed by Wheaton's breadth, intelligence, and way with words, had asked the candidate to delineate an effective research program. Before submitting a twelve-page proposal, Wheaton showed it to Catherine who did some sharp editing and contributed a few ideas. Three months later, Wheaton moved to Berkeley where he would spend the rest of his life, ending a brilliant career as dean of the College of Environmental Design (CED) from 1967 to 1976.

Today, thirty-five years after its inception, IURD is an internationally acclaimed institute whose director reports to UC's Vice Chancellor for Research. It is composed of members of the CED faculty plus representatives of such diverse departments as political science, education, geography, and public policy. Participants include research associates from various professions and visiting academicians from around the world. Its mission statement stresses research that "is directed to urban growth and land use; sustainable development; transportation alternatives; information technology; disaster preparedness; social and economic impacts of changes in urban life; defense conversion; evolving patterns of suburbanization and central city reconstruction; analysis of regional growth patterns using Geographic Information Systems; social policy and urban poverty; and improvements in methods of analysis, evaluation, and planning."[114] The IURD brings together local communities and academic institutions to do applied research to encourage sustainable economic and social development. Six local community organizations are included, among them the Campus-Community Coalition and Defense Conversion Program. Now located in Wurster Hall on the Berkeley campus, the institute represents Catherine's vision realized beyond her greatest dreams.

John Dyckman, who had left the University of Pennsylvania to direct San Francisco's urban renewal program for Arthur D. Little, became the first head of IURD's Center for Planning and Development Research. The centre received a grant of $200,000 from the Ford Foundation for an eighteen-month study of the explosive growth of California's suburbs, "to analyze the social and economic forces represented in the State's mushrooming metropolitan fringe and to recommend legislation."[115] Leading suburban home builder and developer, Edward P. Eichler, was appointed to conduct the study under Dyckman's direction. It would prove to be an innovative partnership between academia and marketplace.

In November 1962, two months after IURD was formally launched, Bill Wurster announced his retirement from the College of Environmental Design, effective June 1963. He had passed retirement age and recently been diagnosed with Parkinson's disease. A selection committee for a new dean was formed under Walter Horn, professor of Fine Arts History, with Fran Violich representing CED. Several candidates were brought forward, among them G. Holmes Perkins, Martin Meyerson, and Jack Kent, who had expressed his interest to Catherine. She entered the fray with endorsement or opposition for several of the candidates whom she knew quite well. The hardest letter she ever had to write, she told her daughter, was the one opposing Kent's candidacy. Although she regarded him as one of the strongest leaders for urban planning in the Bay Area – he had a major hand in promoting the transit system project, later known as BART – she had serious doubts about his leadership style. She once described it to Clark Kerr as "gradual and non-flamboyant, with a bias toward local self-determination ... too conservative to cosmic reformers like me." Catherine came out squarely behind Martin Meyerson, who was awarded the appointment. Bill welcomed Meyerson as his successor. "Meyerson has rapidly become perhaps the most brilliant and broad-gauged leader in this field [of planning]," he wrote to Charles Moore, chairman of the architecture department.

Catherine felt strained. She was tired and often depressed over Bill's declining health, though she preferred not to discuss this with even her closest friends. Elizabeth Winston, a friend from Vassar College days, recalls a visit from the Wursters to her home in Minneapolis during this period. While Catherine was out of the room, Bill shared the diagnosis with Elizabeth, whose husband had also suffered from Parkinson's. She told Bill of an operation he had undergone, in which a hole was drilled into his skull. It was quite gruelling, she recalled, and he was free of symptoms for just one year. Bill turned away from her.

But when he returned home, he discussed the operation with his doctor and was referred to a leading neurosurgeon, Dr. Irving Cooper, who performed the thalamotomy procedure at St. Barnabas Hospital in New York. A deep lesion is made in the basal ganglia of the brain through a perforation in the skull. The Wursters decided to try it, and after consultation with Dr. Cooper the surgery was scheduled for mid-October 1963. Meyerson recalls driving Bill to the airport. "He was in a wheelchair, he couldn't speak or eat properly, it was terrible to see." Two days after

Bill's surgery, Meyerson happened to be in New York and visited him at the hospital. "He jumped out of bed and grabbed my hand. Catherine and I just pranced around in delight, celebrating the miracles of science." For the first time Catherine was able to discuss Bill's condition and surgery with her friends, but her good spirits were short lived. Bill's symptoms gradually returned. Two years later his request for another operation was denied; he was considered too old.

Martin Meyerson arrived at the Berkeley campus during the summer of 1963 just as a new building was being constructed for CED. For the first time all the departments, including the new IURD and its center for planning, would be under one roof. Bill and Catherine were delighted and honoured that it would be called Wurster Hall. Catherine had officially become professor of urban development on July 1, 1962. Eighteen months later Meyerson created the post of assistant dean for her, thinking that eventually she would become dean. Most of all, he wanted Catherine to work with him and the faculty on long-term planning for the college. And she was a unique resource. "Sometimes the most interesting people in a company are made vice-chairman so they don't have too many day-to-day responsibilities, but can make important contributions," Meyerson says of Catherine.[116]

At first she was pleased by the new appointment, though it was not a position to which she would have aspired. She thought she had left administration behind when she fled her post as director of Research and Information for the USHA twenty-five years earlier. Meyerson couldn't fail to notice her stress, which he correctly identified as a symptom less of work than of life in general.

As always, Catherine was over-committed. She was a member, with her friend Kay Kerr, of the Committee to Save the Bay, as well as the Advisory Committee on Problems and Needs of Urban Expansion for the Housing and Home Finance Agency (HHFA). In September 1963, she accepted an invitation to participate on the visiting committee for MIT's Department of Planning. She was also working frantically to finalize details for the Metropolitan Future conference scheduled that month at UC Berkeley.

The years following the India trip saw a subtle change in Catherine's demeanour. The trip had been a high point in every way. She had made good contacts, collected useful information, been treated with respect, and thoroughly enjoyed travelling on her own, just as in Europe during the 1930s. She had returned on a high, but gradually showed signs of strain – being uncharacteristically short with colleagues, many of whom were close friends. She publicly cut people off over differences of opinion and refused to talk to Ernest Weissmann after the paper she wrote for his Tokyo meeting was omitted from his *Regional Planning-Tokyo* volume.

Catherine was so universally admired that her sharp words visibly wounded their targets, and more than a few times she was obliged to apologize. "Profound apologies for Sunday night ..." she wrote to Mel Webber, a faculty associate whom she respected, "I acted like a martyred termagant ... I was literally half dead ... I had just taken a ridiculous hike up Tamalpais, 2,000 feet on the steep trail in a broiling sun at a hundred degrees, and was practically out when I crawled into the car at the top."

She had retained her youthful passion for hiking, but increasingly lacked the stamina for it. Mount Tamalpais tested her limits. Catherine would drive up Ridgecrest Boulevard, park her car and walk downhill along the steep Willow Camp Trail, enjoying the spectacular ocean view. That day, the arduous trudge back to her car almost defeated her. "The experience was probably a salutary shock for a 58-year old lady who has smoked too much for 40 years, but still had a romantically sporting self-image in the back of her mind."[117] Having tried and failed to quit, she was now smoking fifty cigarettes a day.

Charles Abrams, an old friend and housing ally, was another victim of Catherine's wrath. Together they served on a special commission for which the consensus report was now long overdue. Catherine became impatient. Their exchange of words is not recorded, but Abrams's letter suggests he'd been cut deeply. "I suppose what is happening between us has happened before between good friends," he wrote, in a feeble attempt to make peace. Catherine's reply was profuse. "Charlie darling: Please, please don't be so hurt and worried. I shouldn't have kept on attacking you and wouldn't have if the whole Friday thing hadn't been so exhausting and nightmarish .... I guess I'm rather difficult (of course we're all prima donnas and never had to act like a team before)." Further down in her letter comes a clue to her depression. "*I* was the one who was lonely for the past ten years, pushing the issues regarding growth and metropolitan structure that interested absolutely no one."[118]

If Catherine ever discussed personal feelings with friends or family, it was in the lightest, most dismissive way. She was not much given to introspection, at least not since her youthful romance with Lewis Mumford. It was Mumford who now triggered a relapse. He wrote her a letter seeking permission to describe their romance in his autobiography, a draft chapter of which he enclosed. He promised her anonymity by changing her name to "Tess." Horror was her first response: she knew that colleagues would recognize her, which would lead to nasty gossip. But this reaction gave way to a kind of intellectual fascination. "Since I still live in the present," she told Lewis, "a great deal of our joint history was deeply buried."[119] Although she did not believe in exposing personal pasts, she did concede that his chapter would "bring out certain inherent qualities of an affair like that which have more than personal interest and significance."

Bill had no objection to such a revealing chapter because he was a "sure enough man himself to have no twinges about my past," she wrote Lewis. But both Wursters were concerned about how Sadie would react and agreed to stop him in his tracks. Catherine thought he ought to reconsider for his own sake as well. "I have never liked the self-analysis side of your work even when it had nothing to do with me. This may well be due to my own emotional inhibitions, but there always seems to be something more behind it ... a touch of self-pity or self-punishment, even of confessional exhibitionism. Anyway, I've never felt that they do you justice."

She went on to share some thoughts about their relationship. "I always knew there was an unbridgeable gap between us ... we had an extremely important and intensive intellectual and sexual relationship, but essentially of a master-pupil nature rather than an enduring husband-wife emotional unity." That is why she and Sophie could be friends, Catherine concluded. She admitted to several affairs, all of which were working or intellectual relationships with bachelors who, like her, were not looking for marriage. "I was never promiscuous or 'wild' in the party-binge or predatorial sense ... I learned something from most of them and do not look back on them with distaste or embarrassment."[120]

From Lewis Mumford she had taken a deeply anti-technocratic philosophy. He had helped her see how thin and sterile aesthetic dogmas were and how corrupt in practice. She felt their goals were always close, but their approaches different. "I am temperamentally a deep-dyed rationalist, while you (with all your remarkable, intensive knowledge) are essentially appealing to faith from a set of emotional convictions not subject to serious testing or qualification by factual experience or evidence." She had learned much from his brilliant powers of observation and analysis, but could not accept many of his judgments. "This is not to say that you may not be right. It may require emotional conviction and leadership rather than tested knowledge and rational persuasion to solve the problems of either cities or peace. You would have been an early Christian in the days of the Roman decline while I would not, and you would have been right."

All Catherine's encounters with Lewis ended on a note of fond forgiveness. "I agree almost wholly with your judgments about cities (and atomic threat)," she had written earlier. "But I just can't blame people quite so much. I'm essentially a creature of the times, not a prophet crying in the wilderness, so I tend to have more sympathy than contempt for the rest of us, even our stupid leaders."[121]

In the end Catherine offered to return all of Lewis's letters, which she had kept filed away in a folder marked PRIVATE, "against a day when I'll want to go through it all myself." She added, "I'd have sent you your letters any time: I thought you knew I had them." The day never came, and no one touched the folder until a letter arrived for Bill from Lewis, in September 1965, asking for the return of his letters. Lewis was circumspect in his request: he had definitely decided to eliminate the more personal chapters of his autobiography out of respect to the Wursters, but the letters would help him reconstruct the period from 1930 to 1934. He assured Bill that he would not mention Catherine, but wanted them "to complete my own picture of myself." He concluded by quoting Catherine's earlier offer to return the letters. Bill did not react until a follow-up letter came from Sophie Mumford, supporting her husband's request. Today the entire Bauer-Mumford correspondence of the early 1930s resides at the University of Pennsylvania in the Special Collections division of the Van Pelt Library.

In 1962 Clark Kerr and Catherine agreed to stage a conference on "The Metropolitan Future." It would be the fifth of seven statewide conferences discussing "California and the Challenge of Growth" as it faced an unprecedented population explosion. Today Kerr credits Catherine with the idea of convening such a conference on the Berkeley campus because "she had energy and ideas and was always future oriented. Anything she did would be done with a lot of enthusiasm. Catherine was clearly in charge." An ambitious conference, long remembered by all who participated, was packed into two days shortly before Bill's neurological operation in New York.

Catherine articulated the conference's theme in her preface to the proceedings. "To the world, California was a symbol of the old American frontier: wagon trails, gold rush and the wild west ... but now, within a century we have become another kind of frontier, nearly fifteen million of our seventeen million live in the vast and spreading metropolitan complexes on the northern and southern coasts, and in a few smaller urban concentrations in the Central Valley. Within a few decades the urban population is likely to double again ... Many problems may be magnified many fold, but growth also brings the chance for improvement."[122] Many of the 350 participants were Catherine's personal friends, including Earl Warren, chief justice of the United States Supreme Court. The theme of the conference had been taken from Warren's Charter Day remarks at UC Davis in 1962, so it was fitting that he deliver the closing address. Governor Edmund G. Brown addressed a luncheon.

The list of participants was a veritable Who's Who in government, public administration, and planning from North America and Europe. President Clark Kerr convened the meeting on September 26, 1963. Sir Edwin

Herbert, chairman of the Royal Commission on Local Government in Greater London, delivered the keynote address. His speech examined the nature and functions of a Royal Commission: a group of people with wide and diverse experiences yet not closely identified with the subject matter of their inquiry. Royal Commissions do not legislate, but make recommendations to Parliament for consideration and, hopefully, action. Catherine had often expressed the wish that commissions of inquiry be organized in a similar fashion in the United States to advise Congress.

Five major themes were explored by conference participants. The first session, "The Future of American Cities: Alternatives," was chaired by UC Regent Edward Carter, a prominent California business leader. Ed Bacon, executive director of the Philadelphia Planning Commission, spoke "In Defense of Big Cities: Urbanity or Suburbanity." Peter Self, professor of public administration at the University of London, described "New Towns, Greenbelts, and the Urban Region." Professor Jacobus P. Thijsse, deputy rector of the Institute of Social Studies in The Hague, discussed "A Planned Complex of Real Cities and Real Country," advancing Holland's experience with conurbation and the rim metropolis. Scott Greer, professor of sociology and political science at Northwestern University, questioned "Decentralization: The End of Cities?" With decentralization comes the freedom to sprawl, he cautioned. Only a metropolitan perspective could deal with the continuing dichotomy of centralization versus decentralization.

The second session, "The Good Environment," was chaired by Mortimer Fleishhacker, planning advocate and leading Bay Area philanthropist. Steen Eiler Rasmussen, professor of architecture at the Royal Danish Academy of Fine Arts, provided "Lessons for Modern Urban Design." James Rouse, a Baltimore mortgage banker and shopping mall developer, warned "It Could Happen Here." The prospects for a healthy environment by 1980 are not very good, he said, because cities were already oppressively out of scale with people. Justin Herman, director of San Francisco's Redevelopment Agency, declared that the emerging urban renewal process should be utilized for people via moderately priced private housing, scattered public housing, recreation facilities, and cultural activities.

Catherine's good friend, publisher Alfred Heller, came with copies of his newly released book, *The Phantom Cities of California*. At the conference he expressed concerns about the urbanization of northern California where "since world war two we have added about 3.5 million urban acres ... with almost total disregard of their effect on the urban regions."[123] Heller forecast that by 1985 an additional 4 million acres of open space would be consumed by metropolitan growth. (This turned out to be a conservative estimate, highlighting the continuing tug-of-war between metropolitan growth and efforts to safeguard California's rural landscape.)

The third session, "Metropolitan Trends, Problems and Tools," was chaired by UC Chancellor Edward Strong. Robert Weaver, administrator of the Housing and Home Finance Agency, discussed "Social Issues: The Disadvantaged and the Amenity Seekers." Harvey Perloff, director of regional studies at RFF, addressed "Economic and Technological Trends: Implications." William Wheaton, director of IURD, discussed "Political Structure and Planning." He deplored the political fragmentation of American metropolitan areas. Despite "an enormous body of critical opinion, research, proposals for reform, and earnest and hard-fought political campaigns," observed Wheaton, "the number of metropolitan areas which have achieved any real measure of political integration is insignificant."[124]

The fourth session, "State and Federal Roles in Metropolitan Development," was chaired by UC Regent Norris Nash. Governor Edmund Brown's contribution was "Guiding Future Growth: The Division of Responsibility." He advanced the success of recent state legislation to (1) put brakes on haphazard metropolitan growth through local agencies, (2) review and pass on all proposals for the incorporation of new cities, (3) create new special districts, and (4) annex territories to existing cities.

Governor Brown's presentation and others drew critical comments from John Dyckman, director of the Center for Planning and Development Research. He blamed exponential growth in metropolitan areas on the vast employment opportunities created by federal financing through the Department of Defense and NASA. California's high consumption of public and private services demanded state planning "because the balance [between costs and benefits] is precarious and because judgments and commitments made for the year 2000 may commit us to an unattainable and unsustainable pattern of growth."[125]

The final session was devoted to discussion groups that reviewed the presentations and added collateral topics. For example, IURD's Wheaton drew a distinction between housing needs and market demands. Needs are reflected in social, health, and environmental standards, he said, whereas housing demands are controlled by consumers' willingness and ability to pay. He predicted an enormous urban impact from the 30 to 40 million dwellings that would be required to house the next generation – an amount equivalent to all American urban areas in 1950. When various processes in the housing market were reviewed, Catherine aired one of her major concerns: The "filtering-down" process would never meet the needs of low-income housing, she argued. The government must intervene.

Victor Jones, professor of political science, stressed the importance of the nascent Association of Bay Area Governments (ABAG). He saw it as (1) an essential tool for involving elected officials of local governments in regional problems and decisions, (2) a protection of county and city home rule, and (3) an extension of home rule to the metropolitan region. With a view to the future, Catherine agreed that the creation of ABAG was one of the most promising developments in the government of metropolitan areas.

Dean Martin Meyerson of CED summarized the conference highlights. "We are trying to understand the problems so well that we can solve them better than by instinctively reacting to the itch of land speculation, or the bite of public expenditures, or the pressure of an expanding population."[126] He applauded the broad cross-section of participants who represented diverse points of view and experience, and revealed "the rising sophistication of the American urban dweller." The metropolitan community of the future, Meyerson predicted optimistically, would "maximize the choices of the diverse groups of people who will live and work in the metropolis."

The conference concluded with Chief Justice Earl Warren's address, "A Vision for California." During his lifetime, California's population had grown from 1 million to 18 million people, from a frontier community to a "dynamic commonwealth of tremendous proportions in the life of the U.S., economically, culturally and politically."[127] He sided with those who demanded rational systematic planning, rather than a patchwork of partial solutions in the nature of a crazy quilt. Chief Justice Warren suggested that "cities must be studied as a living organism, with a body, a heart, a bloodstream, a nervous system and a brain," reminiscent of Patrick Geddes's biological model that compared urban structure with the human body. He drew special attention to the pollution of waterways and of the "very air that we must breathe" and echoed Heller's concerns when he spoke of California's increasing conflict between metropolitan sprawl and suburbanization, which resulted in the loss of agriculture and the destruction of landscape. The chief justice applauded the University of California for bringing together "all the disciplines that can evaluate the elements for a good life … and thereby can develop a vision for the future of our state."

Not a single paper was delivered by a woman, though this would not have troubled Catherine and might not even have caught her attention. She was often the only woman presenter on a panel or at a conference and was likely the only one at the India seminar. Her sister Betty, who was sensitive to women's issues, once asked her how it felt being the only woman in these various situations. The question startled Catherine, as though she had never noticed, but after a moment admitted she had never felt any discrimination because of her gender.

The conference was a major success. It squarely faced problems first discussed during the 1920s by an eccentric and esoteric group of eighteen, at informal gatherings of the Regional Planning Association of America in Clarence Stein's New York City apartment. In 1931, recognizing a rising star in the field of regionalism, RPAA appointed Catherine executive secretary, and Clarence Stein made her his research assistant. RPAA's faith in the fledgling planner was amply rewarded. Thirty-two years later Catherine had become the preeminent professional in the field of housing and planning.

Now she was charged with consolidating the conference proceedings for publication. But she had other matters to attend to, such as Bill's operation in New York, the MIT meeting, and a paper to complete for the Agency for International Development (AID) on "The Pattern of Urbanization in Developing Economies." There was also an address for the San Francisco Planning and Urban Research organization (SPUR) on the question "Are Housing and Renewal Regional Problems?" Yes, she would argue, because the rapid population growth in the Bay Area would lead to regional problems in transportation and housing, especially as there was a dearth of decent old housing.

Although much of her time and attention were consumed by academic work, Catherine's loyalty was increasingly drawn away from the ivory tower – back into the practical world of professional housers. "Houser" was certainly not a familiar term to most citizens, yet as redevelopment took hold in metropolitan regions the houser's job became more urgent than ever. City boundaries had become blurred except where nature forcefully marked boundaries with bodies of water or mountains. The houser's job was to bridge and monitor the work of architect, planner, engineer, and, often, politician – not necessarily in that order. The houser collected census data, understood population distributions, and worried about displacing people as renewal projects undermined old habitats especially in city cores. The houser was the gadfly who kept her sights on the larger picture and was often the voice of conscience. Catherine would ask: What about the people who are most seriously disadvantaged, the unskilled and uneducated, the families with problems, the hard-core central city slum dwellers, the people who require expensive services and most need new opportunities? These were questions raised by housers, and ones she hoped would be addressed by academic research institutes in partnership with local government. Although she called herself a planner, in her heart Catherine considered herself to be a houser first.

In 1964, Alan Temko, San Francisco's leading architectural critic and urban thinker, wrote an article called "San Francisco Slums and Their People."[128] Fifteen thousand poor people were about to be forcibly displaced as the city built low-cost housing in the Western Addition neighbourhood and a brand new business/culture centre in a blighted area of flop houses, bars, and welfare "hotels" south of Market Street. Catherine agreed with his assessment and advocated a houser's approach. It was axiomatic, she said, that ambitious redevelopment programs require comprehensive housing programs. This entails an overall analysis of present and future housing needs, not just an ad hoc effort to cope with immediate relocation problems. What was called for was a broad-gauged, imaginative housing agency capable of administering the tools for citywide rehabilitation, inducements for needed commercial and nonprofit housing enterprise, and a positive strategy to combat discrimination.[129]

President Kennedy had signed an executive order in 1961 on Equal Opportunity in Housing, outlawing racial discrimination in all new FHA and Veterans Administration properties. Catherine had supported this position for years. "Housing and structure of cities are very closely interrelated," she told the Oakland Junior League in a 1964 talk titled "Are Cities Obsolete?" Historically, housing problems meant slums, which were considered solely an issue of physical health and welfare. This view held until the passage of the US Housing Act of 1937, which responded to conditions created by the Depression. By 1964, because of higher incomes and education, slum living correlated more dramatically with mental and emotional problems, and school dropout and delinquency. Still, the majority of slum dwellers were "non-white" people. Blight could no longer be remedied by providing indoor plumbing. As federal aid focused on salvaging central cities, the chaotic forces of metropolitan expansion were overlooked. President Johnson signed the Civil Rights Act of 1964. Four years later the Fair Housing Act would outlaw housing discrimination and give the Housing and Urban Development (HUD) department, founded in 1965, responsibility for all fair housing programs.

Those who moved into beautiful homes in spacious suburbs were those who could afford to. Once these mostly middle- and upper-class white people settled in their new neighbourhoods, they often passed exclusionary ordinances. They shopped in new suburban shopping centres, leaving inner cities to rot. It was clear that problems spread because what happened in blighted areas depended directly on what happened in suburbia – all of which pointed to the need for regional approaches to metropolitan housing.

Her talks never lost their lustre or their popularity. By 1964 Catherine began to look back, not to the "good old days" but to the forces that shaped her life, as though she sensed that her days were numbered. She spoke of the mistakes of early housers and encouraged young people to face the fact that the United States was an urbanized and metropolitanized nation, and that man-made environments affected everything else and vice versa. Jurisdictional disputes among different professions, which she had experienced in her lobbying days, were largely gone. Even the feud between rural and urban domains was declining. "The dynamic process of urbanization" became a catch phrase, and most modern problems – slums, traffic, etc. – were related to the concept. Catherine praised the intellectual sophistication of Robert Weaver and his staff at HHFA, and predicted that sooner or later a federal department of urban affairs would be created.

Jane Jacobs, author of the book that swept North America, *The Death and Life of Great American Cities,* applauded Catherine's viewpoint in the early 1950s. "Catherine Bauer's thinking [about cities] is the start of a new direction and I think it is very exciting," Jacobs wrote to the editor of *Architectural Forum,* Douglas Haskell, after reading her article. By 1964 Catherine's thoughts had crystallized after her research on India. She was convinced that Americans had failed to take urbanization per se very seriously until recently, when they began to study the problems of developing nations. Just as modern medicine was informed by pathology, modern regionalism found its roots in India's poverty.

The spring of 1964 found Catherine busy giving speeches, reporting on research, and writing papers. The chore of writing an introduction to the proceedings of Metropolitan Future conference hung over her, and by the summer she felt terribly pressured and emotionally drained. She was also losing weight, which she attributed to a "glandular disturbance." In September she rushed back east for a week to keep vigil with her sister, whose husband lay dying of cancer at the University of Pennsylvania Hospital.

In October Catherine secured a leave of absence from UC, partly to regain her strength, but more importantly to complete her stacks of unfinished work. Her first task was to write a long-overdue note to Barclay Jones, associate director of the Centre for Housing and Environmental Studies at Cornell University, to thank him for dedicating *City Design Through Conservation* to her and Bill.

Catherine looked drawn and depressed to her friends and family. To Margy Meyerson, her close friend and confidante, she complained that her energy was gone; further, her doctor was not taking her seriously by suggesting she was simply getting older and would have to get used to it. Catherine recognized a qualitative decline that seemed different from gradual aging, and she returned to her doctor several times. He ran a variety of tests until finding something and prescribing new medication. She soldiered on, but with waning energy and self-confidence.

On a Saturday afternoon in late November she finally settled down to

SEA DRIFT
BEACH HOUSE

Sea Drift is a spit of land on the Marin coast north of San Francisco. Bill had designed the house: an informal and low-maintenance dwelling that reflected the life-style valued by its occupants.

write the conference piece. Her thoughts were flowing smoothly when Bill insisted on spending the weekend at their Sea Drift retreat, a place he was more and more drawn to in his retirement years. Sea Drift is a spit of land on the Marin coast north of San Francisco. Bill had designed the house: an informal and low-maintenance dwelling that reflected the lifestyle valued by its occupants. Two unusual features distinguished the beach house. It had an open plan and no interior corridor: most of the rooms were accessible only from the outside, which encouraged interaction with the out-of-doors. The other feature was a glazed enclosure: a sleeping porch that faced the beach and was sheltered from the wind.

Although she loved their place at Sea Drift, Catherine wanted to stay at home in Berkeley that weekend, thinking that she might finish the project at last. But Bill prevailed. He sat in the car until she was ready to drive. Tension between them mounted that afternoon, and Catherine sought the solace of nature to regain her composure. Promising to be back at Sea Drift by five o'clock, she left for a walk in the wilderness she cherished. She drove to the nearby seaside community of Stinson Beach, stopped for a chat with the hardware store owner, bought some groceries, and continued the drive to Mount Tamalpais. After parking near the base of its western face, she climbed the steep ascent. It was the Willow Camp Trail, the one she had hiked in the scorching sun a year earlier, which she had admitted was too strenuous for an aging lady.

By five o'clock, the light was fading rapidly as mist climbed up the slopes of Tamalpais. Catherine had not returned. Sea Drift had no telephone so Bill went next door to call for help. Within minutes a search began and continued fruitlessly through the night. Early Sunday morning, November 22, 1964, Bill phoned Sadie who drove up from UCLA. Next he phoned Thelma, who enjoyed Sea Drift and often hiked with Catherine. (That weekend she had begged off to attend a Harry Belafonte concert.) Thelma was stunned by Bill's call.

"You can't find Mrs. Wurster?" she echoed in disbelief.

"Yes, Catherine went out for a hike and didn't come back," Bill said. Thelma recalls that she somehow "found a ride out to Sea Drift and soon the house was full of people, just looking and wondering."

Word that Catherine was missing spread quickly through the academic community of Berkeley, and by mid-morning Sunday a search force of 250 students and faculty had joined a posse of 75 to comb the trails and underbrush of Tamalpais's western slopes. Bill remained mute, in his chair, comforted by friends Martin and Margy Meyerson and architecture professor Dick Peters. Other colleagues and friends, including Alan Temko, Jack Kent, and Don Foley, joined the search.

Forced to turn back by nightfall, the search party set out again at

VIEWS FROM MOUNT TAMALPAIS

Promising to be back at Sea Drift by
five o'clock, she left for a walk in the
wilderness she cherished.

daybreak on Monday with waning hopes. At 10:30 a.m. three shots rang out signalling the end of the search. Catherine's body was found by Larry Fong, a nineteen-year-old Berkeley sophomore. She was lying, face down, in a small depression at the 1,200-foot level near Laurel Dell Canyon. Clad in blue jeans, high-top sneakers, a grey sweatshirt and an old olive-green jacket, she was hidden in a patch of scrub oak, five miles from her car. Her reading glasses were found about a quarter of a mile uphill on the trail, suggesting that she was on her way down when she stumbled over a rockfall and hit her head on a blunt rock. She sustained a concussion and never regained consciousness, according to Coroner Frank Keston. Death came from exposure to freezing rain.

Michael Warnum, an architect who had just earned his masters degree from the College of Environmental Design, came up right behind Fong. Fearful of finding Catherine, because he had never seen a dead body, Michael gained strength from what he saw. "She had a smile on her face," he recalled. Moved by this vision, he wrote to Bill:

I climbed up the side [of the slope] and there just below she lay. It was a very peaceful scene, even quieter than before, as no one said a word. She lay full length as if asleep with an arm outstretched. Her clothes were faded and fitted into the colors of the ground, the gold of the grass, the lichen on the rocks, and the moss on the trunk of the oak, under which she lay. It was a beautiful spot itself, level with soft grass and sheltered by the oak tree, the sort of spot one would have chosen to sit down and rest.

Catherine's world was shocked and stunned by the news of her sudden death. It was also a death that was veiled in mystery. Why did she climb the mountain so late on a damp November afternoon? Why would an experienced hiker stumble and fall from a well-trodden path? Were thoughts of Bill's failing health and her own frailty swirling through her mind? Was her judgment clouded by depression? Her sister vaguely spoke of suicide. The mystery of Catherine's death lingers, but her spirit of hope and adventure lend a sense of immortality to her ideas.

Memorial services were held on Sunday, December 6, the first event in the courtyard of brand new Wurster Hall. Close friends Martin Meyerson and Alexander Meiklejohn gave eloquent and heartfelt eulogies. Meiklejohn began by quoting two passages from Ecclesiastics, then added his own words and read Michael Warnum's letter to Bill. Meyerson recounted Catherine's life with high praise:

We often forget that the responsibility of the professor is to profess – to declare openly beliefs and commitments to principles. In this sense, Catherine was a professor long before she joined the faculty of the University of California and long before she taught at Harvard. She was one who professed, who declared her allegiance and engagement throughout her career.

Sadie, Bill, and Thelma sat together at the service, a closely knit family whose bonds were strengthened by their enormous loss. Ten years her senior and in failing health, Bill never dreamed he would survive his wife. He continued to live in their home on Greenwood Terrace, where Catherine's ground-floor study was converted into a comfortable little suite for him. After finishing college Sadie moved back to Berkeley and settled nearby. Thelma remained in the Greenwood house, and UC students lived there to help. Nurses assisted Bill with daily routines. One in particular, Odell Taylor, provided so effectively for Bill's well-being that he became a family friend.

He continued to go to Wurster, Bernardi, and Emmons until his condition prevented his active participation. He was kept informed about the firm, world affairs, and people around him by loyal friends such as Vernon DeMars, his wedding witness, whose indomitable spirit and sense of humour meant a great deal to Bill. Always her father's daughter, Sadie and Bill grew even closer during his last nine years. Having lived to see her happily married in 1973, Bill died peacefully at home a few months later, at the age of seventy-seven.

Douglas Haskell, editor of *Architectural Forum*, eulogized Catherine Bauer Wurster in the magazine's April 1965 edition. He began with a letter he had written to her: "I wish you could come here more often. Things seem to light up when you arrive and the sun begins to shine brighter for the many people who know you." Haskell continued:

A generation occasionally produces a rare creature with the capacity for providing such a light, and Catherine was one of these creatures. She had wisdom and courage, an original mind, a capacity to inspire as well as to lead. Pressed pitilessly to advise, write, teach, administer, and give of herself, she never surrendered to the fatigue her genius exacted. Her loss is an irreclaimable deprivation to the society ... Her works are people, students, ideas that have shaped institutions, vital courses which, but for her counsel, might have strayed. Her works are in a piece of nature that was spared, a young life stimulated into achievement, an older one bequeathed a memory that makes the years more endurable.[130]

Four years after her death, on the afternoon of September 6, 1968, John Edelman, Catherine's cohort from Philadelphia in the 1930s, spoke to a large assembly of her friends and admirers at the unveiling of a portrait bust of Catherine Bauer by Oscar Stonorov. He dedicated it to the family with the words: "Catherine now is in Valhalla." Cast in bronze, the sculpture was placed in the lobby of the new headquarters for Housing and Urban Development in Washington, DC, as a permanent memorial. Her friend, Robert Weaver, first secretary of HUD, made the arrangements. Another cast of the bust sits at the hub of the library in Wurster Hall on UC Berkeley campus.

At the HUD gathering, Edelman said some people today may find her ideas too "dewy-eyed" for this tough period of city riots. He differed. "Couldn't we have avoided much of all this if we had the far-sightedness … to implement the ideas, the teachings of Catherine Bauer Wurster?"

The engraved dedication mounted on the wall behind Catherine's bust reads:

Catherine Bauer was the moving spirit of housing in the United States who helped win recognition of the national responsibility for urban development. Behind the physical fact of a building, she never forgot the human needs that the building was meant to serve. Her vision of a unified human and physical urban environment inspired a wide following and led to national acceptance of that vision.

PORTRAIT BUST OF CATHERINE BY OSCAR STONOROV

Stonorov dedicated it with the words: "Catherine now is in Valhalla."

POSTSCRIPT

In the three decades since Catherine Bauer's death, urbanization has radically changed the landscape of the United States and the world. Access to shelter is still a major urban issue that lacks a champion pressing for equitable solutions. North America's social conscience has changed. Today there is increased reliance on the market economy to solve economic and social problems.

Downsizing, globalization, aggregation of cities, and gyrating stock markets coexist with hard-core unemployment, homelessness, local political instability, and regional disparities. At the end of the twentieth century, the United States, the world's strongest and wealthiest country, faces an ever-widening gap between rich and poor, and between rural and urban life.

American cities have also become great democratizers where people of different cultures with different values and languages meet, mix, and learn to cooperate. Metropolitan centres produce and accumulate unprecedented wealth; they nurture the nation's innovative genius even while other parts of urban society are left behind. Catherine Bauer identified these disparities early in her career. Urban society's lowest income group is still the most vulnerable, and their shelter needs remain the same: the marketplace cannot produce housing that is affordable enough that poor people are not deprived of cash for minimum food and clothing. Their journey to work is exhausting and expensive. National and state housing programs are shrinking as available public housing supply is reduced and downgraded.

Metropolitan housing surveys, championed by Catherine, reveal a stark truth. A growing underclass – underhoused, undernourished, and undereducated – is unable to compete in the global market of production and distribution. While housing was her major concern, Catherine stressed interconnectedness: the interdependence of shelter, employment, and education, strengthened by community support of those in need. A common thread throughout her writing was twinning social with economic assistance, and providing housing subsidies to consumers not producers.

In contemporary terms, Catherine pressed for place-based strategies that complemented people-oriented initiatives. She assigned the cost of slum and blight to the general public purse so that inner-city problems were borne by taxpayers everywhere. Today inner-city housing and poor living conditions have spread to the suburbs and beyond. However, this trend also represents a new geography of opportunity for employment, social diversity, and environmental adaptation.

Catherine saw the city as a whole. Her interests progressed from design in architecture to a deeply held concern for social justice in housing. She was among the first to call for a renewal of the American city through public policies and focused governmental intervention. Her teaching inspired the young and trained leaders of the next generation. Her multidisciplinary approach in the selection of faculty, students, and curriculum, and her insistence on fieldwork and structured research, have become staple practices in the education of planners and housing administrators. Today the entry requirement for professional practice in urban and regional planning is a postgraduate degree, thanks to the efforts of people like Catherine.

She anticipated the role of nongovernmental organizations in pushing for social and political changes in North America. She predicted the urban tidal wave engulfing the world, but underestimated the rate of change and its cumulative impact on the quality of life. At the time of her death California's population was 17 million people, with 15 million classified as urban. By 1996 it had grown to 32.2 million with 29 million urbanites; by the turn of the century that figure will have doubled since Catherine wrote her 1964 report on the "Metropolitan Future." Problems and issues have intensified as urban demographics have drastically changed.

In l990 about a third of Americans who lived in metropolitan areas were central-city residents, down more than half from 1950. Also in 1990 median incomes in central cities across the US were almost 30 percent lower than in the suburbs. Twenty percent of central-city residents were African-American and 11 percent were Hispanic, while suburban communities averaged only 6 percent African-American and 5 percent Hispanic. Poverty analysis shows the same profiles.

After the very survival of HUD within the federal cabinet was threatened, Congress turned around and passed "The Quality Housing and Work Responsibility Act of 1998" on October 5, 1998, signed two weeks later by President Clinton. It renovates the public housing system. The bill had languished for months as disagreements were hammered out by fiercely partisan lawmakers until the compromise version finally passed.

With bipartisan support, Congress agreed to expand the availability of subsidized housing, a cherished Bauer ideal, for the first time in a decade. The act removes disincentives for residents to work and become self-sufficient. It provides rental protection for low-income residents, and deregulates the operation of public housing authorities. Catherine would have applauded these changes. The act also authorizes the creation of mixed-finance public housing projects and gives more power and flexibility to local governments and communities to operate housing programs. The new legislation, after a decade of frustrating debates and public scandals in which housing, as a basic human right, had slipped from the public policy agenda, was welcomed by HUD Secretary Andrew Cuomo, who declared "we are back in the housing business." The *New York Times* praised Cuomo for streamlining HUD and reaffirming its mission to provide decent housing to families shut out of the regular housing market. At the presidential signing ceremony, Cuomo declared the bill a "historic victory for President Clinton and the Democrats who stood firm in support of his policies to transform public housing, expand the supply of affordable housing, and increase homeownership."[1]

Homeless people, long a visible symbol of cynical indifference in an age of affluence, have been given new hope. Catherine Bauer's legacy continues to animate the political debate.

NOTES

ABBREVIATIONS FOR NOTES

CB	Catherine Bauer
CBW	Catherine Bauer Wurster (after marriage)
CBW Coll.	Catherine Bauer Wurster Collection, Bancroft Library, University of California in Berkeley
CS	Clarence Stein
EJB	Ernest J. Bohn
GFA	J.S. Guggenheim Foundation Archives
HAM	Henry A. Moe
IURD	Institute for Urban and Regional Development
JLPUE	*Journal of Land and Public Utility Economics*
LHK	Leon H. Keyserling
LM	Lewis Mumford
LM Coll.	Lewis Mumford Collection, Van Pelt Library, University of Pennsylvania
MOMA	Museum of Modern Art (New York City)
n.d.	no date
NS	Nathan Straus
pvt. coll.	private collection
RFF	Resources For the Future
RM	Robert Marshall
SCL-CWRU	Special Collection Library, Case Western Reserve University, Ernest J. Bohn Collection
SS-PC	Sadie Super, Private Collection
TJK	T. Jack Kent, Jr.
UCB	University of California in Berkeley
WWW	William Wilson Wurster

CHAPTER 1: EARLY YEARS (1905-26)
All letters quoted in this chapter are from the private collection of Sadie Super.

CHAPTER 2: LEARNING YEARS (1926-30)
Unless otherwise designated, all letters quoted in this chapter are from the private collection of Sadie Super.
1 *New York Herald*, Paris ed., 15 May 1927, 5.
2 *The Comet* article draft, CBW Coll.
3 L. Münz and G. Künstler, *Adolph Loos: Pioneer of Modern Architecture* (London: Thames and Hudson, 1966), 226-29.
4 CBW to "Dear Olis," letter, 12 July 1939, SS-PC.
5 *The New York Times Magazine*, 15 April 1928, 10, 22.

6　Ibid.
7　Matthew Josephson, *Life among the Surrealists* (New York: Holt, Rinehart and Winston, 1962), 368-69.

CHAPTER 3: ROMANTIC YEARS (1930-33)

1　Donald Miller, *Lewis Mumford: A Life* (Pittsburgh: University of Pittsburgh Press, 1989), xiii.
2　CB, "Art in Industry," *Fortune* 3, 5 (1931): 94.
3　P.G. Rowe, *Modernity and Housing* (Cambridge, MA: MIT Press, 1993), 130.
4　CB, *Modern Housing* (Boston: Houghton Mifflin, 1934), 279.
5　Rowe, *Modernity and Housing*, 143.
6　CB, *Fortune* article draft, p. 7, CBW Coll.
7　Ibid., 9.
8　LM, "Personalia," 24 January 1932, LM Coll.
9　Clarence Stein Archives, 20 December 1992, Cornell University.
10　Miller, *Mumford*, 191.
11　CB, "Art in Industry," *Fortune*, 110.
12　CB, "Who Cares about Architecture?" *New Republic*, 6 May 1931, 326.
12　Ibid.
14　CB, "The Americanization of Europe," *New Republic*, 24 June 1931, 153.
15　CB to HAM, letter, 16 June 1931, GFA.
16　CB application, 2 November 1931, GFA.
17　Ibid.
18　Ibid.
19　CB to LM, letter, January 1932, LM Coll.

CHAPTER 4: POLITICAL YEARS (1934-36)

Unless otherwise designated, all letters quoted in this chapter are from the private collection of Sadie Super.
1　Donald Miller, *Lewis Mumford: A Life* (Pittsburgh: University of Pittsburgh Press, 1989), 328.
2　CB, "Are Good Houses Un-American?" *New Republic*, 2 March 1932, 74.
3　LM, "European Housing: England," *Fortune* 6, 5 (November l932): 32-37, 82-84.
4　Ibid., 32.
5　Ibid.
6　Ibid.
7　LM, "Machines for Living," *Fortune* 7, 2 (February 1933): 78-88.
8　Ibid., 78.
9　LM, "Taxes into Housing," *Fortune* 7, 5 (May 1933): 48, 86-89.
10　Ibid., 89.
11　CB to F. Gutheim, letter, 19 November 1932, SS-PC.
12　CB, *Modern Housing* (Boston: Houghton Mifflin, 1934), iii.
13　Mary S. Cole, "Catherine Bauer and the Public Housing Movement, 1926-1937" (Ph.D. diss., George Washington University, 1975), 132.
14　LM to CB, letter, 31 July 1933, LM Coll.
15　Cole, "Catherine Bauer," 264.
16　CB, *Modern Housing*, xv.
17　Ibid., xvi.
18　Ibid., xvii.
19　Ibid., 92.
20　Ibid., 95.
21　Ibid., 97.
22　Ibid., 106.
23　Ibid., 107.
24　Ibid., 115.
25　Ibid., 255.
26　R.L. Duffus, *New York Times Review of Books*, 23 December 1934, 3.
27　Douglas Haskell, "Housing in America," *The Nation*, 20 February 1935, 228.

28 Albert Mayer, "A Man's House," *New Republic*, 13 March 1935, 136.
29 Albert Guerard, "Cities, Houses, and Homes," *The New York Herald Tribune* Books, 12 May 1935, 19.
30 "Evolution of Role of the Federal Government in Housing and Community Development" (Washington, DC: Government Printing Office, 1932), 1.
31 "Catherine Bauer Wurster 1905-1964," *Architectural Forum*, April 1965, 79.
32 "Mr. President," 17 May 1934, signed J.L. McDevitt, N. Blumberg, J.W. Edelman, and C. Bauer, CBW Coll.
33 John Locher to CB, Hearings Committee on Education and Labor, US Senate, 74th Congress, 2nd Session, S 4424 (Washington, DC: Government Printing Office, 1936). Read into record by CB.
34 CB to EJB, letter, 6 January 1935, SCL-CWRU.
45 Cole, "Catherine Bauer," 382.
46 Ibid., 386.
37 CB to Charles Ascher, letter, 12 September 1934, CBW Coll.
38 Douglas Haskell, "Catherine Bauer Wurster: An Appreciation," *Architectural Forum*, April 1965.

CHAPTER 5: LEGISLATIVE YEARS (1936-38)
1 Mary S. Cole, "Catherine Bauer and the Public Housing Movement, 1926-1937" (Ph.D. diss., George Washington University, 1975), 402.
2 CB to EJB, letter, "Sat. A.M.," January 1935, SCL-CWRU.
3 CB to EJB, letter, 6 March 1935, SCL-CWRU.
4 CB to EJB, letter, 24 March 1935, SCL-CWRU.
5 CB to Mrs. Smith, letter, n.d., 1935, SS-PC.
6 Cole, "Catherine Bauer," 404.
7 "Facing Forward," *Public Housing Progress 1*, 15 February 1934, 1.
8 Cole, "Catherine Bauer," 459.
9 Ibid., 470.
10 Ibid., 472.
11 Ibid., 476.
12 CB to EJB, letter, 7 October 1935, SCL-CWRU.
13 CB to EJB, letter, 10 October 1935, SCL CWRU.
14 "Low-Cost Housing and Slum Reclamation," *American City* 51, 2 (1936): 43-45.
15 CB to Father Moore, letter, 11 January 1936, SCL-CWRU.
16 Cole, "Catherine Bauer," 493.
17 Ibid., 499.
18 Ibid.
19 Ibid., 504.
20 CB to EJB, letter, 22 March 1936, SCL-CWRU.
21 Cole, "Catherine Bauer," 509.
22 Ibid., CB to Herman Wolf, letter, "The Socialist Call," 10 April 1936, 518.
23 Ibid., 519.
24 Ibid.
25 Ibid., 531.
26 Ibid., 533.
27 *United States Housing Act of 1936*, 74th Congress, 2nd Session, S 4424 (Washington, DC: Government Printing Office, 1936).
28 CB to EJB, letter, 8 April 1936, SCL-CWRU.
29 CB to EJB, letter, 23 January 1936, SCL-CWRU.
30 Senate Committee on Education and Labor, *United States Housing Act: Hearings on S.R. 4424*, 74th Congress, 2nd Session, 1936, 13.
31 Ibid., 160.
32 Ibid., 160-61.
33 Cole, "Catherine Bauer," 550.
34 Ibid., 549.
35 Ibid., 552.
36 Ibid.
37 Ibid., 558.

38 RM to CB, letter, 28 June 1936, CBW Coll.
39 Stephen Fox, "We Want No Straddlers," *Wilderness* (Winter 1984): 5.
40 CB to J.S. Guggenheim Foundation, application for fellowship, 1936, GFA.
41 CB to Mr. Moe, letter, 18 March 1936, GFA.
42 LHK to CB, letter, 16 July 1936, CBW Coll.
43 LHK to CB, August 1936, CBW Coll.
44 CB to Mr. and Mrs. Bauer, letter, November 1936, PC-SS.
45 CB to Philip Johnson, letter, December 1935, MOMA archives.
46 Cole, "Catherine Bauer," 554.
47 "The President Pledges Further Aid to Housing," *American City* 51 (1936): 5.
48 Cole, "Catherine Bauer," 567.
49 Ibid., CBW to George Leighton, letter, 29 November 1944, 582.
50 Senate Committee on Education and Labor, *To Create a United States Housing Authority; Hearings on S.R. 1685*, 75th Congress, 1st Session, 14 April 1937, National Archives, Washington, DC.
51 Ibid., 83.
52 Harold Ickes, *The Secret Diary of Harold L. Ickes*, vol. 2, *The Inside Struggle, 1936-1939* (New York: Simon and Schuster, 1954), 218.
53 "Catherine Bauer," CB to Mrs. Roosevelt, letter, 15 June 1937, 606.
54 Ibid., 610.
55 Ibid., 620.
56 Ibid., 621.
57 Ibid., 626.
58 Cole, "Catherine Bauer," 632.
59 CB, "Now At Last Housing: The Meaning of the Wagner-Steagall Act," *New Republic* 92 (1937): 119.
60 Cole, "Catherine Bauer," 636.
61 CB, Notes, Western Trip, 1937, CBW Coll.
62 RM to CB, letter, 26 August 1937, CBW Coll.
63 Ibid.
64 Fox, "We Want No Straddlers," *Wilderness* (Winter 1984): 7.
65 RM to CB, letter, 26 August 1937, CBW Coll.
66 *New York Times*, 18 April 1939, 1, 3.
67 CB to EJB, letter, 4 January 1938, SCL-CWRU.
68 Ibid.
69 CB to EJB, letter, March 1938, SCL-CWRU.
70 Ibid.
71 Winston S. Churchill, *The Second World War*, vol. 1, *The Gathering Storm* (London: Cassell and Co., 1948), 273.
72 CB to Uno Ahren, letter, 17 September 1938, CBW Coll.
73 Nathan Straus, address to the Architectural League, 3 February 1938, Records Relating to the History of the Agency: "Historical Files," Box 2, National Archives, Washington, DC.
74 NS to Crane, memo, 9 September 1938, CBW Coll.
75 NS to CB, memo, 26 October 1938, CBW Coll.
76 CB to Uno Ahren, letter, 17 September 1938, CBW Coll.
77 Ibid.
78 Ibid.
79 EJB to CB, letter, 19 June 1939, SCL-CWRU.
80 EJB to Vintons, letter, 23 June 1939, SCL-CWRU.
81 CB to parents, letter, 9 July 1939, SS-PC.
82 CB to family, letter, 18 August 1939, SS-PC.
83 EJB to CB, letter, 1 August 1939, SCL-CWRU.
84 CB to EJB, letter, 17 August 1939, SCL-CWRU.
85 CB to family, letter, 18 August 1939, SS-PC.
86 EJB to CB, 17 August 1939, SCL-CWRU.
87 *Congressional Record, House*, 3 August 1939, vol. 84, part 10, 76th Congress, 2nd Session, S 591, p. 10956
88 LHK to CB, letter, 12 August 1939, CBW Coll.

89 EJB to CB, letter, n.d., CBW Coll.
90 Ibid.
91 Kerstin Ahren to CB, letter, 11 November 1939, SS-PC.

CHAPTER 6: TRANSITION YEARS (1939-42)
1 CB to Jacob Crane, letter, 11 September 1939, CBW Coll.
2 Ibid.
3 Ibid.
4 Ibid.
5 Ibid.
6 Ibid.
7 Ibid.
8 CB to HAM, letter, 5 December 1939, CBW Coll.
9 CB to EJB, letter, 31 October 1939, CBW Coll.
10 CB, "European Housing: 'Post-War' to 'Pre-War,'" speech, Ohio Housing Authorities conference, Cincinnati, OH, 10 November 1939.
11 Ibid.
12 Federal Works Agency, *Seventh Annual Report, 1946* (Washington, DC: Government Printing Office).
13 National Housing Agency, *Second Annual Report, January 1 to December 31, 1943* (Washington, DC: Government Printing Office).
14 Federal Works Agency, *Ninth Annual Report, 1948* (Washington, DC: Government Printing Office).
15 Federal Works Agency, *Sixth Annual Report, 1945* (Washington, DC: Government Printing Office).
16 Walter H. Blucher, "Planning and Zoning Developments in 1948," in Clarence Ridley and Orin Nolting, eds., *The Municipal Yearbook, 1949* (Chicago: International City Managers' Association), 253-93.
17 T.J. Kent, Jr., "Planning Renaissance in San Francisco," *Journal of the American Institute of Planners* 14, 1 (1948): 29-32.
18 Deil S. Wright, *Understanding Intergovernmental Relations*, 3rd ed. (Pacific Grove, CA: Brooks/Cole, 1988).
19 Alberta Bauer to CB, letter, n.d., CBW Coll.
20 "Marshall Bequest to Preserve Wilds," *New York Times*, 1 December 1939.
21 "A Communication," *New Republic*, 12 December 1939.
22 CB to EJB, letter, 31 October 1939, SCL-CWRU
23 CB to parents, letter, 16 January 1940, CBW Coll.
24 CB to LHK, letter, n.d., CBW Coll.
25 CB to Robert G. Sproul, letter, 26 October 1939, CBW Coll.
26 CB to H.M. Cassidy, letter, 27 November 1939, CBW Coll.
27 Ibid.
28 CS to CBW, letter, 12 January 1940, Clarence Stein Archive, Cornell University.
29 CB to LHK, letter, 21 January 1940, CBW Coll.
30 CB to family, letter, "Friday Evening," n.d., SS-PC.
31 CB to LHK, letter, n.d., SS-PC.
32 Ibid.
33 CB to family, letter, "Friday Evening," n.d., SS-PC.
34 CB to HAM, letter, 5 December 1939, CBW Coll.
35 CB to LHK, telegram, 18 July 1940, National Archives, Washington, DC.
36 LHK to CB, letter, n.d., National Archives, Washington, DC.
37 Louis Bauer, interview by authors, 25 September 1992.
38 CB to WWW, letter, 30 July 1940, CBW Coll.
39 CB to Alberta Krouse, letter, 10 August 1940, SS-PC.
40 CBW to Ahrens, letter, 10 May 1941, SS-PC.
41 Vernon DeMars, interview with author, 19 July 1992.
42 CBW to Ahrens, letter, 10 May 1941, SS-PC.
43 "William Wilson Wurster" brochure, MIT Museum exhibit, February to March 1993.
44 Donn Emmons, interview with authors, July 1993.
45 CBW, private notes, n.d., SS-PC.
46 Betty Bauer Kassler to "Dear Mr. and Mrs. Woooooster," letter, n.d., SS-PC.

47 Fritz Gutheim to CBW, letter, 17 August 1940, SS-PC.
48 EJB to CBW, letter, 24 September 1940, SCL-CWRU.
49 Donn Emmons, interview, July 1993.
50 Ibid.
51 CBW to Uno Ahrens, letter, 10 May 1941, SS-PC.
52 Ibid.
53 CBW to Joseph Hudnut, letter, 17 February 1941, CBW Coll.
54 WWW to CBW, letter, "Saturday afternoon, 4:20, Wyoming," n.d., SS-PC.
55 CBW, personal notes, n.d., SS-PC.
56 Lloyd Rodwin, interview with authors, autumn 1995.
57 CBW to Dearest Bobby, letter, 10 May 1941, SS-PC.
58 CBW to Herbert Emmerich, letter, 1 April 1942, CBW Coll.
59 CBW to Miss Chase, letter, 8 May 1941, CBW Coll.
60 CBW to Eliot Noyes, letter, 11 March 1942, CBW Coll.
61 CBW to Dear Infant [Jake Crane], letter, 31 August 1941, CBW Coll.
62 CBW to Frank Ingram, letter, 4 March 1941, CBW Coll.
63 CBW to Herbert Emmerich, letter, 1 April 1942: CBW Coll.
64 CBW to "Dear Nathan and Lang," letter, 28 June 1941, CBW Coll.
65 CBW to Coleman Woodbury, letter, 15 April 1942, CBW Coll.
66 CBW to Dr. Winslow, letter, 7 July 1942, CBW Coll.
67 Ibid.
68 CBW to LHK, letter, 19 September l942, CBW Coll.

CHAPTER 7: ACADEMIC YEARS (1943-64)

 1 WWW to Hudnut, letter, 29 October 1942, SS-PC.
 2 Martin Wagner to WWW, letter, 21 June 1944, SS-PC.
 3 CBW to Langdon Post, letter, 3 March 1943, SS-PC.
 4 Barbara Clements to CBW, letter, 16 August 1943, SS-PC.
 5 Ibid.
 6 CBW to Barbara Clements, letter, 24 August 1943, SS-PC.
 7 CBW to Inspector of Income Tax, Ottawa, Canada, letter, 25 May 1943, CBW Coll.
 8 Mrs. Jacob Bauer to "My Dear Catherine," letter, n.d., SS-PC.
 9 CBW to "Dear Mother," letter, 27 February 1944, SS-PC.
10 CBW, "The Politics of Planning: A Study of Land, Cities, and Housing in the U.S.A." Rough outline, unpublished, n.d., CBW Coll.
11 LM to CBW, letter, 22 October 1943, CBW Coll.
12 Ibid.
13 Ibid.
14 CBW to LM, letter, 26 October 1943, LM Coll.
15 LM to Frederick J. Osborn, letter, 2 September 1959, LM Coll.
16 CBW to "Dear Mother," letter, 26 March 1945, SS-PC.
17 CBW to "Dear Mother," letter, 16 May 1945, SS-PC.
18 Dorothy Liebes to CBW, letter, 9 November 1945, CBW Coll.
19 CBW to Robert Mitchell, letter, 12 September 1945, SS-PC.
20 CBW, "Good Neighborhoods," *Annals of AAPSS* 242 (1945): 104-15.
21 Ibid.
22 G. Holmes Perkins, interview with authors, 21 September 1992.
23 CBW to G. Holmes Perkins, letter, 29 May 1945, CBW Coll.
24 Ibid.
25 WWW to Joseph Hudnut, "Dear Vi" letter, 25 January 1945, SS-PC.
26 CBW to G. Holmes Perkins, letter, 5 December 1945, CBW Coll.
27 CBW to G. Holmes Perkins, letter, 29 September 1946, CBW Coll.
28 CBW to LHK, letter, 4 February 1946, CBW Coll.
29 Lloyd Rodwin, "Garden Cities and the Metropolis," *JLPUE* (August 1945): 268-81.
30 Catherine Bauer, *Modern Housing* (Boston: Houghton Mifflin, 1934), 111.
31 CB, "Cities in Flux," *American Scholar* 13, 1 (Winter 1943-44): 70-84.

32 Rodwin, "Garden Cities," *JLPUE* (February 1946): 272.
33 Ibid.
34 Ibid., 281.
35 CB, "Garden Cities and the Metropolis: A Reply," *JLPUE* (February 1946): 65-66.
36 Ibid.
37 Ibid.
38 LM, "Garden Cities and the Metropolis: A Reply," *JLPUE* (February 1946): 69
39 LM to CBW, letter, 29 December 1945, LM Coll.
40 LM, "Garden Cities," *JLPUE* (February 1946): 69
41 Rodwin, "Garden Cities," *JLPUE* (February 1946): 71-77.
42 CBW, "Are the objections to S1592 valid?" lecture notes for Housing 7, 30 January 1946, 1, CBW coll.
43 Ibid., 11.
44 Ibid.
45 Ibid., 13.
46 CBW, "Condition of Rural Farm Housing Indicated by 1940 Census of Housing," paper presented to the Rural Housing Conference, 12-14 April 1946, Littauer Center for Public Administration, Harvard University.
47 CBW to WWW, letter, 13 October 1946, CBW Coll.
48 CBW to Ellie Haas, letter, 26 June 1948, CBW Coll.
49 CBW to "Dear Lydia and Curt," letter, 18 June 1942, CBW Coll.
50 CBW to "Dear Betsey [Church]," letter, 14 March 1950, SS-PC.
51 WWW to CBW, letter, 21 January 1959, SS-PC.
52 Gropius to WWW & CBW, letter, 25 October 1950, CBW Coll.
53 CBW lecture schedule SW 190 spring 1940, CBW Coll.
54 Ibid.
55 CBW mid-term exam SW 190, 26 February 1940, CBW Coll.
56 CBW final exam SW 190, 13 May 1940, CBW Coll.
57 CBW first session CRP 222, 15 February 1955, CBW Coll.
58 Clark Kerr, interview with authors, 18 June 1992.
59 Don Foley, interview with authors, 16 July 1992.
60 Jack Kent, interview with authors, 15 July 1992.
61 Resolution adopted by Regents of University of California, 21 April 1950, CBW Coll.
62 Statement by E.C. Tolman at meeting of Non-Signers, 29 June 1950, CBW Coll.
63 Ibid.
64 Proposed resolution, 6 July 1950, CBW Coll.
65 "UC Loyalty Oath Held Unconstitutional by Court," *San Francisco News*, 7 April 1951, 1, 3, CBW Coll.
66 *Partial Report of the Senate Fact Finding Committee on Un-American Activities in California*, 1, CBW Coll.
67 "Filmfolk Listed as Party Liners," *Boston Herald*, 9 June 1949, CBW Coll.
68 *Partial Report of the Senate Fact Finding Committee,* 151, CBW Coll.
69 *New York Times*, editorial page, 8 October 1950, CBW Coll.
70 CBW to [sister] Betty, letter, n.d. [1951], CBW Coll.
71 Ibid.
72 Ibid.
73 WWW to Col. Harry W. Gorman, MPC, Department of the Army, Washington DC, letter, 20 January 1953, CBW Coll.
74 Security Board of the Department of the Army to WWW, letter, 7 August 1953, CBW Coll.
75 CBW, "Notes for August 26, 1953, 1.30 pm Room 309, Federal Office Building," CBW Coll.
76 Ibid.
77 Ibid.
78 Ibid.
79 Ibid.
80 Lee Johnson, letter of support for Catherine, 20 August 1953, CBW Coll.
81 LHK, sworn statement, 18 August 1953, CBW Coll.
82 Nathan Straus, "To Whom It May Concern," letter, 19 August 1953, CBW Coll.
83 EJB and Henry C. Bates, "To Whom It May Concern," letters, 24 August 1953, 20 August 1953, CBW Coll.

84 Gordon Stephenson, *On A Human Scale: A Life In City Design* (Fremantle: Fremantle Arts Center Press, 1992).
85 Ibid., 238.
86 Gordon Stephenson, letter to authors, October 1994.
87 CBW to Wilfred Owen, letter, 30 August 1960, CBW Coll.
88 CBW, speech to AWS conference, San Francisco, 6 April 1961, CBW Coll.
89 From CBW speech to Oakland Junior League: "Are Cities Obsolete?" 14 January 1964.
90 CBW to Ford Foundation, letter, 20 November 1954, CBW Coll.
91 CBW to Charles Abrams, letter, 8 June 1951, CBW Coll.
92 Charles Abrams to CBW, letter, 24 October 1951, Cornell University Archives.
93 CBW, summary of proposal to RFF, April 1956, CBW Coll.
94 Charles Abrams to CBW, letter, 8 March 1954, Cornell University Archives.
95 CBW to Oliver C. Winston, president of NAHRO, letter, 28 September 1954, NAHRO Archives.
96 NAHRO 1954 award, 10 October 1954, Philadelphia, NAHRO Archives.
97 "News," *Planning*, April 1988, 22.
98 "Dear Mrs. Bauer," from CB Bear, General Manager, *Architectural Forum*, n.d., typed on the *AF* subscription offer and returned to *AF*, Avery Library Collection.
99 Dorothy Gazzolo, interview with authors, 23 March 1993.
100 Robert A. Caro, "The City-Shaper," *New Yorker*, 5 January 1998, 43, 44.
101 WWW, "Row House Vernacular and High Style Monument," *Architectural Record* (August 1958): 141.
102 CBW, "Report to the Institute of International Studies," 12 February 1960, CBW Coll.
103 CBW to "Dear Chris," letter, 11 September 1959, SS-PC.
104 Arthur T. Row, "An Evaluation of the Calcutta Planning and Development Project," Ford Foundation, October 1974, 1, Arthur T. Row pvt. coll.
105 Ibid., 3.
106 Ibid., 7.
107 Ibid., 8.
108 CBW to "Dearest Mary," letter, 12 January 1960, SS-PC.
109 "Implications of the Delhi Experience for a Calcutta Program, 19 March 1961, CBW Coll.
110 CBW to Paul [Ylvisaker] and Ned [Echeverria], letter, 19 March 1961, Arthur T. Row pvt. coll.
111 CBW to Clark Kerr, letter, 3 February 1960, CBW Coll.
112 CBW to TJK, letter, 13 February 1960, CBW Coll.
113 CBW to Clark Kerr, letter, 4 May 1960, CBW Coll.
114 *IURD Annual Report, 1996-1997,* UCB.
115 Office of Public Information, 17 January 1964, UCB.
116 Martin Meyerson, interview with authors, 22 September 1992.
117 CBW to Mel Webber, letter, 19 June 1963, CBW Coll.
118 CBW to Charles Abrams, letter, 15 October 1962, CBW Coll.
119 CBW to LM, letter, 7 March 1963, LM Coll.
120 CBW to LM, letter, 27 April 1963, LM Coll.
121 CBW to LM, letter, 29 October 1961, LM Coll.
122 "The Metropolitan Future: California and the Challenge of Growth, Conference Five, Berkeley," 26-27 September 1963, UCB, vii.
123 Ibid., 103.
124 Ibid., 121.
125 Ibid., 159.
126 Ibid., 190.
127 Ibid., 204.
128 Alan Temko, "San Francisco Slums and Their People," *San Francisco Chronicle*, 23 April 1964.
129 Catherine's response to Temko's article, *San Francisco Chronicle,* 23 April 1964, 38.
130 Douglas Haskell, "Catherine Bauer Wurster: An Appreciation," *Architectural Forum,* April 1965.

POSTSCRIPT

1 Press Release, HUD #98-509, Wednesday, October 21, 1998.

SELECTED BIBLIOGRAPHY

BY CATHERINE BAUER WURSTER
Catherine Bauer Wurster wrote and published more than 115 articles, books, and reports between 1928 and 1965. Extensive bibliographic lists are contained in two books:

Frieden, Bernard J., and William W. Nash, Jr. (eds.). *Shaping an Urban Future: Essays in Memory of Catherine Bauer Wurster*. Cambridge, MA: MIT Press, 1969.
"Catherine Bauer, 1905-1964: A Bibliography." *Vance Bibliographies*, Architecture Series: Bibliography #A 2256.

The following is a chronological selection of works by Catherine Bauer Wurster, delineating her career and contribution to housing and planning literature:

"Machine-Age Mansions for Ultra-Moderns: French Builders Apply Ideas of the Steel and Concrete Era in Domestic Architecture," *New York Times Magazine* 10, 1 (1928): 10, 22.
"Prize Essay: Art in Industry," *Fortune* 3, 5 (1931): 94.
"Are Good Houses Un-American?" *New Republic* 70, 900 (1932): 74.
"Exhibition of Modern Architecture, Museum of Modern Art," *Creative Art*, 10 (1932): 201-206.
"Slum Clearance or Housing?" *Nation* 137, 3573 (1933): 730-31.
Modern Housing. Boston: Houghton Mifflin, 1934.
"Housing: Paper Plans or a Workers' Movement?" In *America Can't Have Housing*, ed. by Carol Aronovici, 20-23. New York: Museum of Modern Art, 1934.
"Now-at-Last: Housing: The Meaning of the Wagner Steagall Act," *New Republic* 92, 1188 (1937): 119-21.
Labor and the Housing Program. Washington, DC: US Housing Authority, Division of Research and Information, 1938.
"A Year of the Low-Rent Housing Program," *Shelter* 3, 4 (1938): 4-6.
A Citizen's Guide to Public Housing. Poughkeepsie, NY: Vassar College, 1940.
"What Every Family Should Have: Two Federal Experts Tally Up the Standards, from Cellar to Garret, from Neighborhood to Community, What We Mean When We Discuss Everything from Our Own Homes to Homes Fit for a Democracy." Co-authored by Jacob L. Crane. *Survey Graphic* 29, 2 (1940): 64-65, 136-39.
"Columbia Basin: Test for Planning," *New Republic* 107, 10 (1942): 279-80.
"Public Housing." In *Homes or Hovels*, ed. by Anthony Adamson, 21-32. Toronto: Canadian Institute of International Affairs and the Canadian Association for Adult Education, 1943.
"Memorandum on Basic Weaknesses in Current Legislative Proposals for Urban Redevelopment, N[ational] H[ousing] C[onference] Attacks 3 Errors in Postwar Bills," *Public Housing* 9, 6 (1943): 2, 7.
"Planning is Politics but ... Are Planners Politicians?" *Pencil Points* 25, 3 (1944): 66-70.
"Housing in the United States: Problems and Policy," *International Labour Review* 52, 1 (1945): 1-28.

"Good Neighborhoods," *Annals of the American Academy of Political and Social Science* 242 (1945): 104-15.

A Housing Program for Now and Later. National Association of Housing Officials and National Public Housing Conference, Joint Committee, Washington, DC, 1948.

"The Current Change in Civic Hopes and Attitudes," *Housing and Town and Country Planning* (Bulletin No. 1), 35-37. Lake Success, NY: UN Social Affairs, 1948.

"Some Notes on Social Research re: Community Planning," for Philadelphia, PA, Citizens' Council on City Planning. Cambridge, MA, 1949.

"Housing and Health: The Provision of Good Housing," *American Journal of Public Health* 39, 4 (1949): 462-66.

"Social Research as a Tool for Community Planning." In *Social Pressures in Informal Groups: A Study of Human Factors in Housing,* by Leon Festinger et al., 181-201. New York: Harper, 1950.

"Redevelopment and Public Housing," in *Planning 1950,* 39-44. Chicago, American Society of Planning Officials, 1951.

"The Social Responsibility of the Planner," *Town and Country Planning* 20, 96 (1952): 169-73.

"Housing Policy: Toward Feudalism or Democracy? (Or Old Cities Face New Problems)," in *Proceedings, May 1952,* 43-49. National Committee Against Discrimination in Housing, Fourth Annual Conference on Discrimination in Housing, New York, 1952.

"Redevelopment: A Misfit in the Fifties." In *The Future of Cities and Urban Redevelopment,* ed. by Coleman Woodbury, 7-25. Chicago: University of Chicago Press, 1953.

"Swing Low, Sweet Architect: The First Lady of Housing Discusses Flaws in Public and Private Design." In *Housing Yearbook 1954,* 40-41. National Housing Conference, 1954.

"The Case for Regional Planning and Urban Dispersal." In *Housing and Economic Development,* ed. by Burnham Kelly, 39-51. The Albert Farwell Bemis Foundation, Cambridge, MA.: MIT School of Architecture and Planning, 1955.

"Housing Policy and the Educational System," *Annals of the American Academy of Political and Social Science* 302 (1955): 17-27.

"The Pattern of Urban Economic Development: Social Implications," *Annals of the American Academy of Political and Social Science* 305 (1956): 60-69.

"The Dreary Deadlock of Public Housing," *Architectural Forum* 106, 5 (1957): 140-42, 219, 221.

"The New Art of Urban Design: Are We Equipped?" Co-authored by Ernest van den Haag, Jose Luis Sert, and Louis I. Kahn. New York: Columbia University, 8 December 1960.

"Framework for an Urban Society." In *Goals for Americans,* 223-47. US President's Commission on National Goals, New York: Prentice-Hall, 1960.

"Urban and Regional Structure: The Belated Challenge and the Changing Role of the Physical Planner," 2-13. Keynote address to American Institute of Planners, Washington, DC, 1961.

"Urban Living Conditions, Overhead Costs and the Development Pattern." In *Seminar on Urbanization in India: India's Urban Future,* ed. by Roy Turner, 277-98. Berkeley: University of California Press, 1961.

"The Form and Structure of the Future Urban Complex." In *Cities and Space,* ed. by Lowdon Wingo, Jr., 73-102. Baltimore: Johns Hopkins Press, 1963.

Housing and the Future of Cities in the San Francisco Bay Area. Berkeley: Institute of Governmental Studies, University of California, 1963.

About Catherine Bauer Wurster

The following is a selection of publications about Catherine Bauer Wurster, listed alphabetically:

Birch, Eugenie L. "Women-Made America: The Case of Early Public Housing Policy." *AIA Housing Journal* 44 (1978): 130-44.

"Catherine Bauer," *National Cyclopedia of American Biography,* 268-9. New York: James T. White, 1984.

"Catherine K. Bauer," *Macmillan Encyclopedia of Architects,* 1: 154. New York: Free Press, 1982.

"Catherine Krouse Bauer." *Notable American Women: The Modern Period,* 66-68. Cambridge, MA: Belknap Press, 1980.

Cole, Mary Susan. "Catherine Bauer and the Public Housing Movement, 1926-1937." Ph.D. diss., George Washington University, 1975.

Elsen, Sylvia. "Early Heroics: Catherine Bauer." *Working Woman* 7 (1982): 72-73.

"Housing: A Memorandum," *California Arts and Architecture* 60 (1943): 18-19, 41-42.

"Housing's White Knight," *Architectural Forum* 84 (1946): 116-19, 148, 150.

Mumford, Lewis. *My Works and Days: A Personal Chronicle.* New York: Harcourt, Brace Jovanovich, 1979.

–. *Roots of Contemporary American Architecture,* 421. New York: Reinhold, 1952.

Oberlander, H. Peter, and Eva Newbrun. "Catherine Bauer's Harvard Years: The GSD's First Woman Professor." *GSD News,* Harvard Graduate School of Design (Summer 1993): 27-29.

–. "Catherine Bauer Wurster: CEDs First Lady – 1905-1964." *CED News* (College of Environmental Design, UC Berkeley) 12 (1994): 4-9.

–. "Catherine Bauer: Ahead of Her Time. Profile of a Pioneer." *Planning* (American Planning Association) 61 (1995): 10-12.

"Portrait," *Architectural Forum* 75 (1941): 10.

"Portrait," *Architectural Forum* 77 (1942): 10.

Stephens, Suzanne. "Voices of Consequence: Four Architectural Critics." In *Women in American Architecture,* ed. by Susana Torre, 136-43. New York: Whitney Library of Design, 1977.

Stevens, Mary Otis. "Struggle for Place: Women Architects, 1920-1960." In *Women in American Architecture,* ed. by Susana Torre, 88-102. New York: Whitney Library of Design, 1977.

"Woman Hiker Dead: Aided Three Presidents on City Planning." *New York Times,* 24 November 1964.

CONTEMPORARY ISSUES IN HOUSING AND PLANNING

The following is a selection of current literature on housing and planning that reflects Catherine Bauer Wurster's wide-ranging intellectual and professional interests and legacy:

Advisory Commission on Regulatory Barriers to Affordable Housing. *"Not in My Back Yard": Removing Barriers to Affordable Housing.* Washington, DC: US Department of Housing and Urban Development, 1991.

Apgar, William C. *The State of the Nation's Housing 1990.* Cambridge, MA: Joint Center for Housing Studies at Harvard University, 1991.

Apgar, William C., and Matthew Franklin. *Creating a New Federal Housing Corporation: A Summary of Eight Public Forums on the Future of FHA.* Washington, DC: US Department of Housing and Urban Development, 1995.

Baku, Esmail, and Marc Smith. "Loan Delinquency in Community Lending Organizations: Case Studies of NeighborWorks Organizations." *Housing Policy Debate* 9, 1 (1998): 151-75.

Bauman, John F. *Public Housing, Race, and Renewal: Urban Planning in Philadelphia, 1970-1974.* Philadelphia: Temple University Press, 1987.

Bauman, John F. "Public Housing: The Dreadful Saga of a Durable Policy." *Journal of Planning Literature* 8 (1994): 347-61.

Bothwell, Stephanie E., Raymond Gindroz, and Robert E. Lang. "Restoring Community through Traditional Neighborhood Design: A Case Study of Diggs Town Public Housing." *Housing Policy Debate* 9, 1 (1998): 89-114.

Briggs, Xavier de Sousa. "Brown Kids in White Suburbs: Housing Mobility and the Many Faces of Social Capital." *Housing Policy Debate* 9, 1 (1998): 177-221.

Carter, Tom. "Current Practices for Procuring Affordable Housing: The Canadian Context." *Housing Policy Debate* 8, 3 (1997): 593-631.

Cisneros, Henry G. *Interwoven Destinies: Cities and the Nation.* New York: Norton, 1993.

Davis, Richard. *Housing Reform during the Truman Administration.* Columbia: University of Missouri Press, 1966.

Downs, Anthony. *Opening Up the Suburbs: An Urban Strategy for America.* New Haven: Yale University Press, 1973.

–. *Why Keeping HUD Is a Good Idea.* Washington, DC: Brookings Institution, 1995.

Gelfand, Mark I. *A Nation of Cities: The Federal Government and Urban America, 1933-1965.* New York: Oxford University Press, 1975.

Haar, Charles M. "Judges as Agents of Social Change: Can the Courts Break the Affordable Housing Deadlock in Metropolitan Areas?" *Housing Policy Debate* 8, 3 (1997): 633-50.

Hall, Peter. *Cities of Tomorrow: An Intellectual History of Urban Planning and Design in the Twentieth*

Century. Oxford: Basil Blackwell, 1988.

Hayes, R. Allen. *The Federal Government and Urban Housing: Ideology and Change in Public Policy.* 2nd ed. Albany: State University of New York Press, 1995.

Joint Center for Housing Studies. *The State of the Nation's Housing.* Cambridge, MA: Harvard University, 1996.

Keating, Dennis. *The Suburban Racial Dilemma: Housing and Neighborhoods.* Philadelphia: Temple University Press, 1994.

Lang, Robert E., and Steven P. Hornburg. "What is Social Capital and Why Is It Important to Public Policy?" *Housing Policy Debate* 9, 1 (1998) 1-16.

McDonnell, Timothy L. *The Wagner Housing Act: A Case Study of the Legislative Process.* Chicago: Loyola University Press, 1957.

Meehan, Eugene J. *The Quality of Federal Policymaking: Programmed Failure in Public Housing.* Columbia: University of Missouri Press, 1979.

National Association of Housing and Redevelopment Officials. *The Many Faces of Public Housing.* Washington, DC, 1990.

Oberlander, H. Peter (ed.). *Improving Human Settlements – Up with People.* Vancouver: UBC Press, 1976.

Oberlander, H. Peter. *LAND: The Central Human Settlement Issue.* Vancouver: UBC Press, 1985.

Plunz, Richard. *A History of Housing in New York City: Dwelling Type and Social Change in the American Metropolis.* New York: Columbia University Press, 1990.

Putnam, Robert D. "Social Capital: Its Importance to Housing and Community Development." *Housing Policy Debate* 9, 1 (1998): v-viii.

Quercia, Roberto G., and George C. Galster. "The Challenges Facing Public Housing Authorities in a Brave New World." *Housing Policy Debate* 8, 3 (1997): 535-69.

Rodwin, Lloyd, and Donald A. Schön, eds. *Rethinking the Development Experience.* Washington, DC: Brookings Institution; Cambridge, MA: Lincoln Institute of Land Policy, 1989.

Rohe, William M., and Michael A. Stegman. *Public Housing Homeownership Demonstration Assessment.* Vols. 1 and 2. Washington, DC: US Department of Housing and Urban Development, Office of Policy Development and Research, 1990.

Rowe, Peter G. *Modernity and Housing.* Cambridge, MA: MIT Press, 1993.

Saegert, Susan, and Gary Winkel. "Social Capital and the Revitalization of New York City's Distressed Inner-City Housing." *Housing Policy Debate* 9, 1 (1998): 17-60.

Servon, Lisa J. "Credit and Social Capital: The Community Development Potential of U.S. Microenterprise Programs." *Housing Policy Debate* 9, 1 (1998): 115-49.

Smith, Robert, Margaret Griffiths, and Tamsin Stirling. "Social Rehousing Policy in Britain: Needs, Rights, and Choices." *Housing Policy Debate* 8, 3 (1997): 679-95.

Stegman, Michael A. "The Role of Public Housing in a Revitalized National Housing Policy." In *Building Foundations: Housing and Federal Policy* by Denise DiPasquale and Langley C. Keyes, 333-64. Philadelphia: University of Pennsylvania Press, 1990.

–. *More Housing, More Fairly.* New York: The Twentieth Century Fund Press, 1991.

–. (ed.) *Cityscape: A Journal of Policy Development and Research. Commemorating HUD's 30th Anniversary* 1, 3 (1995).

Temkin, Kenneth, and William M. Rohe. "Social Capital and Neighborhood Stability: An Empirical Investigation." *Housing Policy Debate* 9, 1 (1998): 61-88.

Von Hoffman, Alexander. "High Ambitions: The Past and Future of American Low-Income Housing Policy." *Housing Policy Debate* 7, 3 (1996): 423-42.

Weaver, Robert. "The First Twenty Years of HUD." *American Planning Association Journal* 51, 4 (1985): 463-74.

Wood, Elizabeth. *The Beautiful Beginnings.* Washington, DC: National Center for Housing Management, 1982.

In addition, consult the Web site of the National Low Income Housing Coalition (www.nlihc.org), especially the weekly memos to members during September and early October 1998.

Acknowledgments

This book owes its creation to mentors, colleagues, friends, and family. Each contributed generously to the manuscript's evolution. The authors offer their sincere thanks for the time spent and care taken in reading all or parts of the manuscript. Any flaws or errors are solely our responsibility.

We wish to record our warm appreciation for financial assistance from the Architectural History Foundation, New York; the Graham Foundation for Advanced Studies in Fine Arts, Chicago (two grants); the Canadian Studies Program at the University of California, Berkeley (two grants); Mr. Alfred Heller, Corte Madera, California; and the Human Solidarity Foundation, Tacoma, Washington.

Much of the information in Chapters 4 and 5 was derived from the excellent unpublished Ph.D. thesis of Mary Susan Cole: *Catherine Bauer and the Public Housing Movement, 1926-1937*, Parts 1 and 2 (George Washington University, 1974). Frederick Gutheim was Dr. Cole's research director.

Invaluable editorial assistance was provided by experienced authors and editors. They are:

Paula Brook	Evangeline Leash	Herbert Winter
Sherril Jaffe	Adolf Placzek	

The manuscript was based on many thoughtful interviews among those who knew Catherine throughout her distinguished career. They include the following:

Edmund Bacon	Elizabeth Bauer Kassler	Gordon Stephenson
Louis and Babs Bauer	Jack and Mary Kent	Georgiana Stevens
Tasha and Michael Churchill	Clark Kerr	Betty Stonorov
Vernon DeMars	Philip Klutznick	Sadie Wurster Super
Louis and Cushing Dolbeare	Ferd Kramer	H. Ralph Taylor
Donn Emmons	Sylvia McLaughlin	Alan Temko
Donald Foley	Martin and Margy Meyerson	Francis Violich
Dorothy Gazzolo	Sophie Mumford	Robert C. Weaver
Frederick and Polly Guttheim	G. Holmes Perkins	Melvin Webber
Alfred E. Heller	Richard Peters	Elizabeth Melone Winston
Elfriede Hoeber	Thelma Redd	Coleman and Josephine
Edward and Anne Howden	Lloyd Rodwin	Woodbury
Victor Jones	Morton Schussheim	

The evolving manuscript was read by many of our colleagues, friends, and family. Their suggestions and encouragement contributed immeasurably to the formulation of our text. They include:

Edward and Mary Barnes	Linda Lyons	Judy Oberlander
Janice Bolaffi	Susan Margolis	Don and Helen Olson
Grady Clay	Scott McIntyre	Abraham Rogatnick
Mary and Arthur Q. Davis	Ira Nadel	Harry Seidler
Sheila Dickie	Annie Neubrunn	Doris Shadbolt
Bette Hanson	Deborah Newbrun	Mark Wexler
Ruth Knack	Ernest Newbrun	Lisl Winter
Nancy Levinson	Cornelia Oberlander	Max Wyman

Essential assistance was provided by many who contributed to the production of the manuscript, the reliability of information, and the historical data. They are:

Joanne Addison	Shirley Marcus	Arthur T. Row
Drori Eitan	George Oberlander	Peter Rowe
Sidney Gottfried	Wendy Oberlander	William Slayton
Janet and Andrew Katten	Nelson W. Polsby	Michael Stegman
Arthur E. Lyons	Chester Rapkin	Israel Stollman

The list is long, but each person made a unique contribution which we wish to acknowledge. We are grateful for the time and effort spent by these busy people. We owe a special debt of gratitude to the librarians of the Bancroft Rare Book Collection of UC Berkeley, which holds Catherine Bauer's archives. We also acknowledge the generous help of librarians at the following institutions:

American Heritage Center, University of Wyoming
Archives, Ford Foundation
Archives, J.S. Guggenheim Foundation
Avery Library, Columbia University
CED Library, UC Berkeley
Fine Arts Library, University of British Columbia
GSD Library, Harvard University
Institute of Governmental Studies, UC Berkeley
Library of Congress, Washington, DC
National Archives, Washington, DC
Department of Manuscripts and University Archives, Cornell University
Special Collections Department, Van Pelt Library, University of Pennsylvania
Special Collections Library, Case Western Reserve University
Vassar College Alumni Association Library

Early versions of parts of our manuscript appeared in *GSD News* (Summer 1993), *CED News* (Spring 1994), and *Planning* (Spring 1995).

We wish to record our deep appreciation for the help extended by Catherine's family throughout the research and development of the manuscript, in particular, Sadie Wurster Super for her account of life with her mother and for the loan of boxes of her mother's correspondence and photographs. We thank Louis and Babs Bauer for their hospitality and for the long-term loan of their precious copy of *The Bauer Family, Descendants of Johann Jacob Bauer*, by Harriet Stryker-Rodder, Certified Genealogist, 1969. Elizabeth Bauer Kassler's untimely death on February 7, 1998, left many bereft. She was happy to share memories of her dear sister and sent us annual letters of encouragement. The last arrived less than three weeks before she died, applauding our progress and looking forward to the publication of her sister's biography. We deeply regret that she did not live to read the completed manuscript.

A special word of thanks goes to George Oberlander for his tireless pursuit of housing legislation leads in Washington for authors residing 3,000 miles away, and to Adolf Placzek for his early spirited encouragement.

The guidance, support, and encouragement of UBC Press throughout the production of the book are gratefully acknowledged. In particular we wish to express our gratitude to Jean Wilson, senior editor, Holly Keller-Brohman, managing editor, Nancy Pollak, our devoted copy editor, and Peter Milroy, director of UBC Press. We sincerely appreciate the generous and supportive comments of two anonymous readers of the manuscript who spoke well of Catherine's life as a source of inspiration.

This book took eight years to evolve from an idea into a concrete form. We must thank our spouses, Cornelia Oberlander and Ernest Newbrun, for bearing with us all these years. Their patience, which was sometimes stretched to the limits, endured. That helped more than they can imagine.

Our list of acknowledgments is as inclusive as possible. We deeply regret any oversight for we truly appreciate the wonderful encouragement from all who became acquainted with our project.

H. PETER OBERLANDER, VANCOUVER, BRITISH COLUMBIA
EVA NEWBRUN, SAN FRANCISCO, CALIFORNIA

ABBREVIATIONS

AAPSS Annals of the American Academy of Political and Social Science
AFL American Federation of Labor
ASAP American Society of Architects and Planners
ASPO American Society of Planning Officials
CED College of Environmental Design, UC Berkeley
CHA California Housing Authority
CHPA California Housing and Planning Association
CIAM Congrès Internationaux d'Architecture Moderne
CIO Congress of Industrial Organizations
CMPO Calcutta Metropolitan Planning Organization
DCRP Department of City and Regional Planning, UC Berkeley
FHA Federal Housing Administration
FPHA Federal Public Housing Authority
FRA Farm Resettlement Administration
FSA Farm Security Administration
FWA Federal Works Agency
GSD Graduate School of Design, Harvard University
HHFA Housing and Home Finance Agency
HLIO Housing Legislation Information Office
HR House of Representatives
IIS Institute of International Studies
IURD Institute for Urban and Regional Development
LHC Labor Housing Conference
NAHO National Association of Housing Officials
NAHRO National Association of Housing and Redevelopment Officials
NHA National Housing Agency
NLRB National Labor Relations Board
NPHC National Public Housing Conference
PWA Public Works Administration
RFF Resources For the Future
S Senate
TVA Tennessee Valley Authority
USHA United States Housing Authority
WPA Works Progress Administration

INDEX

Set in Fairfield by Aitken+Blakeley
Printed and bound in Canada by Friesens
Copy editor: Nancy Pollak
Indexer: Patricia Buchanan